T0355616

The Return of Resentment

the
LIFE
OF
IDEAS

Series Editor: Darrin McMahon, Dartmouth College

After a period of some eclipse, the study of intellectual history has enjoyed a broad resurgence in recent years. *The Life of Ideas* contributes to this revitalization through the study of ideas as they are produced, disseminated, received, and practiced in different historical contexts. The series aims to embed ideas—those that endured, and those once persuasive but now forgotten—in rich and readable cultural histories. Books in this series draw on the latest methods and theories of intellectual history while being written with elegance and élan for a broad audience of readers.

The Return of Resentment

THE RISE AND DECLINE AND RISE AGAIN OF A POLITICAL EMOTION

Robert A. Schneider

THE UNIVERSITY OF CHICAGO PRESS

CHICAGO AND LONDON

The University of Chicago Press, Chicago 60637

The University of Chicago Press, Ltd., London

© 2023 by The University of Chicago

Published 2023

Printed in the United States of America

32 31 30 29 28 27 26 25 24 23   1 2 3 4 5

ISBN-13: 978-0-226-58643-4 (cloth)

ISBN-13: 978-0-226-58657-1 (e-book)

DOI: https://doi.org/10.7208/chicago/9780226586571.001.0001

Library of Congress Cataloging-in-Publication Data

Names: Schneider, Robert Alan, author.
Title: The return of resentment : the rise and decline and rise again of
a political emotion / Robert A. Schneider.
Other titles: Life of ideas.
Description: Chicago : The University of Chicago Press, 2023. | Series:
Life of ideas | Includes bibliographical references and index.
Identifiers: LCCN 2022023735 | ISBN 9780226586434 (cloth) | ISBN
9780226586571 (ebook)
Subjects: LCSH: Resentment—Europe—History. | Resentment—
Political aspects—Europe. | Political psychology—Europe—History. |
Resentment—Political aspects—United States. | Political psychology—
United States. | BISAC: LANGUAGE ARTS & DISCIPLINES / Linguistics /
Etymology | PHILOSOPHY / Political
Classification: LCC BJ1535.R45 S36 2023 | DDC 179/.8—dc23/eng/20220629
LC record available at https://lccn.loc.gov/2022023735

♾ This paper meets the requirements of ANSI/NISO Z39.48-1992
(Permanence of Paper).

For John L. Pacheco

.

Resentment is like drinking poison and waiting for the other person to die.

Ascribed variously to an AA sponsorship guide, Carrie Fisher, Malachy McCourt, Saint Augustine, and others

The mass of men are guided, or, more accurately, acted upon, by instinct, passion, sentiments and resentment. The mass do not know how to think nor do they care to. They know only one thing: to obey and believe.

ALEXANDRE KOYRÉ, *Réflexions sur le Mensonge*

Resentment had erased all ambiguity in our encounters with people like him; we had been polarized into "us" and "them."

AZAR NAFISI, *Reading "Lolita" in Tehran*

Richard Nixon was a serial collector of resentments.

RICK PERLSTEIN, *Nixonland*

Resentment is a union of sorrow and malignity.

SAMUEL JOHNSON, *Selected Essays*

Nothing on earth consumes a man more quickly than the passion of resentment. Mortification, morbid susceptibility, the inability to wreak revenge, the desire and thirsts for revenge, the concoction of every sort of poison—this is surely the most injurious manner of reacting which could possibly be conceived.

NIETZSCHE, *Ecce Homo*

Resentment seems to have been given to us by nature for defense, and for defense only; it is the safeguard of justice, and the security of innocence.

ADAM SMITH, *The Theory of Moral Sentiments*

You often doubt if you really exist. You wonder whether you aren't simply a phantom in other people's minds. Say a figure in a nightmare which the sleeper tries with all his strength to destroy. It's when you feel like this that, out of resentment, you begin to bump back at people.

RALPH ELLISON, *Invisible Man*

Contents

Preface

Readers might approach this book with a couple of questions. A general reader might very well wonder what I could possibly mean by a "return" of something like resentment—that is, an emotion. In short, does an emotion, or this particular one, have a history, and if so, in what sense? To this sort of reader, all I can say is: read the book.

A tiny subset of readers, however—that is, those who know something of the author's background—might ask another question. How is it that a historian of early modern Europe has come to write about a political emotion with such contemporary relevance? (Those readers understandably uninterested in autobiographical reflections are invited to skip the next few paragraphs.)

The prominence of the concept of resentment in our public life, especially since 2016, is, I believe, evident to anyone sensitive to its meanings. My interest in this subject, however, predates the politics of today, extending back to the 1980s. For it was then that the rise of both Christian and Islamic fundamentalism—phenomena with powerful political implications—took most informed observers by surprise. How could such seemingly atavistic religious movements emerge in the "modern" world, especially in the West, where religious observance had been steadily waning, and religion itself increasingly relegated to the private realm? For many, these movements represented a challenge to their way of thinking about the world: how could they have been caught so intellectually flat-footed?

I was one of them. Like many of my generation of historians, I had been instructed in the methods of social history, which emphasized the collective action of ordinary people and looked with suspicion upon psychological explanations for their motivations. In particular, we largely rejected the approach of an earlier generation of social scientists and historians for whom a psychological—even psychoanalytic—interpretation was their stock in trade. Perhaps the most prominent of these was the great American historian Richard Hofstadter (1916–70), who wrote about the "paranoid style" of American politics and "anti-intellectualism" in American life, concepts that, in fact, have regained popularity in the face of present-day right-wing movements. (I deal with Hofstadter and kindred academics in chapter 5.) While, like most, I appreciated Hofstadter's magisterial approach to history and especially his luminous prose, I joined in rejecting both his disparaging view of Populism and an overgeneralizing psychological interpretation of social movements.

There is the clichéd warning about "throwing the baby out with the bath water," and I think that's what we have done with an approach like Hofstadter's. Our rejection was simply wholesale. And while it is by no means an easy task to confront the psychological and emotional dimensions of collective life, the fact that many historians and social scientists weren't really prepared to do this—were even resistant to thinking in these terms—meant that we only perceived a whole set of consequential movements once they had shaken the very foundations of our world. In a sense, we have been playing catch-up ever since. In part, this book represents my own reckoning with this missed opportunity.

Along the way I have relied on the help, advice, and wisdom of many. Suzanne Marchand and Priya Nelson encouraged this undertaking when it was just an ill-formed proposal. And throughout, Darrin McMahon has been a much-appreciated critic and supporter. At the University of Chicago Press, Mary Al-Sayed has been everything anyone would want in a book editor. Darrin and Mary have been especially crucial in encouraging me to craft this book for what Virginia Woolf called the "common reader"—something of a challenge for an academic long accustomed to the scholarly mode. Whether I have succeeded is for that kind of readership to decide, and whether I have cut scholarly corners in doing so will be the gleeful task of my scholarly colleagues to point out. The team at Chicago, including Tristan Bates, Tamara Ghattas, and Fabiola Enríquez, has been helpful and efficient in turning this undertaking into a real book. I thank Mariah Gumpert for her deft and unobtrusive copyediting.

At Indiana University Bloomington, my academic home since 2005, I am happy to acknowledge a grant from the College Arts and Humanities Institute.

Sometimes in stray conversations, other times in more prolonged encounters, I have learned much from many friends and colleagues: Gary Gerstle, Oz Kenshur, Michael Kimmage, Jim Kloppenberg, Herbert Marks, Robert Peretsky, Roberta Pergher, Mark Roseman, and Johannes Turk, among others. I also want to thank Sebastian Aeschbach, Dan Degerman, and Sjoerd van Tuinen, who generously shared their work with me. I am also grateful for invitations to present my often-inchoate ideas to several audiences at various institutions: the European Workshop in the Department of History, Indiana University; the Thumos Seminar, University of Geneva; the Centre for the Study of Emotions, Queens College, London; the Cambridge American History Seminar, Cambridge University, and the Max Planck Institute, Berlin. I am alone responsible for all errors and excesses.

On the domestic front, I hope that my preoccupation with this topic has not been resented by those who matter to me most, Sarah, Kate, and Laura; if it has, I am very sorry, but this at least allows me the opportunity to once again thank you for your love, support, and forbearance. Laura has been my steadfast and expert go-to person on all matters digital. Kate has shared her astute insights into the murky depths of psychology and interpersonal dynamics. Sarah, my best and sternest critic, continues to be the dearest of sounding boards.

The name of my friend John Pacheco and the word "resentment" do not belong in the same sentence. Other words come to mind: piety, loyalty, and integrity, both personal and artistic. But I promised myself that I would dedicate my next book to him—to honor a friendship which has meant so much to me over the years. Fate threw us together in New Haven long ago, and our brotherly bond has comforted and enriched me ever since. Thank you, John.

Introduction

"The Resentment that Never Sleeps," read the headline of Thomas B. Edsall's column in the *New York Times* in December 2020. Edsall frequently reports on recent social science research on contemporary matters; in this piece he gathers evidence suggesting that "rising anxiety over declining social status tells a lot about how we got here and where we're going."[1]

As I write these words, "resentment" is part of the vocabulary that describes the moment. In October 2021, David Brooks, also of the *Times*, proclaimed, "'Some days American politics seems to be a futile clash of resentments."[2] Brooks's and Edsall's colleague Maggie Haberman announced in the title of a column in early 2020: "Trump Adds to Playbook of Stoking White Fear and Resentment."[3] At the peak of the coronavirus pandemic, former president Barack Obama decried then-president Donald Trump for fomenting "anger and resentment,"[4] and weeks earlier, as Black Lives Matter protests racked cities across the US, the then-presumptive Democratic nominee for president, Joe Biden, condemned Trump for turning "this country into a battlefield driven by old resentments and fresh fears."[5] Commenting on the situation in the US, a foreign paper's headline read: "Trump Fans Flames of Resentment and Hatred."[6] In recent years, "resentment" has been a go-to ascription for the collective sentiment that animates Trump's base and carried him into office. Following the election in November 2016, it readily flowed from the pens of editors and op-ed commentators. David Remnick, the editor of the *New Yorker*, vilified the victorious candidate as a "slick performer" who essentially duped his followers by being "more than willing to assume their resentments, their fury, their sense of a new world that conspired against their interests."[7] "Resentment is no excuse for bald-faced stupidity," wrote a guest columnist in the *Washington Post* two days after the election.[8] Writing in the same paper the next day, Leon Wieseltier urged liberals to "stay angry," offering this indignant commentary: "The scapegoating of otherness by miserable people cannot be justified by their misery. *Resentment, even when it has a basis in experience, is one of the ugliest political emotions, and it has been the source of horrors*."[9] Citing recent research, the news site Vox announced, "Trump won because of racial resentment."[10] During the first impeachment proceedings, the historian Michael Kazin was quoted in the *Atlantic*: Trump "speaks to a lot of the same resentments and a lot of the same themes as previous conservative populists, but he is politically more divisive."[11] The ascription goes beyond Trump: "Cultural Resentment is Conservatives' New Religion," asserted the *New Republic* in October 2020.[12] It wasn't only the American political scene that occasioned the use of this concept. The UK's vote to leave the European Union—a vote that was as unanticipated as the Trump victory later that year—was made retrospectively comprehensible by calling upon the same emotion: "Wigan's Road to Brexit: Anger, Loss and Class Resentments," proclaimed the *New York Times*.[13] So, too, with the Yellow Vest protests in France: "I believe that resentment," wrote a journalist in the British paper the *Observer*, "—a sense of being slighted or ignored or despised or abandoned or humiliated— explains the Yellow Vest movement more than any other particular grievance."[14] A column in the *Guardian* in December 2017 by Dayna Tortorici was titled "Reckoning with a Culture of Male Resentment."[15] Taking in a range of ills, *Foreign Policy* laconically noted, "The West Has a Resentment Epidemic."[16]

Today, "resentment" seems everywhere, but it wasn't always so. Just a few years ago, evoking the sentiment in order to explain people's grievances and discontents struck many as a misstep—the wrong sort of analysis which disguised more than it revealed. In 2008, then-senator Obama gave a talk before a crowd of wealthy donors in San Francisco in which he reflected on his recent trip to small towns in Pennsylvania and the Midwest, whose inhabitants felt let down by successive administrations and their repeated promises of regeneration: "So it's not surprising then they get bitter, they cling to guns or religion or antipathy towards people who aren't like them or anti-immigrant sentiment or anti-trade sentiment as a way to explain their frustrations."[17] The reaction was swift. A *Huffington Post* journalist called the speech "a problematic judgment call," reminding readers that for his well-heeled California audience his description of working-class resentment was couched entirely in "pure negatives: guns, clinging to religion, antipathy, xenophobia."[18] And Leo Ribuffo, the late historian of the American Right, lamented this throwback to the discredited political sociology of another generation which dismissed "church attendance, ethnic solidarity, and other allegedly atavistic behavior as socio-psychological symptoms devoid of any sensible rationale."[19] As recently as 2008, then, it was considered somewhat ill-advised to deploy a psychological diagnosis which smacked of resentment—which dared to suggest that many downtrodden Americans might be suffering from misdirected animosities that distracted them from their real interests. To evoke resentment was to assume a condescending attitude toward people whose values were simply different—and whose grievances were real, not delusions.

Clearly, whatever reluctance, inhibitions, or other obstacles to deploying this concept—and its attendant emotional and psychological associations—have been dispelled. "Resentment" is back.

But what do we mean by resentment, particularly in a political context? This book is devoted to exploring this question. Throughout, I strive to explain both the usefulness and meaning of resentment as it has been understood and experienced in the past as well as in recent times. Several concerns, questions, and qualifications will guide my exploration:

One has to do with what set me on the course of this investigation. Like most people, I vaguely know what commentators mean by "resentment" when they evoke it, especially in the political sense. I am, however, troubled by its casual, sometimes unthinking deployment. It's like inflation: when we use something too frequently its value is diminished. Does it really clarify people's motivations? Might it not obscure more than it illuminates? And its potential to obscure is compounded by the complexity of this particular emotion. For example, it is clearly akin to anger; perhaps, as some have suggested, it's a subspecies of anger, but this then leaves us wondering what defines it as distinct. Is being resentful the same as being angry? Clearly not—but why not? (I will explore the difference between anger and resentment below.) The fact that a wide range of commentators gravitate toward "resentment" over "anger" as an insight into the present moment clearly suggests a meaningful distinction. Still, the distinction remains merely implicit, if not entirely vague.

One thing seems clear to me, however: unlike other negative emotions such as anger—but also fear, disappointment, and sadness—to be called "resentful" is often, perhaps even usually, demeaning. It's hardly an emotion that people are happy to "own." This is why, as several commentators have noted, it has often been used to delegitimize or discount people's grievances. On the other hand, in some situations, resentment is useful as a prompt for the recognition of injustice, suggesting a more elastic sense of the concept. We should remain alert, then, to the range of modes and moral valences of resentment, for I want to be sure that we don't assume for it purely negative connotations.

Throughout this study, I will be focusing for the most part on the political, and therefore the collective phenomenon of resentment. This does not mean that there is an absolute distinction between the resentment of individuals in interpersonal relationships and public expressions of this emotion; it is still the same emotion. But there is a difference, nevertheless. Whether personal or political, individual or collective, however, resentment implies, again unlike some other emotions, a relationship to another person or persons. One can be angry at the weather, or fearful of climate change; one can be simply hopeful or anxious in an existential sense without the implication of a particular person or agent as responsible for one's own hope or anxiety. But like other emotions—humiliation, jealousy, envy—with resentment there are always others or another—usually real, sometimes imagined—in the wings.

It may be that resentment, unlike some other emotions, is complicated by its compound nature. That is, it is usually a mix of several emotions: anger, to be sure, but perhaps as well two emotions that are often confused with one another, envy and jealousy. We should be wary, however, of simply conflating resentment with seemingly kindred emotions. The early twentieth-century philosopher Max Scheler, probably the most-cited authority on *ressentiment* after Nietzsche, insisted that the resentful were at base profoundly envious; in his view, it is the envy of the poor, the weak, the generally discontented toward their social betters which gives rise to modern resentment. But while this is surely the case *sometimes*, it is just as surely often not. For example, I don't think that today's anti-vaxxers, resentful of being told to submit their bodies to the ministrations of medical experts, are *envious* of the unflappable Dr. Fauci. The same might be said of jealousy, which should be distinguished from envy. Envy implies wanting something you don't have, while a jealous disposition arises when what you do have is threatened by the affections of another. A jealous person might very well become resentful of their rival, but not all instances of resentment entail rivalry; and while the challenge of dispossession often lies at the heart of resentment, this is not always the case. Shakespeare calls jealousy "the green-eyed monster which doth mock/The meat it feeds on."[20] But those lines are uttered by Iago, the quintessential man of resentment, to Othello, a man in the grip of murderous jealousy. It is as if Shakespeare is drawing a distinction with these two characters between two highly vexed but (here at least) distinct emotional states.

Resentment has a history—at least this is one of my guiding assumptions. It has a history in a dual sense: both as a concept and as an actual, collective emotion. I will argue as well that there are periods in history when resentment is more pronounced as a collective emotion, and times when it is less prominent or relevant. It may very well be, as I will suggest, that it is characteristic of the modern age. But one of the unavoidable aspects of thinking about the history of resentment is Nietzsche's formulation, primarily in *On the Genealogy of Morality* (which I shall look at in a subsequent chapter). Nietzsche didn't find a comparable German word for the disposition he wanted to describe, so he used the French word *ressentiment*. Many have followed him and thereby make a distinction between our ordinary understanding of the emotion "resentment" and an emotion characterized by bitterness, a festering desire for revenge, and a twisted sense of what or who is responsible for one's suffering, which they call "*ressentiment*." This is more than a difference in degree; it implies a deepseated, self-defeating psychological state that ultimately informs one's entire outlook on the world. In this study, however, I have decided not to use it as opposed to "resentment." Indeed, I think that relying upon the Nietzschean term prejudices in advance our sense of what emotional or psychological state it means to evoke, assuming a level of disparagement that is not always warranted.

In this book, I will be toggling between two levels of analysis. On one, this is an intellectual history of the *concept* of resentment—how it has been understood and interpreted by commentators and how it has been deployed as a means of understanding puzzling political movements, ideologies, and popular sentiments. (In the latter sense, we might think of this as "resentment-talk.") Still, to pursue this line of inquiry without attending to these movements, ideologies, and sentiments themselves strikes me—as it undoubtedly would strike most readers—as an exercise in pure and pointless intellectual abnegation. Why not strive to discover the reality of this emotion as a component of politics in past times and, most urgently, our contemporary era? This is what I will attempt to do. It must be acknowledged, however, that accessing the reality of a collective emotion is not a simple task, especially in the past. Even the most public aspects of people's experiences across time are accessible to us only through the documents they leave behind. If, as it is said, the past is a foreign country, we can only visit it virtually, with documents as our passports. For the present state of affairs, however, I will be relying on the many excellent studies produced by social scientists and journalists— studies that seem to appear almost daily—which reveal a lot not only about what our contemporaries think or what they believe in but also sometimes what they feel.

This leads to a final qualification. This book is informed and inspired by the field of the study of emotions in the social sciences and humanities, a relatively new approach to understanding the workings of society.[21] Its newness might puzzle some readers: How could scholars not take into account people's feelings, especially today, when passions clearly run so high in the byways of public life? This is certainly a legitimate question. One answer is that acknowledging the role of emotions in motivating people is one thing; actually giving a comprehensible account of their meaning and impact is another. It's even more difficult when dealing with the past. But another has to do with long-standing assumptions seemingly fundamental to our ways of thinking about the human experience. At least since the seventeenth-century philosopher Descartes (and probably before), the tendency to divide body and mind has marked Western thought. And the long legacy of the Enlightenment only reified this distinction. As Jan Plamper, one of the leading historians of the emotions, writes, in the Enlightenment, "the canonization of reason demanded sacrifice, and the strict separation of reason and feeling was one such sacrifice."[22] This might seem like merely an intellectual disposition based upon a particular, and historically very persuasive, conception of human nature, which indeed it is. But it has gathered strength, bolstered by other somewhat tendentious views, more prescriptive than descriptive in nature: that we ought not to recognize feelings, passions, and emotions on the same level as reason; that legitimizing emotions in public life has produced disastrous results; that an inclination toward the emotive is characteristic mostly of "uncivilized," uneducated, or lower-class social elements which have not achieved the stage of development where they are primarily governed by reason; and that, finally, the long-term social development, at least in the West—the so-called civilizing process—favors the rise of self-control and a commensurate decline of emotions as governing human behavior. This many-faceted bias against studying emotions has only recently been overcome. That it prevailed for so long into the twentieth century might be explained precisely by the experience of those who lived through this tumultuous period, when nationalist, fascist, and populist movements offered a cautionary lesson against allowing emotions to gain the upper hand in public life.[23] In any case, the concept of emotions now has a secure place in our intellectual toolbox. This does not mean that its use is unproblematic. Is it meaningful to invoke "emotions" as an overarching category, or do specific emotions differ so fundamentally as to defy a general approach? It may be that, like "religion," a notoriously difficult concept to define in the abstract, we can only treat emotions in their particular forms.

RESENTMENT OR ANGER?

Between 1872 and 1980 in the field of experimental psychology—and within the limits of only English-language publications—there were apparently ninety-two definitions of "emotion," which is all the more reason not to consider "the" emotions as a generic category.[24] The issue is further complicated by the realization that however we think of emotions, they are never a matter of pure feeling alone. Accordingly, like others, I will sometimes refer to emotions as people's psychological dispositions. Indeed, a blurring of the two terms suggests an important insight that psychologists and others who study emotions have pursued, helping once and for all to break down the venerable divide between mind and body. Emotions are never absent cognition: we think at the same time as we feel. But it is also likely that the balance between feeling and thinking is not always the same with each emotional state. Here we can begin to explore the difference between anger and resentment as a means of establishing the particular nature of the latter—its distinctiveness in relation to other negative emotions.

As normally understood, anger has many faces. "In English one might think that these are some of the species of anger," writes the moral philosopher Owen Flanagan: "rage, outrage, hatred, fury, indignation, irritation, frustration, resentment, prissiness, impatience, envy, jealously, revenge, and vengeance."[25] There are, it seems to me, at least four ways we can distinguish resentment from the rather broad range of feelings classified as "anger."

First, resentment is relational. To be sure, this is often the case with anger. We are angry at someone who has hurt or disappointed us, who has thwarted us in our goals, who has spoken unkindly or has slighted us, who has failed to acknowledge our suffering, who persists in ignoring our presence, and so forth. We can even be angry at ourselves for, say, forgetting to do something. But just as often, anger is merely anger, without any agent responsible for provoking it. As Peter Strawson has noted in a foundational essay in the field of moral philosophy, resentment differs from general anger in the same way that indignation differs from it.[26] To be indignant is to react to harm not done to you but to someone or some group with which you identify. Resentment, then, names an emotion, a kind of moral anger, at something done to me by someone else intentionally. If someone steps on my foot on purpose, the physical hurt is the same as if they had done so accidentally. In terms of pain, there is no difference. In the latter case I might be momentarily angry; in the first, however, there is cause for resentment, a sense of moral injury.

This suggests a second way of distinguishing resentment from anger or realizing how anger can morph into resentment. Rather than two protagonists—the aggrieved and the victimizer—resentment often, perhaps even usually, involves a triangular relationship, where the third element could be a person, persons, or even something abstract like a value system or an ethos. This is best illustrated by the following scene: Say I (a professor) bump into a student and fail to excuse myself; my exalted status assures me that such a courtesy on my part is simply not warranted, at least not to a lowly undergraduate. Though hurt and insulted that I should treat him so thoughtlessly, the student feels he cannot protest because he is constrained by an obligation of deference, even to the point of stifling his legitimate anger, which then turns to resentment. While my action is the cause of his upset, his low status—which is to say an entire ethos of hierarchical values—is what precipitates his resentment. The third term, then, is this constraining ethos. Consequently, we might consider that in many cases resentment is frustrated anger, which often consequently seeks to place blame on someone or something else.

A third way resentment can be distinguished from anger, or at least be seen as a special species of anger, is precisely its level of cognition. Some moral philosophers have identified "cognitively sharpened" forms of anger, "partially constituted by a judgment about responsibility, wrongdoing, and/or blameworthiness of the offender."[27] By extension, then, resentment (like indignation) is pointedly "sharpened," not only by rendering a judgment of responsibility and blame, but with an added measure of conscious, often persistent, even cultivated grievance. The eighteenth-century Anglican preacher and philosopher Joseph Butler, whose views we shall examine below, argued favorably for a "settled" sort of resentment which implied a "conscience" that both gives rise to it and guides it within acceptable bounds of expression. And despite Nietzsche's disparagement of *ressentiment*, he still acknowledged its creative potential in fashioning, via the machinations of the "priests," a new morality. Whether seen in a favorable or unfavorable light, resentment implies an additional cognitive stage beyond sheer anger—an awareness of, or at least some reflection on, the provenance, cause, or reason for your misfortune.

There is, finally, the element of time or duration to consider. Anger might persist, of course; it can be sustained and nurtured, then becoming lodged as a defining feature of one's personality—an angry person. As Pankaj Mishra has argued, an entire "age" might be characterized as "angry" (although here some allowance should be made for overstatement in what was merely the title of his 2017 book, *The Age of Anger: A History of the Present*).[28] Usually, however, we think of anger as momentary: an outbreak, as in a "flash" of anger. In any case, anger that persists likely changes its emotional valence, becoming perhaps a "simmering" anger, or something akin to indignation or resentment, especially when the aggravating harm remains as an irritant. The specificity of resentment, it would seem, relates to this sense of duration, of a continuing feeling or emotional state. This reminds us that the original meaning of resentment has to do with reexperiencing something, as in the French word *ressentir*, which preserves the notion of repetition, or, literally, "returning to a feeling." When we consider this aspect of resentment, especially as a political and collective sentiment, however, there is the added complication that its persistence within a populace may very well be contrived, or at least encouraged and nurtured by powerful political and media forces. To distinguish between authentic collective emotions and those orchestrated from above is notoriously difficult. How can we really separate what people feel "on their own" from what they're told or encouraged to feel? Despite this difficulty, we must remain alert to the vexed nature of the problem.

Like the study of any emotion, then, resentment presents many obstacles to serious study. There is nothing tidy or well-defined about people's emotional states. This is perhaps why what best captures the lived experience of a feeling, especially as reflected upon in human consciousness, is literature—in characters fashioned by their creators as living in the grip of emotions which prove decisive in the narrative course they are set upon. Literature has been described as creating "simulations" in which readers might experience, possibly even viscerally, characters' emotions and conflicts—the psychological depths of their travails.[29] Let us turn for a moment to a canonical depiction of resentment, which indeed proved momentous in the destiny of a whole people. We might even call this biblical tale a founding myth of resentment.

JOSEPH AND HIS BROTHERS

> Now Israel loved Joseph more than all his children, because he was the son of his old age: and he made him a coat of many colors. And when his brethren saw that their father loved him more than all his brethren, they hated him, and could not speak peaceably unto him. And Joseph dreamed a dream, and he told it his brethren: and they hated him yet more.[30]
>
> —Genesis 37:3–5

There are many characters and episodes in the Western tradition that offer representations of resentment. Shakespeare, for one, presents us with a series of resentful protagonists: Iago, Cassius, Coriolanus, and Hamlet stand out in this respect. (In a subsequent chapter I shall look more closely at Hamlet, whose simmering resentment pursues him throughout the play.) Milton's Satan certainly seethes with resentment, unable to abide his subservience to God. ("Better to reign in hell, than serve in heaven.") The Jewish Bible is particularly rich in pairs of figures where one has reason to resent the other: Cain and Abel, Esau and Jacob, Leah and Rachel. But perhaps the portion of the Bible that most richly presents us with an unfolding saga where resentment haunts the series of events virtually every step of the way is the story of Joseph and his brothers. Looking at these chapters in Genesis, we get a good sense of some of the possible grounds for resentment, its potential dimensions, how its effects can resonate across time, and even, in this foundational story for the Hebrew people, its political implications.

"Unlike the other major units of Genesis," writes Herbert Marks in his brilliant commentary on this text, ". . . the story of Joseph is an extended narrative, at once a folktale illustrating the workings of providence and a precursor of the modern novella, remarkable for its subtle psychology and deft manipulation of the plot."[31] Indeed, a red-thread of resentment runs through the plot, starting even before Joseph's birth. For Jacob, Joseph's father (also called Israel), has two wives: Leah, whom he has been deceived into marrying by her father Laban; and Rachel, Leah's younger sister, whom he originally coveted and certainly favored. Leah has borne Jacob many sons, while Rachel has remained barren for many years. But then "God open[s] her womb" and Rachel gives birth to a son, Joseph, and then another, Benjamin. Jacob loves Joseph "more than all his children" because Joseph is "the son of his old age," we are told (37:3).

Because we know the backstory, we realize that this explanation for Jacob's favoritism fails to tell all. Even before Joseph begins to exhibit the obnoxious signs of his favored status, his brothers have reasons to resent him, if only because he is the child of the wife their father clearly prefers over their mother. The family itself is divided into two clans—the offspring of Leah (and her handmaiden) and the two sons (Joseph and Benjamin) of Rachel. Thus, rivalry and resentment characterize this family romance from the start. Jacob only confirms Joseph's favored status over his older brothers by granting him the "coat of many colors," proof that their father "love[s] him more than all his brethren." Consequently, "they [hate] him, and [cannot] speak peaceably unto him" (37:4).

Joseph then proceeds to add irritation to injury. He recounts not one but two dreams, each a revelation of his claim to superiority over his siblings. In the first, he says, his brothers' sheaves of wheat "made obeisance to my sheaf." To which they respond, "Shalt thou indeed reign over us? or shalt thou indeed have dominion over us?" In the second dream, he says, "the sun and the moon and the eleven stars made obeisance to me." This perplexes even his father: "Shall I and thy mother and thy brethren indeed come to bow down ourselves to thee to the earth?" With the first dream, the text reveals that the brothers hate him "yet the more for his dreams, and for his words," making clear that their animus is already well-established (37:8). After the second, the passage concludes, "And his brethren envied him" (37:11).

At this point in the story, the ten brothers remove themselves to Shechem, quite a distance from their father's lands in Hebron. In Thomas Mann's extensive elaboration on this saga in his epic novel *Joseph and His Brothers* (published in four volumes, 1933–43), he casts their departure as a deliberate act in reaction to Joseph's insufferable exhibition of his superiority. As Reuben, the eldest, thinks to himself: "Away with them all, in self-imposed exile from their father's heart. That . . . would be a dignified and powerful demonstration, the only possible answer on their part to this abomination."[32] Instead of protesting the injustice of their brother's claims or reacting in a forthright and meaningful way to the arrogant presumptions of their *younger* brother, which flies in the face of every established notion of familial order and traditional hierarchies, they simply leave. Manifestly long-standing, their resentment has been nurtured over the years, provoked both by their brother's words and actions and their father's favoritism. And yet, as is often the case with resentful people, they find it difficult to engage with the source of their grievance.

Of course, the story has its dramatic denouement when the brothers finally decide to deal with their upstart sibling. Jacob sends Joseph to seek out his brothers in their self-imposed exile. Their bitterness has not cooled. As they spy Joseph approaching in the distance, they comment: "Behold, the dreamer cometh,"—literally, "lord of dreams," which, Marks notes, is a "sarcastic play on Joseph's pretensions."[33] Even then, they prove to be less than decisive, stopping short of murdering him, and instead sell him into slavery, whence begins the story's sequel in Egypt.

The story of Joseph and his brothers exhibits the depths and dimensions of a collective sense of resentment, tells us something about the special nature of this emotion, and suggests why it deserves particular attention as a potent political force across time. For one thing, we see in the brothers' various expressions of animus toward their brother a complex set of feelings, which, we might surmise, they themselves have trouble grasping. Their hatred is compounded by not only envy but also pain in the face of what is a humiliating demotion in their father's eyes. With

Joseph's designation as their father's favorite, their world has been turned upside down. This, then, suggests another common cause for resentment: that the natural order of things, or at least people's time-honored expectations, are being challenged, if not entirely upset. We see too, most obviously, that resentment almost always presupposes a relationship between people or groups of people; a sense as well of proximity, such that an enduring feeling of aggrievement arises not simply from the injury or hurt itself but from the assumption that its infliction is intended. Here, too, the relationship is structural—rooted in familial cleavages across several generations—and intimate as well. This, then, underscores the dynamic of deflection with resentment: the brothers' grievance should have been placed at the feet of their father, whose emotional self-indulgence sets the whole sordid cycle in motion. Instead, they turn against Joseph (who, it must be said, gives them plenty of cause with his irritating boastfulness). While Joseph is clearly the hero of the story, we cannot help but feel some sympathy for his brothers, who, until they sell him to a slave trader, are entirely blameless, virtually blindsided by his rise in their father's esteem. Their sense of victimization, then, cannot be ignored, just as people's resentment more generally must be acknowledged, even if we wonder about its legitimacy or how it is expressed. The brothers' resentment is conveyed in a long narrative arc which drives home the nature of this emotion as enduring, in this case extending back across the generations even to the original conflict between Esau and Jacob, when the latter usurps the former's birthright. It even carries forward in time, setting the stage for Joseph's reconciliation with his brothers in Egypt, whence begins another chapter in the saga, culminating ultimately in Exodus and the formation of the Jewish people under both Moses and the Mosaic law.

*   *   *

In the chapters that follow I will explore resentment as both a concept and an actual sentiment, focusing for the most part on its collective and political expressions across time. In "Sensible Resentment in the Age of Sensibility," I start in eighteenth-century Britain, where philosophers interested in exploring the moral basis of sociability considered the balance between legitimate feelings of resentment in response to injury and what they saw as an unacceptable and socially damaging desire for revenge. Following this, in "Contentious Resentment," I look at several examples of collective resentment from the sixteenth to the early years of the nineteenth century, where resentment played a role in people's collective action, from the persecution of witches to forms of popular protest and revolution. Turning then to the modern period, starting in the nineteenth century, in "A Specter is Haunting Europe," I discuss the emergence of "the people" in the aftermath of the French Revolution as a new force in history, a force whose threatening presence was often framed in terms of resentment. This, then, sets the stage for the chapter I call "The Nietzschean Moment": a consideration of the German philosopher's formulation of the notion of *ressentiment*, especially in *On the Genealogy of Morality* (1887), but also its reformulation by another German philosopher, Max Scheler, in his book *Ressentiment* (1911, 1915). Together they have left a legacy which, for good or for ill, defines resentment negatively—as an emotion most people would not be very happy to "own."

The last four chapters take us from the middle decades of the twentieth century to the present. In "The Rise and Decline of the 'Resentment Paradigm,'" I trace how a group of influential social scientists and historians explained social movements, from American Populism in the 1890s to radical right-wingers in the post–World War II era, largely in terms of status anxiety and consequent resentment. Their "paradigm" reigned for several decades until it was met with a forceful critique by a younger generation of scholars, who dismissed this condescending and overly psychological approach to social movements. Consequently, I argue, "resentment" receded as a meaningful and serviceable concept in the toolbox of the social sciences. The following chapter, "The Uses of Resentment," returns to what we might consider a benign form of resentment, similar to Joseph Butler's formulation in the eighteenth century. In various ways, in the writings of various figures in the twentieth century—from Jean Améry to Frantz Fanon to participants in Truth and Reconciliation tribunals—we see resentment marshaled as a claim for recognition, justice, or even new assertions of collective identity. In the next chapter, "The Two Sixties and Resentment," I argue that there were indeed two aspects of this tumultuous decade. The one we usually think of—the time of protest and the counterculture—was decidedly *not* characterized by resentment. Other emotions prevailed. But there was another sixties, the one of Nixon's 1968 presidential campaign, the "silent majority," and the backlash against leftist protest movements—all marked, as I will suggest, by an effort to orchestrate a politics of resentment. This politics had a certain half-life, but it was eventually eclipsed among conservative Republicans by Reagan's "morning in America." Indeed, in the last decades of the twentieth century, I hope to show, resentment lost its purchase, both as a concept and as an ascription that resonated politically. Finally, in "The Return of Resentment," I try to attend to its many expressions evident in our present-day politics—the movements behind not only the election of

Donald Trump but also Brexit, Islamic fundamentalism, populism, identity politics, and the persistence of anti-Black racism, as well as other, less political modes of resentment. In the conclusion, "Thinking about Resentment Today," I offer some thoughts about how we might consider this vexed emotion, especially in its political context.

*   *   *

The question may still linger—why resentment? The answer, in the first instance, as I have noted, points to its prevalence as a description of our present rather fraught political moment (that is, the surfeit of "resentment-talk"). This book represents a modest attempt to clarify a term that has implications of which, I suspect, many who deploy it are not aware. Which leads to the other reason—to simplify what is obviously a complicated field of inquiry: there are some emotions or psychological dispositions that are more complex than others. Fear, anger, and disappointment, or joy, happiness, and contentment do not evoke subtle shades of meaning, obscure depths of feeling, or complex relationships. With something like resentment, however—and here kindred emotional states might include humiliation, jealousy, envy, and certainly others—there are interpersonal and even intrapersonal dynamics in play. There is as well a psychological element that places this emotion, maybe more than most, on the vexed border between feeling and thinking. In short, "resentment" carries with it a lot of baggage. If this book makes readers aware of the weight of that baggage, I will have accomplished something.

But this modest goal is hardly enough to justify a whole book. So let me lay my cards on the table, so to speak, in the form of three lines of argument.

One is still somewhat modest in scope and simply cautionary in nature. The characterization of "resentment" can mislead us in two diametrically opposed directions. On the one hand, it might serve to explain away violent, extreme, intemperate, or simply criminal impulses and behaviors with the excuse, "Oh, they're just acting out their resentment." Of course, this sets before us the fraught issue of determining the moral frontier between psychological motivations and profoundly deleterious actions, hardly an issue I will be able to settle here. But it is important to remain alert to the potential role of "resentment" in distracting us from terrible consequences that can't be ignored and shouldn't be explained away. On the other hand, the diagnosis of resentment has frequently been deployed in order to dismiss or delegitimize people's grievances and hurt: "Oh, we can ignore their complaints—they're just resentful [of us]." Both cases should serve to warn us about citing "resentment" too casually.

My second argument is a stronger claim: resentment is a condition of modernity.[34] Here there are three aspects of this particular argument. First, resentment is modern because it most readily arises when the principle of equality prevails as the reigning political ethos. In a premodern society, with little chance for social mobility and an entrenched hierarchy enforcing vast social differences, it was highly unlikely that ordinary people would resent the privileges or status of their social superiors. Although peasants surely felt miserable and oppressed, and might have hated their feudal lord as well, their limited expectations gave them little grounds for resenting someone whose position was so much beyond their reach. Only in the last two centuries, with the spread of democratic ideologies vaunting the principle of equality, has resentment emerged as an aspect of popular discontent, as a bitter reflection on the gap between what is and what should be. Second (and overlapping with the first), populism and popular mobilization, both distinctively modern phenomena, often embody resentful impulses, usually directed against distant, seemingly uncaring elites. As we shall see, with the appearance of "the people" in the wake of the epoch-making French Revolution, the concept of resentment emerged as one explanation for their often contentious presence. Finally, the velocity of change, a signature feature of modern times, not only has meant, as Marx eloquently wrote, that "all that's solid melts into air"; it more specifically means a never-ending dynamic of upturning or rearranging existing hierarchies, of undermining traditional cultures, of destroying long-standing communities. Sometimes extolled as a process of "creative destruction," this inexorable feature of modernity has also left repositories of resentment in its wake.

A caveat is in order here: Despite my overall assertion regarding the "modernity" of resentment, readers should not be misled into concluding that premodern people were somehow immune to this disposition—a patently absurd assumption. Resentment, like all basic emotions, can arise wherever and whenever people find themselves in vexed social relationships—even in biblical times, as illustrated by the tale of Joseph and his brothers. And in a subsequent chapter I shall show its episodic relevance in early modern times (the sixteenth through the eighteenth centuries). The point, rather, is that resentment more readily characterizes the modern condition not so much in merely interpersonal ways but as a psychological disposition that increasingly inflects modern politics. Even more, we might conclude from observing the dynamics of contemporary populism that it especially thrives in the context of political polarization generated more by moral outrage than political interests.

My final argument regards how we might think of the emotional range and moral implications of resentment. While it is usually understood as an unedifying emotion, a psychological predicament that most people would be loath to accept as an accurate description of how they feel, we will also encounter examples of very different understandings of this state—as a useful way of conceiving one's position in the world. In other words, resentment is not always negative; it can be purposeful, if also usually unpleasant, and even at its most unappealing it conveys a moral stance, a sense of being morally wronged, that cannot be ignored.

The following chapters will weave in and out of these three sets of arguments, with one or the others—and other times somewhat different reflections—occupying our attention. While it is apparent that present-day concerns motivate this study, I am intent on casting these in a historical light. This is a history of the present, a history that begins in the eighteenth century.

CHAPTER ONE

Sensible Resentment in the Age of Sensibility

The Eighteenth Century

The temperately revengeful have leisure to weigh the merits of the cause, and thereby either to smother their secret resentments, or to seek adequate reparations for the damages they have sustained.

RICHARD STEELE, *The Guardian*, August 8, 1713

Robert Solomon, one of the most important and prolific contemporary philosophers of the emotions, defines "resentment" in rather categorical terms. It is, he writes, "the villain of the passions." It poisons "the whole of subjectivity with its venom . . . maintaining its keen and vicious focus on each of the myriad of petty offenses it senses against itself." Though it is not considered one of the seven deadly sins, "it is surely the deadliest, stagnating self-esteem and shrinking our world down to a tightly defensive constricted coil, plotting and scheming to the exclusion even of pride, making all trust, intimacy, and intersubjectivity impossible, except for the always untrustworthy alliances it forms in mutual defense and for the purpose of expressing its usually impotent schemes of vengeance."[1]

Solomon's depiction of resentment, which continues for several pages anatomizing the emotion's corrosive, devious, and life-denying ways, largely conforms to our contemporary sense of resentment as an unappealing and fundamentally undesirable disposition. Few people today would want to admit harboring deeply resentful feelings. Indeed, this book is largely informed by an attempt to explore our various understandings of this emotion—to see if we can discern shades of its implications beyond the merely negative, disparaging meanings we normally associate with it.

It is interesting to note, however, that a dark view of the emotion was not always the case, for in the late seventeenth century, which is really when a continuous intellectual history of the concept begins, it first evoked a range of meanings, some of them benign or at least neutral.

Thomas Blount's 1661 *Glossographia* defines resentment as "a full taste, a true feeling, a sensible apprehension of a resentment." This is echoed in Edward Phillip's *The New World of Words*, published in 1678, which understands it as "a sensible feeling or true apprehension of any thing." The dictionary of the French Academy (1694) explains *"ressentiment"* as "a sense of injury received," but offers the qualification that it is the memory (*le souvenir*) of either injuries or blessings (*bienfaits*). It can be understood as the experience of recognizing or acknowledging something either good or bad ("La reconnaissance est un ressentiment qu'on a du bien que quelqu'un nous a fait").[2]

These early understandings of resentment, then, imply a meaning of the concept which maps onto more general notions of perception, recognition, or other ways in which the world is simply encountered and mentally experienced. It did not then imply a negative or disagreeable sentiment but was rather capacious in its reach. In this context, it is useful to be reminded that its Latin root, *resentire*, merely meant "to feel." This should not be entirely surprising, for, as Thomas Dixon has shown, it was only in the nineteenth century that the concept of "emotions" emerged as a catchall category "conceived as a set of morally disengaged, bodily, non-cognitive and involuntary feelings . . ." It was only then that the distinction was fixed between feelings and emotions on one side of the phenomenological divide, and mind or reason on the other. Before this, the terrain of what we consider "emotions" was a much broader, nuanced, and varied landscape described by such terms as "affections," "moral sentiments," "passions," and others that "could be understood as both rational and voluntary movements of the soul, while still being subjectively warm and lively psychological states."[3] In keeping with this longer history of "sentiments" and the like, we should not be surprised if the concept of resentment once conveyed a more expansive range of dispositions than in more recent times.

By the eighteenth century, however, a subtle turn was apparent in its meaning, or rather the emphasis was now more consistently on the negative, deleterious aspect of resentment, suggesting a sense of being wronged. For example, the 1730 *Dictionarium Britannicum* defines it as "a sensible apprehension of an Injury offered, or a revengeful Remembrance of it." Samuel Johnson's *Dictionary of the English Language* (1755–56) exhibits the somewhat skewed interpretation of its current meaning, but makes a point of noting the recent modification. "To take well or ill" is his first definition, which preserves the sense of moral ambivalence. The second, however, adds some precision: "To take ill; to consider as an injury or an affront." Johnson then comments, "This is now the most usual sense."

The French *Encyclopédie* (1756 edition) maintains a neutral view of the term, but also confirms its relationship to injury. Resentment is "a lasting movement of indignation and anger, which prompts us to retaliate either immediately or in the aftermath of an act of injustice against us." It is "a passion that nature has placed in human beings for their defense." But the definition adds a limiting proviso that instruments of justice should preempt personal retaliation for wrongs: it is actionable only in a state of nature, for "the law, which assumes the responsibility for my vengeance, has taken the place of resentment."[4]

Despite some qualifications, the eighteenth-century understanding of resentment, while not positive, recognized its potential usefulness as an emotional instrument of self-defense against injury. It certainly did not exhibit the entirely negative, disapproving view expressed by Solomon— and formally given a foundational formulation by Nietzsche (as we shall see). This is in keeping with what emerged in this period, the "Age of Sensibility," when the complexity and variety of feelings and "passions" were the order of the day, the stuff of countless philosophical treatises, medical tracts, sermons, novels, and the like.

It is not surprising, then, that resentment should find a place in the writings of two of the most important moral philosophers of the eighteenth century, both fundamental in the development of "sensibility" as a signature feature of the period—Adam Smith and David Hume. They were preceded, however, by a more obscure figure who nevertheless ranks as the thinker who perhaps began the modern history of the concept of resentment, the Anglican bishop and philosopher Joseph Butler. In contrast to how we usually think of resentment, Butler took pains to justify it as necessary and valuable in assuaging grievances and seeking forgiveness, as distinguished from an instrument of malice or revenge, which he condemned.

JOSEPH BUTLER: "SETTLED AND DELIBERATE" RESENTMENT

The son of a linen draper, Joseph Butler (1692–1752) was raised a Presbyterian and educated first in a local grammar school and then in a dissenting academy in Gloucester (later moved to Tewkesbury). Before entering Oxford, and perhaps in order to be admitted, he decided to conform to the Church of England. Graduating from Oriel College, Oxford, in 1718, he was ordained as a priest that same year. In 1733, he earned a doctorate in civil law. His first appointment was as a preacher at the Rolls Chapel, Chancery Lane, London. Having gained some distinction for both his preaching and writings, he still seemed to languish in obscurity. When he was recommended to Queen Caroline for an ecclesiastical appointment, she responded that she thought he was dead. "No, Madam," her adviser replied, "but he is buried."[5] Subsequently, he rose through various positions: the see of Bristol, the deanery of St. Paul's Cathedral, the clerk of the closet to the king, and, finally, the see of Durham in 1750. He died two years later.[6]

During his lifetime, Butler was well known as a theologian and apologist, taking special interest in refuting Deism and countering the moral implications of the philosophies of both Thomas Hobbes and John Locke. He is considered one of the leading moral philosophers in the Anglican tradition. In the nineteenth century, Cardinal Newman described him as "The greatest name in the Anglican Church."[7] While he wrote extensively on a range of issues, a good deal of his renown stems from the *Fifteen Sermons*, published in 1726 and subsequently reissued several times. These he delivered before a congregation of lawyers and law clerks of the Court of Chancery at the nearby Rolls Chapel in London in 1719; hence the learned tone and content of the sermons, which dealt with a range of moral themes, from human nature, compassion, and self-deceit to the "love of our neighbor" and the "love of God."

The topics of sermons eight and nine, "Upon Resentment" and "Upon Forgiveness," are the most pertinent for us here; in both, the sentiment of resentment receives a sustained treatment which is still influential today, primarily because he was one of the first writers who understood resentment as not only natural but also often necessary in insuring moral justice.

It is worth stepping back to consider why Butler was moved to ponder the purposefulness and meaning of resentment, to regard it with a steady gaze and, moreover, with such sympathy. Like many of his contemporaries, especially devout Christians, he was troubled by the implications of Hobbes's philosophy, with its bleak, one-dimensional view of human sentiments, a view that saw people as fundamentally motivated by selfish desires, individual interests, and fear. But he also rejected the pessimistic view of human nature characteristic of a harsher brand of Calvinism that prevailed under the Puritans. Like many others of his generation, he was influenced by the Earl of Shaftesbury, who, even though Locke was his tutor, rebelled against his "foster-father" in rejecting a philosophy that espoused an image of human sensibility devoid of any moral ballast. Shaftesbury argued for a "moral sense," the sense of right and wrong that was a "first principle" "in our constitution," "implanted in our heart."[8]

Shaftesbury rejected both Locke and Hobbes, but despite their differences, all of these writers were responding to a century of religious strife, civil war, and the fractiousness and violence that seemed endemic in an increasingly complex society. It was no longer possible to rely on either the ideal of public virtue or the efficacy of heavy-handed authority, nor, certainly, on the obligation of Christian obedience. In this period, the order of the day for philosophers and moralists of various stripes was to figure out how the vicissitudes of human interests, appetites, and proclivities could be squared with the sociable demands of a "polite and commercial society," in the famous words of the eighteenth-century jurist William Blackstone. In the course of their exploration of this problem, they generated a sophisticated and finely tuned approach to human behavior that, in fact, furnished the foundations of both modern psychology and moral philosophy.

Butler, like Shaftesbury, Thomas Reid, and later David Hume and Adam Smith, took up this line of concern. Unlike these others, he was a member of the clergy and a Christian divine obligated to frame his arguments in Christian terms. But unlike some of his contemporary theologians, especially so-called religious revivalists like Jonathan Edwards and Isaac Watts, he preferred to rely upon reason rather than scripture, philosophical arguments rather than theology. Butler approached the subject armed not only with traditional theology and the nostrums of Christian morality but also with an awareness of the philosophical discussions on the passions and the vagaries of human nature swirling around him. Still, he did see providential design in what he insisted, against the Hobbesian view, was the essentially benevolent disposition of humans, a virtue instilled in us by God. On the other hand, departing radically from most Christian moralists, he viewed self-love as a benign, natural passion, drawing upon the same inclinations as benevolence: just as self-love prompts us to seek gratification as individuals, so benevolence moves us to want happiness for others.

God wants us to love our enemies, he reminds his listeners several times in these sermons, and implicit in this injunction is the Christian imperative of forgiveness. There is, however, an obstacle to this obligation: resentment. For Butler, resentment and forgiveness are tethered to each other. Unlike other moralists, he refuses simply to condemn resentment, despite his acknowledgment that it is "harsh and turbulent," unique insofar as "no other principle, or passion, hath for its end the misery of fellow-creatures." It is, he avers, incompatible with good will. Alert to the complexities and caprices of human nature, he nevertheless understands it as natural and instinctual—even children and animals (!) are capable of it. This, then, prompts him to ask: Why has God endowed us with this terrible disposition, "which appears direct contrary to benevolence?" (8:1, p. 68). There must be a purpose to His design.

Parsing the nature of resentment, he meditates on the different forms and expressions it can take—or at least he insists on a distinction between two sorts. One is what he calls "hasty and sudden" resentment; the other is "settled and deliberate" (8:4, p. 69). The first is an almost instinctual reaction to "opposition, sudden hurt, and violence" (8:5, p. 69); it also leads to "malice and revenge." The second is a more reflective, measured response to wrongdoing, as much informed by reason as by passion. It is this second sort, instilled in us by our Creator, that Butler enshrines as natural, reasonable, purposeful, and innocent, "a weapon put into our hands by nature, against injury, injustice and cruelty" (8:8, p. 71). Citing the injunction of the apostle Paul, "Be ye angry and sin not," he comments, "Yet here is evidently a distinction made between anger and sin; between the natural passion, and sinful anger" (8:4, p. 69). Resentment is that "natural passion." Just as we are right in feeling indignation when others are unjustly harmed, so, too, resentment is both reasonable and right when it comes to ourselves. "It is one of the common bonds by which society is held together; a fellow-feeling which each individual has in behalf of the whole species, as well as of himself" (8:7, p. 70).

But in his sermons he goes beyond this distinction, pursuing a consideration of the nature of "settled" resentment as a justified response to injury or wrongdoing, that is, as an instrument of self-defense. Here he looks as much at the wrongdoer as the victim, offering a realistic view of the recalcitrance of evildoers. Neither reasoning nor an appeal to morality could be expected to have a modifying or deterrent effect on them, he acknowledges. And, though good Christians might be tempted to offer pity or compassion toward offenders, this too will likely yield little in the way of satisfaction (8:13, p. 73). Moral evil, he insists, deserves a severe and commensurate response. Thankfully, God has endowed us with an instrument for reprobation—that is, resentment, which he calls, in a telling phrase, "not only innocent but generous movement of the mind" (8:17, p. 74).

Butler's endorsement of resentment is qualified throughout; it is defined as much by what it is not as what it is. Above all, he insists that it should not include the passion for revenge. "Resentment is not inconsistent with good will," he proclaims. "We may therefore love our enemy, and yet have resentment against him for his injurious behavior towards us. But when this resentment entirely destroys our natural benevolence towards him, it is excessive, and becomes malice or revenge" (9:13, p. 78). Here, I think, we have an aspect of his understanding that many commentators, especially moral philosophers who focus mostly on the discursive arguments of his position, tend to miss. For they ignore the broader social context of an early modern European society, which indeed helps us understand some of the distinctions he asserts.

Butler makes two pertinent distinctions. The first is to rule out revenge as a component of resentment, for this would be to endorse not only the intemperate, impulsive, "instinctual" face of resentment but also thereby to cause "pain and misery" in the wrongdoer, something beyond the purview of a good Christian (8:3, p. 69). "Hatred, malice and revenge are directly contrary to the religion we profess, and to the nature and reason of the thing itself" (8:3, p. 69). Butler goes to great lengths in describing the "abuses of anger," the "rage and fury," the "peevishness," the "monstrous" resentment, "this distemper of the mind" that "seizes them upon the least occasion in the world, and perpetually without any reason at all . . ." (8:10, p. 72). The worst of these excesses is to persist in retributive anger when it is evident that the injury is not deliberate, when it is clearly the result of "error or misunderstanding" (8:12, p. 71).

But all of this is not meant to rule out punishment or sanctions against wrongdoers, it only means that personal revenge should not be the means. This is the second way Butler distinguishes his understanding of resentment—or rather how it should be expressed—from its typical consequences. Rather, he endorses an "administration of justice," meaning recourse to a public sphere where there are instruments—that is, the law—for judging and punishing wrongdoers. The proper use of resentment "stands in our nature for self-defense, and not for the administration of justice." To be sure, in the "uncultivated parts of the world, and, where regular governments are not formed," the sanctions prompted by resentment are necessary, for there "to be passive is certain destruction . . . sudden resistance is the only security" (8:6, p. 70). But eighteenth-century Britain was not one of the "uncultivated parts of the world" without a "regular" government. Indeed, someone like Butler, a high churchman of the established church, embodied the gentlemanly values of a society that aspired to the highest standards of civilized sociability—and this was a society where the savage, "uncivilized" instinct of revenge could have no place.

His distinctions, then, are twofold along two axes defined by fundamental categorical antinomies: reason ("settled and deliberate" resentment) and passion (revenge), and the private (where an individual expresses resentment for a wrong) and public (where the wrongdoer is punished).

Even a casual understanding of eighteenth-century Britain—and in fact any Western European society of that time—yields an appreciation for Butler's worry that "intemperate" resentment would likely lead to revenge.

His distinctions were indeed pertinent, not merely a matter of abstract philosophizing. Disorder and violence were perhaps the greatest concerns of the day. From routine brawling, rioting, and the excesses of popular celebration in city streets, to highway robbery and the vendettas and dueling of aristocrats, to the threat of civil war—the memory of which was still alive in the minds of his fellow English men and women—this was a society that was only barely pacified. Even at the highest, presumably most "civilized"—or at least gentlemanly—level of society, that of the political elite, there was a deep-seated and much mooted concern with "faction" and "parties" that in fact increasingly characterized the milieu of the English Parliament. "Popular libertarianism, religious conflict, party strife, dynastic instability, all remained features of the decades following the Revolution of 1688," writes a major authority on the period.[9] Butler, like many of his contemporaries, strove to cast society as a peaceable union of sociable citizens, which was, of course, more an ideal than a lived reality. But it was an ideal that, as a high churchman of the established church, as a member of a ruling elite that saw itself as a civilizing influence on a sometimes unruly society, he was duty-bound to promulgate—thus, his insistence on the imperative of forgiveness. Because he also recognized resentment as a natural, innate human disposition, despite its great potential for harm, he offered a highly qualified endorsement of its legitimacy as a moral passion. And because he also saw that it could serve a purpose precisely in evoking or even ensuring true forgiveness, he deserves to be considered a foundational figure in the intellectual history of this emotion.

ADAM SMITH: RESENTMENT AS A NATURAL PASSION

Adam Smith (1723–90) is best known for *An Inquiry into the Nature and Causes of the Wealth of Nations*, published in that epochal year 1776, a book that set the course for modern economic thought and policy. But the importance of this professor, a major figure in the Scottish Enlightenment, is not restricted to his teachings on economics. He ranks as one of the leading moral philosophers of his time, responsible for formulating a sort of secular conscience, embodied in his concept of the "impartial spectator," or the "fair and impartial spectator," which should guide us as we dispassionately "endeavour to examine our own conduct."[10] In 1759 he published *The Theory of Moral Sentiments*, based on a series of lectures delivered at the University of Glasgow. Like Butler, he concerned himself with the moral basis of human behavior, especially in light of the views of philosophers from Hobbes in the seventeenth century to his contemporary Rousseau, both of whom viewed egoistic instincts as a fundamental obstacle to a peaceable society. Smith, too, recognized self-love, or self-interest, as an intractable element of humans' disposition, but he did not see it as antithetical to harmonious relationships, for his understanding of self-interest was quite broad—so much so that it included the sense of "sympathy" for others. We naturally share in their pain and pleasure. Indeed, in Smith's view, an innate sympathy for the feelings of one's fellows provided the basis for a guardedly optimistic outlook on the prospect for a healthy civil society.

Smith acknowledges Butler as "a late and ingenious philosopher," and like Butler, Smith concerned himself with the moral dynamics of human interactions, which include a consideration of resentment.[11] This Smith does in the first part of *The Theory of Moral Sentiments*, where he examines what he calls "unsocial passions." Resentment ranks chief among them. Along with anger, ingratitude, and other emotions that disturb our equilibrium and disrupt our relationships, it does not attract our sympathy, quite the contrary. Resentment, he repeats several times, ranks as perhaps the most "odious" of these sorts of unsocial passions. It brings to mind "something harsh, jarring and convulsive, something that tears and distracts the breast, and is altogether destructive of that composure and tranquility of the mind which is so necessary to happiness . . ."[12] Like gratitude, which is an "instrument" of happiness in others, resentment is an "instrument" too, but of misery in others. Following Butler, Smith contributes to the negative definition of resentment as a morally problematic disposition that undermines peaceable sociability, which was the understanding of the concept that had definitively emerged by the mid-eighteenth century.

But Smith also sees the positive side of resentment. Again, like Butler, he appreciates it as a natural passion that serves as a warning or defense against injury and injustice. There is, he notes, something "contemptible" in the man who "tamely sits still, and submits to insults." Even ordinary people—the "mob"—cannot abide witnessing someone "patiently" submitting to "affronts or ill-usage." "They desire," he writes, "to see this insolence resented, and resented by the person who suffered from it." What Smith really means here is not solely resentment as the indignation of onlookers at someone unjustly suffering.[13] Smith takes the part of the injured and those observing them alike, both of whom experience resentment in a salutary fashion. It is useful to the individual, "by rendering it dangerous to insult or injure him," and to the public, as a means of ensuring or promoting justice "and of the equality of its administration."[14]

But it is also useful to the perpetrator, potentially contributing to their moral regeneration and thus to the moral health of society. Attention to the moral state of those who injure us, however, is first raised because of the personal nature of an injury, which gives rise to resentment. It is not simply a matter of the injury, nor even of the intended injury. "What chiefly enrages us against the man who injures us," he writes, "is the little account which he seems to make of us, the unreasonable preference which he gives to himself above us . . . that other people may be sacrificed at any time, to his conveniency or his humour."[15] This "little account" prompts the implicit disrespect and disregard that, with resentment, inflicts more pain than the actual injury. Beyond this, Smith's estimation of the effect of resentment is quite ambitious. A wrongdoer must experience "shame, and horror, and consternation," without which their moral rehabilitation cannot be accomplished. This is the work, the effect, of resentment, which Smith describes in an elaborate, florid passage where he imagines the psychological and emotional pilgrimage of the wrongdoer laboring under its powerful influence. Once the demented passion that drives them to their misdeed cools, the "violator of the more sacred laws of justice" begins to reflect on "the unhappy effect of [their] own conduct;" they even come to share the feelings of others who "have rendered [them] the proper object of the resentment and indignation of mankind." Isolated and scorned, plagued by their own black thoughts of regret and remorse—the "most dreadful of all the sentiments which can enter the human breast"—their punishment is total and profound. But this is not effected by the instruments of formal justice; rather, it results from a "consciousness of the justly provoked resentment of all rational creatures."[16]

This is a lot to expect from the passion of resentment, all the more so because Smith wants to keep this passion under wraps, so to speak, carefully "humbled" and rendered rational. For as much as he urges us to appreciate the positive work of resentment, he is also concerned with its potential excesses and deleterious consequences. In order to be useful and socially acceptable, it must be tempered. Somewhat strangely, given his acknowledgment of its "odious" nature, he proposes that it can become "graceful and agreeable" as long as "it is brought down below that pitch to which it would naturally arise." He seems to be making the same move as Butler here, asserting a distinction between an emotional, angry, and unpremeditated resentment and an expression of resentment that is measured, deliberate, and properly calibrated to the injury received. One cannot escape concluding that Smith has in mind a class distinction cast in emotional terms, with the cultivated gentleman uniquely equipped to channel this "unsocial passion" constructively and "agreeably," while "the greater part of mankind" remains incapable "of exerting so much self-command over one of the most ungovernable passions of his nature." This is indeed rare. Thus, when "the animosity of the sufferer exceeds, as it almost always does, what we can go along with . . . we necessarily disapprove of it."[17] Resentment is fine; just not *too much* resentment.

His worry about "too violent resentment," of course, is that it leads to revenge, "the most detestable of all passions—the object of the horror and indignation of every body."[18] Again we see the concern for public order, the fear of "civil society [becoming] a scene of bloodshed and disorder, every man revenging himself at his own hand whenever he fancied he was injured . . ."[19] But it is a concern compounded by Smith's mission to moralize sentiments—to argue for a sense of public morality that was both formal and informal, both buttressed by the legal instruments of law and the power of the state but, more profoundly, also underwritten by a common appreciation of the salutary effect of benevolence. Resentment is condoned, but only if it can be conveyed within the bounds and with the intent of benevolent expression.

DAVID HUME: RESENTMENT AND SOCIAL PROXIMITY

In a letter to Adam Smith, his fellow Scottish philosopher, David Hume thanks him for his "friendly Resentment against" Rev. John Oswald. In what was apparently a convoluted tangle regarding some unspecified insult, Hume, prompted by Smith's intervention, was prepared to forgive the right reverend's brother James for having failed to apologize for John's behavior.[20] Despite the opaque nature of this interpersonal contretemps, we can infer that Smith's expression of resentment facilitated Hume's expression of forgiveness, or so he was ready to assume. Like Smith and Butler, Hume acknowledged the usefulness of resentment in effecting a sort of reconciliation.

While Hume's relationship, both personal and intellectual, with Smith is well-documented, in his writings he did not acknowledge Joseph Butler, the Anglican divine whose productive meditations on resentment are noted earlier, and whom Smith himself recognized as an influence. This is somewhat surprising, for, like them, Hume contributed to a nuanced understanding of this problematic passion, adding his own appreciation of the role a certain conception of resentment could play in achieving justice.

In *A Treatise of Human Nature* (1739–40), Hume considers the different kinds of resentment, while first bundling it with other "certain calm desires and tendencies." These are "instincts originally implanted in our natures," identified as "benevolence and resentment, the love of life, and kindness to children; or the general appetite to good, and aversion to evil, consider'd merely as such." Resentment stands out amid this list of fundamentally positive "instincts" as emotionally unpleasant. Clearly, however, he is speaking here of a moderate, or, as he has it, a "calm" expression of resentment, the kind that causes "no disorder in the soul." Indeed, he likens it to the same "faculty . . . which judges of truth and falsehood."²¹

But resentment has another face, one that is decidedly less calm. Hume writes, "When I receive any injury from another, I often feel a violent passion of resentment, which makes me desire his evil and punishment, independent of all considerations of pleasure and advantage to myself."²² It would seem, then, that Hume makes the same kind of distinction offered by both Butler and Smith; that is, a distinction between resentment at two different registers of emotion, one "calm," the other "violent." One commentator, however, interprets this distinction as a way of recasting what he disparagingly refers to as the "struggle of passion and reason, as it is call'd," into one between two sorts of passion.²³ In this case, unlike Hume's near-contemporaries, the distinction does not seem to generate the same conclusion regarding the proper, preferred, or ethically valid form of resentment, which is to say, its modulation in deliberative or rational expression. For, at least in this context, Hume maintains a descriptive rather than a prescriptive stance, with the aim of arguing for an understanding of the passions that still "operate on the will," even if contrary to people's "interests and designs."²⁴ This is in keeping with his overall philosophical agenda aimed at elevating the passions above reason; or, as he famously put it, "Reason is and ought to be, the slave of passions."²⁵ With regard to resentment, unlike Butler and Smith, Hume seems unconcerned with the danger of it prompting revenge. Whether someone's experience or expression of resentment is calm or violent has less to do with the circumstances or nature of injury than "according to the *general* character or *present* disposition of the person."²⁶

Like Smith, Hume sees resentment as provoked not simply by those who harm but those who have injured us with "a particular design and intention."²⁷ An accidental injury does not warrant, nor does it normally cause, this kind and level of response. But Hume frames this unremarkable insight with a concept that is central to his philosophy. We usually make a distinction between someone who steps on our toe accidentally and someone who does so intentionally, even if the pain is of the same magnitude. Resentment, or at least sustained and targeted anger, would be the expected emotional response in the case of the latter but not the former. Moreover, with such intention as the precipitating condition of the injury, the victim's reaction shifts from the hurt to the person who caused the injury. This reflects Hume's general argument that moral judgments are generated not from social utility, self-interest, or reason but from the passions themselves, which is to say that passions create passions. "By the intentions we judge actions," Hume writes, "and according as that is good or bad, they become causes of love or hatred." This is crucial, for it is the malicious intention to harm which gives rise to a sense of injustice that is the ground of resentment, not the ephemeral injury, which, while perhaps painful, does not provoke the same response. More than this, Hume wants to argue that, like all passions, resentment is communicated by what he calls "sympathy," a fundamental term for his whole philosophy. Just as we sympathetically feel another's joy or sadness, so it is with resentment, only here it is the sentiment of wanting to inflict pain or otherwise harm that is communicated. "Hatred, *resentment*, esteem, love, courage, mirth and melancholy; all these passions I feel more from communication than from my own natural temper and disposition."[28]

But this, then, begs the question of whether emotional communication of this sort can take place across an entire society, especially one characterized by vast differences of class and culture, as in eighteenth-century Britain. In general, Hume seems to argue for a generous understanding of the byways of sympathy, based upon "a great resemblance among all human creatures. . . . We never remark any passion or principle in others, of which, in some degree or other, we may find a parallel in ourselves." Elsewhere, however, he qualifies this assertion, suggesting that a "society" characterized by such sympathy presupposes a degree of equality, or at least proximity. Otherwise, the expression of resentment, for example, would not be felt by its intended target; which is to say that resentment as an expression of injustice would be ineffective. It might be thought, he writes, that great disparity creates, by the mere "disproportion," a greater sense of envy, jealousy, or resentment. But this is not true, he responds, for such distance "diminishes the effects of the comparison." And this leads to a general proposition that "resemblance and proximity always produce a relation of ideas together; and where you destroy these ties, however other accidents may bring two ideas together; as they have no bond or connecting quality to join them in the imagination; 'tis impossible they can remain long united, or have any considerable influence on each other."[29]

With this, Hume offers an insight that will become more relevant later in the eighteenth century and beyond, as notions of equality, rights, and democracy, usually embodied in the revolutionary tradition that emerged at the end of the century, become the order of the day. Then, as we shall see, and as such trenchant commentators as Alexis de Tocqueville observed, the prospect and promise of equality as a principle, if not a reality, virtually guaranteed that the sentiment of resentment would grow as citizens were more and more invited to compare themselves with their presumed equals, even though this presumption was belied by the profound differences that distinguished them. With this, we are prompted to acknowledge that resentment as a social phenomenon truly has a history—that it is not merely a perennial and timeless feature of human interactions and the vicissitudes of human psychology. And in this respect, at least, it differs from anger, humiliation, hatred, and other related emotions. It is—perhaps uniquely—a symptom of a modern and modernizing society insofar as an egalitarian ethos encourages people's aspirations for the social advancement once denied them by the barriers of traditional legal and social hierarchies, even, or especially, as those advantages are rarely delivered. "Resentment" has a history and so does resentment—both of which we will explore in the following chapters.

*　*　*

The version of resentment offered by these eighteenth-century moralists seems to adhere mostly to individuals and interpersonal relationships. Butler, Smith, and Hume are interested in the moral integuments of an increasingly complex society, and they acknowledge that the emotional dynamics governing human interactions are indeed one aspect of its complexity, which cannot be controlled simply by political fiat or religious injunction. In this sense, even if they don't address politics or collective emotions, their meditations on this subject certainly have implications for how one should think about civility, justice, and other issues relating to the moral foundations of society.

Their formulation of resentment might not square with common understandings of this emotion. I begin this chapter by quoting Robert Solomon, a reliable source on the philosophy of emotions, who has provided us with a quite negative definition of resentment, one which, I think, would not surprise most of today's readers. But Solomon acknowledges another face of this emotion, which in fact echoes the views of Butler, Smith, and Hume. This is resentment as "the gateway to a sense of justice—or, more accurately, a sense of injustice . . ." An "extremely philosophical emotion," resentment "is quite conscious of not how things are but of how they might be—and, most important, of how they ought to be."[30] And this points to interesting shadings of resentment—not only the revengeful sort that mainly worried Butler, Smith, and Hume, but rather its potential as an instrument of justice. These eighteenth-century writers addressed emotions in the context of their own society, or at least the ideal of a "polite and commercial society." But as Solomon's comment implies, and as we shall see later, a modulated or even moderate resentment could still have teeth. Even in social contexts worlds apart from the genteel circles informed by eighteenth-century "sensibility," forceful expressions of resentment could work as effective irritants on quiescent or majoritarian sentiments that refuse to recognize the grievances of others.

Looking forward, it is of more than passing interest that this connection between justice and resentment would be asserted by Eugen Dühring, the nineteenth-century German philosopher, but remembered by posterity, if at all, as the target of Friedrich Engels's *Anti-Dühring* (1878). And it was Dühring's rather benign, or at least instrumental, interpretation of resentment that would provoke Nietzsche to write *On the Genealogy of Morality*, which, as we shall see, took a very different, decidedly negative view of this emotion. In our day, even the philosopher John Rawls, who, as a good Kantian, strove to emphasize the reasonable, rational basis of justice, acknowledged resentment as a psychological component of justice. Resentment can work to reveal the reality of injustice: "If we resent our having less than others, it must be because we think that their being better off is the result of unjust institutions, or wrongful conduct on their part."[31] Nietzsche's view of the role of resentment (or *ressentiment*, as he called it) in the moral history of the West would prove to be decisive; the sheer force of his formidable exposition tended to eclipse any other interpretation of this emotion. This is, then, all the more reason why we should underscore the eighteenth-century "civil" view of resentment. It is a view that will have a subsequent history.

But a more immediate subsequent history brings us to the end of the eighteenth century, and an event which demonstrated to many that a surfeit of feeling could disastrously break through the polite constraints of sensibility, unleashing terrible destructive emotions the likes of which Butler, Smith, and Hume could hardly have anticipated but certainly feared. Hume in particular, like many of his fellow *philosophes*, expressed great wariness of "enthusiasm."[32] And if nothing else, the French Revolution unleashed enthusiasm in epoch-making proportions. In the wake of this upheaval, it is difficult to imagine writers in the mold of these commentators embracing even a restrained resentment, so attuned were they to the vengeful passions many saw at the heart of the Revolution.

In the next chapter, we will eventually encounter the French Revolution in order to consider the role resentment might have played in its advent. Leading up to this crowning event of the century, which in so many ways redirected the course of Western history, or at the very least set the agenda for the century that followed, I want to look at other sorts of conflict, some political, others not, where we can observe the workings of resentment as a factor in setting people against one another. Here, then, we turn from the intellectual history of the concept of resentment—the way it was defined and reconsidered by various thinkers—to the experience of resentment itself—the ways people's resentful feelings spurred them to contentious action. And we begin with one of the most curious and disturbing conflicts, which indeed was fraught with emotional and psychological elements—the prosecution of so-called witches in the sixteenth and seventeenth centuries.

CHAPTER TWO

Contentious Resentment

*Acting Out Resentment in
the Early Modern Past*

In its widest sense rebellion goes far beyond resentment.

ALBERT CAMUS, *The Rebel*

A common analysis of the role of resentment in contemporary politics and political movements, especially in the wake of the 2016 election in the US and Brexit in the UK, hinges on its supposed formative place in the emotional makeup of those who feel "left behind." Left behind by what? Economic changes, the advance of technology, higher skill levels, more demanding credentials—in short, a bundle of factors, some rather too conveniently subsumed under the ideological mantle of "neoliberalism," that have ravaged many communities especially in the US heartland, creating legions of economic "losers," downwardly mobile workers, who once had a reasonable prospect of securing a foothold in that quintessentially American firmament of the "middle class." Left behind by these distant forces with supranational sources well beyond their control or understanding, these are people who seethe with righteous resentment at having been demoted in the social order, even as they observe "others"—immigrants, women, unfairly (in their view) favored minorities—surpassing and displacing them.

There is much that is compelling in this analysis, which I shall return to in the final chapter. But for the moment, it is important to remember that being "left behind" has been the lot of many people throughout history, not only in the present or in recent times. Indeed, one might well write the history of the modern world with this as a guiding theme: that the collateral damage of deep-seated and long-term changes—social, economic, political and cultural—often, in fact, those transformations associated with "progress" and "modern" development, can be located precisely among those groups that, for whatever reasons, miss out on its positive effects or disapprove of the direction of change, or are otherwise profoundly disturbed by the way things are going. It might be surprising to some to realize that this reaction is hardly particular to the present, that it can be observed as far back as the sixteenth century.

In what follows, I look at some historically distant examples of resentment in political and social life, in part because such distance offers a more dispassionate view of an emotion that, especially now, tends to be freighted with ideologically charged assumptions. A historical perspective can help us avoid pathologizing this phenomenon; that is, seeing it primarily as a disturbed symptom or maladjustment to the progressive march of history (which is how it is often looked upon today). My account, however, will be challenged by the tricky task of locating resentment in times when "resentment" was not deployed as a term of analysis. What follows, then, is an attempt to discover how this emotion is enacted without contemporaries invoking it. The assumption will be that people often demonstrate resentment even when the concept itself is absent from their discursive universe.

One insight that helps us get closer to appreciating the likely context for the emergence of this emotion brings us back to the last chapter and David Hume's assertion that resentment thrives in the soil of "proximity and resemblance," not social distance or disparity. In other words, it depends upon relationships of mutual awareness or relative equality, or at least closeness in status, where people have a sense of being within a range of comparison, emulation, or competition. And this underscores an aspect of its difference from other emotions of political relevance—anger, hatred, or vengeance. One place to look for resentment, perhaps even to expect it, then, is within the confines of a single class or relatively homogeneous community, in which people have a tendency to look upon each other with the expectation, as a starting assumption, that fundamental disparities just simply ought not to be.

RESENTING NEIGHBORS AS WITCHES

I begin with a kind of contentious relationship where social proximity, even intimacy, is fundamental. And, like other sorts of conflicts characterized by resentment, the psychological dimension looms large. This takes us into the vast and vexed topic of the witch hunts of the sixteenth and seventeenth centuries in both Europe and New England, a topic that has given rise to some quite ingenious interpretations, as historians try to explain this largely imponderable phenomenon. One approach has been to delve into the social life of villages and small towns where the conflicts that bred witchcraft accusations emerged. For it is clear that despite whatever was going on in these sordid and deadly conflicts—belief in the devil, entrenched superstitious beliefs, the manipulation of the clergy—they thrived in the soil of deep divisions that ultimately stemmed precisely from those fundamental "modernizing" transformations just alluded to.

The notorious case of the Salem witch trials in 1692 offers probably the best illustration of this connection between individual accusations and conflicts and these deep-seated changes. At least this is borne out in the classic work by Paul Boyer and Stephen Nissenbaum, whose close study, *Salem Possessed: The Social Origins of Witchcraft* (1974), reveals a small-scale society riven by personal and familial squabbles and resentments, and subject to outside economic and social pressures as well. Their analysis is complex and, as these historians have warned in responding to their critics, too easily reduced to a simplistic formulation pitting tradition against modernity in the guise of rural values versus a commercial orientation toward the larger world. But the outlines of their conclusions are clear. The town of Salem, which faced an Atlantic world of increasingly lucrative commerce, was growing away from the agricultural economy of the inhabitants of Salem Village further inland. As a result, the commercial forces emanating from Salem Town worked their way into the social fabric of the village, with some villagers more engaged with commerce than others, more able to take advantage of Atlantic trade, more, then, identified with values that seemed a departure from traditional, "Puritan" ways. According to their finely grained sociological analysis, it was the latter who for the most part found themselves accused of witchcraft. But this division not only ran through the village, it was also internalized by many of the inhabitants themselves—most traumatically by those who saw themselves as steadfast, righteous defenders of the path of their forefathers. "The menace they were fighting off had taken root within each of them as deeply as it had in Salem Town," Boyer and Nissenbaum write. And they link these men, in particular the Puritan clergymen most energetic in persecuting witches, with their coreligionists in England, who were likewise engaged in a struggle against what they saw as pernicious, ungodly innovations. They "were part of a vast company on both sides of the Atlantic who were trying to expunge the lure of the new order from their own souls by doing battle with it in the real world."[1] In 1692 Salem, that battle, however, was an oblique one, only secondarily with the "real world" and more directly with their neighbors.

Samuel Parris, the pastor of the Salem Village church and a leading protagonist in this battle, was instrumental not only in the witchcraft persecutions themselves but also in expressing, in moral and religious terms, the resentment that lay at the heart of the social conflicts that animated these trials. As Parris's biography attests, he was a complex, even tortured figure. Having immigrated to New England after experiencing failure in a Caribbean commercial venture, he developed bitter feelings toward the market-oriented enterprises he saw as encroaching on his traditional Puritan society. In a sense, we can see him acting out the role of the fox in Aesop's fable, with the sour grapes as the despised fruits of capitalism. And here, his sermons display a bitter resentment of the values associated with commerce and trade—activities he cast as tantamount to a betrayal of Christ. "Christ . . . knows who they are that have not chosen Him, but prefer farms and merchandise above Him and above His ordinances," he pronounced in a sermon in 1692, in the midst of the witch trials (172).[2] His sermons then and before are marked by a persistent identification with Jesus the victim: betrayed by Judas, persecuted by the powerful, and scorned by the crowd—the Son of God unjustly brought low by the high and mighty who countenanced money changers in the Temple. In another sermon he evoked the obscure conditions of Jesus's birth: "The Inne that it may be was full of rich folks" (82). It should be noted that the Inn on Ipswich Road was licensed to John Proctor, one of the accused witches executed in 1692, and it was a place of commerce precisely associated with the sorts of activities many in the village found suspect. In 1691, Parris took as his text Psalm 110: "Sit thou at my right hand, till I make thine enemies thy footstool" (171). A year later, he pronounced, "Hence it is that no Seldom great hatred ariseth from nearest Relations" (184). Write Boyer and Nissenbaum, "Did he discover in Christ's earthly sojourn resonant parallels to the experience of the London merchant's son, the nephew of a great Barbados planter, who had himself failed so miserably to make his mark on the world of commerce and who now found himself embroiled in a demeaning controversy in an obscure farm village on the outskirts of a thriving commercial center?"[3] If so, he channeled this sense of failure into a resentful worldview which proved crucial in his role as one of the main animators of the Salem witch trials.

The Salem trials weren't the only instance of witchcraft prosecutions in seventeenth-century New England; they were episodic throughout the colony, especially in the second half of the century, when, as was usual in these cases, many more women than men found themselves on the docket. And here too, resentment played a role in bringing neighbor against neighbor, especially when traditional values and expectations, both Puritan and patriarchal, were challenged. Carol F. Karlsen, another historian of New England witchcraft, has shown, in fact, that property was frequently the issue that stood behind these accusations. Women who inherited property, especially where male heirs were not apparent, found themselves the object of their neighbors' envy, suspicion, and resentment. To be sure, there were usually other factors that contributed to their victimization, but these, too, added to their reputation as "unruly" women. They might have been outspoken, perhaps somewhat eccentric in their behavior, or merely recalcitrant with regard to conforming to the standards of female propriety and docility. In some cases, their sexual comportment provoked the charge of "fornication." And some, indeed, attracted suspicion because they dabbled in folk aspects of the occult. In any case, as Karlsen demonstrates in her book *The Devil in the Shape of a Woman*, in many of these cases any charges leveled against these women were compounded by their status as sole possessors or controllers of property, itself a violation of the implicit norms of a patriarchal social system. Many sons found themselves pushed aside by their fathers, or otherwise passed over in the transmission of property. But they directed their resentment elsewhere—typically against women. "If men found it hard to acknowledge let alone express their resentment against other men, they encountered less difficulty in expressing their resentment against women," writes Karlsen. "These resentments came out," she continues, "but they were not directed at the men who were their principal sources. Rather they were expressed as witchcraft accusations, primarily aimed at older women, who, like accusers' own mothers vied with men for land and other scarce material resources."[4]

While surely rooted in the conviction that the devil was active in their midst, accusations of witchcraft throughout New England often channeled neighborly, familial, and intergenerational conflicts over property and inheritance. To the existential insecurities that characterized a premodern society—illness and disease, sudden and unexplained death, the threatening vicissitudes of nature, continual warfare with nearby Indian tribes—should be added the material insecurities of living in a society where property and the yield of the land were crucial. And when these economic insecurities were most intense, as they increasingly became in an economically developing New England, women were often to blame. "Puritan belief made it easy to hold women responsible for the failures of the emerging economic system," writes Karlsen. "Discontent, anger, envy, malice, and pride were understandable responses to the stresses of social and economic change. Yet the clergy's repeated descriptions of these responses as sins against the hierarchical order of Creation . . . encouraged the conviction among men that if anyone were to blame for their troubles it was the daughters of Eve."[5] In our own day, it is certainly not unusual to hear women—especially feminists—also blamed for the misfortunes of men—resentful men, who find themselves displaced by females in what were traditional bastions of male exclusivity. Now, as in the seventeenth century, resentment often finds both its source and target in "unruly" women.

Neither in England nor New England were Puritans avatars of capitalism, despite the fact that they are so often cast in that role; rather, they emerge as resisters of new trends, a resistance that goaded them to ratchet up their religious commitments such that the Puritanism of the seventeenth century was a much more intense iteration of Calvinism than in the previous century. In either case, their resentment was provoked not merely—or perhaps not at all—by the worldly success of others, but in reaction to the latter's betrayal of established ways. The Salem case shows us, however, that this resistance was as much internal as external, as much a struggle with themselves as against others. This psychological insight adds a further dimension to the emotional dynamics in play, for their resentment derived not solely from their self-righteous judgment of their wayward neighbors; it was laden with the guilt of harboring an enemy within. And it was this guilt that they then turned outward in the form of the witchcraft persecutions. Their Puritanism was more a *response* to these subversive values than an expression of them. In a more recent commentary, Boyer and Nissenbaum have suggested that their interpretation of these late seventeenth-century New England Puritans might be helpful in understanding Islamic and Christian fundamentalism in our day, insofar as these movements are responses to "the pressures of globalization," employing modern innovative techniques "to hasten the coming of a simpler, purer world."[6] This is an insight we will want to recall in later chapters.

WHO'S IN AND OUT AT THE ENGLISH ROYAL COURT

Let us look at another historical experience where, like the conflict over witchcraft, tensions arose among people of generally similar standing, those whose relationships are characterized by social proximity, not distance. Here, it will be possible to see resentment as a catalyst of political change, even of a revolutionary sort. This has to do with the evolving fate of the ruling classes in early modern Europe. A through line of development in European history over the last four centuries follows the ultimate decline of the traditional aristocracy, a decline which in some places, like Britain, really did not manifest itself definitively until the early twentieth century. But as important as its decline, and the ways it was challenged by various forces and classes, are the internal cleavages and conflicts that render its history rather fraught. Here we can observe how political and social changes fostered its fragmentation and division, giving rise to resentments that had explosive potential. And one institution that generated this contention, and the commensurate discontent, was the court.

Imperial, royal, and princely courts grew dramatically in the early modern period in almost every Western European country. The court, of course, was not simply the abode of the ruling family; it was the seat of government, replete with an expanding entourage of courtiers, royal relatives, officials, bureaucrats, and resident members of the nobility, not to speak of legions of servants and functionaries who carried out the mundane tasks of such a gigantic and complex enterprise. It was a place of work and residence for thousands. And courts' exponential growth was a symptom of the growth of centralized monarchies and the demands of state-making in a period when the modern nation-state was coming into being. Louis XIV's Versailles, a sprawling palace that constituted a veritable city with over ten thousand residents, was the prototypical royal court in the seventeenth century, emulated by other princes and monarchs in Europe. But even before the Sun King, these centers of monarchical and princely power cast a long shadow over a society that was still largely rural and still dominated by a landed aristocracy, with few institutions that could rival it.

The dynamic of courtly expansion generated a sustained critique, especially as its growth seemed to come at the expense of those who were excluded from its privileged precincts but nevertheless burdened by its burgeoning expenses. Often this critique was expressed as a moralistic condemnation of those courtiers who pullulated in this arena, where flattery, dissimulation, jockeying for position, conspicuous luxury, and loose morals appeared the rule. The Dutch humanist Erasmus took aim at these puffed-up superfluities. "Though they are for the most part a base, servile, cringing, low-spirited sort of flatterers," he writes in *Praise of Folly*, "yet they look big, swell great, and have high thoughts of their honour and grandeur."[7] In royal courts, he comments in *The Complaint of Peace*, "it is all paint and varnish. Everything is corrupted by open faction, or by secret grudges and animosities."[8] But Erasmus was only one in a long line of critics who attacked the court as an odious place that brought out the worst in men. Antonio de Guevara, a Spanish humanist, wrote several treatises on court life, which circulated widely in the sixteenth century. His critique is unsparing: At court, he writes, "He who is called 'Monsieur' rather merits the appellation 'executioner.'" There, "if one wants to commit adultery, you'll find accomplices; if you want to fight, you'll find company; if you're inclined to lie, you'll find those who will approve your untruths; if you want to conceal something, you will be instructed in thousands of subtle ways to do this . . . if you swear and give false testimony, you will find those who will encourage you. In short, if you wish to indulge in all sorts of evil and sin, you will find true models and examples . . ."[9] After being dismissed from service to the prince of Wales (the future Charles II), a veteran English courtier let loose with a bitter screed: "Were I to live a thousand years I would never sett my foot with a court againe, for there is nothing in itt butt flattery and falsehood."[10] And a member of the parliamentary opposition in England in 1628 rendered his critique in verse:

> The Court is fraught with bribery, and hate,
> With envie, lust, ambition, and debate;
> With fawnings, with fantasticke imitation,
> With shamefull sloth and base dissimulation.
> True Virtue's almost quite exiled thence . . ."[11]

Critics did not limit themselves to a moralizing brief; they drew upon an ancient trope that extolled rural, country life as the virtuous counterpart to the court, that den of iniquity, hypocrisy, and decadence. This merely recast that age-old divide between country and city, which since ancient times has been a perennial source of moral commentary. Rural life, with all its natural charms, peaceful pastimes, hard-won virtues, and communal values, is pitted against urban ways—corrupt, commercial, and cutthroat, where people are simply too busy and too preoccupied with getting ahead, or simply getting, to bother caring for one other. Cultivated across the ages, it is a trope that is alive and well today, a dependable source of moral critique no matter what the context. Indeed, this is a theme that, mutatis mutandis, has proven quite robust, with the divide between the urban and rural informing the politics of resentment in contemporary America.[12]

The juxtaposition of country and city or court was a commonplace of early modern discourse, and it thrived during the Renaissance, drawing upon ancient themes and images, especially in the writings of Virgil, Horace, Petrarch, Tacitus, and others. But in late sixteenth- and early seventeenth-century England it became a potent source of ideological opposition to the Crown, helping to foment the divisions that ultimately led to Parliament's revolt and the English Revolution.

The English court under the Tudors in the sixteenth century, though certainly important, probably lagged behind others on the Continent in terms of size; indeed, for all its prominence in the annals of royalty, and for all the Renaissance splendor we associate with the Elizabethan age, this dynasty did not seem intent on expressing its authority primarily through an expanding court. Elizabeth herself was notoriously abstemious. But under the Stuarts, the court grew in prominence and size, becoming the unrivaled center of power, preferment, and privilege. It also took on a somewhat foreign cast, with a French princess, Henrietta Maria (Louis XIII's sister), installed as the prince of Wales's wife, and consequently as a Catholic presence in this deeply Protestant country. James I even received the pope's diplomatic agents. The king proved himself something of a connoisseur—and big-time collector—of art, though with a taste that favored the continental, baroque, and Catholic style: Rubens, Titian, and Caravaggio, an aesthetic penchant that only inflamed the outrage of the growing Puritan sentiment in the country. And the perceived foreignness of the Stuart court was compounded by new forms of courtly culture: court "masques," orchestrated by the likes of Inigo Jones and Ben Jonson, introduced esoteric imagery and neo-Platonic symbolism—even a whiff of paganism—to the repertoire of courtly entertainment, which confirmed the growing suspicion that the Stuart court was not only excessively large and expensive but decadent to boot. The Stuarts increased the monopolistic power of the court in both political and economic terms. They attempted to impose an "absolutist" style of government, most blatantly exemplified by ruling without Parliament from 1629 to 1640, but also by selling offices and titles and creating commercial monopolies, thus making access to the court and courtly favor a requirement for many avenues of advancement. To add insult to injury, much of this royal patronage and preference was placed in the hands of George Villiers, duke of Buckingham, who, until his assassination in 1628, reigned as the royal "favorite," and thereby served as a lightning rod for an increasingly restive opposition of "mere" gentry and peers alike who found themselves excluded from the spoils and privileges of the court.

Clearly, then, the growing power and prominence of the Stuart court—something of a novelty and innovation in English history—promoted a sense that often characterizes the development of institutions and cultures over time: a perceived difference between "insiders" and "outsiders." This was not primarily a class difference. Though grumbling about the court could be heard in the middling classes, the irritation with its size and nature was most pronounced among their social superiors, especially the so-called mere, or country, aristocracy and gentry. Ordinary people, for all the disapproval they might express, were not affected by the waxing of courtly power. For the elite, however, including ambitious merchants, it could mean the difference between prosperity and decline, survival and demise, favor and advancement for them, their families, and their future heirs—or a bleak prospect altogether. In another context, Norbert Elias notes the psychological aspect of this dynamic, where "losses of power by former establishments in relation to rising outsider groups triggered bitter resistance, a scarcely realistic longing for the restoration of the old order and not merely for economic reasons." Indeed, these groups "[felt] themselves lowered in their own self-esteem."[13]

As one prominent English historian of the period writes, "Popery, painting, and playacting—could anything be more calculated to stir [. . .] anxieties and resentment . . . ? The new Court espoused them all."[14] Discontent was especially rife among the traditional aristocracy, which looked with horror as the court was steadily bloated with "new" men, hardly worthy of the privileges and powers bestowed upon them, especially by the tainted hands of the royal favorite. One of their spokesmen expressed resentment of those whose "riches [were] gotten in a Shop," now ensconced at the very center of power.[15] Another nobleman penned this plaintiff cry, describing the plight of the nobleman who remained in the country, forgoing the lures and advantages of the court: "It is impossible for a mere country gentleman ever to grow rich or raise his house. He must have some other vocation with his inheritance, as to be a courtier, lawyer, merchant or some other vocation. If he hath no other vocation, let him get a ship and judiciously manage her, or buy some auditor's place, or be vice admiral in his county. By only following the plough he may keep his work and be upright, but will never increase his fortune."[16]

Thus, especially in the seventeenth century, voices of discontent, criticism, and moral disapprobation were increasingly heard, targeting the court as the source of all that was wrong with England. And while critiques ranged across the spectrum of perspectives, from political opposition to specific royal policies and religious objections to complaints about royal expenditures and corruption, behind many of these stood deep-seated resentments, especially since they often originated from those who felt excluded from the royal center of power. Their disapproval was compounded by a sense of being demoted, left out, or passed over.

Especially for those associated with the establishment, then, the proper order of things seemed out of joint. In the late Elizabethan and Jacobean periods, this anxiety was often acted out on the stage. Shakespeare's late tragedies in particular depicted a world gone awry. And these plays are rich in resentful characters—Brutus in *Julius Caesar*, Iago in *Othello*, and Coriolanus in the eponymously named play—but none more so than Hamlet, who is especially revealing here because the drama takes place almost entirely in a royal court. Indeed, *Hamlet* depicts the court as a theater of constant conflict and tortured emotions.

At the play's start, Hamlet has just returned to the Danish court from his studies in Wittenberg. He seethes with resentment at his uncle Claudius and Claudius's new wife, Hamlet's just-widowed mother, who have turned not only his world but, we are meant to believe, the whole world—the very natural order of things—upside down. His distress is only inflamed by the pretense, seemingly shared by all the court but voiced especially by his mother and stepfather, that all is well—that his father's death was entirely in conformity with the order of things: "But you must know, your father had a father/That father lost, lost his . . ." (1.2.89–103).[17] And that there is something wrong with him for not acknowledging this: *he* is the problem, not the untimely death of his father and the hasty marriage of his mother. What more effective provocation to resentment than to be told that your grief is unnatural, your filial piety simply inappropriate? It's as if his stepfather and mother are trying to gaslight him.

Moreover, as Richard Van Oort argues in his very stimulating study *Shakespeare's Big Men*, this Danish court exhibits a feature that marks royalty in several of the plays, but especially in *Hamlet*. It is a court where the center, which is to say the king, is vulnerable to attack or otherwise seen as unstable, with a less-than-sure hold on legitimacy and power. Van Oort contrasts this depiction of the power dynamics of the early modern court, what he calls the "neoclassical" view of monarchy, with classical representations, where royalty was not fundamentally challenged. In these Renaissance plays, the center does not hold. In the histories as well as the tragedies, Shakespeare demonstrates an exquisite awareness of the tentative, precarious nature of royal power, which reflects the historical circumstances of his times—not only the uncertain destiny of the Tudor dynasty, with Elizabeth lacking an heir, but also the memory of the long civil wars that had plagued the realm little more than a century earlier. This is surely one explanation why so many of his plays show a contest for royal power, a public way of acting out profound anxieties among his contemporaries about the future stability of the present political order.

Theatergoers might have been anxious. In Hamlet they beheld a character who made plain his resentment from his very first soliloquy. To Hamlet, all the "uses of the world" seem "weary, stale, flat, and unprofitable" (1.2.133–34), and Denmark is "an unweeded garden/That grows to seed" (1.2.135–36). Hamlet indulges in moral polarities that serve to configure the court in clear-cut extremes of good and evil, purity and pollution. Compared to his dead father, a true "Hyperion," Claudius is a "satyr."

And his mother, once besotted with his father, "as if increase of appetite had grown/By what it fed on," has become no better than a "beast," who has compounded base infidelity with incest. Hamlet's diatribe, writes Van Oort, "fills us with indignation towards the centre."[18] In a sense, the whole play consists of the acting out of his resentment. His actions are more "performative" than purposeful, at least in the sense that he cannot seem to bring himself actually to avenge his father's death; rather, the play depicts him in a perpetual state of agitated rumination, self-flagellation, self-doubt, and paralyzing indecision. "Hamlet," writes Van Oort, "thinks about violence more than he enacts it. And he thinks about violence because he is in the first place a man of resentment."[19] This noble Dane, like Nietzsche's slaves, seems incapable of acting on his own behalf. Rather, he indulges in indirection and playacting, in an "attempt to purge himself of the violence he harbors internally as resentment."[20] He projects his misogynistic rage toward his mother upon the virtuous Ophelia ("Get thee to a nunnery."), with fatal results. When he does act, it is again with intemperate, precipitous misdirection, causing the death not of Claudius but of the hapless Polonius, another innocent victim of his thwarted rage. And, instead of decisively exacting revenge upon his stepfather, he orchestrates an elaborate ruse—the so-called Mousetrap play—as a means not of confronting Claudius but of prompting him to betray himself. His desire for vengeance, nurtured throughout the course of this very long play, is only realized in its final scene, and then amid a general carnage ending in his own death. Hamlet's resentment, Shakespeare seems to be saying, yields not justice and certainly not satisfaction but the destruction of a world. Goethe describes Hamlet as "needy and degraded,"[21] which would seem to capture the worst aspects of the "man of resentment," whose soul, writes Nietzsche, "squints."[22]

RESENTMENT AND POPULAR PROTEST

Resentment characterizes other social conflicts in roughly the same period we have just evoked—similar moments where traditional expectations and assumptions were upended by profound social and economic forces. To be sure, those who engaged in these collective actions usually aimed their anger and violence at individuals and groups—local officials, merchants, factory owners, or simply their "betters"—rightly held responsible for the changes that threatened them. But these figures were, in a sense, mere agents of, or stand-ins for, epoch-making transformations which were nothing less than the modernizing commercial and market forces reshaping the Western world. Here, as in colonial New England, it was ordinary people who were most directly affected, and thereby disaffected.

An even greater sense of disaffection was exhibited by workers in England as they experienced the dawning of the industrial age. Luddism was not an ideology as such, but it does describe the disposition and actions of many workers, particularly in the stocking and lace industries, in the early years of the nineteenth century in England, who were confronted with concerted efforts to mechanize their work. These innovations also came in the wake of a prolonged depression caused by the interruption of trade during the wars with France, which only aggravated the workers' discontent at the introduction of power looms and the like. In the years 1811–12, the actions of these workers—from the burning down of mills, the targeted assassinations of mill owners, riots, organization into secret societies, and the mobilization of thousands of armed workers to, of course, the destruction of the machines themselves—represented a sustained and serious threat to both public order and the productive capacity of the industrial heartland of England. In this period alone, workers marching under the banner of the mythical General Ludd destroyed one thousand looms in the area of Nottingham. The threat was so serious that in May 1812, over fourteen thousand troops were called out to quell the uprisings. The Frame-Breaking Bill, introduced into the Commons on February 14, 1812, made these acts of strategic vandalism capital offenses. (In his maiden speech, Lord Byron denounced the bill in the House of Lords, to little effect—except to impress his fellow lords with his passion and eloquence.) As a result, that same year, twenty-four protestors were hanged and thirty-seven were transported to Australia. The historian Edward Thompson writes that Luddism "was a quasi-revolutionary movement, which continually trembled on the edge of ulterior revolutionary objectives."[23] Certainly, in the wake of the French Revolution, the authorities readily suspected the workers of radical designs, even Jacobinism. Eric Hobsbawm's view is more measured: he calls the actions of Luddites "collective bargaining by riot."[24]

The Luddites challenged the authorities, displaying a fearsome readiness for violence, and made no secret of their hatred for the merchant-capitalists who imposed the machines on their workplaces. They also aroused fears of native revolutionary Jacobinism throughout the English countryside, especially as the movement came on the heels of a series of food or grain riots. But to reduce their interests to economic concerns alone is to miss how they were psychologically motivated by a sense of having—collectively—been wronged. Like the grain rioters who drew upon traditional notions of a "moral economy," the Luddites engaged in

machine breaking not simply out of frustration, in acts of wanton violence, but to demonstrate the rectitude of their customary, time-honored
ways of doing their work, and their resentment at having these ways sum-
marily overturned.

For the Luddites believed that they had both tradition and parliamentary legislative history on their side—that textile artisans in particular
were protected by a corpus of constitutional rights. Some of these laws
date to Tudor times, but others were reaffirmed in the eighteenth century, such that shearmen and weavers felt justified using the courts to
prosecute as "illegal" the introduction of such technological innovations
as gig mills and weaving shops. The workers were not only defending the
traditional ways of a craft-based industry, they were also defending a domestic, patriarchal way of life—work in the "little commonwealth" of the
family—as opposed to the factory system, where men, women, and children would be seen as interchangeable, unskilled laborers. The cause was
as much moral as economic, for the factories were seen, so proclaimed a
contemporary, as "nurseries always of vice corruption, and often of disease, discontent and disloyalty." They "deprave the morals of our laborers
and break up their happy domestic labouring parties." Nevertheless, in
1802, the manufacturers and their allies in Parliament attempted to repeal
these old statutes, thus drawing battle lines on the national stage not just
between two sets of interests but between two contrasting conceptions of
the socioeconomic order, with, of course, moral implications.[25]

Today our understanding of this historical phenomenon is clouded
by a contemporary tendency to view these machine-breakers as simply
irrational—either woefully misguided workers who blamed the machines
themselves—inanimate objects!—for their suffering, or people incapable of understanding the advantage of labor-saving devices. It was no
different in the early nineteenth century; when the Luddite movement
was at its peak, the papers in London were prolix in their condemnation,
deeming the workers "infatuated men, deluded men, wicked men, and
ill-designing men."[26] Even Marx looked upon them with condescension:
these confused workers needed to learn "to distinguish between the ma-
chinery and its employment by capital, and to direct their attacks, not
against the material instruments of production, but against the mode in
which they are used."[27] Other supposedly progressive observers, such as
Harriet Martineau and William Cobbett, could not extend their sympathy
for the working class and poor to these rebellious craftsmen, whom they
judged as delusional, beyond reason, or simply desperate. Here, in fact,
we see evidence of a split that indeed becomes apparent in this period,
a fundamental divide that has a lot to do with the emergence of popu-

list movements in our own day. While middle- and upper-class radicals and reformers, like Martineau, Cobbett, and even Marx, certainly didn't share the views of the authorities and factory owners, who were only too happy to send these Luddites to the gallows, they still regarded these machine-breakers with condescension and incomprehension. They were the educated elites, avatars of progress, who knew what was best for the lower classes, and consequently could not countenance their stubborn attachment to traditional, atavistic ways. Their attitude was not so different from that of Voltaire, who was convinced that the rioters protesting Turgot's reforms in 1775—one of the first state-sponsored efforts to create an economic regime of free trade—were in the pay of the royal minister's political opponents.[28]

In our day, "Luddite" has become "an epithet, a convenient device for disparaging and isolating the occasional opponent to progress and a charge to be avoided at all costs by thoughtful people."[29] This assessment, echoing the dominant view two centuries ago, suggests that "resentment" was not solely an emotional disposition on the part of the disgruntled and dispossessed, but also a diagnosis imposed upon these deluded, unreasonable workers who were capable only of demonizing instruments of progress.

Some commentators closer to the time of the Luddites expressed mixed views of them. One of the most interesting observations is found in Charlotte Brontë's 1846 novel, *Shirley*. The novelist's depiction is at once sympathetic and condescending. Early in the novel, Brontë—in her own voice as the narrator—offers the following assessment of these restive workers' plight: "Misery generates hate," she writes. "These sufferers hated the machines which they believed took their bread from them; they hated the buildings which contained those machines; they hated the manufacturers who owned those buildings." And, tellingly, she adds that their hatred was augmented by the fact that the main mover behind these despised innovations, "the man most abominated," was both a "semiforeigner" (his parentage was Flemish) and a "thorough going progressist."[30] Thus, a potent combination: an intrusive innovation, destroying traditional ways of life, introduced by a foreign intruder. What more was needed to foment resentment—and with justice?

But Brontë's portrait of the Luddites ultimately tilts toward a lessflattering depiction, one that highlights the more extreme, even depraved aspects of their collective character. "Most of these were not members of the operative class," observes her main protagonist, the foreign-born mill owner, Gérard Moore. "They were chiefly 'down-draughts,' bankrupts, men always in debt and often in drink—men who had nothing to lose, and much—in the way of character, cash and cleanliness—to gain."[31] She caricatures one of their leaders as a crazed fool, spouting fiery imprecations straight out of the Old Testament, and a known drunk as well. While Brontë might have expressed some sympathy for Luddism, in *Shirley* the Luddites themselves emerge as justly aggrieved but more embittered, violent, and unreasonable than their grievances warrant. Her depiction, in short, amounts to the characterization of a movement where "resentment," though unexpressed, is the damning diagnosis.[32]

Here, then, with the depictions of the Luddites both two centuries ago and today, we see evidence of Frederic Jameson's understanding of resentment as an "ostensible theory" which is "little more than an expression of annoyance at seemingly gratuitous lower-class agitation, at the apparently quite unnecessary rocking of the social boat." Jameson turns the tables on those who would deploy it. It is not an appropriate or accurate description of the psychological state of the oppressed or aggrieved. Rather, he asserts with confidence, "the theory of *ressentiment*, wherever it appears, will always itself be the expression and the production of *ressentiment*." Jameson's pronouncement seems somewhat categorical, ruling out resentment as an authentic sentiment harbored by those who feel overrun by the course of history. And in this sense, it strikes me as rather peremptory, guided more by an ideological disposition than intellectual openness. Still, his assertion should serve to remind us that the charge of resentment can indeed be raised not to understand the aggrieved but to delegitimize and even malign them.[33]

THE DISCREET RESENTMENT OF THE FRENCH BOURGEOISIE

It might be argued that long-simmering resentments played a role in the turbulent politics of seventeenth-century England—and, by extension, elsewhere in Europe where the dynamics of court life and monarchical authority functioned to create schisms among established elites, thereby breeding a toxic measure of discontent. Resentment emerged because deeply entrenched expectations had been violated, especially those grounded in a traditional order where the king and his nobility were supposed to be united in harmonious bonds of affection, mutual support, and protection. For many noblemen, there was a sense of betrayal; the calculus was of the zero-sum sort. Francis Bacon, the philosopher and statesman who suffered his own misfortunes as a result of courtly machinations, was certainly sensitive to the psychological aspects of intra-elite rivalry. "Men of noble birth are noted to be envious of new men when they rise," he writes in his essay "Of Envy." "For the distance is altered," he says, "and it is like a deceit of the eye, that when others come on they think themselves go back."[34] Promoting "favorites," fostering factions, inventing new titles, selling offices, encouraging upstarts and parvenus, creating monopolies: all these innovations, while in many cases legitimate or at least expedient moves in the face of changing circumstances, only served to upend traditional expectations about the proper order of the world. Resentment surely accompanied whatever range of emotions took hold among those embittered elites excluded by these innovations.

When we look to another time and place in the early modern period, the dynamics of resentment are both similar and different. In eighteenth-century France, as in seventeenth-century England, it was also a matter of competition between groups that weren't worlds apart. Social proximity, not distance, as Hume argued, is more likely to breed resentment. The difference, however, is that in this period in France it was those newly seeking power, status, and recognition, not the traditionally privileged, who exhibited signs of resentment. We can see this in two examples.

The first has to do with the Enlightenment, the literary and intellectual culture that developed during the second part of the eighteenth century. Here, the interpretation of Robert Darnton, perhaps the most accomplished historian of that culture, reveals a strain of resentment as a telling feature of its development.[35]

Darnton shows us an aspect of the Enlightenment that is less about high ideals and abstract philosophy and more about naked careerism and a desperate scramble for recognition. This Enlightenment stimulated the literary ambitions of a whole generation of young men, aspiring writers who craved the success of their famous elders such as Voltaire, Rousseau, and Diderot. These well-established, august *philosophes* had helped fashion the Republic of Letters, a supposedly fraternal, egalitarian society where access was determined by talent, not privilege—at least this was the ideal. In actuality, success in this world still depended upon protection and patronage; it still functioned according to the archaic rules of the ancien régime, where appealing to the tastes and mores of the aristocracy, gaining entrée into the leading Parisian salons, or securing election into a royal academy made all the difference between success and failure, between a cushy berth in *le monde* or a catch-as-catch-can existence on lowly Grub Street. Alas, despite the inherent *blocages* of this system, there seemed to be no shortage of young writers on the make. Late eighteenth-century France, Darnton suggests, "suffered from a common ailment of developing countries: a surplus population of over-educated and under-employed *littérateurs* and lawyers."[36]

With the avenues for advancement blocked for these young men, "they cursed the closed world of culture."[37] What took hold, Darnton argues, was an "anti-Establishment feeling"; these thwarted Grub Street writers "seeth[ed] with hatred of the literary 'aristocrats' who had taken over the egalitarian 'republic of letters' and made it into a 'despotism.'" Ultimately, for some at least, it led to a revolutionary hatred of everything associated with the ancien régime: "It was from such visceral hatred, not from the refined abstractions of the contented cultural elite, that the extreme Jacobin revolution found its authentic voice," concludes Darnton.[38]

One does not have to go this far to appreciate the psychological dynamics unleashed by the Enlightenment in several respects. These ambitious, embittered young men can be seen as precocious embodiments of what would be known as "alienated intellectuals," a character type that would loom large in modern times, sometimes viewed as opportunistically working out their own frustrations by stirring up the resentments of the lower classes. As well, their fraught relationship vis-à-vis the privileged *philosophes* took the form of a generational conflict, complicated by what would become another enduring trope: the lure of the capital for the young, and the unanticipated results of expanding educational opportunities. The travails of such aspiring young men became the stuff of literature itself—personified most famously in the following century in the characters of Balzac's Eugène de Rastignac, (*Le Père Goriot* and subsequent novels in *La comédie humaine*), Stendhal's Julien Sorel (*The Red and the Black*) and Flaubert's Frédéric Moreau (*Sentimental Education*). History is a distant mirror. It doesn't take too much peering into it to see a reflection here of the predicament of a generation of young people in the contemporary US and elsewhere, many of whom feel stymied in their even modest ambitions by bleak employment opportunities, a closed housing market, and the burden of student debt.

The eighteenth century offered another conflict that seemed to breed resentment in ways that sharpened its emotional pitch. The French Revolution eliminated the monarchy and established a republic, but revolutionary anger turned most energetically and persistently, especially during its radical phase (1793–94), on the nobility, and everyone associated with it. The Jacobins were expert in stirring the populace against this traditional elite, and, in this sense and others, it is easy to see class conflict, and simply the hatred of the poor for the rich and privileged, as central to this revolutionary moment. But even before the outbreak of the Revolution, tensions between the established nobility and those members of the upper echelons of the Third Estate, especially wealthy financiers, officers of the Crown, and members of the judiciary, while perhaps not as sharp as historians used to think, were still apparent. Historians once framed this conflict in terms of a class conflict between the nobility and the bourgeoisie, defining the nature of this antagonism as fundamentally economic: sclerotic feudalism, which generated wealth for a mostly landed nobility, needed to be overthrown by an economically dynamic bourgeoisie in order to create the new economic order of capitalism. Today this interpretation holds little water; relations between the upper ranks of the so-called bourgeoisie and nobility were hardly so fractious. The existence of a bourgeoisie as a single "class" now seems an invention of an outdated Marxism, its wealth derived more from offices and investments than from capitalist activity. And, perhaps most importantly for our purposes, whatever tensions *did* seem to characterize relationships between nobles and elite non-nobles more likely arose amid concerns over privilege and status rather than economic interests. Resentment, not capitalism, was what came between many ambitious, proud, and accomplished non-nobles and their titled superiors.[39] The diagnosis of the nineteenth-century historian Hippolyte Taine is no doubt dated, but still valid: "The Third Estate, considering itself deprived of a place to which it is entitled, finds itself uncomfortable in the place it occupies and, accordingly, suffers through a thousand petty grievances it would not, formerly, have noticed. On discovering that he is a citizen a man is irritated at being treated as a subject, no one accepting an inferior position alongside one whom he believes himself the equal. Hence, during a period of twenty years, the ancien régime, while seeming to grow easier, becomes even more burdensome and its pinpricks exasperate as if they were so many wounds."[40]

Perhaps the most famous expression of this sentiment, and one of the most successful plays of the last decade of the ancien régime, was Beaumarchais's *Marriage of Figaro* (1778; first performed 1784). In the most-cited passage of that oft-performed play, the hero Figaro, the ambitious, wily "Barber of Seville," rails against Count Almaviva, his unscrupulous, foolish, and sexually predatory master. "Because you've been born a grand seigneur, you think yourself a great genius!" he proclaims with a mixture of both triumph and resentment. "Nobility, wealth, rank, position—all that makes you proud! What have you done to deserve so many advantages?" He answers his own question with what surely struck audiences as a devastating coup de grâce: "You have given yourself the trouble of being born, nothing more."[41]

Now it has long been established that the very success of Beaumarchais's play—precisely among those impeccably noble theatergoers who fell over one another to get seats—should warn us against taking it as evidence of widespread hatred of the traditional nobility. The Count is a caricature, as audiences, both noble and non-noble, realized. Noblemen and women themselves were known to guffaw with pleasure at the play's vicious satire, not because they recognized themselves; quite the contrary. It brilliantly portrayed a noble—or rather, ignoble—"type": an antiquated *seigneur*, a buffoon, who certainly didn't deserve the status and privileges he so flagrantly abused.

But this did not mean that there were no tensions, no lines of fracture between nobles and non-nobles. As Alexis de Tocqueville was later to anatomize, the competition for privileges, fostered by a monarchy that controlled these coveted spoils, gave rise to a political culture which, strangely for such a hierarchical society, was imbued with a sort of de facto equality. All kinds of Frenchmen, regardless of their class or status, found themselves on a level playing field, so to speak, competing for the offices, protections, and favors that conferred the Crown's privileges on them. Equality bred competition. A significant degree of fluidity characterized the upper reaches of the eighteenth-century social world in France, where bourgeois and noble pleasantly socialized together one day and energetically jostled for advantages on another. Nevertheless, it was a world that still subjected non-nobles to demeaning hierarchical restrictions.

This is why prerevolutionary France saw a growing resentment among wealthy non-nobles who, precisely because the political culture of the ancien régime seemed to recognize them as worthy of a whole range of privileges (in part because so many of them simply purchased them), grew irritated at those signs of status and position maintained exclusively by the nobility. They chafed at those often petty or purely ceremonial perks enjoyed by the nobility, or genuinely suffered from exclusionary regulations denying them certain advantages possessed by the noble elite alone. The two most coveted avenues for social advancement in the ancien régime, for example, the upper military and ecclesiastical ranks, were virtually closed to the sons of the bourgeoisie—and those restrictions, if anything, sharpened during the course of the eighteenth century. The 1781 Ségur law reserved entry into the Ecole Militaire—a sine qua non for the officer class—for offspring of families who could prove four quarters of nobility.[42] And by the latter part of the century, the episcopacy, once open to a fair number of non-nobles, had become for all intents and purposes an exclusive noble preserve. The *Parlement* of Paris, too, reversed its long-standing practice and closed its ranks to recently ennobled magistrates. Observes one historian, "In Old Regime society, disdain—and its inevitable complement, resentment—were produced abundantly by the ordinary experiences of bourgeois life."[43] While it might be argued that these tensions were muted for much of the eighteenth century, they certainly sharpened with explosive results in the run-up to the Revolution. And the fuse was lit with the calling of the Estates General to meet in Versailles in 1789.

The story is well known: With the anticipation of the convening of three estates, the assumption on the part of the privileged orders—the clergy (the First Estate) and the nobility (the Second Estate)—as well as the Crown, was that voting would proceed as it had the last time the Estates General had met, in 1614; that is, each order (or estate) would have one vote. What this meant was obvious to everyone: the Third Estate, which represented the millions of Frenchmen and women who were not "privileged,"—from rich merchants, royal officials, financiers, and urbane lawyers to ordinary artisans and peasants—would be outvoted. The counterproposal, then, was to change the rules to voting by head, where the numerous delegates of the Third Estate (whose numbers would be doubled), representing, as it was increasingly acknowledged, the "Nation," would largely determine the outcome of this momentous gathering. The first two estates, of course, wanted nothing of it, leading not only to a stalemate but also to a pamphlet campaign on behalf of the Third Estate decrying the unfairness and unreasonableness of this adherence to such an antiquated arrangement, which clearly did not—and could not—represent the will of the French people.

The most stunning of these pamphlets was also one of the most famous texts to emerge from the French Revolution: Abbé Sieyès's *What Is the Third Estate?* Sieyès frames his argument simply, even modestly, pitching his discourse at a plaintive rhetorical register that belies its actual defiance. "What is the Third Estate?" he asks. "Everything. What has it hitherto been in the political order? Nothing. What does it desire to be? Something." With this, Sieyès essentially radicalized the moment, turning what the privileged orders and the Crown wanted to contain as a matter of political protocol into a confrontation over the fundamental principles of representation and equality.

But *What Is the Third Estate?* was not merely a reasoned case for the recognition of this order. It "managed to catch up the emotions and thoughts that were swirling around him, crystallize them into a powerful and coherent text."[44] And one of those emotions was resentment, which Sieyès channeled effectively, in all likelihood reflecting his own ambivalence, as a man of obscure origins, who was obliged throughout his life to depend on noble and ecclesiastical patronage for his advancement. In a passage that has an undeniably autobiographical ring, he writes that a member of the Third Estate "must submit to every form of contempt, insult, and humiliation. To avoid being completely crushed, what must the lucky non-privileged person do? He has to attach himself by all kinds of contemptible actions to some magnate; he prostitutes his principles and human dignity for the possibility of claiming, in his need, the protection of a *somebody*."[45] As William Sewell notes in his important book *A Rhetoric of Bourgeois Revolution: The Abbé Sieyès and "What Is the Third Estate?"* (1994), "The language of pride and humiliation is ubiquitous." Sewell proceeds to catalog the words which "burst from Sieyès's pen on page after page," evoking the sorts of insults and injuries inflicted on the bourgeoisie at the hands of the aristocracy: "Insult, base, prostitute, servitude, humiliate, vile, fear, degrade, shame, opprobrium, coward, villein, bondage, despise, flattery, mock, brazen, pride, contempt, honor, infamy . . ."[46]

But Sieyès's tract amounts to more than a litany of complaints, a catalog of humiliations. Scorn and contempt increasingly characterize his language. He turns on the members of the "privileged class" with a moralizing *hauteur* that casts them as superfluities, or worse, likening them to a "malignant humour . . . that must be neutralized." *What Is the Third Estate?* ends with this grudging concession to their mere existence, unhealthy as they are, but nothing more: "The word has gone round: you are not yet fit enough to be healthy. . . . Sick as you are then, so remain!"[47]

In a sense, Sieyès's pamphlet was instrumental in setting the French Revolution on its course, a revolution which, as is well known, unleashed a torrent of passions, especially as it became more popular and radical in nature. But surely resentment, bred from close but vexed relationships in the upper reaches of society, was fundamental to how it began.

RESENTMENT AND REVOLUTION

"To what extent do revolutions constitute one of the extreme expressions of resentment? . . . Does the identification of the role of resentment in these events make more intelligible phenomena previously seen as conflicts between orders or classes?"[48] In a book titled *Resentment in History*, the French historian Marc Ferro asks this question, which, unfortunately, he fails to answer, primarily because he sees resentment in virtually every revolution, without telling us what it adds to our understanding of these contentious movements. Let us try to consider it now, asking, in his terms, whether the role of resentment makes these movements more "intelligible." And I mean intelligible not merely in the sense that we might appreciate the experience—or the "phenomenology"—of collective action; that is, not only as an additive, a descriptive gloss to these events, but as a way of deepening our understanding of how and why they come about.

The French Revolution itself was a time of great passions, many of them wild and destructive, and many also expressive of the most ambitious, most world-transforming aspirations not only for the political order, not only for all of French society, but for the whole historical course of humanity as well. The Revolution emerged from an emotional environment known as an "age of sensibility" (as we saw in the last chapter), a time when the public expression of emotions, the acknowledgment of one's sensitivities and feelings, the embrace of those supposedly natural, "sentimental" inclinations of the human heart, were the stuff of literature and moral philosophy—depicted on both the stage and in representational art. "Sensibility" was distinct—explicitly so—from the aristocratic and courtly ethos that regimented and channeled emotions in terms of the standards of honor and ritualized modes of self-presentation. It also informed the nature of the Revolution. For William Reddy, a pioneer in the history of emotions, the period was infused with a surfeit of "sensibility," whereby the entire society was overcome by sentimentalism, especially the dramatic demonstration of fierce emotions. These were taken to be convincing signs not only of revolutionary commitment but of revolutionary sincerity. In the course of the Revolution, however, the emotional overload became conflictual. "Far from providing an emotional refuge," writes Reddy, "the Revolution had turned into an emotional battleground, where everyone's sincerity was suspect, and where working to deflect suspicion, however essential it was to survive, was itself a proof of insincerity."[49] With this, he concludes, the Revolution proved to be a failure in the "navigation of feeling" (which is the title of his book).

For Arno Mayer, another historian, although less committed to the study of emotions than Reddy, a focus on both revolutionary and counterrevolutionary violence yields a somewhat predictable conclusion: It is vengeance that stands out as characterizing the emotional valence of the Revolution. This leads him to evoke Nietzsche, who saw the "avenging instinct" as having such a "strong grip on humanity . . . [that it] left its mark on metaphysics, psychology, historical representation, and, above all, morality." The German philosopher thereby posits this disposition as universal, or at least omnipresent in human history, but most profoundly embodied in the person of resentment. "Disappointed arrogance, suppressed envy, perchance the arrogance and envy of your fathers; in you they break forth as a flame of revenge."[50] Mayer is an accomplished historian, and his book teems with historical details that convince us that certain circumstances are more liable to outbreaks of collective vengeance than others. Even so, one gets the sense from his study that he views vengeance as a disposition always at the ready in society, with revolutions, and other times of popular upheaval and the weakening of sovereign authority, most propitious for its outbreak. Should we conclude, then, that at the heart of the revolutionary impulse lies resentment as expressed through vengeance? The Russian historian Sheila Fitzpatrick, in commenting on Mayer's interpretation, proposes a "two-force theory of revolution in which vengeance is the driving force at the bottom of the revolutionary ocean while ideology is the rational, articulated driving force on the surface."[51]

The issue might seem virtually impossible to resolve: after all, could we really identify the emotional valence of a mass movement like a revolution, where a whole welter of emotions is one way or another in play? If, however, we want to sharpen our understanding of resentment, and in particular how it has been or might be deployed, what better phenomenon than revolution could serve as a sharpening stone? In particular, we might start with the provisional assumption that, as largely forward-looking movements, revolutions *cannot* be dominated by resentment, for this emotional state is fundamentally reactive in nature. Resentment, at least as normally considered, flourishes among the aggrieved who tend to fester in their grievances rather than act purposefully to assuage them.

For heuristic purposes, it might be more productive to consider resentment in contrast with the revolutionary or rebellious impulse. One thinker who, unusually, directly attempted to think through such a comparison is the existentialist philosopher Albert Camus, in one of his most widely read books, *L'homme révolté* (1951), published in English in 1954 as *The Rebel*. Here, Camus explicitly confronts the concept of resentment. He does so because he sees rebellion and resentment as radically different conceptions of resistance and opposition, too often wrongly confused. His aim is to recast rebellion, whether individual or collective, as being existentially meaningful—as, indeed, producing its own meaning, even though its telos may be obscure or problematic. In general, he wants to draw a distinction between rebellion as an attitude or ethical stance, of which he approves, and rebellion as the project of revolution, of which, as a moral witness to the events of the twentieth century, he doesn't. Along the way, however, he draws up something of a balance sheet comparing "rebellion" with "resentment."

While he admits that rebellion "creates nothing," he insists that it is essentially positive nevertheless, "in that it reveals the part of man which must always be defended." Rebellion is as much a mode of being as an activity, but in any case it is forward-looking. Resentment, however, is "completely negative." It merely makes claims against others. It is a form of "autotoxication . . . the evil secretion . . . of prolonged impotence." Rebellion is a different experience altogether, for it allows for one's entire being to be activated; it is existential commitment at its most intense, infused with "superabundant energy." Contrast this with resentment: passive, marked by envy, and stimulated only by a gnawing awareness of what one does not have. The rebel is all about defending not what he has but what he is; it is about recognition, not possession. Rebellion might be unrealistic, perhaps even more so than resentment, which seems down-to-earth insofar as it is animated by palpable desires. But this does not mean that rebellion lacks purpose: for the French writer, the purpose of rebellion lies not in its goal or end but, above all, in recognition of the self, whether individual or collective. Rebellion is the ultimate defense of one's being, while resentment, on the other hand, ultimately forces us to turn inward. Citing Tertullian, Camus asserts that resentment entails taking pleasure in the suffering of the objects of envy, just as the church fathers wrote about the delights of imagining the Roman emperors burning in hell. Rebels, however, refuse humiliation, both for themselves and others. It is true, Camus admits, that rebellion can be, and has been, motivated by resentment, "especially in this age of malice." But, he concludes, "in its widest sense rebellion goes far beyond resentment."[52]

Writing with the Nietzschean formulation of this emotion in mind, with all its disparaging associations and the sense it conveys of inwardness, paralysis, and bitterness, Camus wants to insist on how different it is from the existentially edifying stance of rebellion. But this is to embrace a rather narrow view of resentment, one which does not allow for the more civil, more justifiable modes of this disposition, which, for example, we saw espoused by Bishop Butler. And it is this rather different expression of resentment that we should keep in mind—in a sort of creative tension—as we pursue the course of our investigations in the chapters that follow.

Camus here, however, tries to efface resentment from our conception of rebellion. As it happened, many commentators in the century following the French Revolution came to a very different conclusion. If there's one thing that can be observed about the French Revolution and its aftermath, which brings us closer to the historical role of resentment, it is the social reality it both embodied and produced. In short, with the Revolution, an unleashing of popular energies unprecedented in history, the "people"—their sentiments, their grievances, their potential as a political force—had become an undeniable factor to be reckoned with. There was virtually no commentator in the course of the nineteenth century who failed to grapple with this new presence. Most were troubled by the destabilizing, violent potential of popular mobilization embodied most threateningly in the revolutionary crowd. Some, like Marx, Engels, and other radicals, of course, celebrated its potential—properly disciplined, guided by "correct" ideology—to transform society for the better. Others, like Charlotte Brontë in *Shirley*, were more mixed in their assessment, fearful of the wayward, unthinking, and violent proclivities of masses of restive people while remaining sympathetic to their plight and even hopeful that they could be educated and acculturated into acceptable channels of liberal reform and improvement. The perception of this populace, which cast it as always on the brink of mobilizing in threatening ways, was matched by another, related realization as the century progressed. For it wasn't merely the fact of the revolutionary crowd lurking offstage but a more quotidian reality of a mass society in the making in the course of the century—an increasingly urbanized, mobile society with a mass culture, and a democratizing political culture which colored it. The "people," then, in all their dimensions and meanings, emerge as a challenging feature in the nineteenth-century imaginary.

This has implications for the history of resentment. For, to return to the position of Frederic Jameson, the presence of the people as a historical force—especially the mobilized, revolutionary people—invited observers so disposed to interpret their grievances as merely manifestations of resentment. Nietzsche saw resentment as characteristic of what he called the "herd"—the masses of ordinary people in the thrall of conventional morality, a morality which thwarted the possibility of any individuality of thought or distinction of character. But despite the vaunted uniqueness of his philosophy, he was hardly alone in disparaging the masses, and in this sense, his thinking partook of some rather commonplace assumptions about the nature of the social pressures that defined the modern age. If his diagnosis of resentment as a dominant feature in the emotional and psychological history of Western, Christian society was original—as it undoubtedly was—his interpretation of contemporary society was, then, on the other hand, rather derivative. And yet, it would be difficult to imagine the power and purchase of Nietzschean *ressentiment* absent an appreciation of the reality of a restive, mass society. In order to understand, then, the advent of what I will call the "Nietzschean Moment," when the concept of resentment emerged in its fully developed form, it will be helpful to first look at how various commentators before Nietzsche cultivated this common perception, and how they fashioned a sharper understanding of resentment in the teeth of it.

CHAPTER THREE

A Specter Is Haunting Europe

The Specter of a Resentful "People"

One must retire out of the herd and then fire bombs into it.

D. H. LAWRENCE[1]

On February 27, 1812, the poet George Gordon, the 6th Baron Byron, rose to address the House of Lords with his maiden speech. The subject was the Frame-Breaking Bill, which called for the death penalty for machine-breakers, or so-called Luddites. Byron opposed it. His ancestral residence, Newstead Abbey, was located in the heartland of the beleaguered hosiery manufacturing district, so he knew firsthand whereof he spoke. In the course of his remarks, he ruminated on the common ascription for those crowds of ordinary people who demonstrate their discontent, sometimes violently, always energetically, who often disturb the peace and threaten the equanimity of the authorities and people of property alike. When he spoke, after all, it was in the wake of the French Revolution, with images of revolutionary crowds of desperate peasants and bloodthirsty *sansculottes* fresh in people's minds. "You call these men a mob," he said, "desperate, dangerous and ignorant; and seem to think that the only way to quiet the 'Bellua multorem capitum' is to lop off a few of its superfluous heads." But then he chided his fellow Lords: "Are we aware of our obligations to a mob?" he asked. "It is the mob that labour in your fields and serve in your houses—that man your navy, and recruit your army—that have enabled you to defy all the world, and can also defy you when neglect and calamity have driven them to despair!" He concluded, "You may call the people a mob; but do not forget that a mob too often speaks the sentiments of the people." Although his speech was greeted with some acclaim—one Lord said it was the best speech by a Lord since "the Lord knows when"—the bill passed with only a handful of votes opposed.[2]

Just as Byron claimed to possess firsthand knowledge of the people in what he called his "Christian country," a very different poet writing somewhat later in the century made such knowledge a signature feature of his poetic vision. Charles Baudelaire was a self-described *flaneur* in the Parisian metropolis of the middle decades of the nineteenth century. "The crowd was his element, as the air is that of birds and water of fishes," he wrote in "The Painter of Modern Life" (1863). "His passion and his profession are to become one flesh with the crowd. For the perfect *flaneur* . . . it is an immense joy to set up house in the heart of the multitude and the ebb and flow of movement, in the midst of the fugitive and infinite."[3] In a prose poem, "Eyes of the Poor" (in *Paris Spleen*, published posthumously in 1869), he captures the emotionally vexed predicament of many comfortable Parisians finding themselves increasingly confronted with the reality of "the people"—the burgeoning lower-class inhabitants whose unsettling presence was unavoidable in the wake of Baron Haussmann's urbanist projects of the 1850s and '60s, which opened up the city, clearing the way for all sorts of people to intermingle and make their way across the vast cityscape. In this poem, we see a loving couple after a long day of cozy companionship, reposing outside a café on the "corner of the new boulevard still littered with rubble but that already displayed proudly its unfinished splendors," thus evoking, in fact, both the promise and reality of Haussmann's urbanism: "The café was dazzling." But then their self-absorbed reverie is interrupted by the appearance of six eyes—those of a poor, weary father and his two bedraggled young children—"in rags." They look upon the loving couple and the splendid scene with both envy and joy. Their eyes seem to say, "How beautiful it is! How beautiful it is! . . . But it is a house where only people who are not like us can go." The man grows uneasy: "Not only was I touched by this family of eyes, but I was even a little ashamed of our glasses and our decanters, too big for our thirst." And as he turns to his lover, looking into her "eyes, so beautiful and so curiously soft" and seeking, as lovers do, "to read [his] thoughts in them," she says to him, "Those people are insufferable with their great saucer eyes! Can't you tell the proprietor to send them away?"[4]

Though they were kindred spirits in many ways, Friedrich Nietzsche's attitude toward the people resembled more the irritation of the poem's female lover than the solicitous and guilt-ridden reaction of the narrator of "Eyes of the Poor." His philosophical meditations are laced with frequent aspersions bemoaning the presence of the masses in the Europe of his day. "Many too many are born and they hang on their branches much too long," he has his Zarathustra proclaim. "I wish a storm would come and shake all this rottenness and worm-eatenness from the tree!"[5] He also combined his visceral disgust for their proliferation with an equally vituperative contempt for the ideological movements that attracted many of them in the last decades of the nineteenth century: "Morality today in Europe is a herd-animal morality," he writes in *Beyond Good and Evil* (1886). "Witness the ever madder howling of the anarchist dogs who are baring their fangs more and more obviously and roam through the alleys of European cities . . . [the] peacefully industrious democrats and ideologists of revolution, and even more . . . the doltish philosophasters and brotherhood enthusiasts who called themselves socialists and want a 'free society.' . . . They are at one, the lot of them, in the cry and impatience of pity, in their deadly hatred of suffering generally, and in their almost feminine inability to remain spectators, to *let* someone suffer. . . . They are at one, the lot of them, in their faith in the community as a *savior*, in short, in the herd, in 'themselves.'"[6]

This hop, skip, and a jump across the nineteenth century is not meant to suggest an evolution of views of "the people" from benign and solicitous to contemptuous and fearful. Though Nietzsche looms large in any account of the intellectual history of that century, only in certain textbook accounts is he the period's philosophical *terminus ad quem*. In this book, however, his role is pivotal, for it was Nietzsche who endowed "resentment"—in his terms, *ressentiment*—with a measure of both philosophical rigor and world-historical importance which, for good or for ill, has made it a difficult concept to ignore. After him, "resentment" could never be looked upon as it had been before.

For all this, however, for all Nietzsche's genius and intellectual influence—the way he (and his acolytes) saw himself as escaping the stifling confines of his century—when it comes to what was in fact a necessary condition of his philosophical outlook, he was very much a product of his times. Indeed, one might say this condition confers a measure of banality on this philosopher, otherwise celebrated for his brilliance and uniqueness. This critic of modernity was a product of modernity, particularly of one fundamental feature of the modern world—the insistent, unavoidable presence of "the people" on the modern stage.

This chapter, then, is in a sense a run-up to Nietzsche and his powerful fashioning of the concept of resentment, which I will discuss more fully in chapter 4. In his hands it becomes a singularly potent psychological diagnosis of collective life. But this chapter serves, somewhat preemptively, to displace him by suggesting that others before him not only looked upon the "the people" with disquiet and alarm but also responded with their own psychologically inflected analysis.

IT'S THE PEOPLE, STUPID[7]

Would it be fair to designate the nineteenth century the "Century of the People"? The question properly belongs to the purview of textbook writers, their editors, and publishers' marketing departments, and others who are obliged to think in terms of catchall labels which conflate more than they reveal. Still, a case could be made that, from the French Revolution onward, "the people," both themselves and as a set of concerns, became dominant—an overarching presence, a dumb fact, so to speak, which it would be "stupid" to ignore.

Part of the story is quantitative in nature. Population growth in Western Europe reached historically unprecedented levels, more than doubling from 180 to 390 million by the end of the century. Compare this to the increase in the eighteenth century, a time of demographic expansion, of merely 50 percent. Urbanization dramatically augmented the profile of this increase. In France, the share of the population living in cities went from a quarter to almost half; in Germany, from a third to well over half; and in England, the heartland of the so-called Industrial Revolution, accounts show an increase from 40 percent to as much as 80 percent.[8] Writing at the end of the century, H. G. Wells remarked on "the extravagant swarm of new births" as "the essential disaster of the nineteenth century."[9]

Of course, it wasn't merely the presence of "the people," or rather more people, but the social character of this growing population and its impact in myriad directions. As George Rudé writes in his pathbreaking book, *The Crowd in History*, "To name only a few innovations, factory towns, railways, stable trade unions, a labor movement, socialist ideas, and the new Poor Law and police force in England were evidence that a new age was not only in the making but in being."[10] And undoubtedly the most dramatic demonstration of its "being" was its revolutionary character. Revolutions or attempted revolutions punctuated the century in France—1830, 1848, 1871; 1848 was a year of uprisings in just about every European capital. According to Richard Tilly, in Germanic lands nearly a thousand "disorders," most involving several thousand participants, occurred in the period between 1816 and 1913.[11] In England, often (incorrectly) celebrated for its "gradualism" and public civility, acts of collective violence were frequent, from the Luddites and Chartists in the early part of the century, to the contentious gatherings in support of various reform bills, to the large-scale industrial actions staged in the last decades of the century. The response of the *bien-pensants* to these various disorders was not uniform. Liberals were often sympathetic. But then we have someone like Matthew

Arnold, the apostle of "sweetness and light," writing in the wake of a rau-
cous demonstration in 1866 in support of Gladstone's reform bill—a "riot"
that amounted to trampling flower beds in Hyde Park and pulling down
some railings. Approvingly quoting his father (who had been headmaster
of Rugby School), he writes in *Culture and Anarchy* (1869), "As for rioting,
the old Roman way of dealing with *that* is always the right one; flog the
rank and file, and fling the ringleaders from the Tarpeian Rock!"[12]

A mass society was in the making, manifest not only in the collective
actions that episodically challenged the status quo but in the texture and
tone of daily life. An expansion of suffrage, compulsory education, and
the increase in literacy created an enlarged public eager to consume not
only the proliferating commodities, now increasingly available in new department stores, but also news. Cheap newspapers, catering to the tastes
and interests of the "common man," spread throughout Europe (and
America), provoking upper-class contempt for what they saw as emblematic of the degradation of culture as a whole. The rabble "vomit their bile,
and call it a newspaper," opined Nietzsche. "We feel contemptuous of every kind of culture that is compatible with reading, not to speak of writing
for, newspapers."[13] These tabloids, filled with what was contemptuously
referred to as "pictorial journalism," seemed to pander to the degraded
tastes and prurient interests of the masses. It was, as we might say, "a race
to the bottom." The democratizing impulse extended to art and literature
itself, evoking similar scorn. The Irish writer George Augustus Moore, like
others, railed against "Democratic art!" In his *Confessions of a Young Man*
(1888), he writes, "Art is the direct antithesis to democracy. . . . Athens! A
few thousand citizens who owned many thousand slaves, call that democracy! No! What I am speaking of is modern democracy—the mass. The
mass can only appreciate simple and naïve emotions, puerile prettiness,
above all conventionalities."[14]

Moore's language is filled with the sort of banalities that characterized many writers' and intellectuals' view of "the people." It is a discursive
approach that, among other things, we might call holistic insofar as it
describes the poor and working class as an undifferentiated mass, often
evoked by the age-old trope of the "many-headed beast."[15] To be sure,
this approach had its opposite in attempts to discern social distinctions
among "the people," especially as contemporary social reality itself was
generating these distinctions—between the poor, itinerant, and largely
unemployed (on the one hand) and workers; between craft and industrial workers; between peasants and urban workers; between the working
class and petite bourgeoisie; (for Marxists) between the lumpenproletariat
and the proletariat; (again for Marxists) between class-conscious work-

ers and those bereft of it; between the criminal elements and the generally law-abiding; between those deemed pathologically "degenerate" and those untainted by mental disorders; etc. Indeed, it could be argued that the emergence of the disciplines of both sociology and psychology largely stemmed from a taxonomic urge to make sense of this new social reality and all its complexities.

But it is the holistic approach that I would like to focus on, as it ultimately leads us to Nietzsche by way of seeking out the variety of ascriptions that served to underwrite global views of "the people." For there were several. Nietzsche cast them as the "herd," morally and psychologically in thrall to resentment, which only served to lock them into a life-eviscerating disposition responsible for setting history on a decadent course. Others less ambitious in their analysis were content with characterizations—some (though very few) favorable, most disparaging—which in either case seemed to satisfy the urge to corral the vast multitude of peoples into a single, tidy category.

THE PEOPLE BECOME THE CROWD

Whether positive or negative, sympathetic or fearful, depictions of "the people" were often inflected with references to the French Revolution, that touchstone of political culture throughout the nineteenth century. ("The political and cultural history of the long nineteenth century begins not with Victoria, or even Napoleon, but with Mirabeau and Robespierre," proclaims Peter Gay.[16]) For the liberal historian Jules Michelet, the "people" embodied the spirit of republicanism as birthed by the Revolution, a spirit which, in his hopeful view, was alive, well and growing in his century. His immensely popular book of 1846, *The People* (it sold a thousand copies in one day in Paris alone), was clearly conceived as an extended riposte to those who readily disparaged the popular orders. In a typical passage, Michelet acknowledges that "the rise and progress of the people are often compared to the invasion of the Barbarians," seizing upon a conventional negative trope, but then reverses the meaning of this description: "Barbarians! That is to say, travelers marching toward a future Rome, going slowly no doubt, each generation advancing a little and then halting in death, but others continue forward all the same."[17] Unlike Marx, Engels, and other radicals, his social vision is capacious, underwritten by a nationalist sentiment that was still cultivated in generally liberal circles: "One people! One country! One France! Never, never, I beg you must we become two nations!" Here, however, it is the republican nation he wants to evoke, united against the "ever-enduring coalition of aristocracies" who have never pardoned the fact that "fifty years ago"—referring to the Revolution, of course—the people mobilized "to deliver the world."[18] Despite all this, a note of condescension runs throughout *The People*, as, for example, when he compares them to a child, "young and primitive." "Oh, wise men, it is here that we must hold our tongues," he exclaims (Michelet exclaims a lot). "Let us form a circle and listen to this young teacher from bygone ages. He has no need to analyze what he says in order to instruct us, for he is like a living witness . . ."[19] As a crowd, the people might appear as a disordered mass, especially to the bourgeoisie. But this is a misunderstanding, based on a failure to recognize the conditions under which they live and work—their "subjection to the mechanical order which is itself a disorder and a death for living bodies and which thereby provokes a violent return to life in the few moments of freedom."[20] Michelet's "people" are righteous in their anger, harbingers of a better future.[21]

But especially as the century progressed—and particularly after 1848—fewer commentators shared the liberal historian's sunny view of the prospect of social progress borne by popular energies. Michelet's somewhat younger contemporary Hippolyte Taine (1828–93) was his opposite in almost every respect—except for the fact that he, too, wrote copiously on the French Revolution. But his assessment of the great event could not have been more different. In general, for one thing, his vision resonated with Nietzsche, who referred to him in *Beyond Good and Evil* as the "foremost historian now living."[22] It is easy to see why. Taine, despite all his attention to archival sources, was probably the most psychological of historians of his time. To Guizot, he wrote in 1871, "I have done pure psychology and psychology applied to history—nothing more." He declared psychology "queen of the sciences."[23] Despite his impressive forays into this area of study, when it came to the crowd, his analysis was colored more by his politics—and his reaction to contemporary events—than by his studies. He was appalled by the violence during the Paris Commune in 1871, seeing in it yet another egregious example of the bestial behavior demonstrated by the masses in the Revolution. His historical narrative of the Revolution dwelled, almost obsessively, on the violence of the revolutionary crowd— "an elephant on a rampage," he called it—never missing an opportunity to evoke in lurid language the excesses of the "rabble." "Almost immediately," he writes of one particularly violent episode in a provincial city, "another band, screaming for murder, begins its chase and breaks windows. . . . [A] woman throws herself on the crushed old man, tramples on his face with her feet, and repeatedly plunges her scissors in his eyes." He concludes: "Such is public life in France after July 14: in every city, magistrates are at the mercy of a band of savages, often, a band of cannibals."[24]

Taine's writings were enormously influential and widely read. But beyond his strictly historical contributions, he both contributed to and reflected a general sentiment regarding the "people," a sentiment that ultimately yielded what is recognized as the French school of criminality—indeed, the first sustained study of criminal behavior. The subject was encased, however, in a vast intellectual effort to explain not only the nature and motivation of criminals but the psychological and physical basis of madness as well. Beyond this, academic investigators and pundits alike were exercised with the issue of "degeneracy," assumed to be caused by the "ills of modern civilization," patently manifest, they asserted, in the rise of prostitution, alcoholism, venereal disease, poverty, crime and delinquency, and the declining birth rate, as well as social disorders and revolt. It was something like a counternarrative riposte to the Enlightenment prognosis of progress, and its hold on a segment of bourgeois public opinion was tenacious. Central to the paradigm that governed the discourse of degeneracy was the assumption that virtually all of these were hereditary in nature, in keeping with the science of the day which sought to trace maladies, intelligence, and psychological dispositions through familial, ethnic, and racial lines. A prominent Rouennais physician, Charles Féré (1852–1907), writing in 1884, asserted that "great social upheavals can bring to light hereditary, psychic aberrations [*monstruosités*]. . . . One can cite among those who took a particularly evil role in the insurrections of the century a good number of individuals who were treated for insanity or had lunatics in their family."[25] As Ruth Harris concludes, "In sum, the theory of degeneration enjoyed its immense popularity because it provided a secular, scientific language for talking about the problem of recurring revolution and intractable and antisocial tendencies."[26]

Much of this intellectual baggage found its way into the writings of Gustave Le Bon (1841–1931), an immensely prolific author—he published over thirty-five books and scores of articles—and a consummate popularizer who managed to digest and synthesize a couple of generations of psychological and sociological studies in his own, somewhat tendentious fashion. His 1895 publication *The Crowd: A Study of the Popular Mind*, went through twenty-six editions and was translated into just about every European language. Though highly derivative, he put his own spin on the subject. Unlike his immediate forbears among the crowd psychologists, he saw beyond the criminal aspects of crowd action, noting the "heroic and virtuous" demonstrations of popular will in, for example, the crusades or the *levée en masse* that mobilized to defend France during the Revolution. He also was somewhat ahead of his time in appreciating techniques for manipulating and mastering the crowd, thus influencing readers later in the century from Theodore Roosevelt to Mussolini, Lenin, and Hitler. Freud also recorded his debt to Le Bon; the second chapter of *Group Psychology and the Analysis of the Ego* (1922) is titled "Le Bon's Description of the Group Mind."

Like many of his contemporaries, Le Bon subscribed to reigning assumptions regarding racial hierarchies, heredity, and the threat to civilization from "inferior peoples." The latter were both abroad, in colonized lands, and at home, and nowhere more embodied than by the crowd. Without any apparent influence from Nietzsche, he sounds quite Nietzschean when, in his work *The Psychology of Peoples* (1894), he proclaims, "The superior race contains a certain number of individuals with a very developed brain, while the inferior race does not. It is not by the crowd, but by the number of those who stand apart from it, that the races differ."[27]

For the most part, Le Bon depicts the crowd as a historical force whose time has come, ushering in a mass society characterized by a "feminine" temperament, emotion rather than reason, and a disposition to herd thinking. "The divine right of the masses is about to replace the divine right of kings," he asserts.[28] He understood it as a contemporary force that divided his time from previous history, with an appreciation that it was the French Revolution that set this force in motion. In fact, despite its title, his best-known work *The Crowd* is as much about a "mass society" (*avant la lettre*) as it is about the "psychology of the crowd." Le Bon dwells not only on the actual, physical concentration of many people but also on what we would call virtual crowds—that is, the diffuse gatherings of like-minded people or those united only in common beliefs, opinions, and tastes. This was at the root of his mostly disparaging view of contemporary society, marked as it was by the wayward, fickle, and unthinking proclivities of the masses, easily prey to the ephemera of fashion or the seduction of a strong-willed leader. He appreciated the force of the mass media of his day, especially the new popular press. A prolific commentator rather than a heavyweight thinker, he influenced a wide range of writers in the twentieth century, from José Ortega y Gasset and Walter Lippmann to those of the Frankfurt School, who raised the concept of a "mass society" to a fundamental feature of modern social thought and cultural criticism.[29]

These historians and psychologists of the crowd were witnesses to this social phenomenon that, in many ways, defines the period, especially in the last decades of the century. Other perspectives—those from liberals and socialists—echo the same observation, but with a different moral and political valence. And this maps onto our general understanding of this period in European history, the stuff of college textbooks and undergraduate lectures: the second Industrial Revolution, which was transforming and enlarging the working class, giving rise to protests, syndicalism, and other forms of popular opposition and organization; the emergence of populist, nationalist, and anti-Semitic ideologies, which often drew large, angry crowds into the streets; the invention of a popular press, which contributed to mobilization from both the extreme Right and Left; and, more generally, the development of a "mass society," with its attendant features of consumerism, increased urbanization, and the bureaucratization of fundamental aspects of people's lives.

All of this serves as the backdrop for the rise of resentment as both a sentiment and a concept. Ultimately, it takes us to Nietzsche. His genealogy, however, has resentment baked into the consciousness of Western morality from the beginning, with the advent of Christianity or even the Jewish "priests." Others, more attuned to the vagaries of history, identified this disposition with more modern developments—the pressures and strains of modern life in the nineteenth century. This stemmed from an appreciation of the historical novelty of a period characterized precisely by the political and social pressures exhibited by the "people," but added a psychological element that is itself novel. It comes to us first by way of Alexis de Tocqueville, one of the most astute historians and social critics of the period.

RESENTMENT AND THE MODERN CONDITION

It might be surmised that if Tocqueville had been a more systematic thinker—which is to say, if he had been a German—we might be studying a full-blown theory of political development that could rival Marxism's emphasis on economic life. But Tocqueville, more a man of letters than anything, lacked a philosopher's commitment to system building, and thus left us with much in the way of a compelling analysis of democracy and democratic culture in both France and America, but no theory as such. Still, his many *aperçus* regarding the paradoxical nature of modern political development—the tension between equality and liberty in democratic societies—add up to one of the most trenchant and durable political analyses we have.

For all his cold-eyed objectivity, Tocqueville appreciated the emotional and psychological aspects of political life; his works are littered with words like "envy," "jealousy," "indignation," "aggrieved," "passion," "sentiments," and . . ."resentment." This emotive language served his analysis more than simply adding interesting flourishes to historical processes; it was not merely an evocative technique, secondary to his purpose. Rather, emotions and psychological dispositions were at the heart of his analysis, functioning virtually on a causal level. Accordingly, his major works, *Democracy in America* (1835–40) and *The Old Regime and the French Revolution* (1856), provide what is in essence a model for the emergence of resentment as a symptom of democratic development in the late eighteenth and nineteenth centuries.

The model looks something like this: The democratic impulse, with its inherent value which Tocqueville calls "equality of condition," is an inexorable phenomenon of the era, as he makes clear in the opening pages of *Democracy in America*. "The principle of equality is . . . a providential fact . . . it is universal, it is lasting, it constantly eludes all human interference, and all events as well as all men contribute to its progress."[30] But equality yields mixed, even paradoxical results. In economic and social terms, it renders class distinctions meaningless. In America, the ethos of equality was part of the cell structure of its culture (that is, the cells of white men). And in eighteenth-century France, despite its entrenched class hierarchy, the course of material progress and intellectual trends tended to blur differences between the bourgeoisie and the nobility, whose lifestyles and outlooks increasingly converged.[31] It might be assumed, then, that the leveling dynamic would have fostered unity, or at least a sense of common purpose. But in both America and France, this was not the outcome Tocqueville observed. In the young United States, the principle of equality was so dear that it fostered not comity but self-interest, individualism, and an ever-vigilant jealousy, lest any group gain an advantage over another. "The nearer they draw to each other," Tocqueville writes, "the greater is their mutual hatred and the more vehement the envy and the dread with which they resist each other's claims to power . . ." "Envy" as a psychological feature of a democratic society is something he returns to again and again.

> It cannot be denied that democratic institutions strongly tend to promote the feeling of envy in the human heart; not so much because they afford to everyone the means of rising to the same level with others as *because those means perpetually disappoint the persons who employ them.* Democratic institutions awaken and foster a passion for equality which they can never entirely satisfy. This complete equality eludes the grasp of the people at the very moment when they think they have grasped it, and "flies," as Pascal says "with eternal flight"; the people are excited in the pursuit of an advantage, which is more precious because it is not sufficiently remote to be unknown or sufficiently near to be enjoyed. The lower orders are agitated by the chance of success, they

are irritated by its uncertainty; and they pass from the enthusiasm of pursuit to the exhaustion of ill success, and lastly to the acrimony of disappointment. Whatever transcends their own limitations appears to be an obstacle to their desires, and there is no superiority, however legitimate it may be, which is not irksome in their sight."[32]

In France, despite a melding of the upper classes, the "homogeneous mass" was "divided into a great number of watertight compartments, small, self-contained units, each of which watched vigilantly over its own interests . . ."[33] The French monarchy only exacerbated this dynamic by dispensing privileges unevenly among groups, with the nobility enjoying some conspicuous fiscal immunities and otherwise favored with honorific courtly positions. Thus, while the differences between bourgeois and noble were less significant in terms of wealth and power, this only made the existing advantages enjoyed by the latter all the more galling to those denied them. This was especially so, as Tocqueville argues, because the Crown had largely divested the nobility of any real power as a ruling class. It was merely a caste—puffed up with privileges, enclosed upon itself, even lacking in the martial calling that had distinguished the aristocracy of old. "It is easy to see," Tocqueville writes, "why the privileges enjoyed by this small section of the community seemed so unwarranted and so odious to the French people and why they developed that intense jealousy of the 'upper classes' which rankles still today."[34]

This analysis strikes one as nothing less than a variation on what Freud would call "the narcissism of minor differences." In this sense, it adds to the Humean insight regarding proximity and likeness as the typical basis for resentment.[35] (Or, as Aristotle remarked, with regard to envy it is potter against potter.) But Tocqueville saw that it was the principle of equality, not merely closeness, which established this psychological disposition as an ever-present danger in democratic societies. The expectation of equality fosters a hypersensitivity to differences—for any indication of unequal treatment which threatened to promote some over others. And yet, as Tocqueville acknowledged—and as many have echoed since—people's real prospects more often belied this expectation, virtually guaranteeing that resentment would prove endemic to democratic societies. From this, as we have already noted, we can appreciate a fundamental feature of the historicity of resentment as a collective emotion that has influenced political life: its importance in this respect as a *modern* phenomenon. While it is reasonable to assume that, like other fundamental emotions—hatred, fear, love, jealousy—its potential hold on humans' psychological disposition is basic and unchanging, this insight serves to buttress the conclusion that as a widespread phenomenon with political implications resentment is not perennial but belongs to the unique circumstances of modern life.

Indeed, one of the most important diagnosticians of the strains of modern life, Emile Durkheim, echoed this Tocquevillian insight in even more dramatic terms. In his work *Suicide*, published in 1897, he noted the unprecedented developments of the late nineteenth century, when the crumbling of traditional social constraints, increased prosperity, and greater social mobility conspired to unleash the aspirations of groups of people long inhibited by "aristocratic prejudices." This phenomenon was central to the concept most associated with his name—"anomie," the psychological condition in a modern society lacking in norms and limitations. This was, to be sure, a condition of freedom, central to the ethos of a liberal, cosmopolitan culture, largely freed from the prohibitions of religion and other instruments of social control, but it also induced anxiety and even, so he argued, an increased incidence of suicide, a symptom of what he called the *mal d'infini* ("malady of the infinite"). Short of this drastic recourse, he observed that modern people were increasingly prey to jealousy and envy. In *Suicide* he writes, "With increased prosperity desires increase. At the very moment when traditional roles have lost their authority, the richer prizes offered these appetites stimulate them and make them more exigent and impatient of control."[36] The modern condition promotes an unhealthy and unregulated drive toward competition, unleashing aspirations that can only lead to frustration and disappointment. While the French sociologist is not normally considered among those who joined his near contemporary Nietzsche in seizing upon resentment as a fundamental trait of contemporary society, his diagnosis of the modern predicament, with its heavy emphasis on the psychological disposition of the masses, would seem to reflect it in all but name.

*   *   *

Two other important nineteenth-century commentators shared Tocqueville's and Durkheim's sensitivity to the pressing reality of the people, but, unlike them, they belong to the same line of thinkers, sometimes defined in terms of "existentialism," in which Friedrich Nietzsche figures prominently as a precursor. They are Søren Kierkegaard (1813–55) and Fyodor Dostoyevsky (1821–81), each offering a particular version of resentment.

The Danish philosopher Kierkegaard was at his prime, a well-known public figure in Copenhagen in 1845, with his major works—*Either/Or, Fear and Trembling* (both in 1843), and *The Concept of Irony* (1844)—behind him, when he was attacked in the satirical newspaper *Corsair*. His response was a minor publication in his corpus, *The Present Age* (1846), a largely polemical text, the primary aims of which were to excoriate the press and belittle the concept of the public. The press and the public, he asserts in this essay, were elements of the "present age," a passionless time of mere "reflection," not action, and certainly not the rebellious action of a more heroic era. He writes of the present as an age characterized by "levelling," a process embodied by "a phantom . . . a monstrous abstraction, an all-embracing something which is nothing, a mirage—and that phantom is the *public*."[37] He describes it, therefore, as an age of the "indolent mass [which] sits with its legs crossed, wearing an air of superiority . . ." This mass is simply a dumb obstacle to anything approximating meaningful action. Anyone, from kings and poets to officials and teachers "has to struggle to drag the public along with it, while the public thinks in its own superior way that it is the horse."[38]

Kierkegaard, then, for all his originality, echoes the commonplace observation we have already noted: that he is living in a time of "the people"—of rising demands for equality and democracy, of industrial unrest, of public opinion, of "advertisement and publicity," of materialism, of mediocrity and conformity, in short, of all the elements that would come to be associated with a "mass society." But he adds another characteristic, that of *ressentiment*. This is the sentiment that forms when reflection curdles, when envy cannot find a release in action. He writes, "Just as air in a sealed space becomes poisonous, so the imprisonment of reflection develops a culpable *ressentiment* if it is not ventilated by action or incident of any kind."[39] Once it did, Kierkegaard proclaims. In antiquity the people's envy of the "eminent" found an outlet in ostracism: "The outstanding man was exiled, but everyone understood how dialectical the relationship was, ostracism being a mark of distinction."[40] In the present age, however, the "want of character" cannot recognize distinction, or rather it strives to deny it, "to belittle it so that it really ceases to be distinguished."[41] In this sense, resentment is basic to the modern phenomenon of leveling. The passionate age of antiquity, a time of long ago, with "storms ahead setting up new things and tearing down old," was a time of rebellion, heroism, and true action. Not so the present; "it *hinders and stifles* all action; it levels."[42] And resentment, a sentiment of the masses, is crucially instrumental in this dynamic.

It was Kierkegaard, then, not Nietzsche, who first branded his contemporaries with the label of resentment. To be sure, he did not develop the concept as the German philosopher would; Nietzsche raised it to a central feature of Western morality. Kierkegaard's use of it was more mundane, merely a demeaning ascription. But, in this sense, at least, its deployment in his hands reveals its intimate connection to the social reality that it was meant to characterize.

* * *

On February 12, 1887, Friedrich Nietzsche scribbled a note in the margin of a letter to his friend Franz Overbeck. "Have I written to you about H. Taine . . . and about Dostoyevsky?" Earlier that month, he had chanced upon a French translation of a portion of *Notes from Underground* (1864), and immediately recognized a fellow traveler in the psychological exploration of modern life. In a subsequent letter, he avowed that Dostoyevsky was "the only psychologist, by the way, from whom I learned something." He subsequently read all of the Russian novelist's works he could find in translation. Walter Kaufmann even suggests that "Nietzsche conceived of Jesus in the image of Dostoyevsky's *Idiot*."[43]

The Underground Man, the demented protagonist in the extract of Dostoyevsky's *Notes from Underground* which Nietzsche first read, is a fully formed man of resentment. And it is easy to see why Nietzsche recognized him as the embodiment of his most famous concept. There are, of course, important differences: the Underground Man is agonizingly singular in his bitterness and ceaseless rage against those people and forces he holds responsible for his pitiful predicament. While he lavishly recounts his contretemps with others, he is, in fact, entirely alone. Nietzsche's resentful slaves, on the other hand, are members of the faceless herd—the masses in thrall to their life-denying morality. Moreover, while the Underground Man is hardly admirable in any respect—he is at best pitiable; most readers find him repugnant, as well as mad—he is nevertheless something of a hero. Michael André Bernstein, in his remarkable study *Bitter Carnival*, presents him as personifying the "abject hero," a literary type which Bernstein sees as a perennial figure in the Western canon, from the nephew in Diderot's *Rameau's Nephew* to the Underground Man and many others in the twentieth century: "The figure of the 'mad' artist, the uncompromising, single-minded rebel, and the philosopher working at the (appropriately named) 'cutting edge' of the unthinkable have been staples of cultural mythology . . ."[44] Nietzsche's resentful masses embody something entirely different: the very betrayal of heroism in every respect.

Thus, while Nietzsche was inspired by Dostoyevsky's Underground Man, the dynamic of resentment in *Notes from Underground* is quite different. Instead of resentment as a consoling feature of the herd, the lowly, impotent masses, it thrives here in the festering soul of a man who, while

clearly educated and highly intelligent, lives in squalid obscurity, virtually indistinguishable from the great anonymous urban mass. It is not
they who are filled with resentment but himself, though the emotion is
exquisitely honed to an artistic pitch. If the Underground Man is heroic,
then, it's only in the sense that his voluble suffering, his self-pity, his rage
against anything and everything knows no bounds; he is the champion
in the realm of resentment. But all this emotional excess is compounded
by a tortured self-awareness, expressed in his ceaseless, mordant ruminations, which have him obsessively revisit scenes of his various and myriad
humiliations. This awareness might elevate him as someone special, even
unique, except for the fact that he is also aware of his own mediocrity—
that his abjection is just a more pronounced version of the human condition in modern times. Yet there is a perverse sense of pride that his life is
imbued by a profound sense of refusal, of self-imposed inaction: "Now I
am living out my life in a corner, trying to console myself with the stupid,
useless excuse that an intelligent man cannot turn himself into anything,
that only a fool can make anything he wants out of himself. It is true that
an intelligent man of the nineteenth century is bound to be a spineless
creature, while the man of character, the man of action, is, in most cases,
of limited intelligence."[45]

The Underground Man rails against society, but shares nothing with
the reformers, liberals, socialists, and other political activists of his youth,
an earlier generation of student radicals for whom he has nothing but
contempt. He is, nevertheless, a man of his times—the text makes this
clear by situating him among his contemporaries, despite his aversion
for them. But his aversion is sharpened, or rather deflected, finding a target in a "six-foot" officer who, he imagines, has insulted him, not with
any act of aggression but rather by simply failing to recognize him—the
ultimate insult for this little man. For years, he plots his revenge, becoming something like a souped-up Hamlet, consumed with a series of fantasies: a confrontation, a duel. He writes a letter but doesn't send it; he
endures more imagined scenarios, frantic scheming, dreaming, and failed
attempts to even leave the house, let alone act on his rage. Finally, he con-
trives an encounter: for once he refuses to get out of the way of the officer
as he brusquely makes his way across Nevsky Avenue. "I closed my eyes,"
he says, "and we banged hard against one another, shoulder to shoulder.
I didn't yield an inch and walked past him as an equal! He never even
turned around, pretending not to have noticed a thing. But I know he was
just pretending. I'm sure of it to this day."[46]

This produces, of course, no sense of triumph or satisfaction but
only more self-loathing and frustration. Subsequently he is given over to

"dreaming away for three months on end, huddled in [his] corner," still imagining ways to exact revenge.[47] The Underground Man, then, embodies a common feature of resentment, as we have observed: the tendency—indeed something of a compulsion—to deflect one's grievance away from its true source onto a real or imagined other, now found responsible. For him, the imposing officer is a stand-in for a society that refuses him recognition, which relegates him to obscurity, to the nothingness of a debased existence. In this respect, Dostoyevsky is, as he has been hailed, a progenitor of existentialism, only here, it should be noted, it is not the absence of God which renders life meaningless but rather a mass society that fails in conferring meaning. If the Underground Man is heroic in his suffering, it is only made worse by the realization that, like the anonymous mass, he, too, is anonymous, a nobody.

In *Notes from Underground* and his other novels as well, Dostoyevsky presents us with characters marked by resentment, who stand apart from, and outside of, "respectable" society. They are eccentric, singular, allergic to common conventions, self-exiles from the company of their peers and compatriots. In this sense, and again, unlike Nietzsche, Dostoyevsky's Underground Man is the spiritual ancestor of the defiant outsider, the outlaw, the "rebel without a cause"—a figure both feared and celebrated in so many venues of contemporary popular culture to this day. In him we can detect as well the predecessor to the murderously misogynistic "Incel," the Unabomber, the lone gunman, the rogue terrorist.[48]

*　*　*

In their fascinating study *Are Racists Crazy?* Sander L. Gilman and James M. Thomas argue that it was only during the course of the early twentieth century that "experts begin to locate the cause of racism in the crowd or the mob."[49] They note as well that "the crowd or the mob"—as a concept—was created in order "to define a psychological state in the nineteenth century." They further claim that it was a "classification as troubling as race itself," for it ultimately led to the pathologizing of crowds and crowd behavior. But we can add to this line of development, for before racism, "resentment" was, at least for someone like Kierkegaard, a characteristic of the present age of social "levelling." Dostoyevsky's Underground Man is himself the quintessential man of resentment, but here, too, he discloses his twisted psychological disposition against the backdrop of a modern, bustling world with all the features of a mass society. "The ideas of the herd should rule the herd," writes Nietzsche, "and not reach out beyond it."[50]

CODA: FROM POPULACE TO POPULISM

The crowd that most threatened established elites and sent troubled intellectuals frantically scurrying down various explanatory paths was the
revolutionary crowd. But alongside this threat were two other disquieting
manifestations of "the people": the democratic ethos and the principle of
equality, and the phenomenon of a mass society, both signature elements
of a modernity that many of these intellectuals increasingly bemoaned.
In the last decades of the nineteenth century, however, another form of
popular contention appeared on the scene. In France, Germany and also,
of course, the US, Populism became a force to be reckoned with. Here we
find resentment as a potential feature of both its ideological and its emotional character, although the appropriateness of this characterization
has been hotly contested. "Popular" in nature, its place on the political
spectrum is less clear-cut than the socialist, syndicalist, or trade union
movements, for a vexing quality of Populism is its skewed ideological
allegiances—somewhat left but also, in other respects, decidedly right,
with pronounced notes of anti-Semitism, nativism, and xenophobia as
well as an attraction to authoritarian figures.[51]

Despite its different national and even regional contexts, Populism in
France, Germany, and the US stemmed from generally common sources.
It was a "small-owner protest," and, as such, arose in reaction to the remarkable commercial expansion and concomitant economic consolida-
tion which marked the last decades of the nineteenth century—the first
phase of "globalization" in the modern era. Yeomen farmers, craft workers, small shopkeepers: these were the sort of groups most threatened
by large-scale agriculture, industrial-scale production, and the advent of
the department store, that alluring monument to the new consumerism,
memorably celebrated in Zola's *Au bonheur des dames* (1883), as iconic
of fin-de-siècle Paris as its contemporary novelty, the Eiffel Tower. The
collapse of agricultural prices in the 1870s and 1880s contributed to this
consolidating dynamic, which, combined with the extension of railways
and expanding markets, privileged ever more monopolistic tendencies
and large-scale production at the expense of "small owners." Populism
expressed the real grievances of millions of "little people" left behind,
or at least threatened, by distant, often international forces beyond their
control.

But it is precisely its ideological valence, not the legitimacy of its adherents' suffering, that has provoked the most speculation. And here we
can discern a potential shift in the general depiction of "the people." As
I hope we have seen, throughout most of the century, it was the revolu-

tionary, democratizing aspect of an increasingly "mass" society which exercised various commentators, from Taine to Le Bon to Kierkegaard and Nietzsche. And in different ways, many strove to contain the "progressive" potential of the masses by pathologizing them—by the deployment of essentially delegitimizing characterizations backed by the historical and psychological wisdom of the day. The diagnosis of "resentment" was one of these. Nietzsche, to be sure, did not care to observe ideological distinctions, which were simply beneath him; for him, an anarchist and an anti-Semite, a socialist and a national chauvinist belonged in the same "basket of deplorables."[52] But for the most part, his contemporaries readily adopted an ideological outlook which, in this fashion, took aim at popular, democratizing forces. With Populism, however, the arrow turns to the right on the ideological dial. Henceforth, and into the twentieth century, it would be the "left behind," the victims of "modernizing" forces primarily aligned with the populist Right, who would find themselves slapped with the label of resentment. Did this matter? In subsequent chapters I will suggest that it did, that a convergence of factors, both intellectual and political, fostered a readiness to see resentment as fundamental to many right-wing movements, a readiness that in the twentieth century ultimately led to the sharpening of resentment as a powerful and very handy analytical tool.

CHAPTER FOUR
The Nietzschean Moment[1]

> Virtually everything my generation discussed, tried to think through—one might say, suffered; one might also say, spun out—had long been expressed and exhausted by Nietzsche, who had found definitive formulations; the rest was exegesis.
>
> GOTTFRIED BENN, "Nietzsche after 50 Years"[2]

At this point, we can posit four different modes of resentment:

1. Resentment as a legitimate and warranted response to injury. This is, as we saw with Joseph Butler and Adam Smith, a resentment that is moderate in its expression, "civilized," never leading to revenge. It is reasonable in the sense that it expresses a reasonable demand for justice.
2. Resentment as a feature of modern life, where equality or at least close proximity between classes and the prospect of social mobility are the rule, as suggested by Hume and argued more explicitly by Tocqueville.
3. Resentment in the sense embodied by Dostoyevsky's Underground Man: the psychological disposition of an individual who defines himself as an outsider, beyond the constraints, values, and conventions of society. Defiant, angry, and bitter, he tends to nurse his grievances, dwell on his blighted past, and blame others—even all of "society"—for his failed life. In most cases, his resentment remains merely toxic for himself; on occasion, it provokes him to antisocial, even murderous action.
4. Resentment as a collective emotion, the characteristic psychological disposition of the envious "herd," which can only be viewed as negative, even life-denying—a kind of sickness. Which leads us to Nietzsche.

NIETZSCHE: THE PHILOSOPHER OF RESENTMENT

Although others (as we have seen) discussed this disposition as an aspect of human emotion and psychology, it was Nietzsche who raised it to a foundational feature of a whole swath of human history which largely dictated, he argued, the evolution of a total value system that has prevailed since ancient times. And it was a system, crystallized in the Judeo-Christian tradition, that he categorically condemned as tragically antithetical to the life force, the "will to power," the noble mentality that ought to govern truly authentic human beings, or at least those few capable of realizing this heroic potential. Like Marx, Nietzsche's prescriptive philosophy—and he was nothing if not prescriptive—derived its power from a historical perspective offering an evolutionary account of how, across the last two millennia, Europe's system of morality got so totally turned upside down. At the center of that account is his notion of *ressentiment*.[3]

While it appears in other of his works, it is in *On the Genealogy of Morality* where the concept finds its most profound and sustained development. Written over the course of two months in 1887 in a burst of creative frenzy, this book, comprised of three essays, is considered by many to be his most systematic work of philosophy, despite its polemical, tendentious tone, and a rhetorical style that, like all of his writing, is sometimes entertaining, sometimes irritating, and often somewhat ambiguous in meaning. To Arthur Danto, one of Nietzsche most astute readers, it is "the most treacherous book he ever compiled, one almost impossible to read without being cut to ribbons."[4]

In large part, it provides a history of morality through a sort of morality tale—a story that manages to be at once timeless and rooted in a specific historical epoch. Its outlines are as follows:

In an (unspecified) ancient era, society is divided between two classes—masters and slaves. The differences distinguishing the two are stark and categorical: the strong versus the weak; the noble few versus the ordinary many; the "birds of prey" versus the "lambs"; the happy versus the miserable; those who live life fully, unencumbered by regret, guilt, or bad conscience versus the downtrodden whose lives are filled with bitterness, envy and . . . *ressentiment*. But the slaves' psychological disposition, though profoundly enervating, has creative potential. Indeed, resentment, in Nietzsche's view, is enormously productive, responsible for the sort of dramatic "transvaluation"[5] he espoused for his own time.

We need to pause here. Although it is not always clear in *On the Genealogy of Morality*, Nietzsche seems to suggest a periodization in the creative process engendered by resentment. In the first instance, there is resentment pure and simple: "... a whole vibrating realm of subterranean revenge, inexhaustible and insatiable in its eruptions against the happy, and likewise in masquerades of revenge and pretexts for revenge ..." (91)[6] There are other tendencies intrinsic to this basic psychological state: "a yearning ... to anesthetize pain through emotion"; the slaves need to find something or someone to blame for their suffering ("Someone or other must be to blame that I feel ill" [93].). A resentful consciousness is also imaginatively rich. As Nietzsche writes, "All sick people ... enjoy being mistrustful and dwelling on the wrongs and imagined slights; they rummage through the bowels of their past and present for obscure, questionable stories that will allow them to wallow in tortured suspicion, and intoxicate themselves with their own poisonous wickedness—they rip open the oldest wounds and make themselves bleed to death from scars long-since healed, they make evil-doers out of friend, wife, child and anyone else near to them" (94). It is in passages like this where Nietzsche offers comments that beg comparison to the Marxist concept of "false consciousness," which would later be applied especially to extreme political ideologies and movements in the twentieth century.

In any case, while feelings of revenge and a desire to blame seem to sprout from the very soil of resentment, Nietzsche adds another stage in its creative process, one that ultimately produces the "morality" at the heart of this book's concern. Enter the "priest." Left unattended, resentment festers, producing only unfocused yet powerful "emotions." With priestly intervention, it is given shape, content, and direction. Here is where Nietzsche is most "historical," although his account is characteristically vague, pointing to both "the trunk of the tree of revenge and hatred, Jewish hatred ..." and "Jesus of Nazareth ... the pinnacle of [Israel's] sublime vengefulness via this very 'redeemer' ..." (18). As for the priests, their impact is varied. In one voice, they say, "You yourself are to blame." The priest, he writes, "give(s) *ressentiment* a backward direction" (94). Whence the guilt and bad conscience that Nietzsche bemoans as Christianity's most enervating contribution to human history. In another voice, the priests foster the formation of the "herd": "All the sick and sickly strive instinctively for a herd-like organization." Instinctive or not, it is, he adds, "the cleverness of the priests that has organized it" (100).[7] The herd-like organization, of course, contrasts with the nobles' existential individualism, their heroic character, which, as Nietzsche sometimes explicitly suggests, is exemplified by Homer's warrior protagonists. But beyond these creative tasks, the priests are responsible for harnessing the emotive force of *ressentiment* toward the "transvaluation" of the moral hierarchy.

In short, notions of "good" and "bad" undergo a radical transformation. Where before, according to the noble ethos, good meant excellence and all its kindred values—strength, courage, prowess, willfulness, self-sufficiency, beauty, and in general an innate disposition to dominate—the slave morality reconfigures and inverts these values. (Nietzsche in fact objects to these very terms, preferring antinomies such as "health" and "sickness" or "strength" and "weakness" and a grammar of morality that embraces "life" rather than "goodness" as the supreme value: see *Beyond Good and Evil*.) The ultimate success of the priestly caste is in transforming the life-affirming values of the nobles not only into "evils" but into "sins." And the reverse is true as well: the weak, humble, poor, and downtrodden shall now "inherit the earth." Their existential characteristics—inherent in their pitiful station as slaves—are now to be celebrated as "good." The creative potential of *ressentiment* has been realized in breeding a value system that satisfies the slaves' desire to see their suffering as meaningful—as a sign of their essential righteousness—and to cast their more powerful superiors as the embodiment of evil.

There are several things to be noted here, even from this abbreviated account of Nietzsche's thinking. First, as suggested, there is some ambiguity regarding the role of the priests: Are they crucial in bringing *ressentiment* to a level of self-consciousness—an *ein sich* to a *für sich*, so to speak—by fashioning from its animus a value system he calls "slave morality"? Or is the emotive power of festering resentment sufficient toward this end? His focus on the historical role of Christianity would seem to argue for the former, but it is not always clear. Relevant to an understanding of Nietzsche's analysis in *Genealogy*, this question is even more pertinent when we consider the emergence of modern social and political movements, where leaders and opinion makers—secular "priests"—seem to play an instrumental role in raising the simmering emotion of popular resentment to an ideological pitch with great mobilizing potential.

Another feature of resentment emerges in contrast to the nobles' psychological state of being. An aspect of the nobility's superiority lies not only in their innate power but in their mental makeup as well, which is distinguished by a kind of existential self-sufficiency and unselfconsciousness—a spontaneous nature that depends on no one and acts with utter self-determinacy: "All noble morality grows out of a triumphant saying 'yes' to itself . . ." (20). Slave morality, on the other hand, is reactive; it is fashioned in contradistinction to the dominant, noble value system: "Slave morality says 'no' in principle to everything that is 'outside,' 'other,' 'non-self': and *this* 'no' is its creative deed" (20). What this means, however, is that the slave is not only more self-conscious but also, thereby, more complex and more interesting than the noble master.[8] Resentment in the slave fosters a need to make suffering meaningful, something un-thinkable for the noble, who merely accepts defeat, punishment, and pain as a matter of fate. And this search for meaning—for an explanation for suffering—ultimately leads to a moralizing conclusion that is at once con-soling and difficult. Consolation is found in slaves branding their noble masters as evil and themselves as the truly righteous, which in Nietzsche's view fosters a sort of narcotic, soothing effect: ". . . the release of emotions is the greatest attempt at relief, or should I say, at *anaesthetizing* on the part of the sufferer, his involuntarily longed-for narcotic against pain of any kind" (93).

But resentment, then, while both reactive and creative, also, somewhat paradoxically perhaps, condemns those in its thrall to a state of paralysis. True, especially under the aegis of religion (Christianity, in Nietzsche's view), suffering is made intelligible, but the resentful herd remains under the sway of the priests, who preach the life-denying virtues of asceticism, self-blame, and guilt. Though infused with a desire for revenge, *ressen-timent* does not lead to "protective reaction, a 'reflex movement' in the case of sudden injury or peril, such as that performed even by a head-less frog to ward off corrosive acid" (93). This would at least satisfy Nietz-sche's appeal for willful action and self-determinacy as positive human values. Rather, his understanding of this psychological state promises an impasse—abnegation of the life force for the sake of a consoling morality that offers plenty of "emotion" and depths of meaning but no recourse to action.

Nietzsche's anatomy of *ressentiment* in *Genealogy of Morality* is exqui-sitely exact and unsparingly critical; there is no mistaking his utter loath-ing of this cast of mind and the moral ethos it engendered. Of course, to look upon this emotion with such contempt is hardly unusual; it is rare to find resentment celebrated as a virtue. But he also argued for its for-mative place in Europe's moral evolution, acknowledging its historically creative, though problematic, role. His conclusion that it fostered a para-lyzing, anesthetized state of being, however, suggests an obstacle to seeing this psychological disposition as a feature of purposeful political action, which, in my view, preempts a clear-eyed view of the different modalities of resentment. Perhaps this stemmed from his preoccupation with the Judeo-Christian religious tradition and, in general, his attack on the per-sistent grip of guilt and sin on Europeans' moral consciousness. In any case, no subsequent commentator on this psychological state has been able ignore his interpretation, whose seductive power is as disturbing as it is challenging.

MAX SCHELER AND THE PHENOMENOLOGY OF RESENTMENT

Both a follower and critic of Nietzsche, Max Scheler (1874–1928) was a prominent German philosopher and intellectual, known especially for both his phenomenological investigations and his interest in the emotional dimension of the human experience. His death at the age of fifty-four cut short an already productive career; he left behind a large and diverse corpus of works on ethics, the sociology of knowledge, American pragmatism, politics, and history. A student of Edmund Husserl, the founder of phenomenology, he was active in several circles of young phenomenologists that flourished in Germany in the early years of the twentieth century. This philosophical approach—which is not so much a school or a philosophy per se as a style of thought, a mode of viewing the world—emphasizes the phenomena of things and the experience of human consciousness. It rejects a Cartesian distinction between the self and the world of objects, attempting to capture the experience of the conscious subject's "being-in-the-world." Perhaps best known for its formative influence on Heidegger and the existentialists, in Scheler's time it signaled a radical departure from the dominant positivist and Kantian approaches to philosophy. Though largely neglected today, Scheler has been deemed "perhaps the most creative of the early phenomenologists."[9] His commitment to phenomenology is evident in his 1915 study, *Das Ressentiment im Aufbau der Moralen* (*The Role of Ressentiment in the Structure of Morals*), where he applies this method to the experience of *ressentiment*.

This is one aspect of Scheler's departure from Nietzsche's analysis of resentment, which clearly set the terms of his own investigation. Indeed, he begins his study by citing several long passages from *On the Genealogy of Morality*, and, following Nietzsche's lead, frames resentment as a kind of sickness, dwelling on its pathology—a "self-poisoning of the mind which has quite definite causes and consequences" (29).[10] Its overwhelming power defines the very character of its victim, displacing any instrumental logic: "To its very core, the mind of *ressentiment* man is filled with envy, the impulse to detract, malice, and secret vindictiveness. These affects have become fixed attitudes, detached from all determinate objects" (54). But unlike Nietzsche, Scheler is mostly uninterested in the historicity of resentment—that is, its genealogy. His study remains focused on the experience of resentment, its situational conditions, and the variety of its emotional, intellectual, and psychological features, that is, its phenomenology. He also departs from Nietzsche in vigorously denying the link between resentment and Christianity. Scheler's defense of Christianity as characterized not by the base instincts of a slave morality but rather by the higher sentiments of love and grace is passionate throughout; though of Jewish parentage, he was at the time of the writing of *Ressentiment* a Catholic convert.[11] When he turns to bourgeois morality, humanitarianism, and the moral climate of the modern world in general, however, he rejoins Nietzsche in seeing it contaminated with the sickness of resentment.

Scheler's phenomenological approach endows his study with some curious, somewhat off-putting features. Like many, especially early, phenomenologists, his method has virtually nothing to do with actual research, with empirical investigation into the subject at hand. Rather, his "experiment" with the nature of resentment amounts to a sustained meditation on the experience itself, where that experience, it would seem, is the product of his own imagination. Often this leads to astute, sensitive, and eminently convincing insights; sometimes, the results strike one as purely speculative, unfounded, or even silly. A case in point is his assertion that resentment is intrinsic to the feminine experience "because both nature and custom impose upon woman a reactive and passive role in love, the domain of her most vital interest." He compounds this rather maladroit comment by evoking the predicament of the "'old maid' with her repressed cravings for tenderness, sex, and propagation, [who] is rarely quite free of ressentiment" (43). Here as elsewhere, some of his "research" seems nothing more than repeating commonplace assumptions of the day that are as banal as they are bogus.

For the most part, his observations are not so tendentious, offering a more textured sense of resentment than found in Nietzsche's account. One aspect is his emphasis on the emotional trajectory that might, given the circumstances, result in a resentful state of mind; that is, resentment as the end-point of a process: "There is a progression of feeling which starts with revenge and runs via rancor, envy, and [an] impulse to detract all the way to spite coming close to *ressentiment*" (30). To be thwarted or blocked, however, distinguishes resentment from these other emotions; ideally, at least, one finds relief from a desire for revenge once an act of vengeance is carried out: "This vengeance restores his damaged feeling of personal value, his injured 'honor,' or it brings 'satisfaction' for the wrongs he has endured" (32). A lack of relief marks resentment, on the other hand, thus promoting the festering state of paralysis, impotence, and enervating bitterness that Nietzsche also observed. This, in turn, leads the resentful person to devalue, falsify, or scorn values held by the objects of his resentment, which Scheler calls the "specific value delusion of resentment" (40). A resentful person is possessed of "an urge to scold, to depreciate, to belittle whatever he can. Thus, he involuntarily 'slanders' life and the world in order to justify his inner pattern of value experience"

(55). But, in one of his more original insights, Scheler also suggests that this is an "automatic" and "involuntary" process, in which "conscious falsification becomes unnecessary." Even more, "the most honest convictions may prevail on the periphery of consciousness," convictions that are experienced as "entirely 'true,' 'genuine,' and 'honest,'" for the values affirmed are "really felt to be positive" (57). On an experiential level, then, resentment rests upon one's awareness without guile, promoting a deep sense of rectitude.

Scheler leavens his phenomenological approach with a sociological perspective, though it is hardly distinguished by very much rigor. His main assertion regards the potential for comparison with others and the aspiration for upward social mobility as preconditions for resentment, which can only be present in society where the distinctions of class do not preclude people of lesser standing aspiring to or assuming the benefits or goods of those above them. Here, at least, the argument presented is historical, although rendered only in the broadest of strokes. A premodern society, with its rigid and vast social distinctions, hardly invites realistic comparisons or meaningful aspirations on the part of the common people. (And in an obvious critique of Nietzsche, he adds that this is even less likely for slaves.) People then "knew their place." It is not evident that he had Tocqueville in mind, but his analysis certainly has a Tocquevillian ring: A modern, and in particular a democratic society engenders a comparative dynamic, and it thereby gives rise to resentment, especially, as Scheler notes, when there is a disparity between a "formal" principle of equality in the political realm and the "factual," unequal distribution of income or wealth. From this he derives an "important sociological law": that resentment "will spread with the *discrepancy* between the political, constitutional or traditional status of a group and its *factual* power. It is the difference between these two factors which is decisive, not one of them alone" (33). This disparity, of course, only plays upon the consciousness of the socially or economically inferior; the upper classes remain blissfully unaware of it. Citing Georg Simmel, Scheler offers the psychological dynamic of comparing oneself with others as a sort of existential component of the identity of ordinary people (36). The "noble" man, on the other hand, "experiences value *prior* to any comparison, the common man *in* and *through* a comparison" (37). This constant and compelling dynamic of comparing oneself eats away at the man of resentment: "He cannot pass by, he has to look at them, whether he 'wants' to or not. But at the same time he wants to avert his eyes, for he is tormented by the craving to possess them and knows his desire is in vain" (54–55).[12]

This existential torment not only fuels the class envy that stands at the heart of social resentment; it also encourages a tendency to fixate on trivialities or superficialities, as if these were more meaningful than the actual power, wealth, or status of the dominant class: "Any appearance, gesture, dress or way of speaking which is symptomatic of a class suffices to stir up revenge and hatred . . ." (50). In Scheler's view, resentment of this sort haunts the subject, fostering a perverse identification with the envied class or person; it's less a matter of what they have than who or what they are: "It is as if [resentment] whispers continually: 'I can forgive everything, but not that you are—that you are *what* you are—and that I am not what you are—indeed that I am not *you*'" (35). This personalized animus turns "class hatred" into a resentful obsession that governs the subject well beyond the mundane context of the particular social conflict or difference, stamping both the very identity of the subject and the image of the object of his envy.

Scheler devotes much of his study to two goals: to defend Christianity against Nietzsche's charge that it is merely a "slave morality," the product of *ressentiment*, and, more in line with Nietzsche, to cast humanitarianism and other modern, secular ideologies, especially those of a liberal or emancipatory bent, as animated by the resentment of the weak or common against the strong and noble-minded.

As for his defense of Christianity, he insists that, contrary to Nietzsche's claim, it aims for the higher values of love and spiritual transcendence, not those of meekness or a watered-down, socially leveling sense of justice. If the Christian displays solicitous attention to the poor and lowly, there is no risk that he "might impair his own nobility," as it was with the ancients: "He acts in the peculiarly pious conviction that through this 'condescension,' through this self-abasement and 'self-renunciation' he gains the highest good and becomes equal to God" (65–66). Followers of the Gospel are possessed of a "gay, light, bold, knightly indifference to the external circumstances, drawn from the depth of life itself . . . !" [69]. And as for asceticism, which Nietzsche took as exhibit "A" of Christianity's essential denial of life itself, Scheler again attempts to correct his master. Present-day asceticism—which Scheler, following Weber, associates with the Protestant ethic—might, through its ceaseless drive to produce, multiply the "objects of pleasure," but this hardly brings "enjoyment," just more toil. Christian asceticism, on the other hand, promotes a "maximum of enjoyment" by way of restricting access to "*agreeable* and especially *useful objects*," directing one to the "simplest and most accessible things" (125).

As might be surmised from this, Scheler's vision of Christianity is infused with medieval values and associations; he sees it as essentially hierarchical and aristocratic, conducive, indeed quite hospitable, to class differences, even bondage. And insofar as the modern church has abandoned these features, it has diluted its vital ethos with the weak balm of equality and humanitarianism. Scheler is one of the legion of critics that emerged especially in the latter part of the nineteenth and the early twentieth centuries who attacked "modernity" in virtually all of its facets—egalitarian ideologies (especially socialism and feminism), industrial, commercial, and urban forms of social life, the move from "community" to "society" (especially a "mass" society), the supposed breakdown of the family, the intervention of state institutions into the social realm, the waning of traditional allegiances to religion and nation, and so forth. In all of this, like Nietzsche, Scheler sees the work of *ressentiment*. Modern society has exchanged an ersatz universal love of "mankind" for a real love of "community" (99). It is just the same, he argues, with children raised in dysfunctional, loveless homes who, rejecting the family and the natural principle of familial love, turn out to embrace most enthusiastically a meaningless "love of humanity." Whether he offers this vignette as a cause or merely an analogy is not clear.

Scheler reserves his greatest scorn for the leveling effects of egalitarianism and the democratizing ethos which, he writes, always means "selling short"; "It is a law that men can only be equal in their *least* valuable characteristics." The supposedly "good" value of equality is merely a product of resentment whereby those who cannot aspire to higher values bring everyone down to their level: "In reality it merely wants to decapitate the bearers of higher values, at whom it takes offense" (117). His contempt for a mere "society," the "*rubbish* left by the inner *decomposition*" of communities "united by blood, tradition, and history" (136), along with his evocation of "race" and "nation," put him squarely in a line of (mostly) conservative thinkers whose rejection of the modern world was wholesale. From the perspective of the longer history of the concept of resentment, however, his use of this term in the critique of mostly progressive, egalitarian, or liberal movements and ideologies would stand out in contrast to its subsequent deployment in attempts to explain reactionary and right-wing movements later in the twentieth century.

Scheler makes crystal clear his contempt for the values and culture of the world he lives in, seeing it shot through with *ressentiment*, most conspicuous in the egalitarian movements and the mass society of his day. "And that precisely is decadence!" is the last sentence of his book, *Ressentiment*, figuratively slamming the door on modernity. But like Nietzsche, he can be maddeningly imprecise about when, and how far back, history took a wrong turn. The French Revolution? The thirteenth century? Both periods are his candidates for the "fall" into modernity.

Nietzsche, of course, drew the effects of resentment with the broad brush of time starting sometime in Ancient Judaism, but he too made no mistake of his disgust and disappointment with the contemporary world. Indeed, despite the historical imprecision of his analysis, his concept only makes sense as a product of his times—as a diagnosis of the mass society he was so unhappy to live in. And in particular, it was, as established in the last chapter, the appearance of "the people" which gave rise to his baleful scorn.

*   *   *

The political implications of Nietzsche's philosophy have been endlessly debated, with many seeing him as the quintessentially apolitical—or rather, antipolitical—man, who was more a psychologist of the human condition than a philosopher, more interested in aesthetics than anything as mundane as politics; others insist that we take him at his word when he expresses contempt for the masses and disdain for anything remotely related to democratic, progressive politics. And while most of those who are critical of him in this latter sense do not embrace the once-popular notion that he was a fascist *avant la lettre*, whose notion of the *Ubermensch* and the figure of the "blond beast" prepared the way for Nazi race superiority, it is difficult to ignore the inflammatory, deeply prejudicial cast of many of his remarks. As Richard Wolin writes, "More odious still, according to Nietzsche's Olympian ethical calculus, the suffering of the masses is a necessary precondition for the engendering of a handful of 'Higher Men.'" Indeed, Nietzsche proclaims in *The Will to Power*, "A declaration of war on the masses by the *higher men* is needed. . . . A doctrine . . . powerful enough to work as a breeding agent: strengthening the strong, paralyzing and destructive for the world-weary. The annihilation of the decaying races. . . . Dominion over the earth as a means of producing a higher type."[13]

This, then, returns us to where we began: the contemporary relevance of "resentment" as a diagnosis—in tendentious and highly prejudicial terms, to be sure—of a mass society, with all the ideological and psychological challenges that seemed to characterize it. This has been perhaps the dominant way in which this emotion has been deployed ever since. Nietzsche's formulation has remained unmatched. Even those who follow him have tended not to use the concept so ambitiously, as such a sweeping explanation for the whole course of Western morality and with such profoundly negative connotations. Still, for the most part, a disparaging sense of resentment has stuck, even when it is marshaled by commentators with very different ideological orientations. Most evident in Scheler, but also in Nietzsche, is their contempt for the leftist or progressive groups of their day.

In the twentieth century, the arrow of resentment would be pointed in the opposite direction, aimed for the most part at new right-wing and fascist movements. In the United States, it would prove useful to mid-century liberals, as they tried to both make sense of the horrors of the thirties and forties and stave off native right-wing extremism in their own day. These liberal academics, while not explicitly citing Nietzsche, nevertheless latched on to the concept of resentment and enshrined it amid sundry other supporting factors, several psychological in nature, in order to fashion a remarkably robust intellectual paradigm which proved far more analytically potent than the German philosopher's own formulation. It is to the efforts that went into constructing this paradigm that we shall turn next.

CHAPTER FIVE

The Rise and Decline of the "Resentment Paradigm"

> Social groups that are dispossessed invariably seek targets on whom they can vent their resentments, targets whose power can serve to explain their dispossession. In this respect, the radical right of the early 1960s is in no way different from the Populists of the 1890s, who for years traded successfully on such simple formulas as "Wall Street," "international bankers," and "the Trusts," in order to have not only targets but "explanations" for politics.
>
> DANIEL BELL, "The Dispossessed (1962)," in *The Radical Right*

It is often said that generals are always fighting the last war. Is this true for social scientists as well? If so, we might excuse a cohort of sociologically and historically minded American intellectuals who came of age after World War II for turning their analytical sights on the horrors of the period of that "last war," especially as they were for the most part Jewish offspring of Eastern European and Russian immigrants. They were not alone. Indeed, it would hardly be an exaggeration to say that the need to make sense of the Nazi takeover of Germany, the rise of anti-Semitism, and the ensuing genocide exercised a large swath of the transatlantic community of social scientists, historians, and other academics and thinkers in the middle decades of the twentieth century with an outpouring of analysis unequaled in the annals of intellectual history. What distinguished the younger subset of these intellectuals in the US was that the legacy of attempting to understand the recent European past informed and carried over into their analytical perspective on a range of ideological movements, both past and present. The intellectual tools forged to make sense of Nazism and mass racism became their stock in trade, subsequently applied to groups and tendencies well beyond the midcentury European experience. Combining social and psychological perspectives, they fashioned a powerful analytical approach, with resentment as a fundamental feature. I characterize this approach as the "Resentment Paradigm."

*   *   *

The statement by Daniel Bell quoted above, one of the leading figures of this cohort, summarizes the essence of this paradigm. It comes from an essay, "The Dispossessed," published in a collection which he edited. It crisply conveys a solution to an urgent contemporary problem: how to understand the recent (circa 1960) emergence of right-wing extremist groups in the US. Moreover, it suggests an arc across American history from the Populists of the late nineteenth century to what Bell and his associates see as the "radical right" of their own day. But as suggestive as this explanation is, it is only that: it only hints at the paradigmatic aspect of which this explanation is merely a part. It can be likened to the directions supplied to a stranger: it tells one how to get to the desired destination but it doesn't supply the map that would allow this person to get around otherwise. What follows first, then, is an attempt to map out the dimensions and coordinates of a paradigm which, I will argue, came to dominate intellectual and scholarly approaches to certain social and political movements largely of the middle decades of the twentieth century. In the second part of this chapter, however, I will show that this paradigm was subjected to a sustained attack in the 1970s, which essentially undermined its paradigmatic status. With its decline, therefore, we see the "decline" of resentment, evoked in the title of this book.

The book of essays Bell edited has an interesting history, one worth dwelling on for a moment not only because it crystallizes the views and assumptions that went into the Resentment Paradigm, but also because it was itself—*qua* publication—a factor in its development. The book had two incarnations, both edited by Bell. The first, published in 1955 under the title *The New American Right*, with contributions from Bell, Talcott Parsons, Richard Hofstadter, Seymour Martin Lipset, David Riesman and Nathan Glazer (as coauthors), and Peter Viereck, focused mostly on Mc-Carthyism. *The Radical Right*, which appeared seven years later in 1962, republished the original 1955 texts along with new essays and additional contributions by Alan Westin and Herbert H. Hyman. Its main concern, at least in the new essays, was with what the authors viewed as the embodiment of the "new right" at the moment, the John Birch Society.[1]

Clearly, then, the authors believed both that the analysis they offered in 1955 was in need of updating, given the changing face of right-wing extremism, and that, despite the adjustments in their thinking evident in the 1962 essays, their general approach to the problem was essentially correct, serving as a basis for further explorations into the phenomenon of extremist movements—which it did. Indeed, these authors, who by the early 1960s had established themselves in prestigious university positions, as directors of research centers, as editors of influential journals and magazines, and as highly visible public intellectuals, were engaged in a coordinated effort to promote a particular perspective on social and ideological movements. The book itself had an institutional heft, originating in the "University Seminar on the State" in 1953–54 at Columbia University, with many of the essays supported by the Fund for the Republic (1951–59), an organization under the aegis of the Ford Foundation (but reputedly a front for the CIA).[2]

This coordinated effort, compounded by the professional and personal associations among these academics, is one justification for thinking of their analysis in paradigmatic terms.[3] And by this I do mean to evoke the well-known theory developed by Thomas S. Kuhn. The Kuhnian paradigm has, to be sure, suffered from overuse and simplification since the publication of *The Structure of Scientific Revolutions* in 1962.[4] Here, however, I want to deploy it with some attention to the "disciplinary matrix" that, in Kuhn's original formulation, endowed it with an exemplary set of assumptions and procedures that govern an intellectual enterprise. In the realm of science, where Kuhn developed his concept of paradigms, this could include everything from traditions and theoretical and metaphysical perspectives to instruments and prescribed investigative procedures, all undergirded by the institutional support of the established scientific community. Perhaps most importantly, Kuhn proposed an analysis of new paradigm formation, which follows from the inability of a reigning paradigm to solve a newly apparent problem or to account for an accumulating set of anomalies. This movement from old paradigm to new was crucial to his whole intellectual enterprise—to explain "progress" in scientific thinking. Progress is not linear, nor is it a matter of pure "discovery"; rather, its course is characterized by failure, breakdown, competition, and disruption, as the need to solve new problems or accommodate new data gives rise not merely to "solutions" but whole new ways of thinking.

This, then, suggests one feature of the Resentment Paradigm—its emergence out of a frustration with established approaches to explaining populist and extremist political and social movements, especially those marked by fascism and anti-Semitism.

We need to pause here and step back from *The Radical Right* for a moment. As I suggest at the start of this chapter, the memory of Nazism and especially what in a few years would be called the Holocaust cast a baleful shadow over these social scientists and historians, just as it did over others both inside and beyond academia. Established approaches and methods seemed inadequate to the task of making sense of this experience. This sense of inadequacy was acknowledged at the time. Indeed, figures associated with *The Radical Right* urged a fundamental turn in thinking commensurate with the epoch-making disasters of recent history marked by total war, totalitarianism, and genocide. The political scientist David Truman, who led, along with Hofstadter, the "Seminar on the State" at Columbia, explicitly cast his critique and advocacy in paradigmatic terms, calling for a sober moralism combined with a rejuvenated positivism that amounted to a rejection of what he considered the optimistic and uncritical approach of his academic forebears, those of the period from the late nineteenth century to the 1930s. In a 1965 article in the *American Political Science Review*, "Disillusion and Regeneration: The Quest for a Discipline," he cites Kuhn several times, acknowledging what he describes is "loosely analogous to a paradigm." He calls his post-1945 generation to a sense of urgency and engagement in keeping with both recent history and contemporary threats. His prescription is many-pronged, suggesting an appreciation of the psychological dimension of politics (he cites "contemporary Philistinism"), "theory," and a more international, comparative approach to political science, as well as a rejection of narrow empiricism in favor of a renewed interest in "systems."[5] Hofstadter, too, echoed this paradigmatic shift, evident, among other places in his writings, in his rejection of the Progressive historians. "Those of us who grew up during the Great Depression and the Second World War could no longer share the simple faith of the Progressive writers in the sufficiency of American liberalism," he reflects in the preface to his book on these historians. "We found ourselves living in a more complex world."[6]

Evidence of this sense of urgency taking hold in the orbit of the contributors to *The Radical Right* can be illustrated by noting three direct influences on their thinking. Each was forged as a direct response to the rise of fascism, and each engaged in a psychosocial approach which would later find its way into the Resentment Paradigm.

The first is Talcott Parsons, a towering figure in the academic world and beyond, and, conveniently, a contributor to *The Radical Right*. Indeed, Parsons (born in 1902) was the senior member of this group of scholars and especially influential in the intellectual milieu of Harvard and Columbia where most of them circulated. Probably the most important sociologist of the middle decades of the twentieth century, at least in the US, he constructed his own sociological system, canonized in his 1937 book *The Structure of Social Action*, in dialogue with the work of Marshall,

Durkheim, Pareto, Weber, and others—but especially Weber (Parsons translated Weber's *The Protestant Ethic and the Spirit of Capitalism*).[7] If Weber cast a long shadow over the social sciences in the postwar era, it was in no small part because of Parsons's looming influence.

As his writings just before and during the war reveal, Parsons both contributed to and was influenced by the machinations of a discursive community intent on explaining the rise of National Socialism in psychosocial terms.[8] Among his commentaries, "The Sociology of Modern Anti-Semitism" (1942) demonstrates a somewhat altered intellectual posture when compared to his 1937 opus *The Structure of Social Action*—not only a more engaged approach but also a sharpened analysis with regard to contemporary social problems. "Anti-Semitism is a manifestation of social disorganization," he pronounces, reflecting the theme of the disintegration of "traditional" society under the pressures of modernity—the shift away from *Gemeinschaft*, which he routinely evokes. Consequently, "the average person who finds himself in a state of insecurity is as a rule not at all clearly aware of the actual sources of his feelings, if indeed he is aware of these feelings at all. Frustration and a sense of injustice are in turn very closely associated with what psychoanalysts call 'aggression'; that is, feelings of hostility and resentment." Such resentment is not the same as reaction to "a clear and obvious injury." Rather, it "is much more likely to be repressed than to be given vent to. But the more insecure a person is in this sense the more apparently does his aggression tend to be of a diffuse character, a kind of 'free-floating aggression.'" This aggression, then, seeks an outlet, although, Parsons notes, the process of finding a target usually operates on an unconscious level, "determined by the symbolic significance which it has to the actors." Typically, or at least in Nazi Germany, Jews were the targets—Jews "who allegedly monopolize opportunities and favor their own kind," who are responsible for the "unfair competition," the reason for people's low economic status. "They are convinced that if it were not for Jewish competition they would have received economic success."[9] The theoretical purview of *The Structure of Social Action* hardly allowed Parsons to comment on anti-Semitism, so it is not surprising that this scholarly text did not generate such a well-honed analysis of a specific problem. But the threat of National Socialism and all that it entailed certainly did.

The second influence was the work of Erich Fromm (1900–80), a member of the Frankfurt School, whose enormously influential *Escape from Freedom* was published in English in 1941. Like Parsons's contributions, *Escape from Freedom* offers a psychosocial analysis of authoritarian movements in general and Nazism in particular. And like other neo-Freudians,

Fromm broke with his master by shifting the etiology of psychological disorders from the family to society, from the vexed, largely unconscious, sexual tensions between child and parent to the stage of history. His account is quite historical, taking us from the late Middle Ages to the mid-twentieth century, with the narrative configured in terms of the gradual breakdown of familial, work-related and other communal structures that have traditionally offered people both meaning and a sense of belonging. The advent of modernity, defined largely in terms of the rise of an individualistic, capitalist ethos, meant the evisceration of these communal supports, leaving "man" free but increasingly bereft. With freedom came the burden of choice, "to create himself with the world in the spontaneity of love and productive work or else to seek a kind of security by such ties with the world as to destroy his freedom and the integrity of his individual self."[10] The blessings of spontaneous love and productive work are not the fate of modern man, however; in Fromm's reading of history, he is doomed to become a "cog in the capitalist machine." While general, this fate is particularly the lot of the lower middle class. Where once the independent businessman could take pride in his self-sufficiency, his knowledge and skill, his variety of clients and his ability to cater to their needs, and his place in the community, with monopolistic capitalism these men are reduced to mere middlemen constrained in virtually every respect, psychologically demeaned by their dependency on faceless suppliers and bosses, and at the mercy of the imponderable vagaries of distant markets. This analysis leads Fromm to join with others, such as the American political scientist Harold Lasswell, who at the very moment of the Nazi takeover (1933) identified its appeal to the "lower strata of the middle class, composed of small shopkeepers, artisans, and white-collar workers."[11] Adding to the forces that prompted them to follow Hitler, the authoritarian leader who would rescue them from their isolation and the burden of freedom, was a collective resentment, especially among the older members of the middle class. They were bitter and disappointed, not only from their decline in status and economic well-being, but even more from the profound letdown following Germany's defeat in the Great War. Fromm writes, "The sentiment against Versailles had its basis in the lower middle class; the nationalistic resentment was a rationalization, projecting social inferiority to national inferiority."[12]

Like others among his intellectual contemporaries, especially Ruth Benedict and Margaret Mead, and following the example of Freud as well, Fromm latched onto the notion of "character types." At the very start of the book he evokes the "character structure of modern man," and refers several times to the "authoritarian character," which is really a shorthand designation of a contemporary self, the product of history, with certain psychological traits scattered about rather unsystematically throughout the text. Primarily, it is a "weakened self," motivated by selfishness but ultimately frustrated, fearful, isolated, and confused. Most readers tended to interpret Fromm as diagnosing the followers of Hitler or other totalitarian leaders; he was really trying to show them the nature of the modern condition.

The third influence is embodied in both an institution and a major publication. The presence of the Frankfurt School of Social Research, led by Theodor Adorno and Max Horkheimer, in exile at Columbia University from 1934 to the late 1940s, created an intellectual force-field bringing a heady mix of psychoanalysis, Marxism—indeed, the whole European tradition of radical social thought—to Morningside Heights. It might seem odd that the contributors to *The Radical Right*, who almost to a one were staunch Cold War liberals, some later occupying the front ranks of neoconservatism, were so receptive to the psychosocial cultural critique articulated by such left-wing intellectuals, but this speaks to the specialness of the moment, when New Deal liberalism and a palpable fear of resurgent populist right-wing extremism gave rise to a kind of intellectual united front of concerns. Strictly speaking, *The Authoritarian Personality* (1950) was not a product of the Frankfurt School—it was sponsored by the American Jewish Committee's Department of Social Science Research— but Horkheimer and Adorno were presiding influences in the research and writing.[13]

The book, which combined interviews, quantitative analysis, and a psychoanalytic approach, aimed to predict what psychological and characterological factors made individuals compatible with authoritarian, or fascist, tendencies. Interviewees' disposition toward conformism, discipline, efficiency, stability, success, and other personality traits yielded their "f-factor" (for "fascist"). Its guiding intellectual spirit was Freudianism, especially with regard to the social and psychological costs of repression. Here it also drew upon the work of Wilhelm Reich, *The Mass Psychology of Fascism*, first published in German in 1933, as well as that of Erich Fromm. In the original preface of *The Authoritarian Personality*, Max Horkheimer claims that the study has identified a new "anthropological species," combining in a single type "the characteristics of a highly industrialized society with irrational or anti-rational beliefs."[14] Peter Gordon, in his excellent introduction to a new edition of the book, identifies what is perhaps the most important feature of the study—that the key to fascism and its appeal lies primarily in its "pre-political nature," not its ideology, which is to say that its "sources [are] deep within the personality and [thus] relatively impervious to superficial changes in the external situation."[15] In this sense, the study stood alongside others in insisting that a social science that limited itself to notions of rational agency, self-interest, or even ideology would prove inadequate to the task of explaining movements like National Socialism or anti-Semitism.

This suggests a criticism of the book that was leveled by the University of Chicago sociologist Edward Shils: Why did these researchers skew their attention toward right-wing attitudes? What about "left-authoritarianism"? The question was certainly pertinent, given the postwar circumstances, with Soviet Communism imposing its authoritarian rule over most of Eastern Europe. One explanation is simply political and personal: these were refugee (Jewish) scholars who, like many, considered European fascism, with its attendant genocide and, most importantly, its presumed appeal to the irrational impulses of the masses, qualitatively different from Communism, even at its most authoritarian. But one of the contributors to *The Authoritarian Personality*, the psychoanalyst R. Nevitt Sanford, offered a more "objective" explanation, based on his experience with patients: that those on the political left and right "differed widely in psychodynamic structure."[16] This indeed speaks to the larger issue regarding "resentment," and more generally a psychoanalytic approach to people's political orientation: the tendency to apply this sort of analysis to those on the right rather than the left. It is a disposition we shall see with the scholars associated with the Resentment Paradigm.

THE RISE OF THE RESENTMENT PARADIGM

We can now return to *The Radical Right* in order to identify the lineaments of the Resentment Paradigm with some precision, taking care to isolate the several intellectual underpinnings of its paradigmatic analysis. At the risk of a belabored exposition, I want to make clear what these underpinnings were and thus what endowed this analysis with such power. Imagine this paradigm as a platform supported by several struts which rendered it sturdy, each strut composed of somewhat different intellectual material. Sturdy it was, but once those struts were worn away by criticism, the Resentment Paradigm collapsed. In light of our current interest in "resentment" as an explanation for right-wing discontent, however, it is interesting to note the difference between contemporary uses of this concept, characterized, I have suggested, with a degree of casualness that ought to give us pause, and the full-bodied paradigmatic treatment of these mid-century intellectuals.

Status and Status Politics

Richard Hofstadter spoke for the other contributors to *The Radical Right* when he acknowledged that, while economic, social, and political factors should not be dismissed, "none of these things seem[ed] to explain the broad appeal of pseudo-conservatism [*sic*], its emotional intensity, its dense and massive irrationality, or some of the peculiar ideas it generates."[17] Indeed, these authors joined in a refrain, voiced with an undertone of a paradox, even incomprehension, that, unlike earlier extremist movements, both McCarthyism and the John Birch Society emerged during a time of prosperity and "full employment."

That discontent on this scale had no basis in widespread economic misery prompted the authors of *The Radical Right* to look at other ways of evaluating people's motivations. Here we have a fundamental feature of the Resentment Paradigm—the embrace of "status," as opposed to "class" or economic interests, as the focus of its analysis. The origins of this concept are to be found in Max Weber's sociology, with its tripartite system of social classification: "Class, Status, Party" (the title of one of Weber's essays).[18] Status, unlike class, is imbued with the sentiments of honor, prestige, relative social worth, standing, and other subjective values. Weber's formulation of status was fundamentally descriptive.[19] For the contributors to *The Radical Right*, however, it clearly implied negative, or at least problematic associations and aspirations, particularly those that could not be addressed by the political process. Not driven by interest or other "rational" goals, concerns about status were manifested in "anxieties" and other sorts of psychological disquiet. In his essay "The Sources of the 'Radical Right'" (1955), Lipset offers the concept of "status politics," linking it to resentment: "Status politics refers to political movements whose appeal is to the not uncommon resents of individuals or groups who desire to maintain or improve their social status." Governments can do little to mitigate or assuage status anxieties, as these are basically psychological in nature, which then gives rise to movements which appeal to "status resentments . . . irrational in character, [seeking] scapegoats which conveniently serve to symbolize the status threat."[20] Hofstadter voices the same line, asserting that in times of prosperity, when status politics prevail, what results from the discontented is not politics but "grousing." Bell cites evidence from "many observers" who have noted that "groups which have lost their social position seek more violently than ever to impose the older values of a society which they once bore."[21]

Psychologizing Society

While the concept of status, especially as juxtaposed with "class," was meant to suggest another way of conceiving the social order, it clearly implies considerations of a psychological order, another fundamental element of the Resentment Paradigm. It is difficult to underestimate the weight accorded to the discipline of psychology, not only by the contributors to *The Radical Right*, not only across the social sciences in the US, but also by the educated public in the middle decades of the twentieth century—and not merely psychology but psychoanalysis *à la* Freud. Freudianism, whether properly understood or not, was virtually hegemonic, supplying a set of concepts—a discourse—subscribed to by academics, intellectuals, and educated laypeople alike. Terms and phrases like "unconscious," "repression," the "ego, id, and superego," the "Oedipal complex," "Freudian slip," "anality," and others in the Freudian lexicon were part and parcel of the everyday vocabulary of the *bien-pensant* American midcentury.[22] As Dorothy Ross has argued, the embrace of Freud was one avenue that led an educated American public to "modernism," a lane of intellectual and cultural development that ran parallel to—but often also crossed—such movements as existentialism, abstract expressionism, and the literary avant-garde.[23]

Bell and his associates partook of this Freudian mindset as a matter of course. Commenting on the intellectual climate at Columbia in the 1950s and early 1960s as infused with sociopsychological assumptions, the historian William Leuchtenburg recalled, "We were all thinking in that direction; it was in the water."[24] But it was more than just the water in and around Morningside Heights.

Both Hofstadter and Lipset refer to *The Authoritarian Personality* in their essays in *The Radical Right*. As Christopher Lasch later commented, the "scientific" rigor of these findings only encouraged "Hofstadter and other liberal intellectuals to conduct political criticism in psychiatric terms."[25] Hofstadter cites evidence from the study revealing that those susceptible to extreme right-wing views were unconscious of their own "impulsive tendencies" (suggesting Hofstadter and his colleagues' own tendency to presume to know their fellow citizens better than they knew themselves).[26] Their outlook, he asserts, is characterized by ". . . restlessness, suspicion and fear . . ." Such people believe themselves to be living in a world where they are "spied upon, plotted against, betrayed, and very likely destined for total ruin."[27] Alluding to *The Authoritarian Personality* and other studies, Lipset concludes that in a "certain undefined minority of the population various personality frustrations and repressions result in the adoption of scapegoat sentiments." The findings from *The Authoritarian Personality* suggest that there is a "definite personality type that is oriented toward strong leadership, is intolerant, dislikes ambiguity, and so forth."[28] Bell refers to a "little-understood psychological mechanism— the need to create 'fear-justifying' threats in order to explain fright that is provoked by other reasons."[29] Parsons sees a kind of infantile escape into fantasy on the part of those left behind with the structural changes of the century, a regression into a make-believe world where "everything will be alright."[30] These sorts of comments—some based on the evidence in *The Authoritarian Personality*, some from kindred studies, and some merely speculative in nature, but all clearly rooted in the authors' psychoanalytic assumptions about status politics—litter the pages of *The Radical Right*.[31]

Modernization Theory

To a one, these scholars conceived of history and the march of time as an inevitable process of "modernization," a conception of development which formed the basis of the world view of several generations of academics, intellectuals, and policy makers alike. Again, the roots of modernization theory extend at least to Max Weber, with Talcott Parsons's work raising it to a doctrinal status. In essence, it strove to describe the transition of societies from "traditional" to "modern," governed by a conviction that powerful and virtually universal forces guided the course of historical development in ways that were as inexorable as they were desirable, at least for the most part. While theoretically descriptive in nature, this theory was in practice prescriptive, especially when it came to attempts on the part of various ideologues, whether romantic or radical, revolutionary or religious, to alter, interrupt, or arrest the course of history—to divert it from a path of development largely governed by free-market forces, scientific and technological advances, a democratic culture, and the primacy of political stability.

One of the costs of this development, however, as the title of Bell's essay "The Dispossessed" suggests, is that some people would be left behind. While those who embraced modernization theory had little truck with those who lamented the loss of tradition, who took refuge in the hope of a return to simpler times, or who attempted to arrest the ravages of time, they recognized that the results wrought by modernization were not unmixed. Weber expressed a rather tragic view of modernity: inexorable in its course, the secularization, bureaucratization, and disenchantment that characterized modern advancements nevertheless created an "iron cage" of rationality from which there was no escape. The contributors to *The Radical Right* hardly shared Weber's bleak verdict. Nevertheless, somewhat in the manner of Nietzsche, their diagnosis of development certainly allowed for both winners and losers. Moreover, they started with the assumption—embedded in most conceptions of modernization theory— that rapid social change invariably gives rise to discontent and instability. In keeping with the psychological disposition of his co-contributors, Parsons asserted the "well-established" fact that "major structural change" produces "a considerable amount of irrational behavior."[32]

In America, Parsons and Bell argued, the path of modern development meant the destruction of individualism—the "old mythos"—and its replacement with a society organized corporately, with the primacy on such collectivities as corporations, unions, and other group forms of social and economic life. The individual entrepreneur, they said, had given way to the corporation, just as rural society and small towns had been eclipsed by urban centers and large cities. Here they echoed contemporary, widely read studies—Hannah Arendt's *The Origins of Totalitarianism*, David Riesman's *The Lonely Crowd*, and C. Wright Mills's *White Collar*—all published in the years 1950–51, which made the notion of a "mass society" something of a meme of the period.[33] Although they did not share Mills's evocation of an ideal "petty-bourgeois" past, they certainly recognized this Columbia sociologist's depiction of an old, propertied middle class replaced by a new, salaried stratum, rendering once-proud individuals into cogs in the corporate machine, fostering a society that resembled nothing less than the angst-ridden contemporary world of the existentialists.

Bell and Parsons and their colleagues did not share this blanket, somewhat fashionable, diagnosis of their times. This would have been to concede too much to the discontented right-wingers. Rather, they saw the "radical right" as exhibiting *symptoms*, "the sour impotence of those who [found] themselves unable to understand let alone command, the complex mass society that [was] the polity of [their day]."[34] An outdated and idealized sense of individualism—Parsons termed it "regressive individualism"—was the sole refuge of those who identified with the New Right, the appearance of which could be understood simply as a "protest against the fact that American society [was] changing, and against the direction of change."[35] This analysis suggests at least two conclusions. First, in the face of this inchoate, essentially irrational reaction, nothing could be done, certainly nothing that could be meaningfully understood as "politics." Second, those who failed to adapt to the modern world, who could not find a place in the new managerial society of corporations and other groups that comprised the pluralist conception of the political and social order, were candidates for extreme, often mass movements that exploited their discontent, their frustration with a world that had passed them by—which is to say, their resentment.

Antipathy toward American Populism

In his 1973 book *The Coming of Post-Industrial Society*, Daniel Bell offers his view of nineteenth-century Populism in emphatic terms: "It is not *for fairness*, but *against elitism*; its impulse is not justice but *ressentiment*."[36] This tendentious view, while shared by the other contributors to *The Radical Right*, is most associated with Hofstadter, whose work on the subject was enormously influential. His 1955 publication *The Age of Reform* not only took on the early Populist movement (and also Progressivism) but also conveyed the most historically grounded version of the Resentment Paradigm, the influence of which is evident in the pages of *The New Right*. In 1985, Alan Brinkley deemed it "the most influential book ever published on the history of twentieth-century America."[37] It might also be one of the most contested.

Hofstadter wrote *The Age of Reform* as a riposte to the dominant, largely celebratory interpretation of the Populism of the 1890s, which tended to see it primarily as a movement of resistance against the dehumanizing, exploitative forces of modern industry and finance. The older school of historians, the so-called Progressive historians and their followers, had fashioned a cherished image of Populism and Progressivism as reformist and democratic—expressions of venerable American notions of liberty and Jeffersonian agrarianism.[38] They were popular movements motivated by legitimate grievances. While their works belied a sympathy for the traditional values and ideals of rural folk, especially as contrasted with the predatory capitalism emanating from eastern urban centers, they mostly framed these protests in economic terms. Rational interests regarding the material well-being of millions of ordinary Americans lay at the heart of these reformist movements.

This last point is important, for like his fellow contributors to *The Radical Right* assessing the extremists of the 1950s and 1960s, Hofstadter tended to both downplay the material basis of the Populists and focus on the irrational aspects of their protests. Rather than legitimate claims, he saw somewhat desperate attempts to restore a way of life that was, in truth, largely an imaginary concoction, useful mostly as a foil for exercising a collective resentment against modern trends. (A section of *The Age of Reform* is titled "The Agrarian Myth," where he underscores the "mythic" trope.) These popular movements, while originating in a laudable desire for reform, had somehow morphed into expressions of "resentment so inclusive that it embrace[d] not only the evils and abuses of a society but the whole society itself, including some of its more liberal and humane values," he writes in the introduction to the book.[39] "Somewhere along the way a large part of the Populist-Progressive tradition has turned sour, become illiberal and ill-tempered," he adds. He scolds his predecessors for slighting evidence of provincialism, nativism, and nationalism: "Nothing has been said of its tincture of anti-Semitism."[40] Indeed, he asserts that what we perceive as modern anti-Semitism in the US can be found in the Greenback-Populist tradition.[41]

This jaundiced view of American Populism found its way into *The Radical Right*. Parsons claims that the "elements of continuity between western agrarian populism and McCarthyism are not by any means fortuitous."[42] Likewise, Riesman detects among McCarthy's followers "elements of a soured obscurantist populism."[43] And it is evident in Bell's assertion, quoted at the beginning of this essay, that the Populists of the 1890s were like those of the New Right, for, like them, they "seek targets on whom they can vent their resentments, targets whose power can serve to explain their dispossession."[44] Suspicion of popular movements in general, and American Populism in particular, certainly inform the nature of the Resentment Paradigm.

Consensus Liberalism

A final feature of what I am calling the Resentment Paradigm takes into account the historical experience of the group of academics who contributed to *The Radical Right* as well as their wider circle of colleagues. In short, formational to their thinking was their own experience—or rather their reflections on this experience—of the 1930s and their identification with left-wing movements and ideologies. In the post–World War II era they changed their stripes: they retreated from radicalism, repudiated the Old Left (and soon the New), embraced anti-Communism, criticized ideological allegiances in general, voiced great fear and suspicion of mass movements of either Right or Left, and even distanced themselves from the intellectual's role, which they had once relished as engaged critics of the status quo in favor of a stance of critical detachment. Their critics accused them of conformism, complacency, elitism, and capitulation to the *realpolitik* demands of the Cold War. Indeed, Bell, Hofstadter, Lipset, and others now discovered in America—especially an America where, as Hofstadter argued, New Deal liberalism had become part of the "American political tradition"[45]—a social and political order they could live with.

They embraced Arthur Schlesinger Jr.'s notion of "The Vital Center" as a guiding pivot of American politics.[46] Although they insisted on their role as critics, their endorsement of the US "experiment" could turn celebratory when it came to comparing American society to the experimental disasters of the twentieth century, whether Fascist or Soviet. Instead of the radicalism of their youth, they now valued stability, ideological consensus, the two-party system, a "mixed" form of capitalism, pluralism, and, in general, a modern and "modernizing" path of development. For themselves, as intellectuals, in the place of ideological engagement, they offered irony, skepticism, prudence, an appreciation of "complexity," and a realist's outlook on the world in general. In his collection of essays, *The End of Ideology*, Bell writes, "There is today a rough consensus among intellectuals on political issues: the acceptance of a Welfare State; the desirability of decentralized power; a system of mixed economy and of political pluralism."[47]

In drawing the boundaries of rational, legitimate political discourse and competition narrowly—that is, within the limits inscribed by a consensual framework of the American political and social order as it has evolved over time—they delegitimized a whole range of social movements. Foremost among these was Populism, which Hofstadter, as I have noted, took the lead in portraying in highly unflattering terms—"political primitivism" and the like.[48] But underwriting their liberalism as well—that is, beyond a pointed objection to Populism—was a default suspicion of popular movements and the "masses" more generally. They were thus the original (today) much maligned liberal "elites," whose elitism was not only rooted in their hard-won status as public intellectuals but also inflected with a condescending attitude toward the people, especially in contemporary America. Popular grievances, protest, or discontent that fell outside their particular liberal framework they considered merely symptoms of a failure to adapt to the most successful modern society in history. Chief among those symptoms was resentment.[49]

THE DECLINE OF THE RESENTMENT PARADIGM

Published in the early 1960s by a group of scholars whose rise to prominence took place in that decade, *The Radical Right*, in a sense, ran up against *the* "sixties." And it didn't end well, at least for their analysis. Most of the crucial aspects of the Resentment Paradigm, I argue, were rendered "inoperative" in the discursive firmament of the last decades of the twentieth century. Starting in the 1970s, this paradigm—the once-sturdy platform—had several of its struts one by one knocked out from under it.

When Freud Left

Among the dramatic transformations in the intellectual and cultural life of America in the late twentieth century, the decline in prestige of psychoanalysis must rank high. The reason for this decline—circa mid-1980s—might be (briefly) summarized as follows: Doubts arose concerning the scientific validity of psychoanalysis, especially in the wake of subsequent clinical studies. Evidence was adduced, calling into question its effectiveness as a "cure" for psychological problems and disorders. The heroic, benign figure of Freud—humanist scientist *par excellence*—was subjected to often scathing historical revisionism, rendering an image of a scheming, authoritarian, duplicitous careerist, who ruthlessly put down rivals and even abused his patients. Freudian nostrums—dreams as the "high road to the unconscious," the Oedipal complex, and sex as the root of all our psychological ills—began to look like reductionism disguised as science. And "the critique of Freud as hopelessly situated in Vienna and the nineteenth century unite[d] cultural anthropologists, neo-Freudians, and theoreticians of women's liberation."[50] Feminists certainly attacked the patriarchal and phallocentric features of Freudianism, and cast a critical eye on the contemporary practice of psychoanalysis in general (especially as dominated by men).[51] Post- or neo-Freudian varieties of treatment along with "New Age" psychotherapies suggested a competitive field of approaches and theories only relatively effective, if at all. New discoveries in biochemistry and pharmacology had perhaps the most decisive negative consequences. Advances in brain chemistry thoroughly discredited behavioral or "environmental" origins of psychological illnesses such as schizophrenia or bipolar disorder. And to many sufferers, a new generation of Prozac-like drugs made the psychoanalyst's couch and "talk therapy" seem like witchcraft. Funding for the training of psychoanalysts dried up, and research took a big hit.[52]

So much for psychoanalysis. What about the more general sociopsychological approach? Here a turning away is less apparent, but it is important to underscore the primacy and prestige of a psychoanalytic approach—to be sure, somewhat casually and unthinkingly applied—for the fashioners of the Resentment Paradigm. Their method amounted to more than a superficial interest in psychological motivations; it entailed a commitment to psychoanalysis in order to explain unconscious drives and anxieties, repressed feelings, displaced and projected resentments, conspiratorial fears, and other "irrational" dispositions. It was fundamentally and explicitly Freudian, at least according to the often-bowdlerized version of the teachings of the inventor of psychoanalysis among the midcentury *bien-pensants.* In addition, those who operated with the Resentment Paradigm readily arrived at notions of character or personality "types," or other fixed identifications which tended to reify, indeed "essentialize" groups of people as fundamentally disposed to think and act in certain ways. Perhaps the most convincing demonstration of this analytic tendency is *The Authoritarian Personality*, with its f-scale designed to predict those with fascist proclivities—proclivities that, moreover, presumably stemmed from family and child-rearing dynamics. The Resentment Paradigm essentially tells us that there are "dispossessed" people susceptible to extremist ideologies, not so much because of what they think or do but because of who they are, at least defined by their position in society.

The Defense of Populism

Hofstadter's rather negative depiction of American Populism attracted criticism almost from the moment it appeared, and while the Columbia professor continues to be read and cited, his interpretation of this movement has not survived the test of time. The first wave of criticism of *The Age of Reform* came from C. Vann Woodward, the author of a 1938 book on Southern Populism, *Tom Watson, Agrarian Rebel*, and a celebrated American historian in his own right, who called his friend to task for ignoring evidence and overemphasizing, sometimes caricaturing, the Populists' rhetoric at the expense of their real grievances. Their program, he insisted, "was almost obsessively economic and, as political platforms go, little more irrational than the run of the mill."[53] Like other commentators, he was quick to point out the obvious: Hofstadter's jaundiced view of these reform movements was colored by his conviction—shared by Bell and Lipset, among others—that McCarthyism was their present-day echo. As for his charge of anti-Semitism, perhaps the criticism that provoked the most voluble objections, Woodward made an oblique, and rather tendentious, reference to its provenance, noting that among the new critics of Populism, "there are no conscious spokesmen of the West or South, but some are more or less conscious representatives of the urban East."[54]

Woodward had support in his critical rejoinder to Hofstadter and his "school" in the publications of a range of notable historians, William A. Williams, Norman Pollack, Walter T. K. Nugent, David Thelen (on the Progressives), Michael Rogin, and others. Essentially, their critique charged Hofstadter, not only with superficial research, but with caricaturing Populism, miscasting their nostalgia for a bygone era as regressive, even reactionary politics, when in fact their ideological orientation was in keeping with the radical republican tradition with which a wide swath of the working class in nineteenth-century America identified. This interpretation failed to acknowledge the actual political mobilization that characterized the Populists, rooted in a level of organization and ideological self-consciousness that belied the image of a virtually inchoate reaction to forces beyond both their control and understanding.[55] While, as we will see in a subsequent chapter, the nature of Populism continues to be a vexed topic, in the wake of the critique of these younger historians, the Hofstadter interpretation could only be sustained with great difficulty.[56]

New Left Populism Confronts Liberalism

There was, of course, the political shift among the new generation and the emergence of the New Left. Here, then, one intellectual prop of the Resentment Paradigm foundered not only from the force of intellect but with a radical turn in history. The "Movement," as it was called, embodied something unique in the history of Populism, or so observes one of its premier historians: "Never before in the United States had a radical upsurge that sought to win power for the common folk sprung from within the dominant order itself," writes Michael Kazin.[57] The relatively privileged students who filled the ranks of Students for a Democratic Society (SDS), joined the Student Nonviolent Coordinating Committee (SNCC) in registering Southern Blacks, and led the slowly burgeoning anti-war movement in the sixties, embraced a political vision that, at least in spirit, aimed to go beyond the confines and interests of campus life. The notions of "participatory democracy" and "community" were animating principles that signaled a rejection of liberal elitism, reflecting a Populist hope that a broad-based popular movement could transform America. To be sure, this ideal soon spawned contradictions that proved its undoing. Nevertheless, the spirit of the sixties decisively rejected the elitism of the previous generation of liberals—also rejecting their suspicious and condescending attitudes toward popular movements and the American populace in general.

The Death of Modernization Theory

"I believe that the idea of development stands today like a ruin in the intellectual landscape; its shadows obscure our vision," pronounced Wolfgang Sachs in 1990. "It is high time that we tackled the archeology of this towering conceit, that we uncovered its foundations and see it for what it is: the outdated monument to an immodest era."[58] The Resentment Paradigm rested on a concept of historical development, modernization theory, underwritten by a hegemonic intellectual consensus among scholars, policy makers, and intellectuals in the decades following World War II. Sachs's assertion might be overstated, but it is symptomatic of a turning away from this perspective in the last decades of the twentieth century, both as theory and practice. Modernization theory was both predictive and prescriptive. It promised convergence and homogenization on a global scale, and it served as the blueprint for developmental schemes designed to bring (mostly) non-Western peoples into the modern world, conferring upon them the blessings of economic plenty, education, urban living, political stability, and governance not by ideologues but experts and technocrats. Bell's collection of essays *The End of Ideology* (1960) stands as a scholarly monument to this prognosis, a vision of history subscribed to by his fellow contributors to *The Radical Right*.

One might assert that the demise of modernization theory occurred not in the groves of academe but in the rice paddies of Vietnam and in the burning streets of Detroit, Watts, and Newark. In this respect, the contentious 1960s surely undermined the ideological complacency and optimism that buttressed aspirations for a modernizing world. Whether as cause or symptom, however, the critique that emerged was many-faceted, and it unfolded over several decades: modernization was an instrument of American imperialism, a ploy in the theater of the Cold War; at the very least, it was compromised by a Eurocentric schema of history that assumed global consent to Western values and goals. It ignored local traditions and indigenous cultures; it failed to account for subaltern peoples' interests and aspirations. It put excessive emphasis on material and economic development without considering whether this truly yielded general well-being. It prompted a rapid and often violent uprooting of peasants and farmers, disrupting and deforming the countryside, creating bloated urban centers that lacked the infrastructure and general capacity to handle a burgeoning populace of newcomers. Modernizing development also privileged top-down planning and fostered a reign of experts and technocrats, brilliantly evoked in James C. Scott's "seeing like a state."[59] And modernizing policy makers disastrously underestimated the pushback from subject and colonized people, conveniently managing not to recognize the legitimacy of resistance even when it took the form of wars of national liberation. Perhaps most tellingly, by the last decades of the twentieth century, it was clear that the modernization prognosis was woefully misguided and just plain wrong—it blithely predicted "convergence," the result of an inexorable historical development among disparate peoples and nations, where cultural and ideological differences would simply be transcended. In short, the developing world as it actually *had* developed refuted this. By the 1990s, modernization theory seemed as outdated as the Marquis de Condorcet's *Sketch for a Historical Picture of the Progress of the Human Mind* (1794), which, written in the shadow of the guillotine by a man who committed suicide in order to avoid it, confidently predicted the inevitable and endless progress of humankind.

Without the vision of modernization, the Resentment Paradigm was denied much of its persuasive force, for the paradigm depends upon the conviction that the developmental pattern implicit in the modernization vision is not only inexorable but benign. Thus, while those whose lives are not in synch with this pattern might feel aggrieved, their grievances are not really actionable. They result not fundamentally from policies, laws, or other aspects of the political process as generally understood, but from the very course of history. And protesting against the course of history is about as reasonable as shaking your fist at the heavens.

*   *   *

Of course, while the contributors to *The Radical Right* were busy being exercised by the threat of homegrown, right-wing extremism, the "sixties" were happening. Other movements from a rejuvenated Left, the New Left, along with Black activists and second-wave feminists, were about to burst upon the scene, dramatically expanding the terrain of political culture in the US then and for decades to come. And, as suggested above, there was little they shared with these Cold War Liberals; indeed, in many ways student radicals especially seemed to define their ideological outlook in terms of what their elders were not, acting out a sort of Oedipal complex against their intellectual fathers. In short, they did not operate within the Resentment Paradigm, especially as it dictated a decidedly suspicious view of populism in the US and elsewhere. For these young radicals, the Populist tradition was one they wanted to revive, not deride.

In a subsequent chapter I will look at the "sixties," first from the perspective of left-wing activism, where I will argue that we find an emotional regime where "resentment" figures only marginally; and then at what has been called the phenomenon of "backlash" from the supposed "silent majority," which actually exhibited at least an attempt to engineer a politics of resentment.

In the meantime, however, let us turn to a very different sense of resentment, one largely untainted by its negative, unappealing associations, and thus more in line with what some moral philosophers have insisted is its purposefulness in calling attention to authentic grievances and demanding justice.

CHAPTER SIX

The Uses of Resentment

In the midst of the world's silence, our resentment holds its finger
raised . . .

JEAN AMÉRY, "Resentments"

The Nietzschean/Scheler version of resentment is a sentiment that no one
would want to "own." It is a sentiment of the weak, the discontented, the
envious, those mired in their private well of suffocating grievances, unable
to act or rescue themselves from a fate that, if truth be told, they probably deserve. And the sentiment at the heart of the Resentment Paradigm
marshaled by American social scientists and historians to explain the resurgence of right-wing extremism is hardly more appealing: it is a disposition of those embittered by being "left behind" by the inexorable social
transformation of modernization. But, as we saw with the good Bishop
Butler, this is not the only way we might consider resentment. Properly
channeled and modulated, it can serve as sign of injustice, a prompt that
grievances must be addressed. Butler's (and Adam Smith's) justification
of resentment implies that it not be expressed rashly or unthinkingly, and
certainly not with the goal of revenge. Their resentment is a deliberate,
"civil" expression of the sentiment, which thereby distances it somewhat
from how we normally think of emotions.

Indeed, we might consider, as I do in the introduction to this book,
that resentment is unique within the repertory of emotions. We speak of
being "quick to anger," or "falling in love." Hope "springs" eternal. Feelings of shame and humiliation are conditions that happen to people; they
imply the passive voice: you *are* shamed, humiliated. In the realm of the
emotions, of course, definitions and distinctions are blurry. But it seems
as though resentment provides an opening for deliberateness; it invites
us to consider it as an emotion well-suited for its strategic deployment
toward particular ends, especially for those who, for one reason or an-

other, find themselves with few resources to assert their claims, whose marginal status or demeaned position make it easy for the majority to ignore or discount their grievances. Collective, sustained expressions of resentment can serve to force their claims into the public sphere, if only to say, "We are here!" We might consider resentment, then, as one of James Scott's "weapons of the weak." In this chapter we shall consider the "uses of resentment."[1]

JEAN AMÉRY EMBRACES RESENTMENT AS A VIRTUE

Just a few pages into Jean Améry's essay "Resentments" (1966), he confronts, as he surely knows he must, the Nietzschean view of *ressentiment*. The riposte of this Holocaust survivor is brief and, like most of this powerful text, dripping with righteous anger. There seems to be "general agreement," he avers, that the nineteenth-century German philosopher had the "final say" on resentment. He then offers a few choice lines from *On the Genealogy of Morality*: "The resentful person is neither sincere, nor naïve, nor honest and forthright with himself. His soul squints . . ." But Améry is not about to bother with a critique. "Philosophy" is not his game. Rather, he responds with sarcasm and parody: "Thus spake the man who dreamed of the synthesis of the brute and the superman." The German philosopher must be answered by those who "were present as victims when a certain humankind joyously celebrated a festival of cruelty, as Nietzsche himself has expressed it . . ." (67–68).[2] While Améry refuses to grapple with the Nietzschean view of *ressentiment*, he does acknowledge a need to justify this sentiment in the face of modern psychology's consensus that it is "a disturbing conflict." But his goal is even more lofty and challenging: to establish what he fully admits is a "warped state," the product of unprecedented human cruelty, as "a form of the human condition that morally as well as historically is of a higher order than that of a healthy straightness" (68).

More than either Nietzsche or Scheler, the particulars of Jean Améry's biography are crucial in order to appreciate his outlook. The relevant facts can be rendered in broad strokes. He was born Hanns Chaim Meyer (or Meier) in 1912 in Vienna to a Jewish father and a Catholic mother. Although the family was initially well-established and prosperous, after his father's death in the First World War, he and his mother entered a precarious existence. He did manage to begin a philosophy and literature course at the university in Vienna but, forced to abandon his studies and go to work, never completed a degree. In his twenties, he became politically active in left-wing and anti-fascist movements. Then came the Nazi seizure of power. Although he considered himself fully assimilated, with the promulgation of the Nuremberg Laws in 1935 and the coming Anschluss, in 1938 he found it prudent to flee to Belgium with his (Jewish) wife. There, however, he was arrested as a German alien and deported to southern France, where he was interned in several concentration camps— this time as a Jew. He escaped in 1941 and returned to Belgium, where he joined the Resistance. Captured by the Gestapo, he was tortured, first in a Brussels prison, then at Auschwitz. With the liberation of the camp by the British in 1945, he returned to Brussels, where he remained for the rest of his life. After the war, Hanns Meyer changed his name to Jean Améry, an obvious transposition from the German to the French, signaling both his disavowal of German culture and his new identification with a Francophone world. (He would soon prove to be one of Sartre's most dedicated followers.[3]) He earned his living as a journalist and was reasonably well known in European intellectual circles. One of his last works, *On Suicide: A Discourse on Voluntary Death*, was published in 1976. Two years later, in his second attempt, he succeeded in taking his own life.

Améry was a prolific author, a freelance journalist who wrote on a wide range of subjects from old age and jazz to American cinema "teen-idols." Undoubtedly, his major contributions to the intellectual history of the postwar era are his personal reflections on his wartime experience, published in 1966 as *Jenseits von Schuld und Sühne: Bewältigungsversuche eines Überwältigten*.[4] The five essays that comprise this collection (published in an English translation in 1980 as *At the Mind's Limits: Contemplations by a Survivor on Auschwitz and Its Realities*)[5] include an analysis of the predicament of the intellectual in the camps where, somewhat incidentally, he mentions his "barracks mate Primo Levi"; a piece on "Torture"; a chilling account of his own experience and a meditation on the psychology and phenomenology of the "body in pain"; and an essay titled "Resentments."

The immediate occasion of the drafting of these essays was an invitation in 1964 to speak of his experiences at Auschwitz on German radio. But their real origin takes us to the years circa 1960–65, when the Holocaust newly forced itself on German public awareness, prompting an unprecedented level of discussion on the moral status of victims and victimizers both during the twelve years of Nazi rule and, most urgently, in the present. The Eichmann trial (1961) and Hannah Arendt's controversial reportage (*Eichmann in Jerusalem: A Report on the Banality of Evil*, 1963) shattered the silence that had covered the crimes of the Third Reich, making the Jewish genocide and German guilt matters of general concern in Germany and beyond. The so-called Frankfurt Auschwitz trials (1963–65), which generated copious testimony on this most infamous of concentration camps, did the same. But these events also occasioned, even encouraged, comments reflecting the conviction of many Germans, both ordinary people and public figures, that they had had enough of all this talk about German guilt and Jewish victimization. Améry had himself encountered expressions of this sentiment. He writes about a chance conversation with a South German businessman over breakfast in 1958: "Not without first politely inquiring whether I was an Israelite, the man tried to convince me that there was no longer any race hatred in his country. The German people bear no grudge against the Jewish people, he said." Améry comments, "In the presence of this man, whose mind was so at ease, I felt miserable: Shylock, demanding his pound of flesh" (67). Even many prominent Jewish intellectuals, he sadly notes, seemed "eager to reassure their German contemporaries and fellow human beings . . ." He heard their claims that, "Only totally obstinate, morally condemnable hate, already censured by history . . . clings to a past . . ." And he registered with astonishment their conciliatory assessment that this difficult past really amounted to "nothing other than an operational mishap of German history and in which the broad masses of the German people had no part." In the face of these sentiments, Améry could only testify to his "distress." He belonged to "that disapproving minority with its hard feelings" (67).

This, then, is the historical and psychological context of Améry's public reflections on his experience in Auschwitz: not the experience itself, nor even the immediate postwar years, but a position (*Zustand*) of a distance of more than twenty years after his liberation. It was a time, he notes with disgust, that a prosperous, civilized, seemingly tolerant Germany—the "industrial paradise of Europe"—was happy to put its troubled past behind it. In the face of this, he admits, "I 'stuck out.' . . . I persevered in my resentments" (67).

This context helps us identify several particular features of Améry's understanding of resentment, this "special kind of resentment, of which neither Nietzsche nor Max Scheler . . . was able to have any notion" (71). For one thing, it is a *delayed* reaction, the result of a moral reflection that takes place some time after the original trauma of the Holocaust. In fact, Améry notes that in the immediate aftermath of the war, he had hopes that the condition of a defeated and ruined Germany, proclaimed guilty of heinous crimes by world opinion, would allow for a meeting of victims and victimizers on the common ground of utter debasement. But this mutual condition did not last. The Cold War, Germany's rebuilding and remarkable economic recovery, an eagerness to forget and silence the past, and simply the passage of time—all of this worked to dispel the burden of German guilt, leaving the victims as the only ones incapable of "moving on." In this sense, Améry's resentment shares an important feature of Nietzsche's: it, too, is a *reaction*, but with a difference. It is a *chosen* reaction, a deliberate moral stance taken in the face of the world's overwhelming incomprehension and disapproval.

In a complete reversal of the Nietzschean formulation, however, Améry's resentment is an assertion of strength and will. Even more, he insists that "an inclination to be conciliatory" is not only insane, not only a suppression of the natural desire for revenge, but represents an "indifference to life." It is, to use Nietzsche's terms, to join "the herd." Reconciliation, an inert desire to forget, to succumb to the passage of time, to let the past be past—these are the instincts of those who have become "deindividualized," enmeshed in a "social mechanism," rendering them "insensitive and indifferent" to suffering and trauma, even their own (71). Améry's resentment, therefore, is hardly a "slave morality," an ethos of the weak, but an attribute of those with the moral strength to insist that their victimization not be forgotten as something to be relegated to the ever-receding past.

This, in turn, points to a claim that manages to be both mystifying and potent. Time, the past, and history are features of resentment in ways that do not apply to other emotions or psychological states. This is evident, implicitly and explicitly, in both Nietzsche and Scheler. Resentment entails suffering, privation or oppression over time, the cultivation of accumulated grievances, the persistence of memory, a comparison of the relative status of different individuals or groups, again over time; it is the result of a temporal process yielding winners and losers. Améry, however, seizes historical time by the throat and turns it upside down. His resentment does not just strive to resist the passage of time, the sense that "What happened, happened" (72), the "monstrosity of natural time-sense" (81). It is more than an existential protest against the inevitable loosening of the past's grip on the present, people's entirely natural preference for the future over the past—although it is at least this. Rather, it calls for nothing less than "the annulment of time . . . the genuinely humane and absurd demand that time be turned back" (72, 77).

What does he mean by this impossible demand—an impossibility he freely acknowledges? Let us note what should be obvious, that Améry has not written a text that yields detachable conclusions. His intent is to force readers to acknowledge that a capitulation to the inevitable passage of time creates an intolerable psychological reality for victims, who see only moral betrayal in what the world experiences as a perfectly natural temporal process. Améry's resentment, then, embodies an existential protest not only against the outrage of the crime or the forgetfulness that comes with time's passage, but against time itself—hardly a very consoling sentiment. In this sense, one cannot help but think of Nietzsche's slaves, forced into an impasse of their own making as they console themselves with a *ressentiment* that offers them merely the compensation of a "morality." To object to the passage of time is about as effective as shaking one's fist at the heavens. Perhaps. But effectiveness is not his goal, except in the sense of making an emotional impact on readers by putting before them an image of a man whose resentment will not allow him to submit to the outrages of time—the image of a man who, indeed, shakes his fist at both time and history.

On balance, however, Améry does not so completely avoid any sense of purposefulness, and he is hardly as "unreasonable" as some of his assertions might lead one to conclude. He fully recognizes his "extravagant moral daydream" (79). One day, he acknowledges, the Holocaust will be normalized, placed alongside other bloody historical episodes. "Finally . . . it will be purely and simply history . . ." (79). In the meantime, though, he suggests a possible outcome we might consider as not only realizable but, armed with an optimistic view of recent German history, actually realized. "Goaded by the spurs of resentment," he writes, "the German people would remain sensitive to the fact that they cannot allow a piece of their national history to be neutralized by time, but must integrate it" (79). In lifting a finger against the world's silence, resentment would have been more than a hopeless gesture. Then, he hypothesizes, on "the field of history . . . two groups of people, the overpowered and those who overpowered them, would be joined in the desire that time be turned back and, with it, that history become moral" (78). Only then, he concludes, "would our resentment be subjectively pacified and have become objectively unnecessary" (79).

No sooner does Améry revel in this idealistic fantasy than he quickly sobers up: "All recognizable signs suggest that natural time will reject the moral demands of our resentment and finally extinguish them" (79). But we might respond, from our perspective of the early part of the twenty-first century, that Améry's pessimism turned out to be unwarranted—that he was more prescient than he could have possibly imagined. The results certainly can be contested by students of contemporary German culture, but it is hard to think of a defeated country that has gone to greater lengths to acknowledge, commemorate, and otherwise recognize—especially in the realm of public memory and education—the crimes of its past than Germany (that is, before 1990, the Federal Republic). Was resentment the "spur" for these endeavors? One cannot possibly answer such a question. It is, however, historically incontrovertible that justice is almost never rendered without the relentless witnessing of victims, often over very long

periods of time and against the great obstacles of repression, delegitimi-
zation, and mere indifference—a witnessing that usually grates on the
ears and conscience of the majority which would much rather everyone
just "move on." It is, indeed, hard to imagine such sustained mobilizing of
victims without an emotional "spur," whether it's defined as resentment
or something else.

This is a far cry from Nietzsche's pitiable *ressentiment*, which at best
offers a phony consolation for sufferers in a twisted, enervating morality.
At its most purposeful, Améry's resentment is life-affirming and a source
of righteousness, as it surely has been for countless victims in history. As
embodied in his eloquent, powerful text—which even at its most emotional, when it seems simply to cry out, always achieves a pitch-perfect
tone—this sentiment might at times defy logic, but it never grates. This is
resentment as conveyed by a true writer, a master of language, a singular,
original, compelling voice. Would we recognize resentment as a virtue if
it were expressed not by a refined literary artist of Améry's caliber but in
the plaintive, angry, "mad howling" (Nietzsche), perhaps even offensive
voices of the inarticulate?

GERMAN GUILT, THE HOLOCAUST,
AND ANOTHER USE OF RESENTMENT

In 1965, when after a generation of virtual silence there were intimations
that Germany was beginning to recognize the monstrous crimes of its
Nazi past, a young writer published an essay that boldly branded that silence a scandal. Martin Walser, a prolific author who has published more
than sixty books, most of them works of fiction, recognized today as one
of Germany's leading men of letters, was thirty-eight years old when his
essay "Our Auschwitz" appeared in 1965. Just the year before, the Frankfurt trials, which, even more than those held in Nuremburg immediately
after the war, had impressed upon the German public the dimensions of
its criminal past. Walser's voice was one of the most powerful and eloquent in calling his compatriots to the obligation of recognizing "Auschwitz" as "ours."

In that essay, Walser expresses German "ownership" of the camps. He
rejects likening them to Dante's Inferno, or more general allusions to the
"hell" of Auschwitz, as rhetorical tricks to convince Germans that these
were otherworldly experiences, not the deliberate contrivances of their
countrymen. "But Auschwitz was not hell; it was a German concentration camp. And the 'inmates' were not damned or half-damned souls in a
Christian cosmos, but innocent Jews, Communists, and so forth. And the

torturers were not fantastic devils, but people like you and me: German, or those who wanted to become Germans."[6] Perhaps most controversially, he embraces the oft-contested notion of "collective guilt." If terms like the "state" and "Volk" continue to be evoked by Germans as politically meaningful, "then Auschwitz is a collective German phenomenon. Then everyone is to some extent part of the cause of Auschwitz. Then it would be the task of each individual to discover his share of responsibility. One need not have been a member of the SS."[7]

Walser was not entirely alone in expressing these sentiments or in calling his fellow Germans to own up to their past. The Frankfurt trials themselves were part of a movement of deliberate historical recovery—a sustained effort to bring the Nazi past into the (West) German present and demonstrate to the world that the (West) German economic "miracle" (*Wirtschaftswunder*) and stability that marked its postwar political culture did not come without at least a retrospective acknowledgment of the horrors inflicted by Germans only a generation earlier. The process of reckoning with this past had begun outside Germany: the 1960–61 capture and trial of Adolf Eichmann in Jerusalem seemed to unleash the repressed memory of what only then began to be called the "Holocaust." In Germany in 1968, a year of protest and student uprisings like elsewhere in the West, one charge of the young against their elders was their wartime complicity in Nazi crimes. The process reached a kind of popular climax with the broadcast in 1979 of the American miniseries, "Holocaust," with a viewership estimated at nearly half the West German population. Today, Germany is littered with monuments and museums dedicated to the memory of the Jewish genocide; in many cities one sees *Stolpersteine* (literally, "stumbling stones") in front of houses or apartments where Jews sent to concentration camps formerly lived. As I have already noted, it could be argued that Germany has done more to atone for its past than any other modern country whose recent history rests guiltily upon it—certainly more than the other former Axis nations.

Of course, there was hardly a consensus on this score, with everything from Holocaust deniers and neo-Nazis, whose objections were hardly surprising but increasingly shrill, to ordinary Germans, who simply couldn't be bothered to think critically about their vexed past. In 1984, during his visit to Israel, his tour of Yad Vashem, and his address before the Knesset, Chancellor Helmut Kohl certainly demonstrated his impatience at being reminded of this chapter of German history. "I know German history very well," he commented at one point, interrupting Yad Vashem's deputy director. "That was another era, another Germany."[8] The following year, when Kohl orchestrated Ronald Reagan's ceremonial visit to Bitburg, a military cemetery containing the remains of members of the SS, it seemed to symbolize a disposition among at least an element of the German public to put an exculpatory distance between the "New" Germany and the Nazi past. As the historian Charles Maier wrote, "Bitburg [was] a sacrament of resentment, not reconciliation."[9] On the political right, the sentiment was less ambiguous. In 1987, Franz Josef Strauss, the Bavarian minister-president, declared it was time that Germans get off their knees and "walk tall," and that the country should "emerge from the shadow of the Third Reich" and "become a normal nation again." At about the same time, the former West German president and head of state Karl Carstens urged a return to "the old patriotic tradition," regretting that young people of the day had been wrongly instructed, that they failed to understand that the majority of Germans were simply unaware of the "terrible deeds" of the Nazi regime. A leading Christian Democrat, Alfred Dregger, argued simply that Germans should stop being ashamed of their past. As the historian Richard Evans points out, these views figured prominently in Germany's leading newspaper, the *Frankfurter Allgemeine Zeitung*, testifying to the growing disavowal of the "burden" of German war guilt.[10]

One of the flashpoints in this turn of thinking about the German past occurred among historians. This was what is known as the *Historikerstreit*, or the "Historians' Controversy," a dispute of the late 1980s set off by some scholars who strove to recast the Nazi regime and its deeds as primarily a reaction to "Asiatic" Communist Russia. The leading figure in this controversy was Ernst Nolte, who expressed his desire to not only draw a "finish line" under the Nazi German past but also, less innocently, to place the Holocaust in a proper historical "perspective."[11] The historian Peter Gay accused him of humanizing Nazi crimes by "pointing, indignantly, at the crimes made by others."[12]

It was what was called the *Betroffenheitskultur* ("culture of contrition") to which Nolte and others wanted to put an end. In the 1990s, the desire to "draw a finish line" under the wartime and Nazi German past was expressed publicly more and more, especially by those political figures with increased visibility now that German politics, with Helmut Kohl's election, had taken a conservative turn. Konrad Adam, a New Right journalist, wrote in the pages of the *Frankfurter Allgemeine* that Germans, who too readily condemned themselves, suffered from a "guilt mythology."[13] Others wanted to turn the telescope of history around: it was Germans who were the victims of foreign assaults, today and in the past as well. One commentator claimed that the seven million Germans who had died during the war were more than enough "penance" for Nazi misdeeds.[14] Pronounced Klaus Rainer Röhl, "We've had enough of this stigmatizing, of this media dictatorship, of this political correctness."[15] Rainer Zitelmann, a historian, echoed Nolte: "A line has to be drawn against this permanent self-flagellation, which produces Neo-Nazis in the end. We must become normal." Like Nolte, the task of these right-wing journalists and historians was to rewrite history, to construct what one commentator called a "lachrymose history," where Germany was the victim. That Germans had gotten their history so wrong, argued Röhl, and were so full of shame and sorrow, was due in no small part to returning Jewish philosophers like Theodor Adorno, who had their own agenda to pursue.[16]

* * *

And where was Martin Walser in all this—this once-bold decrier of German guilt? He was quite visible; indeed, it might be said that he darkened Nolte's "finish line" with the color of resentment.

On October 11, 1998, he was awarded the Peace Prize of the German Book Trade, an award conferred in Saint Paul's Church in Frankfurt, a venue that resonated with historical memory: it was there that the first democratically elected Parliament met on German soil during the ill-fated 1848 revolution. Present in the audience as Walser spoke was a cross section of the German cultural elite and government class, including representatives of the Jewish community. Walser's remarks created a sensation.

Walser's speech begins ironically. Why not talk about "beautiful things," he muses, like trees, which he knows well through "casual contemplation?"[17] But then he reminds himself that the occasion calls for something different. He is a "Sunday speaker," thus a "critical sermon" is in order. Ruminations follow, some having to do with a general consideration of "atonement," first in a very general sense: "I couldn't live in a world in which everything had to be atoned for."[18] But then it becomes clear that he is thinking about the continuing burden of atonement imposed on Germans and Germany for the Holocaust. He bristles with outrage that unnamed "serious eminences," who call the public to task for not reacting sufficiently to right-wing terrorism, gleefully seem to see their reticence as affirming that "[Germans] dream only of genocide and gas chambers."[19] Walser is not only outraged; he suspects that those who utter such blanket condemnations wish the Germans ill:

> Inside of me an unprovable suspicion begins to take hold: those who come forward with such statements want to hurt us, because they think we deserve it. Probably they want to hurt themselves as well. But us too. All of us. With one restriction: All Germans. For this much is clear: in

no other language in the last quarter of the twentieth century can one speak in such a way about an entire people, an entire population, an entire society. You can only say that about Germans. Or at most, as far as I can see, about Austrians as well.[20]

Then, in case his auditors have missed the point, he utters the word "Auschwitz," adding, "I tremble with my audacity . . ." And what follows did strike many as audacious, at the very least: "Auschwitz is not suited to become a routine threat, a means of intimidation or moral bludgeon that can be employed on any occasion, or even a compulsory exercise. All that comes into being through ritualization has the quality of lip service. But what suspicion does one invite when one says that the Germans today are a perfectly normal people, a perfectly ordinary society?"[21]

As Walser was pronouncing these words, Germans in fact were engaged over a rather contentious discussion over the planning of a Holocaust memorial in Berlin. Except for fringe elements, very few objected to a monument per se. The criticisms were rather about its placement near the Bundestag—thus forcing an association between the Jewish genocide and German democracy—and its proposed, truly monumental scale. Even Gerhard Schroeder, Kohl's socialist successor as chancellor, was not entirely pleased with its proposed size and location. Günter Grass was among a group of leading German intellectuals and writers who argued that the monument should be abandoned. These demurrals formed part of the background to Walser's remarks, where he, too, weighed in on the controversy. He condemned "paving over the center of our new capital to create a nightmare the size of a football field." It amounted to "the monumentalization of our disgrace."[22]

Although Walser's speech certainly strikes one as polemical through and through, a real provocation, it is not devoid of subtlety or insight. In particular, he ruminates on the role of conscience in both the public and private spheres. "Everyone is alone with his or her conscience," he avers. And if we're truly honest with ourselves, we'll admit that even, or perhaps especially, in private our conscience is constantly prone to self-deception and illusion: "Is not each person a conveyor belt for an endless dialectic of truth and lies?"[23] This digression into a consideration of the nature of memory and conscience, however, is merely a pretext for his rejection of the very notion of a public guilt. Whereas in 1965 the crux of his intervention was precisely to call Germans to recognize their collective guilt, a generation later this very notion strikes him as psychologically impossible and morally dubious. Moreover, he expresses his resentment against "soldiers of public opinion"—clearly alluding to such well-known public intellectuals like Jürgen Habermas and Günter Grass—who "with moral pistol extended, force writers into service of opinion."[24] First we had Auschwitz as a "moral bludgeon," now he gives us a "moral pistol," largely in the same cause. Aggrieved and beleaguered by the forces of political correctness, Walser presents himself as a lone voice of integrity, standing up to those who would cynically impose upon Germans the burden of guilt long outdated. While he does allow for a sense of guilt, his insistence that it can only be personal, a matter of interior conscience, thereby lets it "seep into the drain of privacy."[25] Once drained of its guilt, he says, the German nation can "draw a line under its history" and return to normalcy.

As radically opposed as they are, there are interesting parallels in Walser's and Améry's positions, or at least a common concern. In a sense, they both at least implicitly evoke the notion of a public, though they hold opposing views on the possibility or desirability of guilt publicly shared. Améry invests his hope in the vitality of such a public; indeed, this is the only venue that renders his resentment purposeful, that is, more than a *cri de coeur* into the void. This public also functions as the shared vehicle for a living memory that connects the German people to a past that still implicates all of them, including the victims and their descendants. Walser, on the other hand, with his insistence on the interior, private nature of guilt and conscience, has a fundamentally negative view of the public as a sphere of manipulation, deception, and inconstancy. "For Améry, [the public] is an arena with the potential of liberation, while for Walser, it is a force that is falsifying and alienating," writes Aleida Assmann.[26] There is something of a paradox here, for Walser's resentment of the continuing burden of German guilt is in service of "normalizing" Germany as a nation among others, and in this sense it certainly has the nature of a public appeal. But that appeal connotes at the same time a retreat of conscience from the public sphere. Walser can have it both ways because his resentment requires no response; it is merely a negation. For Améry's expression of resentment to have any meaning, on the other hand, it must imply at least the hope of being heard and acknowledged.

RECONCILIATION, REPARATIONS, AND RESENTMENT

For both Améry and Walser, resentment served to process a difficult, contested past, a past that represented an existential reality both for themselves and for the larger collectivity each represented—the victims of the Holocaust for Améry, the German nation for Walser. How they interpreted the past did not really depend on what they knew or acknowledged about history but rather on the emotional valence of their perspectives. Here, resentment—differently expressed, differently felt—was the catalyst that moved them to cast the German past in very different terms.

For all their distinctiveness, the fact that they each looked to the past with such a steady gaze put them in sync with many of their contemporaries in the latter part of the twentieth century. It might be said that a fixation on the past replaced an interest in the future as the temporal orientation of wide swaths of the public, at least in the West. This goes beyond the emergence of a "historical consciousness" in the nineteenth century, or even the ideological use of the past in fashioning national identities—the "invention of tradition" offered by Hobsbawm and Ranger as an explanation for the fabrication of rituals, dress, and other cultural accoutrements to buttress nationalist self-assertions. This isn't simply a nostalgia for times gone by, a perennial disposition that never seems to die. Nor, even, does it lie with a growing disillusionment with assurances of an ever-brighter future by prophets of progress from the Enlightenment *philosophes* to modernizing policy makers, an assurance belied by the experience of what Isaiah Berlin called "the most terrible century in Western history."[27]

Rather, what has directed attention to the past in a way that surpassed all these backward-looking turns is the widespread need to "come to terms" with the past, to reckon with slavery, colonial exploitation, genocide, war crimes, and other human-made ravages which blighted the century at least since the Great War, and even before. It has become less and less possible to deny or dismiss past atrocities. Where once wars might have concluded with treaties, the exchange of prisoners, adjustments in borders, and perhaps the imposition of indemnities on the vanquished, the twentieth century introduced an expectation of reparations, war crimes tribunals, and other mechanisms designed to "make whole what has been smashed."[28] Where once victimized and excluded populations suffered, not in silence, but without really disturbing the conscience of the outside world, now there is a growing sensitivity to, or at least an awareness of, the woeful plight of oppressed and exploited people, even "people without a history."

It was World War II and the Holocaust that forced the matter as a general concern. Reckoning with Nazi crimes emerged as a moral task that went beyond the victors' opportunistic prerogative; it presaged a dawning realization that the past, especially the dreadful past, is—to paraphrase Faulkner—still very much with us. Or, as a jurist who served on the South African Human Rights Commission wrote—in what might be taken as a riposte to Martin Walser—"the past has no finish line: it is always there."[29] Hannah Arendt was perhaps the most forceful in voicing this view. "We can no longer afford to take that which was good in the past and simply call it our heritage, to discard the bad and simply think of it as a dead load which by itself time will bury in oblivion," she writes in *The Origins of Totalitarianism*. "The subterranean stream of Western history has finally come to the surface and usurped the dignity of our tradition. This is the reality in which we live. And this why all efforts to escape from the grimness of the present into nostalgia for a still intact past, or into the anticipated oblivion of the future, are vain."[30]

One result has been a rather remarkable movement across a wide range of countries and locales to confront past atrocities and attempt a reconciliation, in many cases, between perpetrators and victims. In 1983, Argentina established the National Commission on the Disappearance of Persons. The South African Truth and Reconciliation Commission (1994–2000) ranks as probably the best-known and most successful of these tribunals, and it set the pattern for others. Those in Canada and New Zealand dealt with the mistreatment of Indigenous people. In the US, on a smaller scale, there were similar efforts: in Greensboro, North Carolina, a Truth and Reconciliation Commission was established in 2004 to acknowledge the murder of protestors against the KKK in 1979, and in Portland, Maine, the Maine Wabanaki-State Child Welfare Truth and Reconciliation Commission was created in 2012 to confront the mistreatment of Native Americans over the generations. And there have been others, or others like them, in Poland, Rwanda, El Salvador, Argentina, Haiti, Chili, Ecuador, and elsewhere.[31] In sum, since the 1980s, over forty different truth commissions around the world have been in operation—most, it would seem, guided by the sentiment expressed by Archbishop Desmond Tutu, "Without reconciliation we have no future."[32] A sense of the imperative colors these projects—that it is not simply a matter of assuaging or placating the pain and resentment of the past but that without such efforts history will be stalled. Or conversely, put in positive, even utopian terms: that with recognition of the wounds of the past and the concomitant recognition of universal rights, we can envision a new era of political equality and social comity. Clearly, there is much at stake.

How, if at all, does resentment figure in these moves to effect reconciliation between victims and perpetrators? It seems obvious that any account of the emotional trajectory toward reconciliation, forgiveness, or some other attempt to assume responsibility for widespread harm would entail some consideration of anger and resentment, if only to acknowledge these sentiments as bearing witness to the continued suffering of the aggrieved. Resentment is a mode of memory, ensuring that the sins of the past not be lost in the oblivion of forgetfulness. Like Améry's protest against time's erosion of the memory of survivors' suffering, here too, resentment serves as a persistent, sometimes irritating reminder that victims' wounds are still open. In this sense, then, as with Améry, we see resentment framed in positive or at least purposeful terms, not as the demeaning emotion it is usually viewed to be. The philosopher Amélie Oksenberg Rorty helps us appreciate this salutary aspect of resentment. The emotion can be instructive and revealing. If we ignore or slight expressions of resentment, she argues, we are like a physician who dismisses the symptoms of a suffering patient. "Before we attempt to suppress resentment, we should ask: 'What is the likely alternative?'" The answer, she suggests, is silence—a silence that makes "the resentful doubt their right to grievance." Such silence can only serve the interests of the oppressors insofar as its leaves the resentful defenseless, thus "compounding injury upon injury."[33]

Rorty refers to Bishop Joseph Butler's "Fifteen Sermons," where the Anglican cleric expounds on the relationship between resentment and forgiveness. Butler, we should recall, was one of the first to confront squarely the emotion of resentment: he urged his followers to forgive their enemies and not wallow in resentment, which brings misery and bitterness to the aggrieved. Forgiveness comes only when resentment is overcome. But he did not expect them to forgive without reason. In some cases, they are justified in *not* letting go of their anger or resentment; these emotions, though hardly desirable, can serve as a brake on forgiveness too easily conferred. Forgiveness is a virtue but it must be earned, and until it is, the emotion of resentment, however regrettable, is valid. "If forgiveness involves letting go of warranted resentment, then the forgiver needs a good reason to let go," writes Martha Minow, expressing a very Butlerian point of view.[34]

Moral philosophers have explored the tenuous relationship between forgiveness and resentment in ways that offer an insight into the emotional and psychological dynamics of recent attempts at reconciliation between victims and perpetrators. Like Rorty, another moral philosopher, Jeffrie Murphy, takes Butler as a starting point for a more rounded consideration of the role of resentment in preparing the way for authentic forgiveness. And like the eighteenth-century bishop, he sees forgiveness, if not a Christian virtue, as still necessary for a healthy existence. "The person who cannot forgive is the person who cannot have friends or lovers."[35] Here he notes, as a kind of counterexample, the Nietzschean stance, which abhors any concern for forgiveness as unworthy of a truly autonomous, strong person, who would no more resent someone who harmed him than he would take personally the sting of a bug. Nietzsche cites the model of the French aristocrat and revolutionary Mirabeau who could not be bothered to remember slights and attacks—they were simply beneath his concern: "A man like this shakes from him, with one shrug, many worms which would have burrowed into another man."[36] But this only underscores the place of resentment in the moral makeup of the rest of us—that is, those who lead more relational lives than Nietzsche's lonely hero, where an emotional give-and-take will always entail the need for forgiveness.

Murphy's concern, however, again somewhat like Butler's, is that forgiveness might be too easily granted. It might promise the healing of damaged relationships, but if it comes at the cost of the aggrieved still feeling unacknowledged in their pain and suffering, then it does nothing of the sort. It is then something of a lie. Even worse, if forgiveness is granted too readily, it may be a sign that one lacks self-respect; it may indicate that the aggrieved, in not sufficiently resenting injuries done to them, thereby denigrate their own moral worth: "If it is proper (perhaps even mandatory) to feel *indignation* when I see a third party morally wronged, must it not be equally proper . . . to feel resentment when I experience a wrong done to myself?" Murphy turns the dynamic of forgiveness and resentment, in Butler's terms, around. "We may forgive only that which is initially proper to resent," he writes.[37] Rather than overcoming resentment, forgiveness presupposes resentment as a starting point in the process of forgiving. Only that which provokes resentment is worthy of forgiveness. Resentment greases the hinge of forgiveness.

Thus, the eminently virtuous pursuit of forgiveness—acknowledged by all as a desirable task in both private and public contexts—validates resentment as a legitimate emotion. Murphy sharpens his argument by considering ways other than forgiveness by which wrongdoing might be overcome or some sort of reconciliation effected between wrongdoer and victim. A wrong might be excused or justified by circumstances; or someone wronged might choose to exercise mercy in deciding to overlook or otherwise "forget" a harm done. None of these three cases, Murphy argues, are the same as forgiveness, and thus there is nothing to resent. For in each, the responsibility for wrongdoing is alleviated, or at least profoundly mitigated. Forgiveness is required only in situations where the wrongdoer is morally culpable, and moral culpability in turn justifies feelings of resentment on the part of the wronged, feelings for which one is hardly obliged to feel ashamed. On the contrary, such feelings are a sign of self-respect.

Intrinsic to the issues of culpability, and thus the kind of responsibility that can only be relieved by forgiveness, is the nature of what Murphy calls "moral injury." It is not simply that one is harmed or hurt in a sensible way; it is that such an injury also conveys a message beyond the pain. The message says, "I count and you do not" or "I do not care about you," or otherwise tells the injured that they really don't matter. And with this sort of messaging, the injured is not only warranted in feeling resentful; their self-respect obliges them to arrive at this conclusion. "Intentional wrongdoing degrades us," writes Murphy. Resentment, then, results as much from the message as from the injury—or rather, the real injury is to one's sense of self, one's self-esteem.

Like other moral philosophers, Murphy operates on a level of abstraction that exposes the bare bones of tricky emotional and psychological phenomena like forgiveness and resentment, helping us to clarify the meanings of terms that are muddied in common, unreflective usage. And it seems to me that he has accomplished quite a bit in sharpening our understanding of what forgiveness as an emotional process entails, and what the place of resentment is in this process. In the end, he offers a critique of traditional liberalism for neglecting the "moral quality" of citizens' lives—that is, what they think or feel—in favor of what they do. This restrictive interest, he suggests, forecloses any serious understanding of the role of the passions in politics or social life. It would certainly seem to be a blind spot in any political theory that hopes to address such urgent issues like reconciliation between victims and perpetrators, where passions are often raw and the memories of suffering very much alive. But in Murphy's analysis, little attempt is made to engage with real-life experiences, where the waters are usually quite muddied indeed.

Other scholars with similar interests, have done so, coupling a consideration of the psychological and emotional dynamics of forgiveness, including resentment, with more attention to actual attempts at reconciliation, retribution, reparation, and other modes of attaining the oft-vaunted goal of "closure." And here there seems to be an even greater appreciation of the difficulty of moving toward resolution in the form of forgiveness, without taking the measure of the angry emotions of the aggrieved. Much of the rhetoric that informs the reconciliation project raises forgiveness to such a high ethical level—as absolutely necessary in order to move beyond a state of permanent social conflict and enmity—so as to preclude considering the inevitable emotions parties will bring to the process. Archbishop Desmond Tutu seemed to convey this rather peremptory view of reconciliation when, commenting on the South African Truth and Reconciliation Commission, he wrote, "Social harmony is for us the *summum bonum*, the greatest good. Anything that subverts, that undermines, this sought-after good is to be avoided like the plague. Anger, resentment, lust for revenge, even success through aggressive competitiveness, are corrosive of this good."[38] But others involved in the same reconciliation process express more skeptical views, some criticizing the narrow remit of the commission, which limited itself to "gross human rights violations," the "tip of apartheid's iceberg," commented Pregs Govender, deputy chairperson of the South African Human Rights Commission. "Its banal brutalities continue to ravage South African Society."[39]

Held insufficient, however, is not simply the limited purview of some of these commissions; more profoundly, there is a concern that the feelings and grievances of victims are given short shrift. Reconciliation demands, it is argued, that their emotions not only be acknowledged but also dealt with in a deliberate, difficult, time-consuming process that does not immediately lead to resolution in forgiveness. Failing to do so risks rendering these commissions as tools of the powers that be, who have an interest in putting the past "behind them," and dealing with victims' grievances as expeditiously, and as politically cost-effectively, as possible. But beyond this, and more positively, the process can amount to the experience of collective "witnessing," an experience that encourages people to bring their resentments to the table. "'Telling' these stories of suffering," writes Pumla Gobodo-Madikizela, a psychologist at the University of Cape Town, "means that an audience listens and validates the collectively shared loss. The moment of witnessing then creates the possibility for reflective engagement with the past and its intergenerational impact."[40]

The fact is that "forgiveness," as a discourse (or a rhetoric), holds the potential of crowding out the "discourse" of resentment—or at least a political process informed by the former has a tendency to privilege the forgiveness over resentment. This is what concerned Glen Sean Coulthard in his investigation of the 1991 Canadian Royal Commission on Aboriginal Peoples. He takes a rather critical and skeptical view of these sort of commissions, or at least wants to call attention to the alacrity with which the process of reconciliation has, in some instances, moved toward the desired end of forgiveness, thus paying very little attention to recalcitrant voices. But this is not simply an ethical concern. In his investigation, Coulthard found that strong emotions are not merely expressive of deeply held grievances; they are also themselves constitutive of "political subjectivities." He writes, "under certain conditions, Indigenous peoples' individual and collective expressions of anger and resentment can help prompt the very forms of self-affirmative praxis that generate rehabilitative Indigenous subjectivities and decolonized forms of life."[41] And this he observed among the Indigenous peoples he studied. A wave of First Nation militancy and mobilization preceded the calling of the Royal Commission, without which not only would it have likely not been launched but, more crucially, the grievances of the Indigenous peoples themselves would not have had the requisite force and persuasive power. These grievances remain part of the process. The report itself and its recommendations, he observes, "represent a meeting place where anger and resentment might be expressed in ways that could set terms for a new form of political relating between Indigenous and settler communities in Canada."[42]

In an interesting variation on Coulthard's observations, David W. McIvor argues that one positive effect of resentment in these commissions can be seen in the fostering of "holding environments." Following the pioneering psychiatrist Donald Winnicott, he sees the creation of spaces, both real and virtual, in which people can share their pain and grievances, thus creating a sense of "common relatedness." Reconciliation might be the ultimate rationale here, but it is the process rather than the goal of reconciliation that matters, and it is a process that cannot be rushed. Something is created but it does not immediately lead to the soothing elixir of reconciliation. Even if that cherished goal is never achieved, something is accomplished in the way of developing political subjectivities based upon shared resentments. McIvor suggests the emergence of "counter-publics" for those pushed to the margins or excluded from the dominant public sphere. This falls far short of the ideal of reconciliation, but it is preferred to a coerced or mendacious forgiveness which, if not meaningless, certainly serves the interests of the powerful. "A resentment-fueled political psychology of friends and enemies is a means of survival in a brutal world that lacks an alternative mode of stabilization," writes McIvor.[43]

We see, then, that resentment, an often-demeaned emotion, has a place in the universally praised process of forgiveness and reconciliation. In this sense, it gains a positive valence that, historically, it has usually lacked. To dismiss or wish away resentment, or to shame victims into disavowing their resentful feelings, is to make a mockery of the project of reconciliation between victims and perpetrators.

FRANTZ FANON AND DECOLONIZING RESENTMENT

In an account that might make us think of Jean Améry's breakfast encounter with the German gentleman, Frantz Fanon recalls the declaration of a Frenchman in the crowded car of a train where he was sitting: "May the truly French values live on and the race will be safeguarded! At the present time we need a national union. No internal strife! A united front against the foreigners . . ." And then the man added, turning directly to Fanon, "whoever they may be."[44]

The episode is only superficially similar to Améry's conversation in 1958, which brought home the realization that Germans were quite prepared to put the Holocaust behind them and "move on." Fanon did not have to be reminded of the entrenched racism that was at the heart of the relationship between European colonizers and African and Caribbean colonized. His book *Black Skin, White Masks* (1952) is one of the first texts analyzing the psychological nature of racially inflected colonialism, reflecting his own training as a psychoanalyst. In his more famous book, *The Wretched of the Earth*, published eight years later, when decolonization was the order of the day, he presents a case for violence not only as a political weapon but as a means of psychological liberation—as an act of catharsis to release Black colonized people from the chains of otherness and inner bondage. *Black Skin, White Masks* exhibits a somewhat different approach and a different message. Employing the psychoanalysis of his training, with many references to literary texts in the *Négritude* tradition and marked throughout by his personal experiences, this is a work drenched in resentment.

In *Black Skin, White Masks*, Fanon seems to be working out a position that will bring him from the individual and personal to the collective and revolutionary. Much of it is a meditation on what he calls the dual ontology of being Black, which is to say, simply, the state of being Black compounded by being Black in the eyes of white people. This is a variation of the "double consciousness" associated with the writings of W. E. B. Du Bois. The self's encounter with the Other is the common lot of humankind; for Black people, however, it is complicated far beyond common understanding, even for most Blacks themselves. For under colonialism their fate is always to be confronted with "the white gaze." "An unusual weight descended upon us," Fanon writes. "The real world robbed us of our share. In the white world, the man of color encounters difficulties in elaborating his body schema. The image of one's body is solely negating. It's an image in the third person."[45] This "third person" was the Black man fashioned by the "Other"—that is, the white colonial master. With awareness of this dynamic comes a consciousness that transcends the particular self: "I was responsible not only for my body but also for my race and my ancestors."[46] An attentive reader of Sartre, with whom he established a close relationship toward the end of his life, Fanon refers to *Being and Nothingness*, especially with regard to the "gaze" of the Other, although for him it is "The white gaze, the only valid one [. . .] already dissecting me. I am *fixed*."[47]

The chapter titled "The Lived Experience of the Black Man" seethes not only with anger, which is palpable throughout the book, but also with a pronounced sense of resentment. Here, the Black man is depicted as object and victim, as defined, indeed, constructed by "the Other, the white man, who had woven [him] out of a thousand details, anecdotes, and stories."[48] In these pages, Fanon provides a series of increasingly irritating, and increasingly insulting, statements by whites, somewhat fancifully assembled, but clearly drawn from the stuff of personal experience. "Look! A Negro!" he hears, and merely notes, "It was a passing sting. I attempted a smile." But then the same remark is repeated, and then echoed, this time in alarm, "*Maman*, look, a Negro; I'm scared!" He reflects, "Now they were beginning to be scared of me. I wanted to kill myself laughing, but laughter had become out of the question."[49] Another mother, chagrined at the same comment uttered by her child attempts an apology: "Don't pay attention to him, monsieur, he doesn't realize you're just as civilized as we are." Finally, the remarks achieve a kind of grotesque finality. A little white boy, noticing that the man is now trembling with rage, runs to his mother's arms: "*Maman*, the Negro's going to eat me."[50]

"I am overdetermined from the outside," writes Fanon, reworking a Sartrean phrase from *Anti-Semite and Jew*, a book to which he often refers.[51] And this chapter positively overflows in overdetermination. Virtually every page testifies to the Black man's demeaned status and utter debasement: "Shame. Shame and self-contempt. Nausea. When they like me, they tell me my color has nothing to do with it. When they hate me, they add that it's not because of my color." He concludes: "Either way, I am a prisoner of the vicious circle."[52] History is certainly against him. But not only in the sense of the history of colonialism and centuries of oppression and exploitation. It means that Black people, Africans, have arrived too late to the stage of history. Too much has transpired in which they had no agency. He writes, "There will always be a world—a white world—between you and us: that impossibility on either side to obliterate the past once and for all."[53] With the construction of the white fantasy of Black people as exotic creatures, immersed in nature, at one with their bodies, charmingly childlike, naturally authentic, teaming with sexual energy and prowess—all variations on the theme of the "noble savage"—Fanon virtually throws up his hands at having totally lost any capacity to define himself beyond white people's configuration of him. "A feeling of inferiority? No, a feeling of not existing."[54] He ends the chapter with a plaintive declaration, at once expressing the fullness of his desires and his refusal to accede to this "amputation" of his being, but then ultimately acknowledging his awful predicament. "I feel my soul as vast as the world, truly a soul as deep as the deepest of rivers; my chest has the power to expand to infinity. I was made to give," he declares. "And they prescribe for me the humility of the cripple. When I opened my eyes yesterday I saw the sky in total revulsion. I tried to get up but the eviscerated silence surged toward me with paralyzed wings. Not responsible for my acts, at the crossroads between Nothingness and Infinity, I began to weep."[55]

One might describe the emotional disposition expressed here as "anger," but this doesn't do it justice. More than his angry words, it's the music that sings "resentment." Much of this chapter in particular is autobiographical in nature, even when Fanon does not employ the first person. It reveals a man trapped, paralyzed as well as confused, having been thrust into a world where his race, the color of his skin, and the legacy of colonial exploitation thwart any possibility of self-definition or agency.

Interestingly, however, Fanon does not end his book on this pessimistic, resentful note. It is a moment of awareness, a necessary stage of self-consciousness that needs to be worked through in order to arrive at a more promising place where liberation is possible. Colonized Blacks must realize the impasse of their predicament, and this realization breeds a sense of resentment which itself is productive in forcing upon them the urgency of finding a way out.

Like other thinkers in the existentialist tradition, he develops this line of thought by revisiting Hegel. In one of the very last essays in *Black Skin, White Masks*, he meditates on "The Black Man and Hegel," offering his take on the relations between "lord and bondsman" in *The Phenomenology of Spirit*. Fanon, though, is quick to warn us against confusing Hegel's lord and bondsman with the white master and the Black slave. Hegel's configuration entails the dialectical reciprocity of mutual recognition. The lord needs to be recognized as superior by his slave, yet "scorns the consciousness of the slave; what he wants from the slave is not recognition but work." As for the slave, he can achieve a sense of worth in work—an insight that Marx exploited to great effect. But Fanon notes that for the Black slave this option is foreclosed by the very nature of colonial servitude. Rather, "the black slave wants to be like his master,"[56] though not in the sense of merely emulating him in his whiteness but being acknowledged as a desiring subject. "I ask that I be taken into consideration on the basis of my desire," he writes. "I am not only here-now, locked in thinghood [*sic*]. I desire somewhere else and something else."[57]

Most importantly, Fanon's conception of the master-slave relationship implies greater resistance and negation than mutual recognition. And if the contradiction of this relationship is to be resolved—as it must for the philosopher of Black liberation—it will only be through action. Referring to another nineteenth-century German philosopher, a predecessor of

Hegel in the idealist tradition, he writes, "The I posits itself by opposing, said Fichte. Yes and no." But he abruptly moves into an explicitly Nietzschean vein. He proclaims an endorsement of the affirmative—to life, love, generosity—and then adds, "Man is also a *negation*." In either case, he is careful to reject merely the reactive, for, he writes, "there is always resentment in *reaction*," adding, in case the reader fails to get the reference, "Nietzsche had already said it in *The Will to Power*."[58]

This should prompt us to recall *On the Genealogy of Morality* (perhaps even more than *The Will to Power*): there Nietzsche has characterized the slaves' stance as fundamentally reactive, as opposed to the noblemen, whose superiority is manifest, among other ways, in their independence and self-realization. *Ressentiment*, an emotive state characterized by dependency and paralysis, seems to preclude action. Fanon, however, rejects this disposition, and thereby explicitly rejects resentment, as he concludes this passage: "To induce man to be actional [*sic*], by maintaining in his circularity the respect of the fundamental values that make the world human, that is the task of utmost urgency for he who, after careful reflection, prepares to act."[59]

This call to action is the main theme of *The Wretched of the Earth*, and thus the concluding pages of *Black Skin, White Masks* might be read as leading from a rather tortured meditation on the existential predicament of Blacks—psychologically and physically "fixed" by colonial oppression—to the potential release from that predicament in revolutionary violence. And it is a call that Fanon voices first while explicitly acknowledging the emotion of resentment but then boxing it in as merely a way station to concerted action. Writing about revolutionary tactics, he argues, "You can hold out for three days—maybe even for three months—on the strength of sheer resentment . . . ," but this "won't win a national war, you'll never overthrow the terrible enemy machine . . ." Likewise, "a legitimate desire for revenge," fueled by the "resentment" of racial hatred, "cannot sustain a war of liberation."[60] Resentment, while natural and inevitable, is not enough; it must, in good dialectical fashion, be overcome.

Fanon's conception of revolutionary action in *The Wretched of the Earth*, especially his emphasis on the cathartic and psychologically redemptive role of violence, obscures his indebtedness to existentialism. Sartre published the first chapter of *The Wretched of the Earth* in his journal, *Les temps modernes*, and at Fanon's invitation, he also contributed a preface to the book itself. There, interestingly, Sartre begins with a few paragraphs in the style of a parody, expressing feigned astonishment at the newly stirring "yellow and black voices," mouthing "our humanism but only to reproach us with our inhumanity." "We listened," he continues in the same self-mocking tone, "without displeasure to these polite statements of resentment, at first with proud amazement. What? They are able to talk by themselves?" The parody then ends, acknowledging that the phase of polite resentment was a thing of the past. "A new generation came on the scene, which changed the issue."[61]

He returns to the point, and along the way dismisses the factor of resentment, just as Fanon does in the text that follows. He instructs his European readers, all complicit one way or another in the colonial project, all therefore responsible for the violence turned against them, that "they would do well to read Fanon; for he shows clearly that this irrepressible violence is neither sound and fury, nor the resurrection of savage instincts, nor even the effect of resentment: it is man re-creating himself."[62] This strikes at the heart of Fanonian existentialism, which embraces revolutionary violence as the only means of breaking out of the demeaning, paralyzing bind of colonial oppression, which has reduced its subjects to the point where they embody, even more than Europeans or other "free" peoples, the existential dilemma of human existence. At its most basic, revolutionary violence is the ultimate act of existential freedom, not only liberating the colonial subject from the bondage of colonial oppression, but more profoundly liberating him from the bondage within. "At the level of individuals, violence is a cleansing force. It frees the native from his inferiority complex and from his despair and inaction; it makes him fearless and restores his self-respect."[63] Beyond their physical privations and humiliations, the natives are prone to the demeaning sentiments of envy, "dreams of possession," vis-à-vis their white overlords—sentiments that are surely akin to resentment. But this is not, for Fanon, the end of things. He understands revolutionary violence as an existential act that promises liberation, not only from colonial oppression, but from the psychological paralysis, the self-loathing, indeed, the "slave morality," that has for centuries "fixed" natives to their inauthentic state of subservience.

*　　*　　*

Despite Fanon's attempt to distant himself from a Nietzschean perspective, his "use" of resentment actually recalls an aspect of the German philosopher's formulation of *ressentiment* that is normally overlooked. In *On the Genealogy of Morality*, Nietzsche presents the slaves as essentially reactive. Their masters are not only strong, "beautiful," and truly noble; they are absolute masters of their fate, authors of their existence, who depend on nothing but their own strength and their own self-confident sense of themselves. Compared to these noble creatures, the slaves are hyperaware of their demeaned status, always conscious of their dependency on their superiors. In this sense, they seem to be incapable of truly acting on their own behalf. And, indeed, it is the priests who act in their stead. But this very action is in Nietzsche's own formulation profoundly *transformative*, yielding nothing less than the whole edifice of Judeo-Christian morality. His *ressentiment*, then, is not necessarily an obstacle, a cul-de-sac with only paralyzing bitterness at the end. It is revolutionary. To be sure, this sort of revolution hardly met with Nietzsche's approval, but it was nevertheless the kind of epoch-making "transvaluation" he otherwise espoused.

Resentment was not necessarily a dead end, not for Fanon nor for the other figures discussed in this chapter. It could signal a demand for justice and recognition, as it did for Améry and others whose grievances have not been adequately addressed, such as the victims convened at various truth and reconciliation commissions. It could also convey an insistence that "enough was enough"—that a statute of limitations had been reached, a line must be drawn across the page of history, and a nation must be allowed to break away from its compromising past. Such seemed to be the intent of Martin Walser in 1998 in his resentful declarations almost a decade after the reunification of Germany. Or, as with Fanon, resentment was a sort of way station toward the goal of purposeful action. It was itself purposeful insofar as it was necessary for colonized Blacks to experience their resentment as a symptom of the profound impasse of being colonized. Only then could they break free.

CHAPTER SEVEN

The Two Sixties and Resentment

One Without, the Other With

We need, I think, the Existentialist emphasis on our freedom . . .

HOWARD ZINN

Richard Nixon was a serial collector of resentments.

RICK PERLSTEIN, *Nixonland*[1]

What did Daniel Bell, the sociologist who edited *The Radical Right*, which which we discussed in chapter 5, think of "the sixties"? What did he and his colleagues—Lipset, Hofstadter, Parsons, and the rest—make of the student radicals and other activists whose protests and countercultural manifestations racked the country in this period? One might imagine that they readily applied the same diagnosis to the acolytes of, say, the Students for a Democratic Society (SDS) as they did to the McCarthyites and John Birchers. After all, like the discontented right-wingers, these students' grievances were hardly material or economic in nature; like them, their protests took place against the backdrop of a prosperous society and an age of growth. Interestingly, however, while deeply critical of these students—and sometimes personally the object of their rage—Bell, Hofstadter, Lipset, and the rest never found the Resentment Paradigm serviceable with regard to the New Left. This points to one line of argument in this chapter: many attributes might be ascribed to the countercultural and radical "sixties," but resentment is not one of them. This, in turn, underscores one of my larger claims in this book: that regarding a "decline" of resentment in the late decades of the twentieth century.

I mean this in two respects—indeed, along the two tracks which this study follows. On one, as I hope to have shown, what I call the "Resentment Paradigm" had a limited half-life, spanning the middle decades of the twentieth century. By the late '70s, most of the intellectual props that supported it had been kicked away, at least within scholarly circles. Its dependence on modernization theory, its psychologizing, its consensus liberalism, its elitism and contempt for populism, its fixation on status, and other aspects of the approach were abandoned or discredited by a new generation of historians and social scientists. To be sure, "resentment" continued to be deployed in various ways, but hardly as readily as it had in the heyday of the paradigm, or with the same rigor.

The other sense has to do with the nature of "the sixties"—at least the decade as celebrated (or bemoaned) in popular culture and collective memory as a time of protest, radicalism, the counterculture, and other forms of contestation.[2] Whatever passions animated activists in that passionate time, resentment did not rank high, or so I will argue.

But, one might ask, how could resentment *not* have been palpable in the emotional makeup of the enraged, aggrieved, embittered, or just downright angry rebels, activists, militants, revolutionaries, and the legions of other protestors, critics, and reformers whose activities ranged from occupying buildings to blowing them up, from civil disobedience to terrorism, from marching in the streets to rioting in them? How could they not have been resentful—of an interminable war in Southeast Asia, a seemingly intractable regime of racial injustice and inequality for African Americans, the legal and sexual oppression of women, a culture that vilified and persecuted any deviation from hegemonic heterosexuality, a government that drafted eighteen-year-old men into military service but did not grant them the right to vote, a mass society that prized conformism, efficiency, and the profit-motive over spirituality, erotic fulfillment, and the fellowship of authentic community, of a Dr. Strangelove world armed with enough nuclear firepower to render humanity extinct? For many, especially young people, students, Blacks, women, and homosexuals, there was certainly plenty to be resentful about.

But it seems to me that this is to concede too much to a casual, merely vernacular meaning of resentment as simply an emotion akin to a range of negative feelings such as bitterness, indignation, irritation, rancor, or other variations of discontent. In keeping with the overall argument of this book, however, I intend to think of "resentment" more precisely: as a collective emotion often exploited for very potent political purposes that hinges on a sense of being dispossessed, left behind, or demoted; a feeling based on the conviction that the just and proper order of things has been profoundly disturbed; and a belief that those opposing you, the causes of your misery or the instruments of your dispossession, are not only wrong but morally culpable, even to the extent of comprising a conspiracy of evil forces arrayed against you and all other good and righteous people. In this sense of the concept, I will argue that the square peg of resentment did not fit into the round hole of the sixties.

But this is to consider only one aspect of that decade. There was another sixties, marked not by left-wing, countercultural, and liberation movements but rather by the "silent majority" and the rebirth of modern conservativism, both political and cultural, and a "backlash" against progressive movements that has unquestionably played as great a role in the subsequent history of the US (and elsewhere in the West). These two sixties were not just very different, indeed contrary, polar opposite phenomena; they were also related, one giving rise to the other. In short, the radical and countercultural sixties provoked a reaction on the part of "Middle America," though this was hardly a purely spontaneous reaction but very much cultivated and constructed by politicians and complicit media figures. And here, in *this* sixties, we see the emergence of a politics of resentment.

As for the first sixties, while I will provide evidence to support my analysis, readers should be aware that my assessment is somewhat subjective, based, in part, on a participant observer, an informant of sorts. That would be me. In full disclosure, then, I would simply say that my view of the sixties is derived in some measure from my own (very modest) role as an activist in student and civil rights protests and as a close-up observer of groups like the Black Panthers. As I recall these passionate times, they certainly evoke a whirlwind of feelings. But they were emotions that in almost every respect were underwritten by a strong measure of hopefulness, utopian aspirations, and often wildly radical expectations. We were convinced that history was on our side—hardly a sentiment of those who feel left behind, thwarted, or . . . resentful. This is one reason resentment does not fit with the collective mentality that characterized the radical and countercultural sixties: the prevailing sense of being in step with a new and hopeful course of history. Another, perhaps more complicated reason lies with a sort of ethos that took hold among many who identified with the radicalism of the times, an ethos which aspired to "authenticity" as a defining feature of one's relationship to both the world and oneself.

THE SIXTIES AND THE POLITICS OF AUTHENTICITY

In the middle decades of the twentieth century, no philosophy ranked higher in popular awareness than existentialism. Its popularity was one of the period's distinguishing features, for it is hard to think of a philosophy that so easily translated into other disciplines, other genres of expression, or other cultural practices. Existentialism seeped into popular culture, becoming the object of much media attention, even finding its way into the lyrics of a Broadway musical.³ The vocabulary of existentialism entered the vernacular of the times; "existential" became a buzzword mouthed by those who hadn't even heard of Sartre, Simone de Beauvoir, or Albert Camus, let alone read their works. Less a metaphysics, it was more like an ethos, or perhaps even a mood. In a previous chapter, I noted the status of psychoanalysis and Freudianism in the mindset of Americans of a certain level of cultivation, cosmopolitanism or at least self-regard. Existentialism had a similar purchase on their outlooks, with the works of Freud and Sartre and their followers standing side by side on the shelves of many college students and their parents alike. And for many writers, artists, and thinkers, these were somewhat casually combined sources of inspiration, underpinning a general but intellectually pretentious sense of "modernism" that can be seen as defining much of the twentieth century, at least culturally. Think of the abstract expressionists, who, even if they were entirely unschooled in either Freudianism or existentialism, seemed to act out their implications in the art they produced. Willem de Kooning spoke for himself and his fellow New York artists when he declared, "We weren't influenced directly by Existentialism, but it was in the air, and we felt it without knowing too much about it. We were in touch with the mood."⁴

Of all the concepts spawned or touted by the existentialists—and of all those that were lodged in the lingo of the times—"authenticity" is surely among the most common. The command, "Be real!" became something of a mantra of the period. (Indeed, an n-gram shows a precipitous upsurge of "Be yourself," starting in the early sixties.). The intellectual pedigree of "authenticity" is long, extending well before the existentialists, with roots in Rousseau's protest against the citified, alienating conventions of his times, the Romantics' vaunting of the lonely, misunderstood, or heroic individual, Kierkegaard's search for an authentic faith, Nietzsche's celebration of the man apart from the herd, above even established notions of good and evil, and others who, in Lionel Trilling's well-known argument about the shift in moral signifiers in the twentieth century, managed a transformation from "sincerity" to "authenticity."⁵ Perhaps Sartre contributed most in the middle decades of the century to the central place of "authenticity" to the existentialist ethos. In his philosophical works and even more in his novels, he anatomizes the dynamics—or rather the predicament—of being "free," which, given his rejection of any universal, a priori, or transcendental values, means the sometimes terrifying prospect of choosing to act fully for oneself. Even a less philosophically sophisticated understanding of the concept of authenticity appealed to those who rejected being defined "from without," by the "Other," especially when that other was an "Establishment" which imposed cookie-cutter, conformist identities on the young. Holden Caulfield, the sixteen-year-old antihero in J. D. Salinger's *The Catcher in the Rye* (1951), surely one of the most-read novels of the postwar era, repeatedly expresses his disgust at the "phonies" at his prep school, just one indication of how the imperative of being authentic resonated with the temper of the times.

This imperative, to be sure, is rarely a simple matter of choice, as if one could merely decide one day to be oneself or act in accordance with one's "true" values, whatever one eventually decided these were. Easier said than done. On a common sense level it just doesn't make sense: What is the logic of the imperative to "be" what one already is? But in the postwar era, this notion crept into the therapeutic tool kit of existential psychologists who, put off by Freud's dour pronouncements, offered human potentiality, self-realization and other kindred concepts as the pathway to healthy psychological development. While they acknowledged the daunting reality of a modern "mass society," they nevertheless held out an optimistic prognosis that a measure of happiness or at least personal gratification was possible—that is, as long as one struggled against the comforts of conformism, the lure of materialism, or the other soul-crushing blandishments of middle-class society.

But for radicals of the sixties, the search for authenticity was not an individualistic affair, despite its appeal to strong notions of selfhood and personal identity. Marshall Berman has brilliantly explained the convergence between individualism and the social order that was their special achievement. Since the mid-nineteenth century, these were opposed; one was identified with bourgeois society and liberalism; the other associated with radicalism. "Political thought was frozen into this dualism until the cultural explosion of the 1960s redefined the terms," writes Berman. It was the young New Left critics who accused bourgeois liberalism of fostering a fraudulent version of individualism, as it forced people into competitive and aggressive relationships that only thwarted a realization of true selfhood. Their critique yielded a new prospect of individualism that could only be realized in a social order, a radically reformed society, in which an individual's "feelings, needs, ideas, energies" could be expressed. "The moral basis of this political critique was the ideal of authenticity."[6]

It would seem, then, that insofar as being authentic, as a psychological or emotional state, puts a premium on acting and thinking for oneself, it precludes victimhood. For is this not the ultimate concession of being defined from without, of having your identity determined by another or circumstances beyond your control? A sense of victimization is the breeding ground of resentment. Can we conclude that the existentialist ethos is resistant to resentment? Three figures in the countercultural, or radical, "sixties" will allow us to explore this question.

Authenticity and Student Radicalism

Tom Hayden (1939–2016) was twenty-three years old in June 1962 when, by all accounts, he took charge of drafting the Port Huron Statement, the founding document of the Students for a Democratic Society (and the birth certificate of the New Left), a document the historian Michael Kazin has called "the most ambitious, the most specific, the most eloquent manifesto in the history of the American Left."[7] He brought to the writing of this document his experience as one of the "Freedom Riders" in the South and an intellectual formation that especially inclined toward the existentialists. Todd Gitlin, a fellow SDSer, called him a "fervent existentialist." And among the existential philosophers, Albert Camus ranked highest among his influences.[8] But he was hardly alone in his partiality for the Algerian-born French philosopher, the author of such classics as *The Stranger*, *The Plague*, and *The Rebel*, books that were common on the reading lists of college students in the sixties. In his autobiography, *Reunion*, Hayden claims that he shared his predilection for Camus with many of the founders of both the SDS and the SNCC (Student Nonviolent Coordinating Committee). Speaking for all of them, he said they drew upon *The Plague* as an analogy for what they observed in contemporary America, where most people went on with their normal lives, oblivious of, or rather, not caring to acknowledge, the problems and threats that menaced their very existence. Like Rieux, the physician-hero of the novel, who commits himself to treating plague victims in the face of his neighbors' denial of the epidemic, "it was [their] task to awaken the nation to these evils and face them [themselves] through daily personal acts like registering voters in the South."[9] In reading Camus, Hayden writes, he found the philosophy he was searching for: "All I maintain [says Rieux in *The Plague*] is that on this earth there are pestilences and there are victims, and it's up to us, so far as possible, not to join forces with the pestilences."[10] In a speech he gave in Ann Arbor in 1962, he referred to *The Stranger*—surely a book that many of the students had read—and its main character, Meursault, "the man lacking relatedness to anything at all," and held him up as a warning to a "drifting generation whose public lives were underdeveloped" and whose "privately constructed lives" were filled with meaningless routine.[11]

In Hayden's account, the discussions leading up to the drafting of the Port Huron Statement pursued several broad political paths, but "after much introspection and debate," they decided on a way "closer to [their] understanding of Camus." This path combined the personal and the political; it was a commitment to struggle for a better world "*as the only way to live*." Acknowledging Camus's existential dictum that everyone had a choice to be stronger than the conditions of the world as they found them, they vowed to live and act "according to moral values and to create institutions that would advance the process."[12] A Camusian sense of realism and morality informs the Port Huron Statement. Its final sentence fully acknowledges the idealistic, even utopian cast of the program: "If we appear to seek the unattainable, as it has been said, then let it be known that we do so to avoid the unimaginable."[13] As this last proviso starkly connotes, their idealism was qualified by a foreboding sense of menace and deep discontent. The Port Huron Statement raises the specter of nuclear annihilation (a threat that would become all too real in just a couple of months with the Cuban missile crisis in October of 1962), but it is no less alert to other ills and problems: persistent racism, poverty amid plenty, the exhaustion of ideas, the stalemate of the political system, widespread alienation, the degradation and meaninglessness of work, the reduction of human value to the value of things—all seemingly hidden by a blanket of complacency barely disguising an omnipresent despair. Sounding like the students of existentialism that they were, they write, "Loneliness, estrangement, isolation describe the vast distance between man and man today."[14]

Indeed, virtually every step of the way there are evocations of such values as dignity, meaning, and affective relationships. "We regard *men* as infinitely precious and possessed of unfilled capacities for reason, freedom and love," they write. (Throughout, in this pre-feminist era, the male pronoun is meant to denote both men and women.) They "oppose depersonalization that reduces human beings to the status of things."[15] In a passage that could have been lifted from the writings of contemporary existential psychologists like Rollo May, Abraham Maslow, or Bruno Bettelheim, they sound the themes of human potential and authenticity not merely for the individual but as the remit of the social order: "Men have unrealized potential for self-cultivation, self-direction, self-understanding and creativity. It is this potential that we regard as crucial and to which we appeal . . ." Rather than "submission to authority, the goal of man and society should be human independence . . . with finding meaning in life as personally authentic . . ."[16]

Historians have observed that the Port Huron Statement goes in two somewhat different directions. In one, it is primarily a call for participatory democracy, for a renewal of the venerable American tradition of radical republicanism. The other takes us into existentialist territory, with an emphasis on finding meaning in an alienating and conformist society. Both are valid ways of reading the document. It is this latter register of concerns, however, that lifts the statement above previous expressions of radical reform, for its authors refused to accept a division between private, individual concerns and those of a public or political nature. This would, of course, become a signature element of sixties radicalism, an oft-repeated slogan mouthed by student radicals, especially second-wave feminists. (An essay by Carol Hanisch, a member of the collective New York Radical Women, "The Personal is Political," is credited with popularizing the phrase.) As Todd Gitlin, an early leader of SDS, has observed, "Only in America could an organization of the Left have sounded such singing praise of 'human independence.'"[17] But this sense of independence, as the document insists, did not point in the direction of pure individualism. The authentic life—a life lived on one's own terms—could only be realized in a society commensurate with life-affirming moral values.[18]

Second-Wave Feminism: From Anger to Authenticity

In 1970, the radical feminist Robin Morgan wrote in a special all-women issue of the underground newspaper *Rat* an article titled, "Goodbye to All That," "It is the job of revolutionary feminists to build an ever stronger independent Women's Liberation Movement, so that sisters [in the] captivity [of the Left] will have somewhere to turn, to use their power and rage and beauty and coolness in their own behalf for once, on their own terms, on their own issues, in their own style—whatever it may be."[19] The result was the flourishing of female-only "consciousness-raising" groups, "bitch sessions," women's caucuses, and other separatist moves, based on the principle that any real transformation of society had to entail a radical transformation of gender relationships as well.[20]

While not a partisan of the New Left, Betty Friedan also believed that women could not expect to find liberation within a general, even radical movement of expanding rights. "It is a cliché of our own time that women spent half a century fighting for 'rights,' and the next half wondering whether they wanted them after all," she wrote in her pathbreaking best seller, *The Feminine Mystique* (1963) (83).[21] Friedan's book, which sold a million copies in one year, is rightly considered a foundational text for second-wave feminism, a book that belongs on the shelf next to Simone de Beauvoir's *The Second Sex* (1949). "It pulled the trigger on history," pronounced the futurist Alvin Toffler.[22] (In 2005 a conservative publication placed it seventh among the "ten most harmful books of the nineteenth and twentieth centuries."[23]) Friedan went on to occupy the front ranks of the women's liberation movement as a cofounder of the National Organization for Women in 1966 and its first president.

The *Feminine Mystique* argues that women in postwar America had gone backward, that unlike their mothers and grandmothers during the 1930s and 1940s, large numbers of whom found fulfillment in work and careers outside the home, they had succumbed to the "feminine mystique" which celebrated home, family, motherhood—deference to a husband and children in the lulling confines of suburbia—as the alpha and omega of contemporary womanhood. In no uncertain terms, Friedan delivers a sustained denunciation of the life choices of millions of her contemporaries, the overwhelming majority of whom had moved, whether freely or not—and in most cases fairly directly—from their parents' care to caring for husbands and children. The average age of marriage, she notes, had moved decisively lower, compared to that of the interwar years—just one data point in support of her claims.

Here, interestingly, she yokes her analysis to the well-known views of Erich Fromm and others who (as shown in chapter 5) explained the appeal of totalitarian movements as providing comforting refuges to people who found it difficult to manage their own lives in a modernizing world characterized by the collapse of traditional structures and values and, more generally, by the "burden" of freedom. Friedan, indeed, seems to place the blame for women's reactionary choices on women themselves. But hers is an equal opportunity indictment, with men equally guilty of fleeing the realities of contemporary life by crawling into the middle-class cocoons that postwar America offered them. There is more than a whiff in all this of Friedan's radical past, her profound animus for bourgeois culture as well the clichéd assessment of the "fifties" as a time of herd-like conformity and utter complacency. She denounces the "terrible implications" (66) of the constraints on contemporary women, the "stunting or evasion of growth" (77), and the "emptiness, idleness, boredom, alcoholism, drug addiction, disintegration into fat, disease and despair after 40" (175) that often was the lot of suburban housewives, whom she calls "walking corpses" (305). In the "sanctuary" of their suburbs, she writes, they are "trapped within the narrow walls of their homes, dependent, passive, childlike" (307). There, in her gilded cage, the housewife and mother "doesn't feel like she really exists" (308). The feminine mystique, she concludes, "is taking a far greater toll on the physical and mental health of our country than any known disease" (364).

If Friedan had stopped there, with this devastating, pitiable portrait of the American housewife, one would have to conclude that her prognosis for her female contemporaries was a bleak one indeed. "So the aggressive energy she should be using in the world becomes instead a terrible anger that she dare not turn against her husband," she continues, "is ashamed of turning against her children, and finally turns against herself, until she feels as if she does not exist" (308). In this passage, she evokes precisely the thwarted anger, often inwardly turned, that marks the person of resentment. But *The Feminine Mystique* has more to offer these women than a group portrait of desperate housewives. Like many intellectuals of her generation, Friedan was much taken with existentialism, and with existential psychology in particular. While the considerable scholarship that went into this book is worn lightly, as befitting a publication aimed for a mass readership, many of the notes that accompany the text acknowledge the writings of such figures as Abraham Maslow, Rollo May, and other psychologists who were open to the influences of continental philosophy. In one chapter, she dwells especially on the work of Maslow, famous for his humanistic critique of Freud and for espousing the notion of "self-actualization" as a fundamental drive of successful, healthy individuals. According to Maslow, a hierarchy of needs guided the self-actualizing person, from morality and creativity at the top to the basic human needs of security, physical sustenance, and sex at the bottom. In Friedan's view, contemporary American women were stuck with settling on the very least of these. The task, then, was to encourage them to strive for the fulfillment of a higher level of needs, those that could only be realized through creative work *outside the home*. She is rather categorical on that score: "The picture of the happy housewife doing creative work at home—painting, sculpting, writing—is one of the semi-delusions of the feminine mystique" (334).

On one level, then, her reading of Maslow and others allows her to seize upon the notion of "authenticity" to project the ideal of a personality restructuring for women as the only meaningful mode of liberation. Her insistence, or rather hope, that women could, in a sense, "have it all"— rewarding, independent lives along with the emotional rewards of marriage and motherhood—put her at odds with (mostly) younger feminists, who inclined more toward separating entirely from men, experimenting with nonheterosexual relationships, and in general denouncing the "patriarchy" in all its forms—indeed, as the very core of the modern system of oppression of all peoples. Friedan was sensitive to the challenge of these radicals, but she showed them no sympathy. In one of the last passages in *The Feminine Mystique*, she addresses directly her militant sisters. For once citing Simone de Beauvoir (whose *The Second Sex* is barely acknowledged in the book), she brands them with the aspersion of resentment: they are "acting out sexually their rebellion and resentment at being 'underneath' in society generally, being dependent on men for their personal definition." Their anger, she argues, is self-defeating, for "their resentment [is] being manipulated into an orgy of sex hatred that would vitiate the power they now had to change the conditions they resented" (389). It cannot be merely accidental that the one time in *The Feminine Mystique* Friedan brings up the concept of resentment, it is as a term of reproach. For, like other apostles of radicalism in the sixties, she realized that "liberation" could only be accomplished once resentment was overcome.

Robert Moses: A Socratic Existentialist[24]

Robert Moses (1935–2021) was a stalwart of the Civil Rights Movement, among the most prominent young African Americans who filled its ranks in the early years of the decade. After earning a BA from Hamilton College in 1956 and a master's degree in philosophy at Harvard the year after, in 1960 he began working in the Atlanta office of the Southern Christian Leadership Conference. Soon he was on the front lines of the effort to register African Americans in the South to vote. Later he joined the Student Nonviolent Coordinating Committee, suffering beatings and imprisonment on several occasions. (He served as a mentor to the more famous Black activist Stokely Carmichael, who was to become the public face of the SNCC.) By all accounts he was a remarkable leader—quietly charismatic, fearless yet humble—whose profound belief in the justice of the cause was evident to all who encountered him. Commented one activist, "There was something about him, the manner in which he carried himself, that seemed to draw all of us to him. He had been where we were going. And more important, he had emerged as the kind of person we wanted to be."[25] Like Hayden, he was also a devoted reader of Camus, and his own testimony indicates that he derived solace and inspiration from reading the works of the French writer, especially *The Rebel* and *The Plague*, books that always accompanied him down the perilous backroads, and in the jailhouses, of Mississippi.

As we have seen (in chapter 2) Camus offered a somewhat quixotic, but to many a very appealing, brief for action, even rebellion, in a world where meaning and ultimate values are, at best, uncertain. While not a nihilist, Camus was a philosopher who faced squarely the notion of the absurd. The absurdity of the human predicament does not, he insisted, deny the essential meaningfulness of acting, but, as illustrated most profoundly in his "Myth of Sisyphus," it's not the goal or end which confers meaning on action but the act itself. As elaborated in *The Rebel*, rebellion itself strikes at the heart of an existential commitment to life—"I rebel—therefore we exist." But this is not, he repeatedly warns, to follow the path of revolutions and revolutionary ideologues of the twentieth century, whose espousal of absolutes only leads, he writes, to the role of either an oppressor or a heretic.[26]

Time and again in the course of his struggles, Moses finds Camus a relevant reference point. Generally, it seems, he saw the French philosopher as a kindred spirit for whom acting morally in an absurd world was paramount. And this meant the moral imperative of acknowledging and confronting a lurking threat, especially when it would be easier and less disruptive simply to turn away from it, as so many have done in the course of history. On one occasion, he cited Camus during a tense meeting of activists, where the issue before them was rising racial tensions within their ranks. "There is an analogy to *The Plague* by Camus," he said. "The country isn't willing yet to admit it has the plague, but it pervades the whole society. Everyone must come to grips with this, because it affects us all. We must discuss it openly and honestly. . . . If we ignore it, it's going to blow up in our faces."[27]

But it was the prospect of violence, the realization that activists' actions put innocent people at risk or could tempt some of them to breach their vow of nonviolence, where Camus seemed most pertinent. Moses reflected on the importance of Camus in his moral and intellectual development in an interview conducted by the notable Southern writer Robert Penn Warren. It was 1964, in Jackson, Mississippi, at the local office of the SNCC.[28] In the course of their conversation, Warren asks Moses how he copes in the face of constant intimidation and all-too-real threats of violence: "You take it day by day?" he surmises. Moses answers that it has taken him quite a while to come to terms with the moral challenges of a difficult cause, but that he has been helped by the writings of Camus, which he first read in college: "The main essence of what he says is what I feel real close to—closest to." Moses continues, saying that it comes down to maintaining "certain humanitarian values" even in the course of a struggle where these are continually challenged, "and that's what . . . more than anything else conquers the bitterness, let's say." Then he adds, almost as an afterthought, "But there's something more."

"What's that?" prompts Warren. In response, Moses begins a riff on Camus's *The Rebel*, citing the example of the Russian "terrorists" of 1905 and their reputed regard for human life even as they were engaged in life-threatening violence.[29] Camus's account impressed him: these young Russians lived by the rule that if they took a life they offered one of their own in exchange. But what Moses wants to raise is the question of whether one can cease being a victim without becoming an "executioner." "For when people rise up and change their status," he says, "usually somewhere along the line they become executioners and they get involved in subjugating, you know, other people." Stokely Carmichael remembers him saying something similar on several occasions: "If you exploit others, you are an exploiter. If you oppress, you are an oppressor. If you sell out principles, you are a prostitute."[30] Moses, like Camus, is vexed by the implications of wielding power and the likelihood, then, of inflicting harm. This question is never really resolved. But the fact that it hangs over Moses, as it does for Camus, that it continued to bother both the civil rights activist and the existential philosopher, is the essential lesson. More than perhaps any of the leading existentialists, Camus managed to endow his philosophy with a humanist cast, always raising concerns about the moral integrity of the individual trying to act meaningfully in an absurd world. Above all, he put a premium on commitment. Robert Moses, Camus's disciple in the movement in the struggle for Black freedom in the US, read him as an inspiration to keep the faith, despite his "existentialist" qualms, and in the process, to "try to eke out some corner of love or some glimpse of happiness within."[31]

Moses's ruminations might be read as another variation on the master-slave dynamic, for in worrying about exchanging the status of "victim" for "executioner," he seems to be searching for a way out of this sort of asymmetrical, essentially unjust relationship, just as Fanon, more decisively, strove to negate it through revolutionary violence (see chapter 6). Despite their differences, in both cases a rejection of victimhood is paramount. To evoke the terms of Fanonian existentialism, this denial was the same as a rejection of the Black psychologist's reworking of Sartre's "inauthenticity"—the self as "overdetermined from without,"[32] which is to say, by others. Victimhood, as produced by the victimizer, is the ultimate inauthentic state. And a profound sense of being victimized is, as we have seen, a fundamental feature of resentment.

The Emotional Tenor of Black Militancy

It must be acknowledged that Robert Moses was hardly representative of the Civil Rights Movement, especially as it evolved in the course of the sixties, when it was increasingly pulled in the direction of Black nationalism and Third World anti-colonialism. His reflective, nuanced disposition gave way to a more militant, even dogmatic positioning, more in keeping with a rising revolutionary fervor that was global in nature, compared to which aspirations for integration and mere "rights" seemed paltry indeed. Even here, however, in a radical political culture symbolized by the raised, clenched fist, there is evidence that resentment didn't quite have the purchase one might have expected. The case of Huey Newton (1942–89), cofounder and chairman of the Black Panther Party, illustrates the point.

Although he attended community college in Oakland, California, in 1959, Newton admitted to being functionally illiterate well into his late teens. But in his twenties, he quickly made up for the many years when books were beyond him, becoming an avid reader of a wide swath of the Western literary and philosophical canon. Among the texts that most impressed him—and which he applied to his developing conception of Black Power—were the works of Friedrich Nietzsche.

He offers his reflections on the German philosopher in a few pages in his autobiography *Revolutionary Suicide* (1973).[33] Newton appropriates Nietzschean concepts, bending them to suit his own purposes—creatively, but without much concern for the niceties of textual analysis. While the references to specific texts are not clear, he mentions learning from *The Will to Power* that "man attempts to define phenomena in such a way that they reflect the values of his own class or group . . . if it is to his advantage, something is called good, and if it is not beneficial it is defined as evil."[34] He connects this insight to the recent reevaluation among African Americans of their own "blackness" and the very meaning of "black" in contemporary discourse. From time immemorial these were names associated with demeaning and inferior characteristics, but now, Newton writes, "the rising level of consciousness within our Black communities has led us to redefine ourselves"; today they "are sources of pride." He concludes, "This is an example of Nietzsche's theory that beyond good and evil is the will to power." Power, in other words, wasn't instrumental merely in a political sense but also as a means of reshaping a collective self-image.

He also reveals a familiarity with *Genealogy of Morality* and the notion of a "slave morality." Given the African American experience, how could he have not? But he essentially turns Nietzsche's argument on its head, seeing the slaves' adoption of Christian morality of the meek not as a source of weakness but as a clever strategy used against the Romans. "They understood how to make the philosophy of a weak group work for them," he writes.[35] The slaves used this philosophy to weaken the powerful by supplanting the masters' moral code with their own. Nietzsche, of course, viewed this same dynamic as the end of true nobility and the subversion of life-affirming values, a tragic account of epoch-making decline, and he characterized the slaves' *ressentiment* as creating an impasse, thwarting the realization of human potential. Newton, however, makes this into something entirely different—not a dead end but an opportunity to win over and undermine the dominant culture. "We have seen the same principle work on college campuses," he writes. "Many white youths now identify with Blacks; the identification is manifested in clothes, rhetoric, and life styles."[36]

Newton thus associates the transformation of values with power. It is a rather postmodern insight: words, and the values they exemplify, have no intrinsic meanings; they can mean what we say they mean. A feature of the "will to power," then, is the ability to redefine the world in your own terms, to impose your meaning on it. This process, the same dynamic that enabled the slaves to reconfigure Roman morality, lies behind the Panthers' rebranding of the police as "pigs"; it was the same logic that transformed the meaning of "Black" from something shameful to a source of African American pride. And it was also, in Newton's account, how he and his associates arrived at the slogan "All power to the people." While it had a programmatic meaning in terms of the Panthers' policy of armed self-defense and their aspiration for Blacks to control their own communities, Newton ultimately endowed it with a "metaphysical sense" based "on the idea of man as God." This is Huey Newton the revolutionary humanist: "I have no other God but man, and I firmly believe that man is the highest or chief good."[37] And this is Newton the Nietzschean, vaunting a noble, godlike image of "man," only embodied collectively in a reborn Black community. His reading of Nietzsche turned the German philosopher into an advocate of social action spearheaded by an exalted vanguard that interpreted the "will to power" according to its own lights. Newton thus managed to finesse the emotionally demeaning impasse of *ressentiment*, seizing upon the notion of a slave morality as a means of recasting an African American people of former slaves in revolutionary terms.

Martin/Malcolm

More than any other leader in the Civil Rights Movement, Martin Luther King Jr. embodied the spirit that Robert Moses also strove to convey in his conversation with Robert Penn Warren: the desire to act meaningfully and humanely while engaged in an often contentious, sometimes violent struggle. King espoused what the philosopher Martha Nussbaum calls "revolutionary non-anger." For he was committed to harnessing the deep anger and resentment of his followers and channeling these fraught emotions into productive action. This meant acknowledging and expressing people's justifiable anger, but ultimately urging them to overcome it in service to the cause. In "Letter from a Birmingham Jail," King writes, "I have not said to my people 'Get rid of your discontent.' Rather, I have tried to say that this normal and healthy discontent can be channeled into the creative outlet of non-violent direct action."[38] He notes the "strike-back" mentality as an impulse that must be avoided, and not simply for tactical reasons. Indeed, his conception of nonviolence characterizes it as a purifying set of practices, instilling discipline in protestors but also instructing them to separate the "deed from the doer, criticizing and repudiating the bad deed, but not imputing unalterable evil to people."[39] King urged his followers to "keep their eyes on the prize," to strive not for retribution but justice, to hold out for the redemptive future he prophesied in his celebrated "I Have a Dream" speech, which, perhaps more than any other public expression of the day, did more to supplant anger with hope as the emotional temperament of the civil rights movement. To be sure, King's stirring rhetoric, which has been rightly enshrined as one of the greatest oratorical moments in American history, cannot be taken as defining the whole movement for African American rights; it certainly misrepresents the revolutionary and more radical tendencies embodied in the Black Panthers or Malcolm X, who criticized King for his supposed moderation and accommodating spirit. It was, rather, aspirational in purpose, a rhetorical expression of an ideal.

In her book, *Anger and Forgiveness*, Nussbaum uses the example of King (along with Gandhi and Nelson Mandela) in order to fashion her own variation on this ideal. She calls it "Transition" or "Transition-Anger," a way of responding to but getting beyond anger in favor of a productive mode of engaging with a threatening and contentious world. Nussbaum writes as a moral philosopher (which is, after all, what she is), and so she is more interested in these figures as exemplars of this ideal than in whether their rhetoric matched the practice of their followers (a concern more for the historian). She wants to extract from their exemplary ethical stances— their desire not to let anger and resentment be the emotional resting point of their movements—a prescription for how "we" should feel and act in this contemporary world so emotionally charged with angry and resentful voices, so threatened by acts of revenge and retribution.

Although she does not cite him, one might easily suggest Malcolm X as a foil to King—the fiery Black revolutionary who was everything the nonviolent civil rights leader was not. At least this is how the mainstream media often juxtaposes the two, with the not-so-subtle suggestion that Martin's way was preferable to Malcolm's. But recent biographies of the latter show us a complex and interesting figure who was quite attuned to the swiftly changing currents of racial politics in the sixties. To reduce him to an angry militant, uncompromising in his resentment against the white race amounts to a distorting caricature.

For one thing—and this was apparent at the time as part of a larger movement of Black pride—"Malcolm inspired blacks to unapologetically love themselves," writes Peniel E. Joseph in his recent book, *The Sword and the Shield: The Revolutionary Lives of Malcolm X and Martin Luther King Jr.*[40] "His unapologetic insistency on . . . *radical black dignity* marked him as a prophetic visionary in the eyes of a global black community and as a dangerous subversive to the American government."[41] Moreover, Malcolm did not differ so much from King on the goal of integration. As he declared in a debate with James Baldwin in 1963, "If integration is going to give the black people in America complete freedom, complete justice and complete equality, then it's a worthwhile goal."[42] What he objected to was the notion that they had to ask—"beg," he called it—for those rights. "He viewed civil rights at its best," writes Joseph, "as an assertion of black humanity."[43] Finally, and perhaps most dramatically, Malcolm X came to embrace an international perspective that joined up with the global struggle of oppressed peoples—and not only people of color. This was, of course, a revolutionary and potentially violent agenda, even more so than that depicted in the 1959 TV documentary on the Nation of Islam, "The Hate that Hate Produced," in which he was featured. But, especially after his trip to the Middle East, where he was welcomed by Muslims both white and non-white, he abandoned the race-based views of the Nation of Islam and began to espouse a revolutionary ideology more in keeping with the globalist "rainbow coalition" that increasingly defined the program of the Black Panthers and militants of all races. This did not signal a turn away from the angry rhetoric that mostly defined him in the public's eyes. (Although usually overlooked then and now is his quick wit and wicked sarcasm, which was often mistaken for mere contempt.) He would not, in short, win accolades from Martha Nussbaum for the "Transition-Anger" she cherished in Martin Luther King Jr. But Malcolm's insistent anger, which was always purposeful, even programmatic in its focus, does not make him a man of resentment.

*   *   *

It is often said that if you can remember the sixties, you really weren't there. Be that as it may, when one thinks about the presence of resentment in today's political culture and then tries to imagine it having anything close to a comparable weight in the countercultural and radical sixties, one would, I believe, be at a loss. While generalizations, especially about an entire decade, are dangerous and misleading, I think it's safe to conclude that other emotions dominated the collective mood of those passionate times. Resentment was not one of them.

THE OTHER SIXTIES:
INVENTING THE POLITICS OF RESENTMENT[44]

There was, of course, another "sixties" than the one celebrated by popular culture and our collective memory, where—in part in reaction to it, in part the result of a deliberate attempt to mobilize elements of the American populace in support of a conservative, if not reactionary, political establishment—we find fairly robust expressions of deep-seated resentment. The sixties, in short, witnessed, along with everything else that characterized that tumultuous decade, a politics and rhetoric of resentment.

The "Silent Majority" and Resentment

On the evening of November 3, 1969, President Richard M. Nixon addressed the nation on television. His topic was the war in Vietnam, the prospects for peace as well as the growing anti-war movement. Only several weeks before, on October 15, a "Moratorium to End the War in Vietnam" had drawn out millions of protestors around the country in an unprecedented show of public sentiment against continued US involvement in Southeast Asia. Beyond this one-day event, anti-war protests, some violent, most peaceful, created a constant drumbeat of opposition and discontent across the nation, and not only on college and university campuses. It is clear that the Nixon administration, and Nixon himself, felt beleaguered.

Nixon's speech, which has been remembered mostly for his evocation of a "silent majority," ostensibly dealt with the war and his plan to end it on terms favorable to the US. But there is no mistaking his intention to mobilize public opinion against what he tried to depict as a vocal minority of protestors, whose patriotism, moreover, was suspect. "It might not be fashionable to speak of patriotism or national destiny these days. But I feel it is appropriate to do so on this occasion," he intoned from a text apparently written largely without the aid of speechwriters. "Let historians not record that when America was the most powerful nation in the world, we passed on to the other side and allowed the last hopes for peace and freedom of millions of people to be suffocated by the forces of totalitarians." And then he pronounced the phrase with which the speech has been identified ever since: "So tonight, to you, the great—silent—majority of my fellow Americans, I ask you for your support."[45]

Nixon's mention that evening of a "silent majority" had been prepared by similar rhetorical gestures on his part, at least since 1967; his use of "quiet Americans," a "new majority," "forgotten Americans," "the forgotten majority," the "backbone of America," "the non-shouters," and other like phrases meant to evoke a population of solid, hardworking, patriotic citizens who don't go in for protesting against or even criticizing their country. Unmistakable was the sotto voce suggestion that these ordinary Americans had been silent—and put upon—too long. The way had been prepared more recently in the weeks before the speech by Nixon's bulldog, Vice President Spiro Agnew. Speaking shortly after the massive Moratorium Day protests, at a fundraiser in New Orleans on October 19, Agnew homed in on his favorite targets: privileged students and so-called intellectuals. His speech was a tissue of pithy put-downs. "The student now goes to college to proclaim rather than to learn," he declared. "A spirit of national masochism prevails, encouraged by an effete corps of impudent snobs who characterize themselves as intellectuals."[46] Although there were cries of objections from liberals, the speech was a rousing success among supporters of the administration and conservative pundits alike, which only emboldened Agnew further. Several days later he expanded on these themes: "I have no regrets. . . . What I said before I will say again. It is time for the preponderant majority, responsible citizens of this country, to assert *their rights*." The anti-war leaders were "political hustlers . . . who would tell us our values are lies." Their claims to be on the side of the people are patently false, for "they disdain to mingle with the masses who work for a living." They "prey upon the good intentions of gullible men everywhere," and "pervert honest concern into something sick and rancid . . ." They are, finally, "vultures who sit in trees and watch lions battle, knowing that win, lose, or draw, they will be fed."[47]

Lest these be considered merely rhetorical exercises cynically crafted to address a particular moment, the same sentiments found an outlet from a less dubious source. *Time* magazine's "Man and Woman of the Year" were announced in January 1970: "The Middle American"—husband and wife.[48] The editors' portrait of this imaginary pair highlighted their fears and resentments: "They feared that they were beginning to lose their grip on the country. Others seemed to be taking over—the liberals, the radicals, the defiant young, a communications industry that they often believed was lying to them . . ." They were ignored: "No one celebrated them; intellectuals dismissed their lore as banality." They were disrespected, threatened in their own homes: "Pornography, dissent and drugs seemed to wash over them in waves, bearing some of their children away." Now, however, their time had come: "But in 1969 they began to assert themselves. They were 'discovered' first by politicians and the press, and then they started to discover themselves."

The article went on to voice the concerns of these "Middle Americans," some certainly legitimate, others perhaps less so. Taxes were high, yet they felt they had little voice in how the money was spent. Inflation was high as well. Crime was rampant; schoolchildren were being bused out of their neighborhoods by court order; sex education in the schools was an affront to the religious values of many. Drugs and pornography proliferated. Middle Americans "have felt ignored while angry minorities dominated the headlines and the Government's domestic action. If not ignored, they have been treated with condescension." The United States was the greatest country in the world; but its cherished values and traditions were everywhere mocked: "Why were people trying to tear it down?" Quoting the executive vice president of the National Confederation of American Ethnic Groups, the article noted the inevitable backlash—against militant Blacks, white intellectuals, long-haired protestors: "Our families don't have long haired brats—they'd tear the hair off them. Our boys don't smoke pot or raise hell or seek deferments. Our people are too busy making a living and trying to be good Americans."

And then there were policies aimed to help mostly Blacks (or so it was assumed), such as open admission to universities or preferential treatment in hiring, which perhaps more than anything seemed to represent the height of unfairness, a blatant contradiction to the meritocracy that supposedly created a level playing field for all Americans. The *Time* editors quoted the "Futurist" Herman Kahn: "If anything, they believe that a black face helps. A Middle American can't send his kid to Harvard, but he knows the black man down the street can, if the boy is bright enough." The eminent Harvard psychiatrist Robert Coles is quoted as saying, "They say that the Negro should be given jobs, but only so long as he does not go faster than they had to go."

There can be no doubt that *Time's* Middle American belonged to Nixon's "silent majority," and that in their reputed silence they seethed with resentment.

A Philosopher of Popular Resentment

The *Time* article also referred to Eric Hoffer (1898–1983), the so-called longshoreman philosopher, who had become something of a cult figure, mostly to conservatives who relished his blunt-speaking eloquence. "San Francisco State is being destroyed by a bunch of crummy punks," he is quoted as musing. "Who the hell would have dreamt that a thing like this was possible? Ignorant, bedraggled, illiterate punks!"[49] This was typical of the kinds of pronouncements he dispensed at this juncture, which the press ate up. His first book, *The True Believer*, published in 1953, which catapulted him to prominence, was much more measured and thoughtful, offering an interesting if not entirely novel critique of mass ideological movements both right and left.[50] By the late sixties, his books had increasingly taken on a cranky tone, filled with aphoristic put-downs aimed at countercultural and radical elements, and much else. Here the contempt is palpable, the politics wistfully reactionary.

Hoffer delivered his views in pungent prose, swaddling his barbed opinions with musings on modernity, a modernizing society, and nature, as well as wide-optic, somewhat facile speculations on the history and fate of "mankind." But his tone and aim are sharpened in his 1967 book, *The Temper of Our Time*, where he takes on all comers. As the "people's philosopher," in this book he particularly relishes skewering intellectuals, instructing his readers—presumably all "salt of the earth" Americans—that historically, "rule by intellectuals went hand in hand with subjection or the enslavement of those who do the world's work."[51] Intellectuals, he writes, deliberately keep their distance from the masses, with whom they are fundamentally incompatible. When America's influence increases, this is sure to arouse the "fear and hostility of the intellectuals." They are, in short, un-American. "Nothing so offends the doctrinaire intellectual as our ability to achieve the momentous in a matter-of-fact way, unblessed by words. . . . In the eyes of the foreign intellectual, American achievements are illegitimate, uninstructive and uninspiring."[52] Thank God, he muses in a later book, America has been fortunate, unlike the Europeans, in simply ignoring intellectuals and, especially, making sure to keep them out of the corridors of power.[53]

Perhaps to shore up his working-class bona fides, but also to cast himself as the voice of the people, he gives the rich a few whacks. Indeed, in all of his writings, as well as his cultivated public image, Hoffer strives to come off as homespun and plain-speaking—the voice of sixties-style populism of the Right. He wonders how strange it is that today's "dissenting" intellectuals, so critical of virtually everyone and everything in America, are lacking in animus when it comes to the rich. Perhaps this is because, like them, the wealthy have distanced themselves from the common people, and like them as well, they cannot help making a noisy display of their righteousness: "But what they confess in public are not their private sins but the sins of society, the sins of the rest of us, and it is our breasts they are beating to a pulp."[54] In the past, young aristocrats enjoyed the privilege of horsewhipping their peasants, he muses. These days are gone; today, instead it is the children of the rich, "their revolutionary children," who ride "roughshod over community sensibilities."[55] Like *Time*'s Middle American and Nixon's "silent majority," Hoffer's "people" have for too long been made to suffer the disrespect and condescension of pampered elites.

He has, of course, nothing but contempt for these "revolutionary children," but it is the "Negro" problem that provokes his most sustained comment. Here he joins with much of the white working class, especially those whose forbears immigrated in the late nineteenth and early twentieth century, who strenuously disavowed any responsibility for the plight of African Americans. "The majority of us started to work for a living in our teens, and we have been poor all our lives. . . . Our white skin brought us no privileges and no favors."[56] He refers to "[his] kind of people" who don't believe the world owes them anything. And while he concedes that the "Negro" should have equal rights, "he can have no special claim on us, and no valid grievances on us. He has certainly not done our work for us Our hands are more gnarled and workbroken [sic] than his, and our faces more lined and worn."[57]

But Hoffer really hits his stride when he turns to how law-abiding, good Americans have reacted in the face of all the crime and disorder—the "perverse high-jinks of unruly punks who think they can get away with it." Here his analysis turns dark, revealing unmistakable shadows of resentment. For he dismisses any psychological explanations for crime and, in fact, seems to be uninterested in even thinking about causes, motivations, or conditions. What is the reason for the current plague of violence in our cities' neighborhoods and streets, he asks? It's not the "outer manifestation of some dark disorder in the cellars of the mind," but rather "the unprecedented meekness" of its usual targets.[58] It is the failure of the "majority" to act and react in the face of crime, a lack of resolve, that has allowed these unruly elements to run amok, "to stalk older people like animals stalking their prey." And in case we fail to understand, he sharpens his point. "We do not know what is ahead of us," he ruminates. But he's certain that the "violent minorities" will not change their ways. A time of reckoning is near. "There is a vague feeling that a day of wrath is waiting around the corner when the saturated resentment of the long-suffering majority crystallizes in retaliation. It is impossible to say when, where and how the reaction will come."[59]

Updike's Rabbit: The Sixties Breed a Resentful Everyman

It's as if, all these Afro hair bushes and gold earrings and hoopy
noise on buses, seeds of some tropical plant sneaked in by the birds
were taking over the garden. His garden. Rabbit knows it's his garden and that's why he's put a flag decal on the back window of the
Falcon even though Janice says its corny and fascist.

John Updike, *Rabbit Redux*[60]

Harry "Rabbit" Angstrom, John Updike's fictional protagonist in four
novels published across a period of more than forty years (1960–2001), is
twenty-six when he appears in the first of these, *Rabbit Run*, an already-
aging former high school basketball star living in a small town in south-
central Pennsylvania, burdened by a failing marriage and a crummy job,
and profoundly frustrated with his middle-class existence. Ten years later,
he resurfaces in *Rabbit Redux*, published in 1971, Updike's take on the sixties, in which this now thirty-six-year-old Everyman finds himself even
more adrift and confused.[61] It's not only his interpersonal travails or the
enervating discontents with family and work that had troubled him in the
earlier book—though these still gnaw at him with depressing regularity.
Now he's confronted by the teeming counterculture of sex, youth, and
Black assertiveness which has seeped into his sleepy Pennsylvania town.
Its manifestations are everywhere he turns, but strangely for a man who
first comes off as threatened and disgusted by what he sees—though not
so strange for a creation of Updike, this consummate fashioner of characters—in a way he ends up being seduced by this very culture. By the
middle of the novel, this middle-class white guy is sharing his home with
a Black Vietnam vet, hipster, and drug dealer, who constantly taunts him
for his white, bourgeois ways, and a runaway flower child, the offspring of
a wealthy Connecticut couple, who ultimately shares his bed. His suburban house has become something of a hippie commune.

Rabbit is indeed adrift, so it is not surprising that a man so unmoored,
so alienated and confused, should succumb to, even invite, this topsy-
turvy transformation of his domestic life. But even as he is living so in-
timately with these two people, the very embodiments of the most up-
ending features of the counterculture, who, despite their own confused
and disordered lives, goad him into thinking differently about things, his
resentments, as reflected in his ruminations and periodic rants, are never
far from view. African Americans, whose newly conspicuous presence—
they seem to be everywhere: on the bus, in the streets, in the news—

clearly irritate him. "I don't follow this racist rap," he shouts at his wife's lover, who has just provoked him with his liberal views. "You can't turn on television now without some black face spitting on you. Everybody from Nixon down is sitting up nights trying to figure out how to make 'em all rich without putting 'em to the trouble of doing work."[62] In these and in other passages, he sounds like someone who would find Hoffer's rough-shod racism much to his liking.

But his resentment has other targets as well. He has nothing but scorn for the rich, especially those newly ensconced in "those great big piecrust mock-Two-door houses with His and Her Caddies parked out by the hy-drangea bushes. . . . Timbered gables, driveway pebbles, golf clubs fill the sky with debris." Recalling a doctor who came to treat his ailing mother, and then couldn't wait to escape his parents' dismal home, he remembers with chilly contempt the "doctor's irritation at being halted even a second setting a prong of distaste on his upper lip behind the clipped mustache the color of iron." The image, though, conveys a perverse kind of admiration: "His handshake also metal, arrogant, it pinches Harry's unready hand and says, *I am strong, I twist bodies to my will. I am life. I am death.*" Challenged by Skeeter, his new Black housemate, to tell him what he really thinks of the nouveau riche up on the hill, he responds, "I hate those Penn Park motherfuckers. . . . If I could push the red button to blow them all to Kingdom Come . . . I would." Reflecting on the lives of his parents who "lived near the foot of this hill in the dark," his father coming every day from work, "too tired to play catch in the backyard," and now his mother's dying treated like a "game being played by doctors who drove Caddies and had homes in Penn Park," he repeats, "I hate them."[63]

It is only deep into the novel that we learn the extent to which indus-trial "modernization" is steadily draining the economic lifeblood of his little town, just as it was beginning to do across much of middle Amer-ica at the end of the sixties. And the reader is informed of this at the same time Rabbit is, although Rabbit seems rather slow on the uptake. Told of the technological changes coming to the printing shop where he and his father work, his boss has to spell out what it means for him: he is going to lose his job: "I thought I made that point. That's part of the technical picture, that's where the economy comes. Offset, you operate all from film, bypass hot metal entirely."[64] But this impending blow is only the most tangible aspect of the sense of loss and disappointment that suffuses him, as it does Updike's whole tetralogy. Rabbit, the former bas-ketball star, as Morris Dickstein has written, is burdened by an "inchoate quest, his effort to shape his life to the fleeting glimpses of glory he once had."[65] Even a baseball game on a Saturday afternoon in the company of his young son and father-in-law fails to assuage his profound sense of loss. Here, at least, it is supposed to be different: "There was a beauty here . . . a beauty refined from country pastures, a game of solitariness, of waiting . . . a game whose very taste, of spit and dust and grass and sweat and leather and sun, was America . . ." But he slowly perceives that "something is wrong." The crowd, whose "catcalls are coarse and unkind," is pitifully small, made up mostly of drunks or other ne'er-do-wells. "Rabbit yearns to protect the game from the crowd; the poetry of space and inaction is too fine, too slowly spun for them."[66] In Updike's novel, Rabbit's personal "quest" to recover a lost glory, even a lost sense of purpose, mirrors the state of America as it emerged battered and rudderless from the sixties.

Updike was as an astute an observer of the inner life of his country as anyone writing in the postwar era. And it is painfully obvious that, like his white, male, small-town protagonist, he looked upon the recent social and cultural transformations of his nation with deep misgivings. Like Rabbit, Updike came of age in the fifties and grew up middle-class in a south-central Pennsylvania town, and like him too, Updike was a supporter of the Vietnam war, although his support was distinctly lukewarm.[67] And his identification as a Christian—an impressively theologically learned Christian at that—is well known. But it would be absurd to view Rabbit as channeling unrefined Updike's reputed "conservative" views—whatever those "views" were for such a subtle, protean, mostly unpolitical writer. For while, especially in the first part of the novel, Rabbit's various resentments are on display; they are softened by an even stronger emotion, or at least one that evokes the reader's sympathy—an overwhelming sadness that surely stems from the author's own wistfulness about the state of his country, a feeling evident in many of his novels. Updike was no prophet, but I think he was prescient in presenting us with an antihero whose resentments were triggered by the challenging vicissitudes of a turbulent decade, which is to say, the transformations that would continue to ripple across our culture for decades to come. And while Rabbit's resentments cannot be ignored, rendering him rather unappealing for the liberal-minded reader, we come to appreciate that they are secondary in his emotional makeup. That beneath this animus for Blacks, the rich—for so much new swirling around him—lies an amalgam of sadness, confusion, and a sense of loss which would increasingly characterize the psychological disposition of white men for generations to come. Updike was a singular writer in so many ways; it may have been that he was also unique in rendering a contemporary man of resentment in a time when readers were not quite ready to recognize him as such.

Backlash and the "Southern Strategy"[68]

To recall the ways Americans were exhorted to feel resentful in the sixties prompts us to ask whether these amounted to a real *politics* of resentment. To take Nixon's and Agnew's speechifying literally, with its often-inflammatory populist undertones, one would think that the rhetoric and the politics were the same. Research on the grassroots politics of this period, especially in the South, however, casts doubt upon this conclusion. It makes us wonder whether resentment was as pronounced among the "silent majority" as the rhetoric suggests.

During the 1968 presidential campaign, Nixon's electoral guru was Kevin Phillips, a young, Harvard-educated lawyer with a nerdish predilection for maps and statistics, who was committed to engineering a realignment of American politics. His 1969 book *The Emerging Republican Majority* spells out in numbing detail the dynamics of a turn in the electoral fortunes of the Republican Party based on a demographic lock on white voters in the South, Southwest, and Midwest of the country. This transformation, he predicts, would leave the Democrats as a minority party of renegade Yankees, Jews, Blacks, and sundry other, mostly Northern European ethnics, all in thrall to a liberal establishment, "a privileged elite blind to the needs and interests of the range of the national majority." In all of this, race is pivotal. Ethnic and racial differences have long characterized American politics, he observes, but "given the immense midcentury impact of Negro enfranchisement and integration, reaction to this change almost inevitably had to result in political realignment."[69] Based on his demographic reading of population trends in recent years, Phillips asserts that the suburbs had become a "white noose" encircling "the increasingly Negro cities." The "emerging Republican majority," then, would be underwritten by two aspects of "Negrophobia." One was the age-old animosity for Blacks—that is, traditional racism. But the other was somewhat new: white resentment of liberal social policies, mostly associated with Johnson's "Great Society," which had been designed to rectify generations of racial discrimination. Among these the most controversial were various schemes of school busing, housing desegregation, preferential treatment, and affirmative action.[70]

With Phillips's book, the concept of "backlash"—although evoked before—definitively entered the vocabulary of American political culture. And while it was often understood in terms of men's reaction to the challenge of feminism,[71] it certainly also conveyed the sense of animosity and, indeed, resentment on the part of whites who chafed at the recent gains of African Americans from both civil rights legislation and the social programs of the Great Society. Backlash was central to Phillips's analysis, which lay behind the so-called Southern Strategy, a race-based politics which would yoke Nixon's electoral fortunes to the same population who had supported Barry Goldwater and George Wallace; the disgruntled and angry white voters, both working class and suburban middle class, who would emulate their Southern counterparts, yielding what Phillips called the "Southernization of American politics."

Others have contested the validity of seeing these years in terms of a race-based politics of backlash. The historian Matthew Lassiter, for example, offers a grassroots perspective of the politics of the late sixties, which shows suburbanites across the country, North, South, and West, voting not fundamentally in terms of race but rather in defense of their comfortable lifestyles—their safe, economically homogeneous neighborhoods, their neighborhood schools, their corporate jobs. These suburban dwellers, not working-class whites, hard hats and all, constituted his true electoral base. Instead of Phillips's Southern Strategy, Lassiter counters that the Republicans followed a *"Suburban* Strategy," appealing to the interests of a vast suburban population that had grown up around American cities in the postwar era largely because of what Lassiter calls "growth liberalism," which included the GI Bill, military spending, federally funded highway construction, and "regional branch offices that reflected the explosive expansion of the technology-driven and service-oriented sectors of corporate capitalism."[72] In other words, a constellation of public policies favored suburbanization, which in turn gave rise to a middle-class sense of entitlement—residents who identified primarily as homeowners, taxpayers, and school parents. In all of this, race was, to be sure, a factor, especially when it came to court-ordered busing, which suburbanites resisted with zeal and effectiveness. But unlike their working-class counterparts living in cities, they tended to couch their protests in terms that avoided racial overtones, preferring to present their grievances in defense of seemingly race-neutral values such as property rights and neighborhood schools, values that would appeal to "anyone." And in fact, Nixon and the Republican leadership rejected a race-based strategy that pandered to urban white workers, except for the midterm elections of 1970, when the strategy—Phillips's Southern Strategy—proved dramatically unsuccessful. "The suburban strategies that revolved around a color-blind defense of the consumer rights and residential privileges of middle-class white families," concludes Lassiter, "succeeded where the overtly racialized tactics of the Southern Strategy had failed."[73]

Where does this leave the "politics of resentment?" In Lassiter's view, it was a politics that was decisively abandoned; thus, more rhetorical than real. Looking at other studies of working-class, urban communities in the late sixties and early seventies, however, where residents bitterly complained about crime, forced busing, and desegregation of housing, the resentment seems real enough, with a politics aimed to appeal to it. In such journalistic accounts as J. Anthony Lukas's *Common Ground: A Turbulent Decade in the Lives of Three American Families* (1985), which offers an up-close, finely grained depiction of how a group of ordinary working-class people in the Charlestown and South End sections of Boston dealt with the ramifications of court-ordered busing; or the sociologist Jonathan Rieder's *Canarsie: The Jews and Italians of Brooklyn against Liberalism* (1985), which primarily focuses on two ethnic groups in a Brooklyn neighborhood as they react to policies and demographic trends as well as social problems associated with racial integration, we find racism and resentment in equal measure. Indeed, we might surmise that it was resentment that was new—that added to the long-standing, dare we say, venerable racist sentiments harbored by white urban residents, whose exposure to African Americans dated from the Great Migration of the earlier part of the century, was a growing sense of resentment, as demographic changes and public policies increasingly pitted the interests of whites and Blacks against one another.

*   *   *

So the balance sheet on the presence of resentment as an element of the political climate of the sixties is mixed. I have argued that when it comes to the decade of protest and the counterculture, of feminism and the movement toward civil rights for Blacks and Black Liberation alike, it does not seem appropriate as an ascription of the prevailing emotion or psychological disposition in this time of upheaval and hope. For the "other" sixties, however, which might be seen as a reaction to the first, I am suggesting that resentment did indeed raise its vexatious head, mostly as a rhetoric of politics, but also as an emotional component of urban white residents who felt beleaguered by recent social and political transformations, especially the recent gains of African Americans.

But did this effort to mount a politics of resentment stick as a signature element either of the Republican Party or conservatism more generally? If we take someone like Pat Buchanan—speechwriter and aide to President Reagan, candidate for president first under the Republican banner then as the standard-bearer for the right-wing Reform Party, frequent commentator on TV, and more generally, a provocative spokesman for the hard Right—we might conclude, why yes. In his speech at the 1992 Republican Convention, he proclaimed—indeed, seemed to gleefully endorse—a culture war for the soul of this country. "Many people did not like this speech," quipped the leftist columnist Molly Ivins. "It probably sounded better in the original German."[74] And despite the ebbs and flows of the political right in the last thirty or more years, Buchanan has exhibited staying power as a persistent voice for an angry, resentful politics that ultimately triumphed in Trump's election in 2016.

But returning to the last decades of the twentieth century, it is retrospectively clear that when it came to the animating spirit of both the Republican Party and the conservative movement more generally, it was the upbeat legacy of Ronald Reagan, not the resentful rhetoric of Pat Buchanan, that prevailed. It was the sunny "Morning in America" political commercial, not the bitter "culture war" speech, that primarily characterized the Republican Right in this country, from Reagan through George H. W. Bush and his "thousand points of light" to George W. Bush, with his espousal of a "compassionate conservatism." Reagan indeed set the tone. As Mark Lilla notes, "Reagan abandoned the dour, scolding, apocalyptic style of 1950s conservatism and radiated hopefulness. After George McGovern's lame plea, *Come home America!*, after Jimmy Carter's sensible shoes and sensible sweater and sensible advice to lower the thermostat, Reason beamed, 'Twilight? Not in America. Here it's sunrise every day.'"[75]

To be sure, when it comes to the actual policies as well as many of the pronouncements of these presidents and other Republican leaders, the picture looks much different, with plenty of evidence for a politics aimed to undo several generations of progressive legislation and social reform. Not-so-subtle appeals to racism, ethno-nationalism, and cultural resentment are certainly not hard to find in their speeches. And, of course, there was the growing influence of the Jerry Falwells, the Pat Robertsons, the Lee Atwaters and Paul Weyrichs who gave voice, in somewhat different ways, to a revanchist, uncompromising, explicitly reactionary politics that was as angry as it was aggrieved. I am, however, considering not the totality of Republican conservativism in these years but rather the dominant tone, the primary emotional veneer that marked their self-presentation before the American public. Whatever actual policies they pursued, their rhetoric did not perpetuate the dark discourse of resentment as cultivated by Nixon and his acolytes.

It is interesting to note in this regard that, unlike today, in the aftermath of the sixties, "resentment" was rarely used to describe the reactions of aggrieved populations, especially white men. It was rather "backlash," especially "white backlash" that seemed to come into vogue, frequently invoked to explain both their angry reactions and their growing alienation from the Democratic Party. Early evidence of this can be found in a 1964 article by Seymour Martin Lipset, who, let us recall, was one of the contributors to *The Radical Right* and often cited "resentment" to explain right-wing extremism and anti-Semitism, as well as populism. His article, "Beyond the Backlash," published in the British journal *Encounter* in 1964 in anticipation of the electoral face-off between Johnson and Goldwater that year, attempted to explain why he thought the right-wing candidate would not win—that the Goldwater phenomenon, while similar to other movements in American history animated by people threatened by modernizing trends, was really quite marginal in its appeal. It was, he concluded, the "backlash of a dying right-wing elephant."[76]

Even more telling is the 1991 book by Susan Faludi, *Backlash: The Undeclared War against American Women*, a best seller, which won the National Book Award for nonfiction. In Faludi's hands, "backlash" is not merely an opportunistic appropriation of a concept that had already been circulating in the public sphere as a catchall explanation for conservative or reactionary trends, especially in the Reagan era. She means it literally. Recent gains of women are now blamed for a whole host of contemporary ills: the breakdown of the family, the neglect of children, unhappy marriages, discontent among women themselves—indeed, for almost everything that conservatives saw as wrong in contemporary society. "This counter assault is largely insidious," she writes. "In a kind of pop-culture version of the Big Lie, it stands the truth boldly on its head and proclaims that the very steps that have elevated women's position have actually led to their downfall." The success of modern feminism has spelled doom for all that was good and healthy in American culture—this is the backlash's mantra. "It is a preemptive strike that stops women long before they reach the finish line."[77]

Faludi finds the sources of this backlash in various places—the Reagan administration, highly visible anti-feminist figures, conservative think tanks ("The Backlash Brain Trust"), pop psychologists, even some self-proclaimed feminists. The mass media are the major culprit, especially TV and movies (*Fatal Attraction*), the fashion industry, and the whole hegemonic phenomenon of advertising. One of her chapters is titled, "The Politics of Resentment: The New Right's War on Women," and here she refers to the work of Lipset, Hofstadter, and Theodor Adorno on right-wing movements and their followers "who see themselves as social outcasts rather than guardians of the status quo."[78] But it is interesting to note that despite this brief acknowledgment, she does not pursue the thought that backlash might have a social basis—a constituency of "social outcasts"—preferring to aim her considerable critique at a range of establishment institutions, personalities, and forces. Whether, say, ordinary people share this anti-feminist perspective, and, if so why, does not interest her.

In this respect, I believe Faludi's book tells us something about the meaning of "backlash" as it was invoked in these decades—what it was meant to convey and its limitations as well. It connotes a political response to progressive movements or recent gains on the part of groups, such as African Americans or women. While it certainly derives its potency from people's real concerns, these are stoked, manipulated, sustained, and often distorted by political leaders, media outlets, and other formal devices. Thus to name a phenomenon "backlash" is to close off access to understanding what might be the grievances, or at least concerns, that lie beneath these machinations. It is to remain in the realm of a rather circumscribed sense of politics, not straying into the murky depths of people's actual sentiments, the psychological dimensions of their discontents or grievances. For all its problematic aspects, the concept of resentment invites us into these depths. Interestingly, in 1999 Faludi would, in a sense, take up this invitation in *Stiffed: The Betrayal of the American Man*.[79] In this book, an ethnographic study of ordinary men who have found themselves, in myriad ways, bereft, confused, demoted, and disillusioned—in short, men at an entire loss of what it means to "be a man" at the end of this "American century"—she reveals a curiosity and empathy largely lacking in *Backlash*. I would suggest, then, that comparing these two studies, *Backlash* and *Stiffed*, serves to illustrate two significantly different intellectual approaches, with, I am arguing, something missing in the former.

* * *

Let me recapitulate my larger, perhaps somewhat speculative argument here. By the seventies, "resentment" had waned in respect to the two tracks of investigation which configure this study. On one, as I hope this chapter has shown, resentment as a description of the decade of radical activism and counterculture just doesn't fit. Whatever emotions characterized this period, a sense of being resentful—of being left behind, aggrieved, and bitter—was not *dominant*. On the other, as enshrined in what I have called the "Resentment Paradigm," resentment lost its place as an important analytical concept, discredited by its association with an earlier generation of intellectuals such as Bell, Lipset, and Hofstadter, intellectuals associated with Cold War liberalism and somewhat outdated psychoanalytic conventions. In its place emerged the concept of "backlash," a notion with fewer problematic associations but which was also much less revealing of people's sentiments and the psychological aspect of their grievances and discontents.

It is in this dual sense that I mean the "decline" in the title of this book. The "Return of Resentment," however, was in the offing.

CHAPTER EIGHT

The Return of Resentment

Anatomizing a Contemporary Political Emotion

> The feeling saturated our social-media feeds, dominated our conversations with friends, occupied our minds as we struggled to fall asleep and wake up. After Trump was elected, the resentment came to seem less like a state of mind than an ineluctable mood, something we were living in.
>
> EMILY WANG with MATTHEW SHEN GOODMAN,
> "A Note on Resentment," *Triple Canopy*[1]

I began this book with a long list of newspaper articles and opinion pieces which prominently feature "resentment" as a way of getting a grasp on the startling political turn in the last few years, especially with the election of Donald Trump in 2016. Scholars, too, have contributed to what we might call the "resentment vogue"—a newfound embrace of this concept as a catchall explanation for everything from populism, anti-immigrant sentiments, and Tea Party activism to the emergence of "angry white men" as an identifiable voting bloc.[2] If once this tendency to psychologize political groups and positions was considered out-of-line, today its respectability is hardly in doubt.

With few exceptions, however, these works are not very clear about what is meant by resentment. Sometimes, indeed, it's simply another way of saying "anger" or describing the emotions of rage, rancor, or other strong negative feelings. This book has argued throughout that resentment should be understood with a specificity that qualifies it as complex and politically potent in ways that do not pertain to other emotions. Pankaj Mishra vividly describes the depths of its meaning in language that I think most of us would recognize. It is, he writes, a particular attitude toward "other people's being, caused by an intense mix of envy and a sense of humiliation and powerlessness, which, as it lingers and deepens, poisons civil society and undermines political liberty. . . . A compound of

emotions, [resentment] most clearly reveals the human self in its fundamentally unstable relations with the external world."[3]

To put it in more schematic terms, resentment has several facets:
it connotes a grievance resulting from a deeply felt injury suffered beyond the transitory moment; "others" are responsible for this injury and
usually this also implies a relationship between the aggrieved and those
held responsible for their grievances; the affliction entails intentionality,
willful injury, not just accidental harm; the injury itself does not merely
cause pain but denotes a moral wrong, a sense of unfairness or injustice,
a feeling of being demeaned; and resentment, especially as a collective
emotion, endures; often it is nurtured or perpetuated through the media,
in ideological movements, or by political leaders. Resentment entails not
just the feeling itself but also a significant level of cognition or reflection,
perhaps even more than with other emotions.

In any case, "resentment" has returned. This is not, however, the resentment of generations past—of Bell, Lipset, Hofstadter, and the other
sociologists and historians of the post–World War II era we looked at in
chapter 5. Several aspects of how we conceive of it today distinguish it
from their understanding of the psychological disposition of the right-
wing groups and tendencies that exercised them. For one thing, from
their liberal/pluralist perspective, populism and right-wing extremists
were unworthy of their sympathy; they exhibited no inclination to understand these groups on their own terms, or to discover if any genuine
discontents provoked their resentments. In their view, they were merely
misguided, even maladjusted, and their extremism, their anti-Semitism,
their suspicion of outsiders and foreigners, and, in general, their appeal
to people's prejudices and base instincts defined them as simply illegitimate, or worse. Armed with a general, if watered-down, Freudianism,
they readily diagnosed this orientation in psychological terms. As well,
operating within the tradition of the Enlightenment, they were reluctant
to acknowledge the place of emotions in politics, preferring to follow
Max Weber's rather severe prescriptions in "Politics as a Vocation." With
present-day observers, those who have "rediscovered" resentment as a
useful concept, on the other hand, the attitude is quite different. While
almost to a one they look disapprovingly on the political choices of those,
for example, who align themselves with Trump or who voted for Brexit,
they nevertheless strive to understand what motivated these choices. Unlike Bell et al., they are rarely disposed to write off such groups as simply
misled or irrational. They are governed, in other words, by the assumption that there are grievances and discontents beneath these resentments
worth taking seriously. Moreover, the study of the emotions has now been

firmly established in the humanities and even in some significant corners of the social sciences; we consequently recognize the limitations of a strictly rationalist approach. We are much more alert to subjective factors stemming from unconscious biases, group allegiances, identity, honor and shame, respect and humiliation, religious values, collective memory, and other matters that inform people's political orientations.

This leads to a second difference between these two generations of observers. As we saw, for the contributors to *The Radical Right*, the path of history followed the process of modernization, which for the most part they recognized as benign and progressive, fostering economic development and political stability in its wake. The time of their writing, the early sixties, marked the high point of an optimistic view of modernization. To resist or deny it to try to escape its inexorable course, was useless if not delusional. To be sure, they also acknowledged it as a process which inevitably left some people behind. These were the "dispossessed," whom Bell identified as the most susceptible to embrace right-wing extremism. Today's commentators also see dispossession and its attendant psychological ills as a feature of development, but they are hardly sanguine or positive about the nature of the responsible historical processes. Indeed, an aspect of the current discourse on resentment is to yoke it to the economic transformations wrought by globalization and neoliberalism, transformations which they generally bemoan. In this respect, the contrast with the contributors to *The Radical Right* could not be starker.

How, then, to think of "the return of resentment" as a feature of the current political landscape? What developments have rendered it a meaningful concept that describes deep-seated sentiments in play today, primarily in the US but also elsewhere in the world? Here I offer several different sets of circumstances characterized by the kinds of conflicts and consequent grievances which have generated widespread feelings of "resentment," first with regard to right-wing American voters (and in particular Trump supporters) and then to other sorts of people for whom resentment might appropriately describe their psychological motivation. I should note that several of these are overlapping accounts, each offering a slightly different image of the return of resentment. In this respect, then, I would liken what follows to the experience of trying on a new suit or pair of pants in a clothing store in front of one of those three-paneled mirrors, where you can see yourself from several angles. It's still you, but viewed from slightly different perspectives. Likewise, my account will, in a sense, encircle the experience of resentment from many perspectives, offering a range of reflections, with a particular interest in the conditions that give rise to this collective sentiment.

CUTTING IN LINE

The first perspective comes by way of an analysis offered by the sociologist Arlie Russell Hochschild in her rich ethnographic study of Tea Party activists in Louisiana, *Strangers in Their Own Land: Anger and Mourning on the American Right* (2016). For five years from 2010 to 2015, Hochschild embedded herself in the Bayou region of the state, which has suffered vast environmental damage from the petrochemical industry, damage that has profoundly affected the health, livelihood, and quality of life of its inhabitants—something, she found, that most readily acknowledged. Yet—and this is the "Great Paradox" she revisits in the course of her study—very few of them voiced any support for the environmental movement and virtually all rejected outright federal policies that might have mitigated their suffering. Indeed, their opposition to any governmental activism was at one with their contempt for government programs in general, especially those that smacked of welfare or "handouts."

Hochschild found the key unlocking this paradox in a set of assumptions that resonated with her informants, assumptions which spoke to deep-seated expectations about social mobility and worthiness that most believed had recently been upturned precisely by those governmental officials responsible for upholding them. This dynamic is best captured in the following metaphor, a sort of fable:

You are standing in line. The line is long; there are many people ahead of you and many behind. It is moving, surely but slowly. At the end of the line is the American Dream. But wait! All of a sudden, certain people are cutting ahead of you. Who are they? Blacks, women, immigrants, refugees: this is unfair! But then you realize that these people are not cutting in on their own: someone is helping them. "Who? A man is monitoring the line, walking up and down it, ensuring that the line is orderly and that access to the Dream is fair. His name is President Barack Hussein Obama. But—hey—you see him waving to the line cutters. He's helping them. He feels extra sympathy for them that he doesn't feel for you. He's on their side . . ."[4]

When Hochschild recounted this fable to the Tea Party activists, most expressed an immediate sense of recognition: This was precisely what they felt! It is, in fact, a perfect metaphor for conveying a sense of resentment in very mundane terms that anyone could recognize. After all, what better expresses the sort of momentary, if ultimately inconsequential, feeling of resentment that comes from having someone jump the queue? How dare they! In microcosm it is an act that violates the moral order, inverts what is universally acknowledged as right. And yet, on a much larger canvas of experience, this is what the Tea Partiers were claiming: that welfare programs, affirmative action, preferential treatment of minorities, the domestic resettling of refugees—even the EPA's policy of protecting the brown pelican—rewarded those who simply did not earn what was granted to them, especially as it came (so they thought) at the expense of those who had been patiently waiting in line. Their emotional response was resentment; their political reaction was to join the Tea Party.

Interestingly, the metaphor of jumping the queue surfaces in a propaganda clip against Muslim immigrants in Sweden. In a 2010 video, sponsored by right-wing Swedish Democrats, an old white woman is laboriously making her way down a corridor toward an office desk marked "Pensions." Clearly, the viewer is meant to look upon her sympathetically—she is "one of us," perhaps your very own grandmother. As she shuffles along, however, she hears a clattering noise behind her: it's a gaggle of women dressed in burkas, pushing strollers, who virtually overrun her as they arrogantly stride toward a desk marked "Immigration."[5]

Like Hochschild's resentful informants in this blighted corner of Louisiana, the image of the nice Swedish woman almost being trampled by pushy *Muslim* immigrants is quite compelling. But these are merely images of resentment in action, something on the order of metaphors which, while they might capture the experience of feeling resentment, are not too clear about the causes. One of these causes is undoubtedly economic.

THE LEFT BEHIND

Most of Hochschild's informants were basically middle class, and many were employed, or formerly employed, by the very industries that had ravaged their community. Their resentment stemmed from a bundle of grievances, most of which were rooted in a deep-seated distrust, even hatred, of Washington and all it represented. Another demographic of the aggrieved stands somewhat apart from these sorts of people. These are generally members of the working class who in recent decades have been subjected to a range of economic forces, the result of which has been a decline in their material well-being, a loss of status, the hollowing out of small-town communities, especially in the industrial heartland of the US, and even challenges to traditional gender relations in their families.

We tend to group these economic forces under the rubric of "neoliberalism," a somewhat broad (and somewhat vague) term for a whole range of developments, most apparent only in the last decades of the twentieth century.[6] Neoliberalism is best understood by the transformations it has wrought: privatization, deregulation, free trade, globalization, and a rock-bottom faith in the ability of market forces, devoid of any government involvement or regulation, to encourage economic growth. As a corollary to these trends, many governments have turned toward austerity—some in reaction to the budgetary crisis experienced by many European nations in the wake of the Great Recession in 2008, others as simply a matter of policy. In the minds of many, beyond these economic and political developments, neoliberalism has also fostered "financialization," not only in economic terms but also more generally, giving rise to an ethos where money is the measure of all things and where the accumulation of wealth—the more the better—is the prime indicator of a person's intrinsic worth.

Capitalism—and, in fact, all forms of economic development—produces, along with wealth, losers and winners. But under the reign of neoliberalism, while it is true that many populations in the developing world have been rescued from abysmal poverty, others, especially in the US and Europe, have found themselves on a course of downward mobility. It is hardly necessary here to document the fate of whole swaths of the working class in the US as factories have moved off-shore, industrial production is increasingly automated, unions are weakened, companies are bought out by investors and liquidated for cash, the social safety net has frayed, cities and towns are depopulated, the opioid crisis has ravaged communities, and the mortality rate for white men has increased for the first time in generations. These trends have been long in the making, dating as far back as the 1970s; the coup de grâce came more recently, in the subprime mortgage debacle of 2007–2008, when many of these same families lost their homes.

It is generally assumed that white working-class voters were responsible for Trump's victory.[7] Several things cannot be denied both over the short and longer term: in the longer term, since the late 1960s, there has been a steady erosion of working-class identification with the Democratic Party in favor of alignment with the Republicans and, generally, a more conservative orientation (something touched upon in chapter 7); in the shorter term, a significant number of white working-class voters who voted for Barack Obama in 2008 and 2012 cast their votes for Donald Trump in 2016, especially in the Rust Belt region of Pennsylvania, Ohio, Michigan, and Wisconsin, states that put him over the top in November.[8] As sociologists Rory McVeigh and Kevin Estep found, "He tended to gain strong support in counties with relatively high unemployment rates. He also won counties with high median ages, perhaps reflecting the difficulty older Americans have adjusting to the changes of postrecession America."[9] And many commentators have insisted that his appeal was rooted in a long-festering sense that forces beyond their control—forces largely associated with "globalism"—were responsible for the dismal conditions of their lives. Recall that in his inaugural address Trump spoke of "rusted-out factories scattered like tombstones across the landscape of our nation," clearly playing upon a note of general resentment in the heartland. "One by one, the factories shuttered and left our shores, with not even a thought about millions of American workers *left behind*." And he assured his listeners: *"You will never be ignored again"* (emphasis added).[10]

Many observers have seized upon these sorts of statements and concluded that working-class Trump supporters were motivated by economic grievances stemming from long-standing neoliberal policies. There are two problems with this. First, it is simply not true that most working-class people voted for Trump; in fact, Clinton garnered the majority of their support. Only 12 percent of Trump supporters have incomes below $30,000 per year.[11] An interview study of American voters in 2018 found that "devoted conservatives"—the group farthest to the right—enjoyed a higher income than almost any others across the ideological spectrum.[12] It *is* true that in 2016 Trump received more support from white workers than Romney in 2012 and, conversely, that the Democrats lost ground in this group as compared to previous elections. It is also true that those regions, both in the US and the UK, that have fallen behind in the most recent period of economic expansion tended both to vote for Trump and to leave the European Union in the referendum earlier that year. But this does not mean that the *reasons* voters chose—what motivated them—are economic in nature. Correlation is not the same as cause. Which leads to the second point: a survey of voters—particularly working-class voters—reveals that "economic hardship" was at the bottom of their concerns in the 2016 election, far outranked by such factors as affiliation with the Republican Party, anti-immigrant sentiments, or fear of cultural displacement. As this report finds, "A majority (55%) of white working-class Americans in fair or poor shape say Trump does not understand the problems facing their communities well."[13] Another survey reveals that out of a large sampling of voters, a very small portion expressed resentment for the wealthy and the better educated—an even smaller percentage than liberals.[14] It would seem, then, that those who would reach for purely, or mainly, material conditions to explain Trump's appeal are reaching too far and perhaps in the wrong direction. In many cases, this analytical impulse to see economics at the heart of people's political outlook stems from an understandable quest to explain disturbing or seemingly wrong-headed beliefs by way of concrete realities, like economics, that can at least be dealt with in rational terms. But it is an explanation that hardly does justice to the complexity—or even reality—of people's views.

There are, however, other ways we can view resentment as connected to economic conditions. First, it has been noted that while the level of economic well-being does not necessarily indicate whether individuals align themselves with Trump or other right-wing figures or movements, the fact that they live in an economically depressed or declining area often does. Concerns for their neighbors, for the quality of life in their communities, for the evident out-migration of young people, for the decline in public services, for, in short, all the signs that their hometowns—often rurally situated—are just not doing well prompt them to identify with a general sense of discontent, despite the (relatively) comfortable circumstances of their own lives. Another factor related to economics has more to do with expectations than actual conditions.[15] It is indeed clear from survey research that many Americans suffer from a severe case of declining expectations: that the well-being their parents and grandparents enjoyed—and which, they hold, was certainly well-earned—has been unfairly denied them. It certainly will not be the lot of their children. One recent survey found that 47 percent of those polled believed that "their generation will have a worse life than their parents," while 52 percent believed that "today's youth will have a worse life than their parents."[16] Compounding their disappointment with a measure of resentment is the conviction that not only are "others"—immigrants, undeserving minorities—outpacing them economically but that this undeserved gain has been their loss. Finally, people are aware of the global nature of contemporary capitalism. While, despite the perennially insistent wishes of leftists, members of the working class do not generally embrace an anti-capitalist critique, they are hardly ignorant of the global forces and trade agreements that have emptied their towns of stores and factories. Resentment of transnational, distant authorities is at the heart of a growing popular discontent against the European Union, something cultivated by right-wing parties like the Front National (renamed the Rassemblement National) in France and evident, most consequently to date, in the Brexit vote in Britain. In the US, conspiracy theories regarding the reputedly nefarious, mysterious doings of George Soros and other international figures and agencies have only inflamed legitimate concerns about NAFTA and other free trade agreements engineered by distant elites. Recent critics of neoliberalism have argued that its insidious workings have penetrated every level of society, fostering a generalized sense of insecurity which not even the well-provided can escape. Be this as it may, it cannot be denied that working people in the US, but elsewhere as well, have suffered the brunt of the deleterious effects of a global economy.

In all of these cases, we see economic factors cycled through psychological dispositions—identification with a group or region, disappointed expectations, fear and resentment of distant forces controlling your life.

RACIAL RESENTMENT

Another salient condition of contemporary resentment, which if nothing else calls into question a reliance on economic trends, is racial animus. For one cannot deny that the level of material well-being is a weak predictor of people's views on race. Racism runs up and down and in and out of the social fabric of America, hardly respecting the strictures of class. The question here, however, is whether we can make a distinction between racism and racial *resentment.*

The most dramatic expression of white resentment in the US followed Obama's election, which precisely sharpens this point. While it is true that many white working-class voters cast their ballots for him, it is also true that for others—and as time went on, for more and more of the former—he embodied something very disturbing and threatening to their national and ethnic identity. A Black man's elevation to the highest office in the land—the very personification of "America"—just didn't seem "right."

The Tea Party exhibited this sentiment most clearly. After all, the group was founded right after the 2008 election; and although the precipitating factor seems to have been the bailouts and federal expenditures in the wake of the financial crash, researchers have found racial animus, directed at both Obama particularly and African Americans more generally, quite prevalent in its ranks.[17] The Obama presidency provoked resentment among many whites, mostly, it seems, for his symbolic status. The tendency was to see him not simply as wrong-headed or incompetent or objectionable for his policies or his ideological leanings or any other "normal" reasons why we might oppose a president, but as fundamentally *illegitimate.* Only 29 percent of the Tea Party's followers believed he was a Christian; 41 percent did not believe he was born in the US.[18] "Birthers" were fairly numerous in their midst. In their informants, Parker and Barreto found significant evidence of the belief that "Obama, and what his presidency represents, is a threat to the social prestige of 'real Americans.'"[19] At their rallies, they report, participants brandished images of the president as a primate, an African "witch doctor," even as a caricature of Hitler."[20] Resentment arises when something is perceived as *fundamentally wrong,* when a traditional or seemingly fixed order of things has been overturned. For many Tea Partiers and their followers, a Black man in the White House was their (American) world turned upside down.

Going well beyond the Obama presidency, two pronounced sentiments seem to animate anti-Black attitudes: Blacks have benefited from "preferential" treatment; white people are now the victims of discrimination. Vincent, a white technician from New Jersey featured in Michèle Lamont's study, *The Dignity of Working Men: Morality and the Boundaries of Race, Class, and Immigration* (2000), offered these observations about African Americans: "Make them earn their money instead of just sitting around drinking beer, or wine, or whatever, or just collecting [voice raising] *off us poor guys that gotta work*." And then: "You hear it on TV all the time: [Blacks say] 'we don't have to do this because we were slaves 400 years ago. You owe it to us.' I don't owe you shit, period. I had nothing to do with that and I'm not going to pay for it."[21] A rather thorough survey of US voters found that those who "venerate" Trump tend to think that African Americans have been indulged by the government, getting more than they deserve. If they want to succeed, they need only apply themselves instead of waiting for handouts.[22] Another survey of whites revealed that 68 percent believed Blacks used race to get ahead; 58 percent thought that they were responsible for their own failures.[23]

Vincent's comments convey several aspects of racial resentment in the US, which of course is hardly confined to the working class. This is where we need to dwell for a moment on an analytical distinction between animosity, bigotry, superiority, or fear, on the one hand, and resentment, on the other. Can we make a distinction? In other words, can one be racially resentful without being anti-Black, and conversely, is it plausible to think of racism *without* resentment?

The latter seems quite likely. One might feel great aversion for another race, harboring all the stock prejudices, assuming all the well-worn negative stereotypes, convinced of "their" innate inferiority, and so forth, without necessarily feeling resentful of them as well. Indeed, a belief in one's racial superiority would seem to mitigate against such an enervating sentiment, which normally hinges on a sense of victimization—certainly not a characteristic of a self-regarding "superior" race. When and under what circumstances might resentment have become an added ingredient to the racist stew? The German historian Götz Aly has recently reminded us that European anti-Semitism underwent a profound transformation from medieval to modern times. In the Christian Middle Ages, Jews were an alien people—calumniated as Christ-killers, segregated, persecuted, often exiled or killed. In the modern era, with Jewish emancipation and general access to the rights of citizenship, Jews became not so much aliens as competitors, especially as in many countries they seemed to be more in step with the demands of "modernity" than many Christians;

they were now quite educated, more urban, very much engaged in commerce, more cosmopolitan.[24] "As the gap in education closed, the degree of friction between Jews and the majority population increased," writes Aly. "Envy is born of social proximity, not of distance between two cleanly separated groups."[25]

Is contemporary racism likewise inflected more with resentment than prejudice or animosity? That is, has the status or treatment of African Americans today prompted some whites to view them more as rivals than as anything else? The concept of "racial resentment" is designed to suggest this: it asserts that if race hatred or sheer prejudice are still present—as they surely are—the balance of one's disposition is resentment, not pure racism. As David C. Wilson and Darren W. Davis, two social scientists who have been most forceful in arguing for this psychological qualification of contemporary racism, write, ". . . racial resentment differs from old-fashioned racism in that it raises questions about effort and determination on the part of African Americans, as opposed to references regarding genetic or biological differences. Racial resentment features annoyance and fury as its central emotional themes, and these emotions are provoked by a sense that 'black Americans are getting and taking more than their fair share.'" For those whites filled with resentment for Blacks, their attitudes are based on universally acknowledged notions of fairness and justice, not sheer prejudice, which thereby allow them to escape the accusation of naked racism. "By being resentful of any favors," Wilson and Davis write, "especially those based on race, the subtle racist can hold anti-black beliefs without being 'anti-black.'"[26]

In reality, of course, racism is rarely psychologically and emotionally simple. The history of prejudice and racial hatred comes in many shades. It very well might be, however, that over time—and especially with progress in civil rights and increasing integration—the character of anti-Black racism has changed in that simple animosity or prejudice has been eclipsed, though not entirely replaced, by resentment. Here, Vincent's statements imply a couple of resentful assumptions, which could stand in for the views of many others: White people are unfairly forced to pay for the preferential treatment of Blacks (for example, through welfare and affirmative action). And white people are unfairly to blame for the mistreatment of African Americans in the past, a time when their ancestors were still in Europe. In other words, white people are now the victims. The mirror again shows a world turned upside down.

As with Jews and the transformation of anti-Semitism, racial resentment emerges not, say, under the conditions of slavery, when African Americans were hardly in a position to challenge their white masters, but rather when whites begin to perceive Blacks as competitors, as taking something from them that they take to be their moral right, their birth-right. It is typical to date white "backlash" from the late sixties, in the wake of the Civil Rights Movement and federal legislation that challenged segregation and guaranteed voting and housing rights for Blacks. But there was white backlash *avant la lettre*: it dates to the era of Reconstruc-tion following the Civil War, which ended when Southerners managed to reimpose a social control over the Black population. Though ultimately a failure, Reconstruction was an existential threat to the regime of Southern white supremacy. In the sixties, white critics of the Civil Rights Movement recalled this era as a warning against "going too fast." As historian Law-rence Glickman has written, many whites felt that the movement "fore-grounded black civil rights at the cost of white people's peace of mind. They associated civil rights activism with what popular historians and commentators of the day called the 'excesses' of Reconstruction." Mar-tin Luther King Jr. recognized white backlash as "a new name for an old phenomenon."[27] While the backlash did not succeed in blocking the civil rights legislation passed in the midsixties, it did leave a residue of fear and resentment among many whites, who were encouraged to conclude that a zero-sum dynamic defined the Civil Rights Movement: as Blacks gained, whites lost. "White backlashers imagined coercion where it did not exist," Glickman writes. "They embraced a lexicon and posture of victimization that hearkened back to the era of Reconstruction and anticipated the de-ceiving, self-pitying MAGA discourse that drives reactionary politics in Donald Trump's America."[28]

It is apparent, then, that racial resentment as an irritant in American political culture long preceded Trump. Still, a reactionary, race-inflected politics was clearly an element of his success. And as Robert P. Jones has argued, he managed to "convert white evangelicals . . . from so-called value voters to 'nostalgia voters.'" He writes, "Trump's powerful appeal to white evangelicals was not that he spoke to the culture wars around abor-tion or same-sex marriage, or his populist appeals to economic anxieties, but rather that he evoked powerful fears about the loss of white Christian dominance amid a rapidly changing environment."[29]

Here, too, we see another version of what we might call the "relational" aspect of resentment: it is most pronounced when proximity or, in this case, competition and rivalry, rather than distance or hierarchy, charac-terize social or racial differences. Racism in all its manifestations—from structural or institutional racism to white supremacy—certainly persists in the US, perhaps now more than ever. One reason for its present-day vehemence, I would suggest, is that it is increasingly compounded with resentment.

IMMIGRATION, RESENTMENT, AND
THE "GREAT REPLACEMENT"

Without downplaying racism, it is clear that immigration, perhaps more than any other hot-button issue of the day, has aroused widespread concern and resentment, proving decisive in Trump's electoral victory and the Brexit vote, as well as the swing to the right in many European nations. Indeed, as entrenched as anti-Black sentiment is in the US, the fear of "outsiders," whether migrants from Central America or Muslims from the Middle East and Africa, has given rise to what has been called the "new racism," which targets foreigners, especially non-white foreigners, rather than African Americans. And this has fed an even deeper anxiety: that within a couple of decades the US will no longer be a majority all-white nation. Xenophobia, like racism, has a long-standing place in American life; in recent years, however, with both the steady influx of immigrants and this prognostication of an imminent shift in the country's ethnic balance, it has reached new proportions. Where liberals celebrate diversity, others perceive an existential threat to their way of life.[30]

But does resentment underlie this anxiety? Is it that voters for Trump or supporters of Brexit *resent* the presence of foreigners—those whom they are convinced simply "don't belong?" In fact, the situation is not so simple. In one respect, we must acknowledge that undocumented immigrants, in particular, rank among those who, as in Hochschild's metaphor of cutting in line, are seen to have been accorded special advantages, displacing worthy citizens of their rightful place and privileges. And their resentment is reinforced by the realization that the burgeoning presence of these outsiders, often wildly exaggerated, will soon lead to an even more momentous displacement—the (white) majority turned into a minority. The white supremacists at the "Unite the Right" rally in Charlottesville in August 2017 chanted, "You will not replace us!" (or, as was also heard, "Jews will not replace us!"). An extreme expression of the sentiment, to be sure, but it certainly manages to convey a sense of resentment in the face of what the anti-immigration French writer Renaud Camus has called "the Great Replacement." "I totally sympathize with the slogan 'We will not be replaced,' Camus told an interviewer in 2017, soon after the Charlottesville demonstrations. "And I think that Americans have every good reason to be worried about their country . . . being changed into just another poor, derelict, hyperviolent and stupefied quarter of the 'global village.'"[31] Then, they will truly be "strangers in their own land."

But in another sense, the anxiety provoked by the influx of foreigners has less to do with resentment magnified by a fear of "replacement" than simply a concern, usually hyped by the media and political leaders alike, with security. This is the view of the political scientist John R. Hibbing in *The Securitarian Personality: What Really Motivates Trump's Base and Why It Matters for the Post-Trump Era* (2020). Hibbing argues that security from outside threats and outsiders more generally lies at the heart of Trump supporters' concerns. He calls them "securitarians," people on the alert for a range of threatening elements: immigrants, terrorists, criminals, and foreign powers—in general, elements they perceive as originating from beyond the nation's borders. Added to this shopping list of threats are liberals, because they are seen as striving to help outsiders: "The real enemy is not the outsider, but the people who support them." This explains the astonishing finding that about the same percentage of Trump "venerators" who identify immigrants as a threat, 75 percent, feel as threatened by liberals."[32]

Does resentment play no role in the psychological makeup of the securitarians? Comparing four groups—liberals, moderates, "non-Trump-venerating conservatives," and "Trump venerators"—Hibbing finds the last "the least bitter, the least resentful, and the least socially unfulfilled." His query concerning their resentment directs his interviewees' attention to "wealthy people" and "those who do not have to do physical labor," and again, Trump venerators score very low. In response to the question, "I sort of resent those who have lots of education and live in cities on the coast," only 15 percent of those questioned agreed, far less than the liberals. "On the whole, the level of resentment among Trump venerators is remarkably low," concludes Hibbing.[33]

These findings are significant and cannot be dismissed. But there are some nagging doubts concerning Hibbing's interpretation of his own evidence. For one thing, do people's explicit denial of "resentment" preclude their harboring resentful sentiments nevertheless? It is rare for people readily to acknowledge feeling resentful, especially as it often implies a sense of victimization, even defeat. For another, while the Trumpists disavow resentment of the wealthy or those more educated, this certainly does not cover the map of possible targets for this disposition. What about liberals, seen by so many of them as a terrible threat? Is it not likely that their fear is compounded by a resentment of liberals' support of immigrants and other "outsiders?" And surely the immigrants themselves are a source of resentment. Finally, how does time factor into Hibbing's interpretation of the psychological disposition of securitarians? That is, if people for whom security is the paramount concern are convinced that their interests and fears have been neglected—by elites, by the government, by liberals—over a prolonged period of time, wouldn't this likely turn their concern into resentment? How demeaning to their legitimate anxieties; what a flagrant violation of the bedrock responsibility of any government to protect its citizens! How could one not resent those who would, over a long period of time, countenance or even facilitate such a profound reversal of traditional expectations?

In short, people's attitudes toward immigrants are not of a piece; like racism, negative attitudes toward outsiders and foreigners are processed through different psychological channels, and they have different sources as well. Resentment is only one of them. But the much-touted prognostication of ethnic minority status has clearly added something more to age-old xenophobic sentiments. Now it's more than a dislike of foreigners and their ways, more than even a fear of how they might threaten "us." Indeed, that a "Great Replacement" looms is perhaps the most disturbing image in the mirror of being left behind.

RESENTMENT DOWN AND UP

Several studies have shown that, contrary to assumptions regarding Americans' desire for social mobility and envy of the rich, members of the white working class do not as a whole aspire to "move up" into the ranks of the upper, upper-middle, or professional classes. In fact, recent ethnographic work has revealed that their status as working men and women is fundamental to their sense of themselves, a source of pride and solidarity. In Lamont's study, *The Dignity of Working Men*, her findings lead her to conclude that "workers are not condemned to think of themselves as losers due to their failure to realize the material version of the American dream."[34] Rather, their sense of their own worth is rooted in strongly held values of work, independence, family, tradition, and religion, values they hold on to ever more strongly as they sense these are less valued by society at large. This does not imply satisfaction, complacency, or, certainly, approval for the state of affairs in their country. Discontent is rife, as is economic insecurity. And while Lamont's book shows that working-class identity is imbued with these positive values, like all collective identities, it is also affirmed in the disapproval of those outside its ranks, a disapproval often expressed through resentment.

Members of the white working class aim this resentment in two directions, against the poor and against elites. As J. D. Vance writes in *Hillbilly*

Elegy about his experience working as a cashier at a grocery store in his rural community, "[It] taught me a little more about America's class divide, it also imbued me with a bit of resentment, directed toward both the wealthy and my own kind."[35] Resentment of the poor flows from shopworn assumptions regarding government "handouts," welfare fraud, and "freeloaders," and from unfounded concerns that the burden of supporting those who don't work, have too many babies, and the like, is draining the public coffers and squandering the working person's hard-earned tax dollars. (Of course, a good many of these aspersions are racial in nature, and when people complain about the chronically unemployed or undeserving poor, they often likely have Blacks or Hispanics in mind, even when they are careful not to put it in those terms to an interviewer.) Many opposed Obamacare because they became convinced that it was just another way of taxing them to help the poor. Even those willing to admit that expanded healthcare would be of benefit to them expressed reluctance to endorse a program that helps poor people as well, which would, of course, imply being lumped together with them. But as Joan C. Williams points out in her 2017 book *White Working Class: Overcoming Class Cluelessness in America*, working-class people have long harbored the suspicion that the "government" bends over backward to aid the impoverished while doing little for them.[36] "All they see," she writes, "is their stressed out daily lives, and they resent the subsidies and sympathy available to the poor."[37] Vance also shows that even in a small community, even within an extended family, the lines of resentment run deep, dividing those who pride themselves as managing on their own against those who have fallen into a state of dependency or worse. Commenting on poor people he sees using cell phones, he writes, "I could never understand why our lives felt like a struggle while those living off of government largesse enjoyed trinkets that I only dreamed about."[38] Williams quotes a financial counselor whose clients are working-class people: "I found that they were much more likely than the poor to reject the government benefits. . . . They saw it as an affront to their dignity. I heard so often things like, 'I don't want a government handout; I can do this on my own.'"[39] The sentiment is captured in the comment of a civil servant interviewed by Lamont: "I have worked for everything I've got. Nothing was given to me. I did it all myself."[40] These sorts of declarations from the working class are common in the literature, conveying not only a great sense of self-pride but also a resentment of others "beneath" them, a resentment that functions as marking a boundary between themselves and those whose ranks they fear they may fall into one day.

Working-class resentment also aims upward, interestingly not so much at the rich, whom they tend to admire, but professionals—teachers, doctors, "experts," media elites—whom they perceive as "looking down" on them, mocking their values, their religion, their lifestyles, even what they eat. In some cases, this resentment is based on personal experiences. They resent teachers who convey a sense of intellectual superiority, treat them condescendingly or seem implicitly to scold them for not adequately educating their children at home. The same goes for doctors, whose medical advice they interpret as a critique of their lifestyle. Therapists, if encountered, are seen as meddlers. Writing about the 1990s, Barbara Ehrenreich recounts that her working-class father "could not say the word *doctor* without the virtual prefix *quack*. Lawyers were *shysters* . . . and professors were without exception *phonies*."[41] In her study, Arlie Hochschild disclosed that many of her Tea Party informants "felt obliged to try to modify their feelings and they didn't like having to do that, they felt under the watchful eye of the 'PC police.'"[42] Politicians are adept at amplifying these sentiments to their own advantage. In his 2020 senate campaign, Mitch McConnell asserted that Democrats were "looking down their noses at us all in what they call flyover country . . ."[43] What better way to convey a sense of being condescended to than the image of coastal elites literally *looking down at you* from thirty thousand feet!

CULTURAL RESENTMENT

One of our mirrors also reflects a different sort of reaction, this one only partially inflected by race, and more generally by a transformation in values universally recognized as marking the cultural history not only of the US but of the Western or developed world in the post–World War II era. We normally associate a "cultural revolution" with "the sixties," and all that this suggests in the public mind in terms of youth culture, the sexual revolution, feminism, the anti-war movement, Black militancy, gay rights, environmentalism, and more. In retrospect, these changes were set in motion years before that tumultuous decade, and, just as importantly, they have continued to mark Western culture to this day. But just as evident has been a conservative reaction, or backlash, against these trends, a reaction that has mounted a robust defense of "traditional" values, gender roles, and institutions, especially regarding the family, sexuality, and religion. All of this, which we looked at in chapter 7, comprises one of the basic narratives of the history of the last seventy years or so. It is a dual, or intertwined, narrative, which is to say that the "sixties" was not only a time of cultural revolution but of a sustained and powerful conservative reaction.[44]

The question is whether it makes analytical sense to separate out this particular reaction from other pretexts for the same dynamic—in particular, race, immigration, or downward social mobility. It does for several reasons. For one, it is quite plausible to assume that many cultural conservatives harbor few strong feelings about race, immigration, the economy, or other issues we typically think about when we try to understand resentment. Many devout Christians, both Catholic and Protestant fundamentalists, who otherwise might be somewhat open-minded or perhaps merely indifferent regarding these issues, voice passionate dismay when it comes to changes in gender roles, the family, sexuality, and a woman's reproductive rights. Indeed, these are often the single-issue voters who cast their ballots with their opposition to, say, abortion as their sole concern in choosing a candidate. But this single issue usually stands in for a cluster of concerns ultimately grounded in a deeply felt opposition to the revolution in culture of the last half-century. For these people, a world based on traditional values assumed to be part of the natural, God-given order of things has been upturned. The values they hold sacrosanct are no longer respected, but mocked. They feel superannuated, beleaguered, resentful. One of Hochschild's Tea Partiers felt that her religious devotion and family values weren't respected, that "she had to *defend* that devotion from a liberal perspective which she associated with a morally lax, secular, coastal-based culture." Another expressed disapproval of liberals' "moral laxity," but even more resented its imposition: "If you're gay, go be gay. Just don't impose it on me."[45]

Moreover, the belief, often exaggerated and certainly exploited by politicians and conservative pundits, fuels their resentment of powerful forces—often unseen—operating in the culture, not only undermining their values but also prohibiting them from defending and expressing them. Thus, compounding their resentment of a "culture of permissiveness" is their resentment of the silence imposed upon them by so-called political correctness. Self-censorship might be effective, even advised, in some contexts, but if practiced unwillingly, it can only breed resentment. One feels stifled, muzzled, unfree to express one's opinions—and even worse, somehow forced to mouth the pieties of the moment. From her informants, Hochschild concluded that "in the realm of the emotions, the Right felt like they were being treated as the criminals, and the liberals had the guns."[46] The reaction against "political correctness," so much a staple of conservative complaint, underscores a feature of resentment. For nothing is guaranteed more to elicit this emotion than the sense of being forced to hold your tongue. After all, you're an adult! You spent your childhood having your speech monitored at home and at school, in all likelihood. How demeaning to have the PC "thought police" tell you what you can and can't say about various people and issues. Responding to the mandated use of gender-neutral pronouns in Ontario, the contrarian philosopher Jordan Peterson asserted that such imperatives would give rise to "silent slavery, with all the repression and resentment that that will generate . . ."[47]

Finally, as Pippa Norris and Ronald Inglehart point out in their transnational study, *Cultural Backlash: Trump, Brexit, and Authoritarian Populism* (2019), especially among the older generations, and increasingly over the years, there has developed a dawning realization that all that these sorts of people hold as dear and true has steadily given way to what the authors call a post-materialist set of values embraced by the young.[48] Moreover, by the new millennium, these had become dominant. This is, then, another variation of the theme of the "left behind." Only here it is not so much a matter of being surpassed by outsiders, minorities, or immigrants— "intruders," those jumping the queue, who might well stir their ire. Rather, it's the sense of being culturally left behind by values and behaviors you hold to be immoral, threatening, and simply contrary to the traditional order of things. You are now a stranger in your own world. Indeed, in April 2022, seven out of the eight conservative men who participated in a discussion with reporters from the *New York Times* answered affirmatively to the question "I feel like a stranger in my own country."[49] The values you consider precious and that have guided you and your parents throughout their lives are now declared antiquated by the young, even mocked. It seems you see yourself and those like you in a kind of rearview mirror.

"SOMEWHERES" AND "ANYWHERES"

Norris and Inglehart emphasize age cohorts and generational differences as determinants to peoples' cultural orientation and the degree to which they identify with a "cultural backlash." Of course, like others who study such movements, they also acknowledge other factors, such as race and education, but also geography. And here the divide falls largely between rural and urban. In *The Politics of Resentment: Rural Consciousness in Wisconsin and the Rise of Scott Walker* (2016), Katherine J. Cramer considers "place" as fundamental to people's sense of themselves and ultimately to their political outlook, especially for those living in small towns. Cramer spent several years interviewing "ordinary people" in the rural part of her native state. Like Hochschild, she was concerned with the polarization that characterizes the American voting public, and again like Hochschild, she wanted to engage with voters she normally would not encounter in her largely liberal university town of Madison. She was guided by the hunch that observers like Thomas Frank, whose enormously popular book *What's the Matter with Kansas?* argues that people like this have been basically "hoodwinked" into voting against their interests, were wrong. And in her study, she concludes that these supposedly duped voters are in fact motivated by real interests and concerns beyond economics. "People *are* taking economics into account," she writes. "But their considerations are not raw objective facts. Instead, they are perceptions of who is getting what and who deserves it, and these notions are affected by perceptions of cultural and lifestyle differences. That is, in a politics of resentment, people intertwine economic considerations with social and cultural considerations in the interpretation of the world they make with one another."[50]

Their resentment, she finds, is rooted in a "rural consciousness" politically animated against elements they identify with Madison, Milwaukee, and urban centers in general, but in particular those associated with the state government. Their animosity is particularly sharp for public employees and bureaucrats, university faculty, state agencies like the Department of Natural Resources (which oversees hunting, fishing, and the environment) and anything else governmental and urban. They resent the intrusion of state agencies into their affairs, and they are also convinced that they are not getting their "fair share" of state revenues as compared to urban populations. Here, of course, racial overtones often inflect their resentment: when they criticize the allocation of tax revenues to "city people," they really mean "undeserving" minorities. As *New York Times* columnist Charles Blow writes, rural residents are "suspicious of big institutions and big government . . . located in big cities with big populations of people who don't look like them."[51] Cramer concludes that these rural inhabitants of Wisconsin are not, by and large, motivated by libertarianism, not by an ideology of "the less government, the better," but rather by a resentment against a government which, they firmly believe, serves others, not them.

This resentment is also cultural and, as always with this disposition, psychological in nature. The sociologist Robert Wuthnow has argued in his book, *The Left Behind: Decline and Rage in Small-Town America* (2018), that rural residents live in what he calls "moral communities." By this he does not mean that they are somehow better than urban people or that the latter are immoral, and he does not mean "moral" in the sense of good or righteous; it is not a value judgment. Rather, he means that these are communities characterized by an ethos of cooperation, mutual obligation, and belonging derived from a sense of place as crucial to their lives.

They are quite aware of the value of their communities and their virtues, just as they insist that what they have is peculiar to "the country," as opposed to the city. This awareness, however, is increasingly fraught with a sense of fragility. "The moral outrage of rural America is a mixture of fear and anger," writes Wuthnow. "The fear is that small-town ways of life are disappearing. The anger is that they are under siege. The outrage cannot be understood apart from the loyalties that rural Americans feel for their communities. It stems from the fact that the social expectations, relationships, and obligations that constitute the moral communities they take for granted and in which they live are year by year being fundamentally fractured."[52]

Wuthnow wants to emphasize the virtues of his now beleaguered "moral communities," but the disapproval and dislike of "others," especially city people and "outsiders" more generally, is inescapable, as is the sense of a divide between "us" and "them."[53] We can see this division in larger terms than the difference between rural and urban; indeed, for the British journalist David Goodhart, this is a distinction between those from "somewhere" and "anywhere." And this distinction implies an interesting reversal of values. Since virtually the beginning of human history, the characteristics of "civilization" were associated with rooted people, those living in permanent settlements and ultimately in (usually) walled cities, while nomads, itinerants, migrants, or those simply without fixed abode, were considered inferior, lacking in higher skills and capacities, and often threatening as well. Today, however, the values implicit in this distinction seem reversed. The "Anywheres" are those who early on in their lives are marked or (in most cases) primed for success—passing exams (often with the help of tutors), going away to college, following a career path to an urban center or perhaps even abroad (often supported by their well-endowed parents). "Such people have portable 'achieved' identities, based on educational and career success which makes them generally comfortable and confident with new places and people," writes Goodhart.[54] The "Somewheres," on the other hand, are the people they leave behind, whose identities are connected to family and community, who do not necessarily aspire to upward social mobility and increasingly find themselves estranged from forces and trends that more and more dominate the culture, that is, those associated with "Anywheres." The Anywheres are contemporary cosmopolitans, while Somewheres are rather provincial in their orientation (although anyone who has encountered the entrenched provincialism of many New Yorkers will wonder about this distinction). In any case, this is a distinction which, while obviously reflecting ideal types, suggests a whole bundle of factors beyond the merely economic—cultural, psychological, and geographical—giving rise to contemporary resentment.

POPULISM AND RESENTMENT

I love the poorly educated!

DONALD TRUMP[55]

The only thing is the unification of the people . . . the other people don't mean anything.

DONALD TRUMP[56]

You're stronger, you're smarter, you've got more going than any-body. And they try and demean everybody having to do with us. And you're the real people, you're the people that built this nation.

DONALD TRUMP[57]

Much of what we have encountered so far in this chapter might be sub-sumed under the rubric of populism. For animating the populist spirit is the conviction that the world is divided between "us" and "them," with the latter serving as a catchall category containing—either at once or at different times—liberals, the rich, cultural cosmopolites, experts, govern-ment officials, "Anywheres," and indeed any group that might be config-ured in the populist imaginary as distant elites, whose values, policies, and practices stand opposed to the righteous interests of "the people." Resentment against elites, of course, is a perennial feature of populist politics dating at least to the last decades of the nineteenth century. As the historian Michael Kazin points out, on the right there has long been "a deep suspicion that those who become real decision makers in the fed-eral government want to push their plans or ideas on ordinary people." The demagogue Joe McCarthy cast ordinary, right-thinking Americans as victims of the foreign policy elite: "Those who have all the benefits that the wealthiest nation on Earth has to offer—the finest homes, the finest college education and the finest jobs in government."[58] And it is a theme that has been revived under Trump, especially as elites now have been branded as stalwarts of the "deep state." As one of his prime defenders, Newt Gingrich, said on Fox News during the first impeachment hearings, "There is an entire class of people who believe that they should be making the decisions . . . and that the elected officials chosen by the American people are inferior to the brilliance of the career civil service."[59]

Those who study populism—especially those who perceive it as a threat to liberal democracy—view this animus toward, or suspicion of, elites as one of its distinguishing features. But this is not sufficient to explain the appeal of populist movements, for this anti-elite (not simply anti-elitist, which is something else) disposition has a necessary corollary which exalts the "people" as good or pure, or "real," or otherwise the moral opposite from those evil, corrupt, impure, or foreign elites. As Jan-Werner Müller has emphasized in one of the best recent treatments of the subject, populism is always anti-pluralist, which is to say, among other things, that it conceives of the people as an organic whole, as a sort of giant tribe of a unified populace that knows no real differences or distinctions.[60] "Put simply," he writes, "populists do not claim 'We are the 99 percent.' What they imply instead is 'We are the 100 percent.'"[61] Populism not only finds a way to demonize elites but to transform the weak, downtrodden, simply those reputedly ignored into the true heroes of the day—the "real" Americans, the "silent majority," "our" people. This is, then, a variation on the Nietzschean theme of the slaves overturning the hierarchy of values by recasting their own weakness as morally superior to the heroic ethos of their noble masters.

Nietzsche, of course, saw *ressentiment* at the psychological heart of this transformation; it was the disposition that allowed the priests to manipulate the slaves into viewing their oppression as a moral strength, not the utter debasement it really was. And as we have seen, the view of populism held by Bell, Hofstadter, and others—or at least the American, nineteenth-century version—branded it with the label of resentment, which they then transposed to other, right-wing movements. Are today's populists, with their inveterate animus toward elites, inherently resentful?

Populism has commentators lining up for and against. On one side are those who see authoritarian rulers such Bolsonaro in Brazil, Duterte in the Philippines, Erdoğan in Turkey, Modi in India, Orban in Hungary, Trump in the US, and others as populists of a sort, but populists who manage to exploit democratic methods in order to enact essentially illiberal policies. They embody, in this view, a somewhat new phenomenon—"illiberal democracy."[62] But there are others who hold out for a revival of the populist spirit of earlier times, an animus of ordinary people directed not so much against governmental or technocratic elites, experts, or well-educated inhabitants of the coasts, but rather at the rich, global corporate interests, and more generally against those people and policies responsible for the growing economic inequality in much of the developed world.

One of the newest champions of populism is Thomas Frank, the author of the 2005 best seller *What's the Matter with Kansas? How Conservatives Won the Heart of America*. In his most recent book, *The People, NO: A Brief*

History of Anti-populism (2020), he urges the revival of an older American populism, precisely the sort denigrated by Hofstadter and, in turn, celebrated by his New Left critics. Indeed, Frank rehearses the generational conflict between the older and younger historians—just as I do in chapter 5—decisively coming down on the side of the latter, whose political sympathies for the populism of the People's Party of the 1890s translated into a desire to see a renewed populist spirit in the sixties. Alas, Frank doesn't see that decade in those terms, but instead reminds us that student radicals, for one, regarded white workers in the image of the hippie-bashing, flag-waving, resentful hard hats who backed Nixon and his war—the shock troops of the "silent majority." Even worse, Frank bemoans the fact that recent expressions of populism—championing the working class, taking aim at corporate interests—have, rhetorically at least, been mouthed by such right-wing, Republican stalwarts like Pat Buchanan and, later, Steve Bannon. He sees these figures for what they are, disingenuous outliers in the orbit of conservative republicanism. Their populism is a "phony populism of the right." What he would like is something entirely different: a populism, perhaps as embodied by Bernie Sanders, but in any case a movement which harkens back to the Democratic Party before the seventies, a party, he insists, that worked for the interests of a broad expanse of the American populace of all races and ethnicities, especially working people. A party, in other words, that vaunted class and economic issues above those of culture and identity. "The populism I am describing is not formless anger that might lash out in any direction. It is not racism," he concludes. "It is not resentment. It is not demagoguery. It is, instead, to ask the most profound question of them all: 'For whom does America exist?'"[63]

It isn't just Frank or the New Left historians of the late sixties who reject a fundamental link between populism and a spirit of resentment. Even someone like Müller, who is no champion of populism—his book is a cogent brief against it—denies the usefulness of seeing this movement in psychological terms, that is, as symptomatic of an inability of people to keep up with demands of modernity. "One should at least face up to the political consequences of such psychologizing diagnoses," he warns. And one consequence is an essentially undemocratic impulse among liberals, who fail "to take ordinary people at their word, preferring instead to prescribe political therapy as a cure for fearful and resentful citizens." This is to deny as well what liberals would hardly deny for themselves: that especially in political matters there are reasons for strong emotions. "Simply to shift the discussion to social psychology," as Müller writes, ". . . is to neglect a basic democratic duty to engage in reasoning." Finally, he charges those "enlightened liberals" who would dismiss populists as filled with resentment of "repeating the very exclusionary gestures" of nineteenth-century liberals "who were wary of extending the franchise because the masses were 'too emotional' to exercise the vote responsibly."[64]

Müller's critique is more effective as a scolding of liberals than as a diagnosis of populism. Should the validity of an analysis really depend on its political consequences? Still, his comments should give us pause in the rush to see resentment at the core of populism—or, indeed, to explain any challenging political movements primarily in emotional terms, or worse, as psychological "symptoms." One of the reasons for writing this book, as I have noted, is my own concern that we deploy "resentment" too quickly, too casually, with little thought given to its disquieting implications.

It must be said, however, that most commentators assume that populism and resentment are joined at the hip. William Galston, a political scientist who served in the Clinton White House, identifies populism in pretty much the same terms that Frank disavows for it: it has always been, he writes, "protectionism in the broad sense of the term," standing "against foreign goods, foreign immigrants, foreign ideas."[65] Moreover, as Yascha Mounk and others have emphasized, at the heart of the rise of populist movements is what Galston calls, as a sort of counterpart to "illiberal democracy," "undemocratic liberalism." This regards the promotion by elites of rights and policies, programs and institutions, which, while furthering a liberal, progressive view of the world, fail to derive their legitimacy from popular support or consultation. That is, they are liberal but not democratic. The European Union is an example; so, too, are various trade agreements, regulatory agencies, court rulings, climate change proposals, lockdowns during the pandemic, and, most dramatically, generous immigration policies which, many people are convinced, not only work against their interests but arise without their consent. Of course, it would be hard to imagine governing a complex, postindustrial society, where technocratic expertise is essential, while at the same time preserving democratic consultation every step of the way. But this creates a situation of once-democratic societies suffering from a "democratic deficit." Liberalism and democracy are what Mounk calls "non-negotiable values," and the assumption in the post–World War II era was that these were inseparable. Recent history, however, has demonstrated that they are not.[66]

As a factor in the rise of populism, "undemocratic liberalism" clearly provides the seedbed for popular resentment insofar as people become convinced that their lives are ruled by distant, sometimes even foreign-based elites who operate in their own interests, according to their own lights. While this conviction can in part be attributed to the policies of neoliberalism and the forces of globalism, the felt impact is not necessarily economic. It is also psychological. Here, the recent book by the Harvard philosopher Michael Sandel, *The Tyranny of Merit: What's Become of the Common Good?* (2020) is helpful in suggesting that a culture of meritocracy—usually viewed as an unmitigated good in fostering a democratic society—actually functions to demean those who fail to succeed by its rules, and thus contributes to the rise of populism.

Sandel's case is a hard one to make, especially for liberal readers for whom meritocracy is an article of faith. A meritocratic system rewards talent, hard work, and everything we associate with "merit," as opposed to inherited privileges, fixed hierarchies, or other entrenched restrictions by which certain groups of people have historically maintained an unfair advantage over others. And who could be against that? However, this sets up another hierarchy, one which deems the success of some as deserved as opposed to others, whose failure is likewise basically warranted. Failure implies not bad luck, having the "wrong" parents, or being born into an inferior class, as it would have in times past. In those cases, you could at least console yourself that your dismal fate was beyond your control. Today, "failure implies a sense of inferiority."[67] Sandel cites the British sociologist Michael Young, who long ago "anticipated the hubris and resentment to which meritocracy gives rise." "It is hard indeed in a society that makes much of merit to be judged as having none," Young wrote in 1958. "No underclass has ever been left as morally naked than that."[68]

This is especially true today when a college degree is vaunted as the surest means to success. Americans are constantly being told that education is the pathway to upward mobility. While this might be true (although Sandel contests this), it is beside the point with regard to the deleterious consequences of a culture of merit. For this merely legitimates inequality: just as earning a degree is the passport for mobility, so the failure to secure a degree justifies one's lower station in life. "Even if meritocracy were fair it would generate hubris and anxiety among the winners and humiliation and resentment among the losers," Sandel writes. There is no doubt that many working-class people are convinced that elites look down upon them. Perhaps worse is that this sense is augmented by the "self-doubt that a meritocracy inflicts on those who fail to rise."[69] Among liberals, prejudice based on race, gender, sexual orientation, or religion is unthinkable. "Credentialism," he asserts, "[is] the last acceptable prejudice."[70]

Sandel prompts us to appreciate the range of possible causes of resentment today. It is not simply economic inequality, nor merely the result of globalism, nor the feeling many have of being left behind. The ethos of meritocracy, a seemingly unassailable value system, also must be considered in the mix. All of these are in play. But beyond these, beyond causes and conditions, his analysis suggests a consideration of the emotional depths of resentment, even surpassing a sense of victimization, so often invoked as part and parcel of this experience. At least for some, it comes emotionally freighted with humiliation. We normally think of humiliation as experienced by individuals—indeed, to be humiliated usually means to be singled out in a most excruciating, isolating way. But it can also provide a sort of glue, a sense of identity for a wide assortment of people who share what is called a "narcissistic fantasy" that they have been unfairly humiliated by those who think of themselves as their betters. And it was a fantasy expertly played upon by Donald Trump and other self-styled populists. We shall return to this "fantasy"—and features of the reality that has given rise to it—in the conclusion.

NORMALIZING THROUGH RESENTMENT, OR "YOU'RE NOT GOING TO EXPLAIN AWAY THOSE ANGRY WHITE MEN, ARE YOU?"

If nothing else is obvious about Trump's base, there is the fact, borne out by countless surveys, that his most stalwart and numerous supporters are white men, perhaps skewed toward those without a college education, but not without significant exceptions among degree holders. Like the factor of racial animus, however, the phenomenon of "angry white men"—as they are so often described—certainly constitutes a potent factor in the growth of right-wing politics in the US, which long predates Trump and the current moment. And, slapped with the label "toxic masculinity," it connotes a much wider phenomenon than implicated in partisan politics. It speaks to the proclivities of a whole gender and leads us into the most intimate spaces of our culture.

Is the concept of resentment helpful in understanding this bloc of "angry white men"? The answer is not as obvious as one might expect, or perhaps it's merely not so palatable to some. On at least one occasion when I have told a female colleague, a feminist scholar, the subject of this book, the response was something on the order of: "You're not going to explain away those angry white men, are you?" In a sense, of course, that's precisely what I'm doing, or at least that's potentially in the offing with the deployment of "resentment" as an explanatory concept. And not just for these men but for any group seemingly animated by bitter, revengeful feelings of being left behind—and wanting "to get back what's rightfully theirs." Even to entertain "resentment" as an underlying condition of their political orientation is to open the door to understanding, which to some people might seem a misplaced, disturbingly suspect indulgence. What's next—"understanding" Nazis, KKK members, Timothy McVeigh, Dylann Roof? "Tout comprendre, c'est tout pardonner?"

Of course, there's absolutely no reason to assume that "understanding" entails or leads to "forgiveness." Most intellectuals and scholars would agree that to attempt to understand highly disturbing, threatening social movements simply enables us better to deal with them, or at least to know what to look for when they appear. "Tout comprendre, c'est tout anticiper." This much would seem uncontroversial, at least for those committed to a reasoned approach to political life. But perhaps this does not adequately resolve the issue.

An alternative to resentment as an explanation for "angry white men" is "toxic masculinity," a blanket explanation for the egregious behavior and attitudes of many contemporary males. The term actually originated in the so-called mythopoetic men's movement of the 1980s, which strove to coax men to a healthier sense of masculinity, allowing them to recover a protective, "warrior" maleness, as opposed to the "toxic" masculinity that fostered anger, aggressivity, and other noxious traits. As the Australian criminologist Michael Salter has pointed out, however, "toxic masculinity" has come to be blamed for "rape, murder, mass shootings, gang violence, online trolling, climate change, Brexit and the election of Donald Trump." It has morphed into something of an intractable feature of men—or at least a significant portion of the male population. "When people use it," writes Salter, "they tend to diagnose the problem of masculine aggression and entitlement as a cultural or spiritual illness—something that has infected today's men and leads them to reproachable acts."[71]

Is it toxic masculinity "all the way down"? The problem with this kind of diagnosis is that, despite scholarly attempts at qualification, it tends to connote an intractable characteristic, indeed, an innate character flaw shared by an entire sex. It does what many up-to-date academics warn against: it "essentializes" maleness in very stark terms. To be sure, this does not characterize serious discussions of the phenomenon: those who consider it with any intellectual rigor tend not to focus on the intrinsic inclinations of men but on the malignant effects of a specific masculine culture. But discussions, especially in the public realm, are rarely rigorous, usually casting "toxic masculinity" as a pejorative diagnosis which does more to blame than to explain. As a foil to this tendency, resentment allows us to appreciate its usefulness: resentment is always a *reaction* to conditions or provocations. (Indeed, the original French root, *ressentir*, conveys this sense of feeling the effects of something.) It may lodge itself deep into one's entire outlook on the world, so much so that every thought is poisoned with resentment.[72] But just as with most criminals, resentful men are created, not born.

What, then, are the conditions that "create" resentful men? They are many of the factors I have already adduced in this chapter, although perhaps in more concentrated terms. The political philosopher William E. Connolly provides a succinct summary of these (to which we might add some). "White workers come to feel caught in a squeeze," he writes. On one side, the forces we could corral under the umbrella neoliberalism—predatory banking practices, deindustrialization, automation, authoritarian managers, decline of union protections, disappearing pensions, lack of health care—have conspired to render their lives unstable, their work prospects uncertain, a comfortable retirement unlikely, and, generally, their status as "real" men called into question. On the other, "they feel underrepresented by noble pluralizing movements in the zones of race, sexuality, gender and religion." He concludes, "A powder keg is thus waiting to be ignited."[73]

Of course, when a powder keg did ignite on January 6, 2021, it revealed that the angry, white (mostly) men were not primarily victims of neoliberalism or declining economic prospects; many were solidly middle class, some were professionals, one was a former Olympic medalist, one was a state legislator, and several were veterans. The overwhelming majority (85 percent) were employed; about a third had white collar jobs. Other forces, then, most ideological, some undoubtedly psychological, as opposed to economic, conspired to bring these men to storm the Capitol that day. Whatever motivated them was a complicated, or perhaps muddled, toxic brew of various resentments. Ostensibly they came with a mission to "stop the steal," under the delusion that the victory of their president had been thwarted by nefarious forces. But they arrived furnished with a bundle of ideological convictions, as publicly espoused by the Oath Keepers, QAnon, Three Percenters, Proud Boys, Nationalist Socialist Club (or NSC-131), No White Guilt, and other sundry groups of so-called militiamen and self-styled "patriots," who turned the 6th of January into a transgressive carnival of white supremacy and ethno-nationalism.[74] Some were likely not so sure why they were there, and many undoubtedly came along for the wild ride, wherever it might take them.

The dividing line between such men, those along for the ride, and those others whose violent, gratuitous actions might only be understood in terms of sociopathology—that is, those who are truly toxic—is not entirely clear. At the outer edge of the latter are men whose inclinations exceed the bounds of human understanding: the murderers and rapists, the wanton terrorists, the sadistic prison guards, torturers, and others whose penchant for violence and cruelty cannot be made comprehensible under the sign of such a universal disposition as resentment. But apart from these truly monstrous figures, there are resentful "little men," as dangerous as they are small, who remind us that Michael André Bernstein's "abject heroes"—all literary figures—have real-life counterparts. Moreover, their particular grievances, such as they are, point to the enormous impact of feminism in the contemporary West—women's gains not only in the workplace but also in establishing control over their own bodies, and how many men perceive these gains as both their loss and a threat. Here we leave the realm that can plausibly be identified with right-wing extremism, those supporting Trump as well as others, and into a much wider arena where the reflections of resentment are quite varied, and hardly limited to the ranks of the extreme Right.

TODAY'S UNDERGROUND MEN: THE "INCELS"[75]

On May 23, 2014, a young man shot to death several undergraduate women at the Alpha Phi sorority near the campus of UC Santa Barbara, and then continued his killing spree down Seville Road in Isla Vista, California. He subsequently died from a self-inflicted gunshot. With this act, Elliot Rodger, a twenty-two-year-old college dropout from a well-to-do family, made "Incels" a matter of public awareness. On October 1, 2015, Christopher Harper-Mercer, a twenty-six-year-old student at Umpqua Community College in Roseberg, Oregon, shot and killed eight students and a professor and wounded eight others. In a message drafted before his suicide, he praised Rodger. On April 23, 2018, Alek Minassian mowed down with his van a group of pedestrians in the business district of Toronto, killing ten and injuring sixteen. He left a message on Facebook: "The Incel Rebellion has already begun. . . . All hail the Supreme Gentleman Elliot Rodger!"

Except in the minds of these and a few other demented young men, there is no "Incel Rebellion." But there are Incels—men who are involuntarily celibate, and blame women, that is, young, conventionally attractive women, for their plight. And while these murderous actions are hardly representative of the behavior of those who identify with Incel culture (such as it is), the rhetoric of its followers suggests a mindset that is quite hateful indeed. Jia Tolentino, a writer for the *New Yorker*, spent time trolling Incel message boards and came up with a sampling of the rants. A typical one reads, "Women are the ultimate cause of our suffering. They are the ones who have UNJUSTLY made our lives a living hell. . . . We need to focus more on our hatred of women. Hatred is power."

Right before his murderous rampage, Rodger emailed a 107,000-word memoir-cum-manifesto to his parents, his therapist, some friends, and former teachers; he also uploaded a video to YouTube, "Elliot Rodger's Retribution." These two sources document in detail his grievances— the injuries and insults he supposedly endured from young women who spurned him, but also his resentment of his male peers who managed to "score." Some passages of "My Twisted World," (a text he posted online) could have been written by the countless alienated, lonely, socially inept young people found everywhere. "All I ever wanted was to fit in and live a happy life," he writes. "But I was cast out and rejected, forced to endure an existence of loneliness and insignificance, all because the females of the human species were incapable of seeing the value in me." He doesn't stop there, however, and his motivations are all too clear. In what he called his "War on Women," he would go after the women of Alpha Phi, "the hottest sorority of UCSB." He writes, "[These are] the very girls who represent everything I hate in the female gender . . . hot, beautiful girls . . . spoiled, heartless, wicked bitches." He would show them and everyone else who was "the superior one, the true alpha male." Those who have studied Incel culture—who have waded into the cesspool of their online postings—have given us a pretty good sense of their twisted mindset. "Misogyny" is only a starting point. Fundamental to their worldview is not only a sense of entitlement to the sexual favors of young, attractive women, but a desire for their utter submission, even degradation. One posting on the MaleForeverAlone reddit reads, "The female part of our species, though technically human, completely and utterly lacks the essence of being that one could call humanity. By lacking all empathy, compassion, self-awareness, and capacity for logic or reason, there is little to separate the femoid from a beast in the field." After the Toronto massacre, some Incels tweeted their support for "a state implemented girlfriend program." Elsewhere, a columnist mischievously mused that if we believed in redistributing wealth, then why not sex?[76]

Two forces at polar ends of the spectrum of factors help us understand this disturbing phenomenon. One, misogyny, is very old, virtually timeless, alas—the hatred, distrust, and debasement of women. The other is the still-new social media environment and various digital platforms— especially reddit, 4chan, and the website Incels.me—that have been absolutely crucial in fostering a sense of commonality among these loners, in lifting these present-day underground men out of their basements and bedrooms into the dark corners of the web, where they have found each other, and where they can cultivate together their twisted thoughts. Beyond these, a range of factors come to mind. Certainly, the various revolutions of the sixties and beyond, especially feminism, have inclined more women to be assertive and discriminatory with regard to their sexual partners. Likewise, the increased social mobility among younger people, especially the college-age cohort, has expanded the range of potential partners for both men and women. And internet dating and hookup sites like Tinder, Bumble, and Grindr have not only increased this range exponentially but tend to match people primarily according to looks. With these digital instruments, in particular, as Tolentino has suggested, "sex has become a hyper-efficient and deregulated marketplace, and, like any hyper-efficient and deregulated marketplace, it often makes people feel very bad."[77]

This perhaps suggests a more general explanation that evokes again the specter of neoliberalism. For the impact of modern globalism is hardly limited to the realm of economic exchange; it has infiltrated every crevice of contemporary life, both public and private. Sociability under neoliberalism has become increasingly transactional, as well as provisionally calibrated according to a person's fluctuating value. Just as millions of young people merely need to "swipe left" or click a mouse to find sexual companionship; digitized pornography instantly offers a dizzying range of sexualized images providing immediate sexual titillation, gratification, or release; and virtually everything can be measured, ranked, exchanged, or monetized, creating, in any case, many more losers than winners, it is hardly surprising that such a culture should stir up the sludgy passions of some of our contemporary underground men who react to this daunting environment with self-hate, envy, and resentment. Here is a broken mirror indeed.

VLADIMIR PUTIN AND RUSSIA'S HISTORICAL "DRAMA" OF RESENTMENT

Of all the violent men whose appalling misdeeds grab our attention, surely none, at the moment of this writing in the spring of 2022, looms larger on the world stage than Vladimir Putin. This martial arts devotee, often photographed bare-chested, at least once mounted on a horse, a self-described "hooligan" in his youth,[78] who is known, according to one news outlet, for "celebrating all things machismo,"[79] and whose most recent biography contains a chapter entitled "Autobiography of a Thug";[80] this former KGB agent and president of Russia since 2012 (and before that between 2000 and 2008), who has hardly made any attempt to veil his scorched-earth intentions in Chechnya and now Ukraine, might be considered as simply hell-bent on imposing his will by any means necessary. Why interrogate his motives or disposition beyond acknowledging him as just another virulently angry man, albeit one with a very large army and, apparently, much of a whole country under his command? Can't we simply brand him an authoritarian bully and leave it at that?

But just as I'm suggesting that the Incels or the "Stop the Steal" insurrectionists of January 6, 2021, cannot be dispensed with such bromides as "angry white men," so Putin, alas, clearly demands a deeper look into his psyche. In fact, Russia's invasion of Ukraine has given rise to commentary which, among other things, brings the two strands of my analysis in this book together—that is, "resentment" as both a concept (or "resentment-talk") and a reality. A range of commentators certainly have deployed it with striking regularity in this context. "Maybe we should see this invasion as a rabid form of identity politics," suggests the *New York Times* columnist David Brooks. "Putin spent years stoking Russian resentments toward the West."[81] The writer on politics and literature Paul Berman is at pains to draw a distinction between the "deep and thunderous fashion of the communists" and Putin's pronouncements. "It is the voice of resentment, directed at the victors of the Cold War," he argues. "It is the voice of a man whose dignity has been offended. The aggressive encroachments of a triumphant NATO enrage him."[82] And Jane Burbank, a Russian historian at New York University, casts his "brew" of "attitudes" and "complaints," especially those that regard Western "decadence," as "developed in the cauldron of post-imperial resentment."[83]

These assertions—and there are many more like them—once again suggest how readily "resentment" has found its way into the vocabulary of our contemporary discourse. But do they really land on target as an accurate and revealing analysis of Russia's, and Putin's, attitude vis-à-vis the West? In fact, a well-wrought reading of Russian history adds depth to this analysis, identifying collective resentment as the source of Russian nationalism, lying at the heart of its political culture since as far back as the eighteenth century.

This analysis is found in Liah Greenfeld's 1992 study, *Nationalism: Five Roads to Modernity*,[84] where she examines the development of national identity in England, France, Germany, Russia, and the United States, all, in her view, set on that course by collective sentiments of *ressentiment*. I have to confess here that, given the prominence of resentment in this well-known study, I originally thought it would find a place in my own account of the political face of this emotion. But further consideration convinced me otherwise, and for the same concern about how it is currently deployed more generally: in attempting to explain too much it tends to explain too little. In Greenfeld's rich comparative study, it seemed to me, behind the development of nationalism lay not so much resentment as emulation and competition. Except, that is, for the Russian case—there the diagnosis of resentment seems to fit. For among the intelligentsia in the late eighteenth and nineteenth centuries, a growing conviction about the superiority of Western ways bred a sense of inferiority which ultimately turned into its opposite—that is, a rejection of European modernity and a commensurate vaunting of Russian traditions and values: the Russian Orthodox Church, the Russian "people," the Slavic "soul." It was a variation on the "sour grapes" syndrome whereby one comes to devalue and despise what was once prized but is now beyond reach. Moreover, Western Europe—decadent, corrupt, even evil—did not deserve its presumptive superiority, a presumption which provoked, Greenfeld argues, a resentment which was formative in the development of Russian nationalism in the nineteenth century and beyond. "Again and again," she writes, "eager to prove its worth, Russia was forced to confront the West on its own ground, only to return, humiliated, to the world of inner glory, where it licked its wounds and thought of revenge. The very same drama was constantly reenacted . . ."[85]

Vladimir Putin has appeared as nothing less than a contemporary reenactor of this venerable Russian "drama." His own resentment against the West, and especially NATO, has been on full display in 2022. In his speech justifying the invasion of Ukraine, he repeatedly cast Russia as victimized by NATO's devious ways: "They have deceived us, or, to put it simply, they have played us . . ." Other comments are grist for Greenfeld's mill, evoking something of a culture war on the geopolitical stage: "they"—meaning the West—"sought to destroy our traditional values and force on us their false values that would erode us, our people, from within, the attitudes they have been aggressively imposing on their countries, attitudes that are directly leading to degradation and degeneration because they are contrary to human values." And he concludes, defiantly, "This is not going to happen."[86]

Putin is hardly alone in expressing resentment of the imperious influence of the West. Indeed, it is apparent that he has received encouragement by various public intellectuals to enlarge his grievances beyond a strategic concern with NATO and the like to embrace not only a "Eurasian" vision of Russia's continental hegemony, not only the ambition to restore "Great Russia," but also to vaunt beleaguered Russia as a moral bulwark against a decadent West. And chief among them is the man called "Putin's Rasputin," Alexander Dugin, a prolific philosopher cum provocateur (he has written fourteen books on Heidegger alone) whose ideological pedigree is firmly rooted the reactionary/fascist tradition that has perennially been a source of inspiration for those with a profound quarrel with the modern world.[87] True to form, Dugin's own quarrel is highly nationalistic and religious in character. According to one knowledgeable commentator, his pronouncements are "spiced with liturgical and quasi-apocalyptic terminology, which originate in a Christian-mystical world he is fond of."[88] In his 2009 manifesto, *The Fourth Political Theory*, where he advocates an alternative to liberal democracy, communism, and fascism, his Russian chauvinism is leavened with a heavy dose of resentment: "Dear Russian people! The global American empire strives to bring all countries of the world together under its control. They intervene where they want, asking no one's permission. They come in through the fifth column, which they think will allow them to take over natural resources and rule over countries, people, and continents." He concludes with this exhortation: "To resist this most serious threat, we must be united and mobilized! We must remember that we are Russian! That for thousands of years we protected our freedom and independence. We have spilled seas of blood, our own and other people's, to make Russia great. And Russia will be great! Otherwise it will not exist at all. Russia is everything! All else is nothing!"[89]

"It is possible that it is being reenacted right now," Greenfeld wrote in 1992 regarding Russia's historic "drama" of *ressentiment*.[90] Given that the Kremlin has proven quite receptive to Dugin's worldview, her words strike one as prescient.

RESENTMENT AND ISLAMIC FUNDAMENTALISM

Among the signs indicating a "return" of the *concept* of resentment, we surely must consider its use as an explanation for Islamic fundamentalism in general and jihadi terrorism in particular. These are not only very disturbing phenomena in Western eyes (and in the eyes of others) but also quite puzzling. How is it that in modern times an ideology based on a doctrinaire, militant, and dogmatic adherence to the (usually distorted) principles of a great world religion like Islam should prove to be such a powerful force, both politically and spiritually, mobilizing millions of people, especially in countries where secularism once seemed to be the prevailing, or at least rising, ethos? One need only think of the city of Lahore in Pakistan, as late as the 1990s a university town with all the trappings of a cosmopolitan culture, now a hotbed of Islamists; or Palestinian nationalism, once dominated by the secular Palestine Liberation Organization, now increasingly challenged by the Islamic Resistance Movement, or Hamas; or Turkey, constitutionally conceived by its founder Atatürk as a secular state, now declared a Muslim nation by its President Recep Tayyip Erdoğan. How did this religious movement—to be sure, hardly monolithic either theologically or politically—manage to establish its hegemony over a large part of the Middle East and beyond, and in such a short period of time? The puzzlement is only compounded by its most disturbing (though certainly not defining) feature, the expression of its militancy in the form of terrorism, especially suicide bombers.

The fact that this movement took Western observers by surprise is perhaps as puzzling, or at least in need of explanation, as the phenomenon itself. In short, "we"—that is, those looking at the post–World War II world with a liberal worldview—simply didn't see it coming. We were intellectually handicapped in two different but related ways. First, it defied the expectations and prognostications of most social scientists and pundits alike that religion would prove to be so robust, such a force in public life; it just didn't conform to the outlook of a modern, modernizing, and increasingly secular world. And this was true, by the way, not only for the Muslim societies but also for the US, where the dramatic emergence of Christian fundamentalism that began in the 1970s proved a potent force in the nation's politics. An inability to grapple with the emotional and psychological dimensions of collective movements points to the second obstacle to our understanding of this phenomenon. As noted in chapter 5, insofar as observers were able to muster an inclination to consider movements from anything approaching an emotional perspective, it was as *psychological* symptoms of maladjustment, irrationality, and abnormality—diagnostic terms hardly conducive to recognizing trends that did not conform to their vision of a modernizing world. As for appreciating specific emotions as a component of collective life, this too did not find a place in social scientists' tool kit, especially as most equated emotions with the irrational. It wasn't until the more recent "emotional turn" in the humanities and social sciences that observers began to entertain emotions as legitimate, important—indeed, omnipresent—factors in social and political life.

Given these obstacles, it is not surprising that one of the first observers to interpret Islamic fundamentalism as a symptom of resentment was close—generationally, intellectually, and in some respects ideologically—to the sociologists and historians I identified in chapter 5 as followers of the "Resentment Paradigm." Bernard Lewis (1916–2018) was a leading scholar of the Ottoman Empire and Turkey as well as the Middle East, a longtime Princeton professor and a public intellectual who often consulted with policy makers and politicians both in the US and abroad. It is said that he was the first to use the term "Islamic fundamentalism" as well as the concept of a "clash of civilizations" to describe the emerging conflict between the West and Islam, a concept that the Harvard political scientist Samuel Huntington would later appropriate for his 1996 book *The Clash of Civilizations and the Remaking of the World Order.*

Lewis first mentioned "Islamic fundamentalism" in a 1990 article in the *Atlantic Monthly*, "The Roots of Muslim Rage," with the unambiguous subtitle, "Why So Many Muslims Deeply Resent the West, and Why Their Bitterness Will Not Be Easily Mollified."[91] It is here that he explains its emergence as primarily a reaction to Western principles and values: "These are indeed seen as innately evil, and those who promote or accept them as the 'enemies of God.'"[92] The Muslim world, he argues—and it is important to note, as his critics did, that Lewis treats this world as a monolith, with little acknowledgment of the vast variety of adherents to Islam—has suffered the humiliating effects of Western advancement and superiority in political, economic, and cultural terms. The fundamentalists believe that two "enemies" confront them, both Western in origin—secularism and modernism. They have been overtaken by the West, suffering a loss of mastery, a loss all the more humiliating in light of the greatness of Islam in past centuries. Lewis dismisses the stock explanations for the sorry plight of Muslim countries today, especially imperialism. The French and British have left; the "Westernizing Shah," too, is no longer a factor. "Yet the generalized resentment of the fundamentalists against the West and its friends remains and grows and is not appeased."[93]

But Lewis does acknowledge the deleterious impact of Western influences on the Middle East: "For vast numbers of Middle Easterners, Western-style economic methods brought poverty, Western-style political institutions brought tyranny, even Western-style warfare brought defeat."[94] In this respect, he differs from his colleagues operating within the Resentment Paradigm, who did not see the resentments of American right-wingers as having any basis in material wants or objective conditions; their suffering, such as it was, stemmed merely from their loss of status. Lewis, however, ultimately discounts what he has just acknowledged: the "clash of civilizations" is rooted in an "irrational" reaction of "an ancient rival against our Judeo-Christian heritage, our secular present, and the worldwide expansion of both."[95] Islamic fundamentalism, not the social, economic, and political conditions in the Middle East, "has given an aim and form to the otherwise aimless and formless resentment and anger of Muslim masses at the forces that have devalued their traditional values and loyalties and, in the final analysis robbed them of their beliefs, their aspirations, their dignity, and, to an increasing extent even their livelihood." And in a passage that many have criticized as recklessly tarring Islam with a very broad brush, he declares that the "dignity and courtesy toward others" that once characterized this world religion has given way "to an explosive mixture of rage and hatred which impels even the government of an ancient and civilized country"—meaning Iran—"to espouse kidnapping and assassination, and to try to find in the life of the Prophet approval and indeed precedent for such actions."[96]

Lewis played an important role as both a public intellectual and adviser on Middle Eastern affairs, especially in the aftermath of the 9/11 terrorist attacks. The *Wall Street Journal* declared US policy in this period was guided by the "Lewis Doctrine." President George W. Bush seemed to evoke the "clash of civilizations" when he spoke in those tense days: "They hate our freedoms," he declared. "This is the fight of all who believe in progress and pluralism, tolerance and freedom."[97] Lewis was one of the strongest advocates for the US war in Iraq in 2003, and consulted frequently with Vice President Dick Cheney in the run-up to the invasion. A Marxist in his youth, Lewis became prominent among the neoconservatives and a familiar figure in the corridors of power in Washington; in this respect, he shares much with several of his intellectual kindred spirits who, at least in the sixties, operated within the Resentment Paradigm. Indeed, I think it's quite plausible to consider his critique of Islamic fundamentalism in 1990 as one of the last manifestations of that paradigm.

How strange, then, to realize that this critique—this evocation of resentment—has been echoed by one of the most celebrated thinkers on the Left in today's world. The Slovenian philosopher Slavoj Žižek, a self-described "radical leftist," who also calls himself "a communist in the qualified sense," holds academic positions at Kyung Hee University in Seoul and New York University. His vast and varied writings—he has written forty-six books, coauthored or edited another thirty-three, and published over four hundred essays and articles—are all over the place, touching upon everything from canonical philosophers, especially Marx, Hegel, and Derrida, to film, current events, and popular culture. He is an iconoclastic thinker, relishing paradox, provocation, and contradiction, inviting controversy, and more than anything resisting any attempt to be pinned down. He manages to stimulate, infuriate, and confuse his readers all at the same time.

Yet when it comes to the Muslim world, his views strike one as rather conventional. Islamic fundamentalism, he writes in his 2008 book *Violence*, is a way for Muslim societies to avoid "a total breakdown" in the face of modernizing forces; it functions as a sort of panic shield, a "psychotic-delirious-incestuous reassertion of religion as direct insight into the divine Real, with all the terrifying consequences that such a reassertion entails, and including the return with a vengeance of the obscene superego divinity demanding sacrifices."[98] This is hardly a measured analysis, to say the least, but then again, Žižek is not a measured writer. Several pages after this intemperate passage, however—"psychotic-delirious-incestuous"?—he manages to stumble upon an insight worth considering. The "terrorist pseudo-fundamentalists" are not even real fundamentalists. If they were—that is, if they were truly secure in their fundamentalist beliefs—they wouldn't be driven to mindless violence by "a stupid caricature in a low-circulation Danish newspaper." "How fragile the belief of a Muslim must be," he exclaims. More than their own beliefs, they are "deeply bothered, intrigued, fascinated by the sinful life of the non-believers," he writes. "In fighting the sinful Other, they are fighting their own temptation."[99]

While, like his other declarations, these are mere assertions devoid of any supporting evidence, this is a worthy point to consider. And he takes it further. Fundamentalists are fundamentally (so to speak) far from feeling superior to the evil Westerners "but rather . . . *they themselves* secretly consider themselves inferior." He goes further yet: Westerners only exacerbate their sense of inferiority with our "condescending, politically correct" embargo on expressing any sense of superiority over Muslims; this "only make[s] them more furious and feeds their resentment." For, he claims, they are really not so committed to preserving their identity; rather, "the fundamentalists are already like us, that secretly they have already internalized our standards and measure themselves by them."[100]

There is a lot that's "secret" here—prompting us to ask how Žižek has managed to gain access to the hidden thoughts of people he gives no indication of having spoken to or even studied. In any case, his analysis should remind us of another case we have encountered where direct testimony interestingly conforms to his analysis of Islamic fundamentalists. Recall the Salem witch trials and the central role of Samuel Parris, the minister in whose house the whole sordid episode began. Parris's sermons, as we noted, richly reveal the psychological complexities that presumably brought him and many of his parishioners to see witches all around them. While their accusations were directed at their neighbors who had broken away from traditional, Puritan ways, it is fairly clear that for many, their fear of witches was matched by a fear of their own potential waywardness and unruly temptations—that is, the devil within. Like most witch prosecutions, the relations between accusers and accused were close, often intimate; the "witch" was one's neighbor. And like all close relations, they were fraught with desires and fantasies, which strongly suggest a knowing fearfulness of and vulnerability to a changing world, which they projected onto others. Islamic fundamentalists are certainly not "our" neighbors, but the nature of the contemporary, media-saturated world means that "they" know the West very well—how could they not? We don't have to take Žižek's word for it that fundamentalists are (secretly) gripped by a conviction of inferiority vis-à-vis the West, but his analysis nevertheless suggests something we have encountered before in this book: that resentment usually entails a sense of proximity and mutual awareness often compounded by envy disguised as a moralizing disapproval.

IDENTITY, RESENTMENT, AND THE *THYMOS* FACTOR[101]

We should resist sequestering the phenomenon of Islamic fundamentalism in a zone of the exotic or uniquely disturbing, for the modern world has produced many varieties of fundamentalism, extremism, and terrorism as well.[102] More productive is to consider it as simply another variation on the theme of identity, an assertion of a particular identification of a group in the face of homogenizing, or in this case, Westernizing influences that are part and parcel of globalization. Just as "Somewheres" chafe at a world that seems to be increasingly dominated by the values and culture of "Anywheres," so adherents to different groups, resisting universalizing trends and assumptions, insist on their particular identities and the acknowledgment of their particular grievances.

It is, of course, not simply a question of "identity" but of "identity politics," a phenomenon which if anything is more pronounced on the left than on the right. Indeed, if there is a single, salient difference between the protests of the sixties and the movements that have continued to contest the status quo in subsequent decades, it is surely the emergence of "identity politics." "Identity" is mixed up with notions of individualism and human self-consciousness; it's been a feature of Western culture since the early modern period. "Identity politics," however, is quite new. But its presence in American political culture (and elsewhere in the West) has only expanded since the 1970s, as different groups have announced themselves, each claiming a distinct identity and a distinct set of grievances. It also continues to be an object of fierce criticism—from both the right and the left. From the right comes the charge of cultural separatism, special pleading, the trivialization of politics—in short, the degeneration of American political life into a "culture of complaint." Writing in the conservative magazine *National Review*, Jonah Goldberg asserts that basing one's politics on one's identity can only yield toxic grievance: it reflects a psychology of blame. And this, in turn, breeds resentment against those who have succeeded. "It is a theory of morality," writes Goldberg, "that says that the success of the successful is proof of their wickedness."[103] To Todd Gitlin, an *éminence grise* of the New Left, it represents a devolution from the Left's embrace of "universalism, common culture, the human condition, liberality, the Enlightenment project," or what he prefers to call "commonality politics."[104] In a 1993 essay in *Dissent*, "The Rise of 'Identity Politics,'" he writes: "The proliferation of identity politics leads to a turning inward, a grim and hermetic bravado celebrating victimization and stylized marginality."[105]

There are, in sum, two critiques of identity politics. The first sees it as lumping people into ready-made categories according to skin color, gender, sexual orientation, disability, or other criteria, thus squashing their individuality, reducing their claims to personhood to the nature of their grievances. The second echoes Gitlin and others: it is a politics of retreat leading to defeat. Identity politics not only signals and exacerbates the further balkanization of the American public into myriad, often competing groups, it also thwarts the kind of coalition building necessary for effective political action. "Moral panic about racial, gender and sexual identity has distorted liberalism's message and prevented it from becoming a unifying force," writes Mark Lilla, a professor of humanities at Columbia, in a much-discussed op-ed piece in the *New York Times*. Identity politics is essentially narcissistic, reflecting an indifference "to the task of reaching out to Americans in every walk of life."[106] Steve Bannon, Trump's onetime *consigliere*, gleefully agrees: "If the left is focused on race and identity, and we go with economic nationalism, we can crush the Democrats."[107]

But a third "critique" brings in the concept of resentment. This assessment is hardly limited to the right; Gitlin's commentary also raises the specter of victimization and marginalization. Is there a way to explore the relationship between identity politics and resentment without frontloading the analysis with a negative value assessment?

In many respects, Francis Fukuyama does just that in his 2018 book *Identity: The Demand for Dignity and the Politics of Resentment*. To be sure, he, too, worries that identity politics both takes our attention away from issues of economic justice and material concerns and undermines a sense of common identity necessary for a functioning liberal democracy. It is hard to escape the conclusion that he would like to see less of it, not more. But along the way, he offers an account that allows us to appreciate its emergence from a deeper sense of history, going back to the Protestant Reformation. Ultimately, it derives from a need for recognition, the "demand for dignity," an impulse he relates to the Greek concept of *thymos* (or *thumos*).[108] This concept is found in Plato, Aristotle, and other Greek writers, and to invoke it is to be reminded of an alternative conception of politics to self-interest or the fulfillment of wants. The Harvard political scientist Harvey Mansfield deploys *thymos* to remind us that politics and political science are not the same thing, especially insofar as the latter is ruled by material factors, quantitative methods, and rationality. "Politics is about what makes you angry," he writes, "not so much about what you want. Your wants do matter but merely because you feel you are entitled to have them satisfied and get angry when they are not. . . . Politics is about who deserves to be more important."[109]

The claim of entitlement, however, has not been equitably acknowledged across history. Up until the modern period, *thymos* was understood in terms of *megalothymos*, which only related to extraordinary figures and classes—rulers and aristocracies, martial heroes, the "great"—who would be recognized as superior. With the advent of democratic societies, *isothymos* more and more defines this impulse, as people expect to be respected on an equal footing with others. But here we see Tocqueville's analysis ratcheted up to a higher level: people are not only irritated by social differences that ought not to prevail among citizens in a democratic society; now we are profoundly miffed because our particular identities— identities rooted in our very bodies—are not accorded the recognition and respect they deserve.

This, of course, is the rub: historically marginalized groups have not been acknowledged in the most fundamental ways. Not only have Blacks, women, Hispanics, LGBTQ people, the disabled, and other "minority" groups been denied basic rights, but their very *identities* have been ignored, rendered invisible, or otherwise demeaned. Resentment, then, not simply anger or other strong emotions, characterizes their response. For at issue is not simply the satisfaction of a want, a set of demands, or the resolution of a particular set of grievances, although these are certainly relevant and important. It goes beyond this to a fundamental claim for recognition of the group's legitimacy, its dignity, its very existence, not only as a constituent member of society, which might risk dissolving its identity into the mass of the majority, but as a particular group with its own status. "A humiliated group seeking restitution of its dignity carries far more emotional weight than people simply pursuing their economic advantage," writes Fukuyama.[110] To be overlooked in this fashion should remind us of the metaphor of the queue: in the lineup of claims to personhood, your particular claim has sent you to the back of the line.

As his comments connote, Fukuyama, like others, tends to see identity politics as strategically co-opted by a politics of resentment. He is very clear in his preference for people "pursuing their economic advantage" rather than focusing their energies on securing recognition for their particular identities, especially when this leads to the splintering of the polity into competing groups. This is, of course, to repeat a common critique of resentment—that it tends to foster a turn inward, thwarting purposeful action, especially when, in the guise of identity politics, it has become in the view of some progressive critics a cheap substitute for serious thinking about how to reverse the thirty-year trend in most liberal democracies toward greater socioeconomic inequality."[111] He readily acknowledges the importance of recognizing the victimization of various marginalized groups of people in the course of American history—"the racism, gender discrimination, and other forms of systematic exclusion [that are] somehow intrinsic to the country's DNA." But he worries that focusing so much on these past (and present) sins will preempt a "progressive narrative" that can and should be told of the "overcoming of barriers and the ever-broadening circle of people whose dignity the country has recognized, based on its founding principles."[112]

It should not be terribly surprising to find these sorts of qualms about identity politics from a traditional liberal like Fukuyama. It *is* surprising to find an even more trenchant critique from Wendy Brown, the formidable theorist of radical democracy, and a fierce critic of liberalism and establishment politics more generally. But identity politics is in her sights: it leads nowhere in terms of a real politics, she argues, or at least a politics worthy of the name, which is to say that which aims not only to contest but to wield power. She wants feminists and others to shift their claims from "I am" to "I want this for us," from past injuries to an imagined future.[113]

Brown arrives at her critique by way of brilliant readings of Rousseau, Marx, Weber, Foucault, and especially Nietzsche. Indeed, Nietzsche, and in particular his concept of *ressentiment*, looms large in her analysis; like the German philosopher, she sees resentment as a twisted, politically unproductive attitude which, while it might provide solace to the aggrieved, ultimately entraps them in the well of their own powerless self-pity. A starting point is her insistence that the liberal notion of rights only "empowers" in terms of what state power can confer. Rights are "among the cruelest social objects of desire," the most devious mechanisms of social control. An insistence on "rights" thus confirms and shores up state power. An identity defined by injury in turn renders one's political persona in terms of victimhood, which then limits political action by the latitude of the injury. "Given what produced it, given what shapes and suffuses it, what does identity want?" she asks.[114] The answer is "protection"—from the state—rather than power.

Brown recognizes the impulses and even virtues of identity politics; certainly, unlike conservative critics, she hardly dismisses the legitimacy of the injuries which energize it. But she finally sees it as a form of retreat, the "instinct for freedom turned back on itself" surfacing "in the form of a cultural ethos and a politics of reproach, rancor, moralism, and guilt," precisely matching Nietzsche's notion of *ressentiment*.[115] As victims, constantly petitioning for redress and protection, partisans of identity politics are not only limited by the purview of their injury; their identities as "victims" call for a commensurately narrow conception of their political opponents. Indeed, these are not really opponents at all; they are not political actors who might be met on the plain of political contestation where the distribution or possession of real power is at stake. Rather, they are "perpetrators," from whom the only response—in fact, the ideal response—is "justice," not power. Identity politics sets up a relationship akin to Nietzsche's master and slave, only here it is between perpetrators and victims. It rewards the impulse of resentment insofar as it motivates a perpetual cultivation of grievance; because the very nature of one's identity rests upon injury, its perpetuation is an existential necessity.

Brown's searing critique of identity politics makes sense only in the light of her radical vision of freedom, a field of virtually endless possibilities, unconstrained by state structures, institutions, and established ideologies. Unlike the "liberal presumption of freedom," largely conceived as a "freedom from," the quest for freedom is a "permanent struggle against what will otherwise be done to and for us."[116] But, one might counter, are not deeply ingrained identities useful in this struggle, as a means of constructing and affirming a necessary level of political self-consciousness? And, one might further ask, to the extent that identities bring to public recognition injuries and other past wrongs, aren't they useful, not only in unmasking the real nature of powerful entities but also in providing the moral basis for contesting them? For this to happen, however, resentment must break loose from the mode of private grievance; it must indeed become *public*, which is to say that it needs to be recast and made articulate and comprehensible to others. As we saw earlier with Butler but also with the Truth and Reconciliation process, with this, resentment in essence becomes something else.

Resentment, then, can play a useful though still somewhat problematic role. For one of the features of a resentful disposition is to configure the world in terms of morally inflected players; it's basically a world that pivots around the opposition between good and evil, or, in this case, between victims and perpetrators. It is, to be sure, a highly simplified world view and one which almost always casts the victims as morally pure, thus encouraging a measure of self-righteousness that often leads to sectarianism, intolerance in the ranks, and a blindness to one's own errors and excesses. Still, a contentious movement purged of resentment would find itself denied one source of moral leverage. Resentment provoked because of a lack of respect and recognition accorded groups of people has surely been a motivating force in political struggles, along with oppression, denial of rights, or material suffering. The moral philosopher Axel Honneth has insisted on the inseparability of "recognition" and "redistribution"; it is not a matter of either/or, as some critics of identity politics have asserted. Rather, "recognition" has to be a component of any political dynamic toward equality. Without it, redistributive justice would be cycled through a hierarchical system marked at best by both paternalism and abasement. In this sense, as a way of demanding recognition, resentment has a fundamental role in the very constitution of political struggles.[117]

RESENTMENT AS A CONDITION OF LATE MODERNITY

Resentment is clearly a capacious concept, and thus susceptible to a range of applications which, simply because of this range and the different experiences to which it can be applied, risks becoming vacuous. Especially in the wake of recent political realities, has its meaning been stretched beyond any sense of usefulness? Does it mean so much so as to mean too little?

Indeed, there are those who would ascribe it to all of us—to you, me, and everyone—who see it as a default disposition of late modernity, as intrinsic to the emotional predicament of living in contemporary times. For followers of Freud, repression, sublimation, and the channeling of desire yielding a general neurosis are the emotional markers of modern civilization. For the existentialists, living in a godless universe is marked by anxiety and insecurity, with humans the only source of meaning in a meaningless world. In both, the individual is the unit of analysis. Another approach sees people's relations with others as key. And here, resentment, growing out of the very nature of any relationship, is both ubiquitous and inevitable.

René Girard (1923–2015), a literary critic and philosopher, is perhaps the most forceful proponent of this relational view of resentment. But it is grounded in his overall "mimetic theory," which strives to do nothing short of explaining the human condition. To be human, according to Girard, is to desire: humans are animals that desire. We don't, however, know what to desire. This can only be supplied by the Other, who, in essence, determines our desire. This suggests, however, more than a dyadic relationship between two people, more than the Self and Other; it is more complicated than that. For the relationship entails a third object—that which the Other has or embodies, which is to say that which they desire. "We assume that desire is objective or subjective but in reality it rests on a third party who gives value to the objects," he writes. "The third party is usually the one who is closest, the neighbour."[118] One admires or strives to imitate the Other—whom Girard designates as the "model." You want to possess what your model has. In the first instance, this entails identification, admiration, veneration, and other positive feelings toward the model, but it also entails envy, which then turns to rivalry: ultimately you cannot possess what your model has. As Girard writes, resentment is "what the imitator feels about his model when the model hinders his efforts to gain possession on which they both converge."[119] As Elisabetta Brighi comments, in an extremely intelligent gloss on Girard's views, "The fact that we imitate the desire of others makes us all ipso facto powerless and weak in relation to our models, whom we come to both admire and detest . . ." She adds, "This is not a characteristic of certain people, but a modality of our mimetic, common human condition."[120]

In this sense, then, unlike Nietzsche, who cast the underclass of slaves as uniquely prone to resentment, Girard does not designate a particular group or class of people as uniquely suited to its effects; it is a universal disposition. He is thus closer to Max Scheler in two respects: in seeing envy as the emotional core of resentment, and in positing that modern, democratic society is more susceptible to this relational sort of resentment, insofar as the ethos of equality invites an intense and proximate level of mimetic desire. In a recent introduction to his own work, he writes, "We live in a world where many people, rightly or wrongly, feel blocked or paralyzed, in all aspirations, obstructed from achieving their most legitimate goals. Individual psychology inevitably ends up resenting this permanent frustration . . ."[121]

It seems to me that one could arrive at this conclusion without the baggage of Girard's rather speculative mimetic theory: he is not a thinker who bothers to engage with the experience of actual people, either in the past or present, preferring to remain within the confines of literary and philosophical texts. One might easily elaborate on Tocqueville's view of democracy and, with some interpolation, come up with a quite similar diagnosis. Indeed, Stefano Tomelleri, a disciple of Girard, sounds very Tocquevillian when he suggests that democratic societies foster a "consolidated" resentment "where the equality that is produced at the level of values contrasts with striking inequalities of power and access to material resources."[122] (Tocqueville: "Democratic institutions awaken and foster a passion for equality which they can never entirely satisfy."[123]) And if we factor in the contemporary phenomenon of social media, with the attendant hyperawareness of what "others" have, do, and accomplish—all the wonderful lives your "friends" are leading, all the experiences they're enjoying without you, all the smiling faces of perfect children and excellent spouses, all the evidence of people busy networking and connecting but somehow managing not to include you, in short, all that digitally reminds you of what you both desire and lack—with all of this, the mounting measure of envy and resentment Girard sees as a feature of the late-modern world seems more than merely speculative.

But is this not, then, to expand the potential range of the resentful— which is to say, to just about every inhabitant of the world of late modernity—to the point where the concept loses all meaning? As I assert at the beginning of this book, we should be wary of applying this emotion so indiscriminately, if only because overuse of anything diminishes its value. If everyone's resentful, no one is; the ascription has to have the quality of a non-vacuous distinction. Still, as I have underscored several times, there is a powerful argument for seeing "modern" trends—the drive for equality, democratization, social leveling, extension of rights—as promoting general expectations which, if thwarted, violated, or ignored, give rise to resentment among the disappointed. On the other hand, my depiction of the many reflections of resentment in this chapter has privileged its presence, with some exceptions, on the political right, which, by all accounts accurately reflects the political temperament of our times.

We might conclude that we are left with two options: either resentment skews rightward politically, in which case its relevance, while certainly crucial, is limited and particular, or it characterizes the modern condition, and increasingly so, as our world becomes more and more a place where people constantly measure themselves against one another. But there is also a third option: that "resentment" is so deeply lodged in our vernacular discourse as to be not merely descriptive but prescriptive—basically functioning as a purpose-built lens which sees what it is designed to find.

Conclusion

Thinking about Resentment Today

We understand certain emotions to be more emotional than others. These are the emotions that tend to be accompanied by acts of violence or obvious somatic disturbances. That is, rather strangely, we most easily see emotions in others when their display engenders in us either fear or embarrassment.

WILLIAM IAN MILLER, *Humiliation*[1]

How narrowly or widely should we draw the circle around resentment? In a sense, each of the two paths of analysis I have tried to follow in this book to explain this collective emotion conforms to one of these options.

The first finds resentment most pronounced among those "left behind" or threatened by myriad and often unseen powers, and thus is somewhat narrow or at least limited in scope. It regards a specific population. These are people who perceive their fate as being at the mercy of various forces—economic, social, cultural—leaving them demoted, surpassed, or otherwise demeaned in ways that violate their fundamental assumptions about their proper place in society. The world has turned to their disadvantage. It has thus become an unjust world, but their sense of injustice is compounded by the conviction that once, in living memory, things were quite different. And not just different but right. Others—unworthy others, moreover—have taken their place. To be sure, as I have suggested, to be left behind is hardly a fate limited to recent times. One could argue that it is intrinsic to the very process of historical development—some people win, some lose. As we have seen (in chapter 2), even aristocrats in the sixteenth and seventeenth centuries could find themselves upended, excluded from the royal precincts of the privileged and powerful, usurped by parvenus and outsiders. Still, chapter 8 shows that the ranks of the left behind have burgeoned in the last few years, fueling the rise of populism and the extreme rightward swing of politics in the US and elsewhere. So if this development has given rise to a somewhat delimited sense of resentment, in our time its range has expanded dramatically, even alarmingly.

The second analytical path toward understanding resentment, however, is even more expansive in its reach. It potentially includes all of us who live in the modern world. For it posits resentment as an inevitable feature of modernity, especially in a democratic culture where the principle of equality reigns as a fundamental ethos. Equality, or relative equality, *should* prevail, but it doesn't, and resentment thrives in the space between "should" and "is." While democracy has hardly installed itself everywhere, the democratic spirit, as Tocqueville argued, is a feature of the modern, or at least the developed, world. There are forces operating almost everywhere which, if they do not necessarily promote democracy per se, have worked to instill in people a sense that they should be recognized and treated like others. But here too, as with the "left behind," these forces are increasing in intensity and reach, fostering an awareness of the lives of others which has penetrated almost every corner of the world. While economic inequality has increased markedly, both within the US and between different parts of the globe, it has also been psychologically aggravated by the perception of *relative* inequality, a perception which, given this imperious awareness, can only be ignored with great effort. And, as social psychologists tell us, perceptions of relative inequality or deprivation—that is, subjective knowledge of the *discrepancy* between your material well-being or status and those of others—play an even more decisive role in determining one's disposition, ill or well, than the objective conditions of one's life.[2]

In fundamental ways, these two understandings of the basis of collective resentment are analytically distinct. To highlight their distinctiveness, let us call them the "Left Behind/Threatened Model" and the "Comparison/Discrepancy Model." For thinking about resentment in terms of each might help us see different aspects of this collective emotion. The most basic difference, as I have noted, is the scope of their potential populations. The "Left Behinds/Threatened" are limited to those who, well, feel themselves left behind and/or threatened—a lot of people these days, but not everyone. With the "Comparison/Discrepancy Model" the feeling of resentment theoretically extends to everyone. But this then suggests differences of a political nature, although the differences are not as clear-cut. The Left Behind/Threatened Model portends a reactive dynamic which may give rise to rather dramatic, perhaps extreme forms of political expression, as outlined in much of chapter 8. It is a matter of people striving to get back what they have lost, or think they have lost, or worse, what they think has been taken from them, or maybe even worse, what they fear is *about* to be taken from them, which tends to promote rather fractious political behavior, as well as line-drawing between "us" and "them." While the Comparison/Discrepancy Model certainly does not preclude either fractiousness or polarization, it more often serves as an alert to injustice or inequity that should and can be rectified. It is here not a matter of getting something back but of getting something that, unfairly, has been denied. It thus can be aspirational. To once again cite the philosopher John Rawls: "If we resent our having less than others, it must be because we think that their being better off is the result of unjust institutions, or wrongful conduct on their part," he writes in *A Theory of Justice*. His conception of resentment is, we should note, mild and conceptually situated within the context of the pursuit of justice. "Those who express resentment must be prepared to show why certain institutions are unjust or how others have injured them."[3] For Rawls, resentment calls attention to injustice, which thus conforms to the Comparison/Discrepancy Model. It is less contentious than the resentment of the left behinds; moreover, as a potential feature of any set of relations where justice is the presumed goal, it is widespread in its purview, and largely agnostic in terms of its ideological orientation.

There are other differences between these two models of resentment, which I will discuss shortly, but for the moment it is necessary to consider how they might be seen together, rather than as distinct. One way is rather schematic, but still helpful. We might think of Comparison/Discrepancy resentment as a kind of baseline, potentially universal mode of the emotion, always at the ready in a society where people assume a level of equality, at least as a principle. It is, however, not an entirely different species of resentment from that suggested by the Left Behind/Threatened Model; it shares a basic emotional and psychological penchant to see a moral wrong and want to right it. Accordingly, I would propose that despite the conceptual distinction between my two models, we should not see them as entirely distinct, but rather residing along a continuum of resentment.

As inelegant (or perhaps even unconvincing) as this formulation might be, I intend it to serve as a necessary warning to those—perhaps many readers of this book—who are inclined to think of resentment as an emotional trait of "others"—which is to say, primarily the embittered and angry "left behind and threatened." In this sense, it is an emotion alien to "us," serving thus to reify the distinction between "us" and "them," in an almost self-fulfilling manner. And along with this assumption is the tendency to think of resentment in pathological terms, as a disorder of the maladjusted. Here, once again, it might be useful to remind ourselves of Frederic Jameson's criticism that resentment is often used to delegitimize people's claims and grievances; that it is "little more than an expression of annoyance at seemingly gratuitous lower-class agitation, at the apparently unnecessary rocking of the social boat."[4] To recognize that the disposition to resent potentially resides in all of us is to be cautioned against deploying the concept with this intent, or rather, to become aware that this is exactly what we might be doing.

But this is not then to suggest ignoring the different expressive modes and moods of resentment. The differences are crucial. In general, resentment of the Comparison/Discrepancy Model is easy to take, not only because the principle of justice finds acceptance almost everywhere, but also because it tends to be more civil, or at least more articulate than that exhibited by the "left behinds and threatened." We have already seen examples of this mode of resentment. Bishop Butler and others in the eighteenth century argued for a mild, "civilized" mode of resentment as a legitimate, even necessary means of having one's injuries recognized and addressed. The Holocaust survivor Jean Améry unapologetically cast his resentment as a protest against the tendency to relegate Nazi Germany's crimes to the oblivion of a fast-receding past; his frankly impolitic assertions were deliberately meant to arouse, provoke, and disturb his complacent contemporaries, demonstrating that sometimes resentment could serve as the weapon of last resort of the weak and forgotten. And similar expressions of resentment have also been a feature of many Truth and Reconciliation Commissions around the world in recent decades, resorted to by aggrieved plaintiffs as a necessary brake on a rush to reconcile with their victimizers without attending to and acknowledging their suffering and hurt.

These examples of resentment are, I would say, "acceptable"—that is, not only are their modes of expression measured, but most people would regard their claims as just and legitimate. But what if resentment is not civil, even if the grievance is acknowledged as just? What if it tends to violate general norms of public comportment, even upsetting them with its rancorous, angry expressions of an intractable discontent? To reintroduce a distinction I have deliberately avoided in this book between "resentment" and *ressentiment*, with the latter endowed with all the negative characteristics posited by Nietzsche: Should we somehow rule *ressentiment* out-of-bounds? Recall the comment of Leon Wieseltier cited in this book's introduction: "Resentment, *even when it has a basis in experience*, is one of the ugliest political emotions, and it has been the source of horrors."[5] The philosopher Sjoerd van Tuinen raises this issue, framing it in terms of the following question: To what modes of resentment do we accord the right of expression in the public sphere?[6] The question obviously breaks down into two parts: Who and by what authority are the "we," and what are the standards that determine the right of access? Time and again, protest movements have had their legitimacy challenged precisely because their mode of self-presentation does not conform to some tacit rules of public discourse and comportment. Just think of how often protesting Blacks or women have been dismissed as "angry"—for their noisy, persistent resentment—where the emotional tone of their claims is used to delegitimize them.

For many, it is easy to dismiss the resentment of the Left Behind/ Threatened Model, either because its mode of expression is angry, uncompromising, and often inflected with prejudice and racism, or because they cannot recognize the grievances expressed as legitimate. William E. Connolly recently encountered an unwillingness of the latter sort when he raised the topic of working-class grievances during a talk to a gender rights group. The response of his audience is telling: he "was told more or less politely by some that white workers have to accept a new position in the new world." This led him to reflect that "it might be pertinent to note how some academics with upper-middle-class backgrounds skate over binds faced by portions of the white working class, even when the academics carefully explore the circumstances of other constituencies in even worse shape." One reason for this "skating," he surmises, is "because the bearers of working-class resentments must not be allowed to disrupt the precarious and variable pluralizing achievements of blacks, gays, transgender movements, women and religious minorities."[7]

Connolly's auditors (a gender rights group) clearly were little inclined to think about these particular "left behinds" with sympathy, or even understanding. He says as much. If we were to interrogate them further they might respond, curtly, "Why should we?" Let us assume (somewhat unfairly, I'll admit) that they took these "working-class whites" to be not simply aggrieved but manifestly racist, anti-Semitic, xenophobic, misogynistic, or simply antidemocratic, and often violent as well. Does calling them "resentful" do anything to get us beyond these negative, irredeemable traits? In other words, what work does the resentment diagnosis do in promoting a deeper understanding of motivations and values of today's "left behind and threatened?"

VICTIMIZATION, HUMILIATION, AND RESENTMENT

You know, to just be grossly generalistic, you could put half of
Trump's supporters into what I call the basket of deplorables.
Right? The racist, sexist, homophobic, xenophobic, Islamophobic—
you name it. And unfortunately there are people like that. And he
has lifted them up.[8]

HILLARY CLINTON, September 9, 2016

"That one comment by itself may have swung enough votes," observed
the conservative commentator Charles Murray regarding Hillary Clinton's
notorious "Basket of Deplorables" speech. "It certainly was emblematic of
the disdain with which the New Upper Class looks down at mainstream
Americans."[9] In turn, Trump and his supporters gleefully jumped on the
occasion, deftly managing to turn Clinton's maladroit comments to their
advantage. "While my opponent slanders you as deplorable and irredeemable, I call you hardworking patriots who love your country," proclaimed
Trump in a speech just following her remarks. Days later he told a gathering that Clinton was herself deplorable because she "viciously demon-
izes people like you."[10] Mike Pence followed suit: "For Hillary Clinton to
express such disdain for millions of Americans is one more reason that
disqualifies her to serve in the highest office."[11] Trump supporters began
sporting T-shirts emblazoned with "I am a Deplorable." His campaign
even worked up a parody of *Les Misérables* titled *Les Déplorables*.

This was not the first time a Democratic presidential candidate mis-
spoke, their words quickly taken as a condescending put-down of their rival's followers. Recall that at the beginning of this book I mentioned then-
Senator Obama's comments in 2008 before a well-heeled crowd of donors
about how people in the small towns of Pennsylvania and the Midwest
"get bitter, they cling to their guns or religion or antipathy toward people
who aren't like them or anti-immigrant sentiment or anti-trade sentiment
as a way to explain their frustrations."[12] In his memoirs, Obama confessed
a regret for his choice of words; he also grudgingly acknowledged that
Sarah Palin's riposte landed on its mark: "In small towns," she said at the
Republican National Convention, "we don't quite know what to make of a
candidate who lavishes praise on working people when they're listening,
and then talks about how bitterly they cling to their religion and guns
when those people aren't listening."[13] In his 2020 memoir, Obama was
succinct in his reaction: "Ouch."[14]

These two incidents are not merely episodes in the sparring matches
between candidates that mark all campaigns. They reveal the potent work-

ings of resentment in the public sphere. And they might help us get "beneath" resentment and discover what other emotional and psychological forces have brought it currently to the fore.

First, they serve as yet another example of what is and has long been a feature of cosmopolitan elites' attitude toward—take your pick: the white working class, inhabitants of "flyover" states, people who watch Fox News, people who eat at Cracker Barrel (as opposed to Panera), people who drink Budweiser (instead of a craft IPA), "rednecks," "yahoos," "hillbillies," "trailer trash," gun-toters, fundamentalist Christians, people without a college degree, people who live in small towns, people who have never traveled outside their home state, people who shop at Walmart, people who ignore the wisdom of experts . . . the list is long.[15] It's one thing when these condescending ascriptions are passed around in college common rooms and over cocktails, but it's never a matter of simply that; the word always gets out. Perhaps long ago, elites felt confident that their disparaging remarks about the lower orders would remain *entre nous*, even when they found their way into print, given the low level of literacy. But in the mid-nineteenth century, looking back on the years before the French Revolution, Alexis de Tocqueville wasn't so sure. In *The Old Regime and the French Revolution*, he writes about elite officials and the privileged few talking openly about things the masses should not hear, assuming they were "not only dumb but hard of hearing." They talked "about them in their presence, as if they were not there."[16] In short, the masses have always been listening. And if they don't quite catch on, today there's always the likes of Tucker Carlson to clue them in.

This, then, lends some credibility to the sentiment that lies at the heart of populism and the resentment upon which it feeds—the perceived chasm, fraught with antagonism, between "the people" and distant elites, a separation that is as much moral as ideological. This kind of talk strongly suggests that this morally inflected chasm is not merely a fantasy of "the people" nor solely foisted upon them by opportunistic media voices. It is real. And if cosmopolitan elites were candid with themselves and a bit more self-aware, they would acknowledge the cost of such public expressions of condescension, even contempt. Of course, distinctions must be made between legitimate criticisms of ideas and attitudes that are simply bigoted, hateful, or dangerous, for which there is no cause for reticence or self-censorship (quite the contrary), and the gratuitous mocking of some people's values, lifestyles or deeply held beliefs. (It's puzzling that the same sorts of people who exhibit a punctilious respect for the traditions and culture of inhabitants of a foreign country they're visiting, even if these are strange and somewhat off-putting, experience no compunction in ridiculing the lifestyle traits of their American compatriots.) The difficulty arises when it comes to something like the proclamation of "white privilege" indiscriminately applied to a whole populace. On a basic level, the assertion is simply true: all white people are indeed privileged relative to Blacks, insofar as they have not been profoundly and woefully disadvantaged by the legacy and persistence of racism in all its myriad forms. But could anyone reasonably be surprised if poor or working-class whites, especially those who in recent years have experienced a precipitous decline in their material well-being and economic prospects, respond to the assertion that they are somehow "privileged" with an incredulous, resentful "Huh?"

How should we understand this response as it relates to resentment? In one sense, it merely shows us one more example of people feeling victimized, which fuels the populist impulse as much as it serves as a prerequisite to resentment. Without the conviction of victimization, resentment is not possible, and this is as true for Bishop Butler's mild, civil understanding of resentment as a necessary goad to justice as it is for today's "left behinds and threatened" who see themselves as victims of liberal elites, government officials, racial preferences, global capitalism, mainstream news media, Hollywood moguls, changes in cultural mores, "caravans" of immigrants, etc. But an added ingredient to being victimized is the sense of humiliation, only here, I would suggest, the degree to which this emotion is pronounced tells us something about—might indeed help us predict—the mode, measure, and mood of resentment.

Trump certainly exhibited an uncanny ability to play upon his followers' sense of humiliation, as was demonstrated profusely in the way he continued to capitalize on Hillary Clinton's "basket of deplorables" remarks. "She and her wealthy donors had a good laugh," he said in a speech in Baltimore. "They were laughing at the very people who pave the roads she drives on, paint the buildings she speaks in, and keep the lights on in her auditorium . . . she mocks and demeans hardworking Americans. . . . She revealed herself to be a person who looks down on the proud citizens of our country as subjects to rule over."[17] Later, he remarked, "The Clintons end up with the money, and America ends up with the humiliation."[18] In his address to the Republican National Convention in 2016, he announced this as a theme of his campaign: Americans had "lived through one international humiliation after another. . . . The humiliation of our country never seems to end. . . . Let us not let our great country be laughed at anymore."[19] Whatever acts of humiliation he was referring to did not really matter; the evocation of being laughed at, a humiliating experience anyone could relate to, did the trick. During the campaign, he did in fact point to the incident of some US sailors being detained by the Iranian navy, and exploited it to discuss an important issue of foreign policy in emotional, even personal, terms: "You see the way they captured our ten sailors 'cause they were a little bit in the wrong waters. And instead of saying nicely, 'Hey, listen. You gotta be over there a little bit,' they humiliated the sailors, humiliated their families, and humiliated our country."[20] And on January 6, 2021, he told his "Stop the Steal" supporters moments before they stormed the Capitol, "You're stronger, you're smarter, you've got more going than anybody. And they try and demean everybody having to do with us. And you're the real people, you're the people who build this nation."[21] A videotaped message later that day harped on the same theme: "I know your pain. I know you're hurt. You see the way others are treated that are so bad and evil. I know how you feel."[22]

Combining victimization with humiliation breeds a very potent version of resentment, indeed. We see it elsewhere wherever resentment adds fuel to division and contentiousness in public life. During the Brexit campaign in Britain, advocates for withdrawal from the European Union played upon the theme with aplomb, casting their country as having been "dictated to" by nefarious elites in Brussels and Strasbourg, unfairly treated by those far-off officials, forced to accept immigrants, and otherwise demeaned by European officials whose interests were contrary (viz., "foreign") to the time-honored ways of "this sceptered isle." Boris Johnson even drew an analogy between the EU and other plans to establish a pan-European entity at Britain's expense: "Napoleon, Hitler, various people tried this out and it ends tragically. The EU is an attempt to do this by different methods."[23] The same combination of victimhood and humiliation was central to the myth of the "Lost Cause" of the defeated Confederacy, which insisted that the American Civil War had nothing to do with slavery but was only a righteous defense of states' rights. If the South was defeated, so goes this myth, it was only because it was confronted by a rapacious Union army which practiced scorched-earth tactics, devoid of any remnant of chivalry, supported by a tyrannical government, and backed by an industrial behemoth which could function only because it exploited the ("real") slave labor of immigrant workers. Not only was the South defeated, but in defeat it was dishonored by the humiliation of Reconstruction and subjected to a demeaning, exploitative misrule by "scalliwags," northern carpetbaggers, and former slaves, which left this once-noble, rich, and pastoral land prostrate, impoverished, and dishonored.[24] The same combination operated in the context of the Holocaust, especially where genocidal actions were staged on the local level between different ethnic communities. In Omer Bartov's study of the mass killings of Jews in the town of Buczacz (then in Eastern Poland, now in Ukraine), we see Poles, Ukrainians, and Jews in the twentieth century in an uneasy set of relationships; depending upon the period and the ruling powers, sometimes the Poles, sometimes the Ukrainians were on top. But animosity between them was still rife: "Each group's conviction in the uniqueness of its own victimhood . . . went hand in hand with a desire to punish those associated with its suffering . . ."[25] Despite their antagonism, however, Poles and Ukrainians grudgingly recognized each other as entitled to rule. Not so the Jews, who nevertheless managed to gain positions of power during the Soviet occupation. With this, Poles and Ukrainians were for once of one mind: to be ruled over by Jews was intolerable. It was a humiliation which would not be forgotten. So once the Soviets were expelled by the German army, the resentments of the Poles and Ukrainians were unleashed in a murderous, face-to-face campaign against their Jewish neighbors.

This last example not only shows us the link between victimization, humiliation, and resentment, it also suggests that with heightened humiliation comes even more vehement resentment. The hurt of humiliation is so profound, so basic in the ways it plays upon universal fears of being exposed, ridiculed, and demeaned, that it can easily produce the kind of rage and even violence that supplies its own justification. And, like resentment, it tends to stick around. "Humiliation lingers in the mind, the heart, the veins, the arteries forever," writes Vivian Gornick. "It allows people to brood for decades on end, often deforming their inner lives."[26] Could we, then, imagine a different register of resentment if absent humiliation? I don't want to propose something like a "physics of resentment," but it might be useful for the moment to entertain a somewhat formulaic approach to this emotional disposition: *Victimization + Humiliation = Extreme Resentment*. And then, contrariwise: *Victimization – Humiliation = Civil Resentment*. Following these formulas, then, the Left Behind/Threatened Model, fraught with humiliation, predicts resentment of a rather disruptive sort, while the Comparison/Discrepancy Model portends a milder expression of the same disposition.

Let us assume that my two formulas are valid. What do they do for us? One might wistfully conclude that it would really be best if our public discourse (such as it is) could avoid the kind of talk that humiliates groups of people who are particularly sensitive to its effects. But, even if this were possible, it does nothing to preempt the way someone like Trump and his acolytes on Fox News and elsewhere so deftly manage to instill in their followers the conviction of grievous humiliation. Or one might draw a conclusion in the opposite direction: a sense of widespread humiliation among your followers is useful in galvanizing them to action—so encourage it! Indeed, we sometimes hear liberals bemoan the fact that their ranks don't seem disposed to display the same noisy, vehement contentiousness of their counterparts on the right. Where are the Tea Partiers of the Left, they ask? In Frantz Fanon, however, we saw something very much like this: how his own very poignant sense of personal humiliation as a colonized Black man bred a righteous resentment, which he then overcame by transforming it into the revolutionary ethos so eloquently prescribed in *The Wretched of the Earth*.

Thinking of humiliation this way, I hope, helps us understand its role in exacerbating resentment—indeed, in fusing with it to produce a rather potent collective sentiment, especially when it is played upon by political leaders and amplified by media outlets. But it should not then furnish us with yet another excuse to exile resentment from our emotional makeup, relegating it to the benighted and alien ranks of the "left behind and threatened." Throughout this book I have tried to push back against this tendency, calling attention to the potentially wide purchase of resentment, in different measures, to be sure, such that it can affect (and infect) all of us. This is only one reason why I have urged that we take care—and perhaps reflect a bit—before we reach for this concept to explain social and political phenomena, especially when they disturb and challenge us.

Indeed, lest some people think themselves immune to a "left behind and/or threatened" syndrome, let us recall that it might be built into the very process of the life cycle. The trope of the conflict between generations, especially between fathers and sons, for example, is as old as time. Freud endowed it with psychoanalytic, if also quite dubious, authority in *Totem and Taboo*, arguing that the prohibition against incest originated in the ultimately murderous competition between the father and his resentful sons over access to women. We saw an element of this in chapter 2, in the resentment of ambitious young Frenchmen in the eighteenth century yearning to ascend into the heights of Enlightenment culture, only to find their advancement blocked by a new establishment of gatekeeping *philosophes*, relegated to the literary lowlife of Grub Street. It's a dynamic that persists today, with several generations of well-qualified young people seeing their prospects frustrated because an aging cohort of baby boomers continues to occupy the positions—and the housing—which by all rights should become available to them in due time. These are young people whose quite natural expectations for progress in life are thwarted by their entrenched, inert elders who seem to be just hanging on for as long as they can. And (note to self), how could tenured professors of a certain age not be cognizant of the legion of newly minted PhDs who look upon them not so much as seasoned scholars valued for their sagacity, but as deadweight obstacles to their career hopes? These young people are not so much "left behind" as simply blocked, "threatened" with failure, and frustrated in their attempts to get on with their lives—a sense of frustration which is certainly fraught with resentment of their elders.

But the generational resentment can work both ways. Indeed, the sentiment of being left behind, strictly speaking, is more likely found in the aging generation as it prepares to shuffle off this mortal coil. At a certain point, one will likely feel superannuated, and resentment is hardly an unanticipated or unusual response. In Elias Canetti's sprawling study *Crowds and Power* (1960), there is a section titled "The Resentment of the Dead." Here the Nobel laureate meditates on the widely observed phenomenon across many cultures of the "universal *fear* of the dead." He writes: "They are discontented and full of envy for those they have left behind. They try to take revenge on them, sometimes for injuries done them during their life-time, but often simply because they themselves are no longer alive."[27] We don't really know if the dead are resentful of the living—as far as I know, no one has yet reported back to tell us. But the same feeling might be assumed for the "not-dead-yet." Many people in their later years come to feel the winds of change passing right over them, sometimes sweeping them off their feet. And while we might imagine this as a perennial sentiment for the older generation, it seems more likely, and likely more intensely experienced, in our contemporary age, with the velocity of change increasing exponentially. What member of the baby boomer generation—those onetime stalwarts of the sixties youth culture, once supposedly suspicious of anyone over thirty—has not experienced a twinge of resentment when confronted by the digitally deft, physically agile, media-savvy, luxuriously hirsute youth of today, whose very speech patterns strain the ears? Like Arlie Hochschild's "strangers in their own land," to be among the living yet a stranger in your own time is a recipe for resentment.

This, then, joins up with a more collective and politically potent kind of resentment, which I allude to in chapter 8. If anything has demonstrated the head-spinning and disorienting pace of change in our day it is the cultural transformations of the sixties, which have continued unabated ever since. That decade gave rise to the much-discussed "generation gap." Parents and children fell out, barely recognizing one another across this yawning divide that had to do with a lot more than long hair and rock music. Today, while age is surely a factor, what we might call the "culture gap" has morphed into the perennial "culture wars," a much more intractable divide. This is a division configured unevenly by several different categories of class, geography, education, religion, and ethnicity.

Those culturally "with it"—happy to embrace the liberating potential of ever-evolving values and new lifestyle choices—tend to be upper-middle-class urban dwellers, with more education and less religion than those who hold traditional values dear. But the fit here is hardly perfect. That, however, is not the point. The point is that the collective resentment of those "left behind" or "threatened" by a hegemonic culture is very much like an older individual's feeling of being beyond their sell-by date, only the political consequences ramify much more broadly. It's something like feeling betrayed by time or history, or, indeed, the culture itself. (One is reminded of Mark Twain's quip, "I'm in favor of progress, it's change I don't like.") Given the profound changes in gender roles, sexuality, sexual identity, reproductive rights, family composition, and other transformations that strike at the heart of intimate life, is it any surprise that those who choose not to embrace these changes do so not only with a strong measure of disapproval but with a pronounced sense of resentment as well? What could be better designed to provoke resentment than the very concept of "wokeness," which, despite all the virtues that might be ascribed to it, pretty much says flat out that those who do not embrace its virtues are, what, asleep? And it is by no means clear that this reaction depends on the vicissitudes of populism, neoliberalism, immigration policy, or any other changes in the offing. The cultural revolution of our day is, to borrow Trotsky's phrase, a "permanent" revolution. The reaction to it, as embodied by the fractious "culture wars," is deeply felt and morally inflected with resentment. It is likely permanent as well.

Both generational conflict and the countercultural legacy of the "culture wars" suggest a structural bifurcation of two blocs pitted against each other. And if these particular blocs don't always give rise to resentment, they might still serve as a model for a dynamic which often does. This evokes the distinction between "us" and "them" which is at the heart of populism, but it suggests a division that goes beyond it. And it is illustrated in the current opposition between those who have welcomed the COVID-19 vaccinations and the significant movement of anti-vaxxers who have not. Like the conflict between generations, resentment here is a two-way street. Whatever one might think of the anti-vaxxers, there can be no doubt that underwriting their resistance is not simply (or only) ignorance, but a fear for their own health and well-being, as well as a politically charged defensiveness of their autonomy—their cherished (if not fetishized) "freedom" as Americans. They resent those authorities who would force them to subject their bodies to this unwanted intervention. Their resistance, to be sure, is often also fraught with loony conspiracy theories—for example, that the vaccine is loaded with microchip tracking devices engineered by Bill Gates—but one must acknowledge that there are more understandable sensitivities in play, such as racially based, historically legitimate wariness of medical abuse, a fear of needles, or simply resistance to having a foreign substance inserted into one's bloodstream, suggesting all sorts of associations with the anthropologically ubiquitous concern with bodily "pollution." However outlandish or plausible these fears might be—or however cynically they may have been fostered and exploited by powerful forces—they have given rise to a collective resentment against those especially distant authorities who have instituted vaccine mandates or prescribed other prophylactic measures such as masking. To the argument that these measures merely serve and protect the good of all society, they answer, as one woman did, "Society will just have to wait!"

But as with resentment and generational conflict, what's sauce for the goose is sauce for the gander: resentment cuts both ways. Who among us who gleefully rushed to get vaccinated as soon as we could has not grown resentful of the anti-vaxxers whose resistance to this effective and reasonable measure is responsible not only for the persistence of this pandemic but for its potential to virally mutate as well? Like the current resistance to universal vaccination, frustration with anti-vaxxers is hardly new. When smallpox vaccination was made available—and backed by legislation in Britain in the nineteenth century—there was a host of resistors, whose obstinacy proved durable even when confronted daily with the horrible effects of this disfiguring disease. Then, too, impatience and frustration grew among those who embraced the new measure as a godsend. When the government relaxed mandates in 1898, Joseph Bell, a Scottish physician (the real-life model for Sherlock Holmes), bemoaned the measure as a "terrific experiment in murder," but then decided that "it may be needed to open the stupid eyes of men apparently impervious to argument or reason."[28] Few of the vaccinated today would admit to feeling pleased at the demise of the unvaccinated (at least not publicly). But if a measure of schadenfreude is really not right, resentment can hardly be a surprising response. Noting the reciprocity incumbent on everyone in society, the political commentator David Frum writes: "Something else [we] do for one another: take health care precautions during a pandemic. The reciprocal part of the bargain is not being upheld." And he concludes, in unmistakable tones of resentment: "Will Blue America ever decide it's had enough of being put medically at risk by people and places whose bills it pays? Check yourself: Have you?"[29]

This returns to something I have been evoking throughout much of this book: resentment's reach is quite expansive, touching even those who believe themselves somehow exempt from its grip. Might it be a symptom not only of ill feelings toward others whose stances provoke moral outrage, but a function of such polarization *tout court*? As Frum observes of the anti-vaxxers, "Pro-Trump America has decided that vaccine refusal is a statement of identity and a test of loyalty."[30] But this clearly goes well beyond the controversy over whether to get vaccinated or not. It's not only a matter of what other people believe or espouse, their opinion on this or that issue, but their identity, indeed, their very being. It was once taken as a truism in American political life that "all politics is local." If Tip O'Neill were alive today, I suspect he would have to concede that, no, it's "all politics is tribal." In tribal America (and elsewhere) where the lines drawn between the opposing tribes cannot be reduced to interests, particular policies, or even something as coherent as ideologies, but are fixed by allegiances to the group and one's identity as a member of the tribe, there can be no dissension without the stigma of disloyalty, even treason. And lest one conclude that this sort of tribalism exists only on the right, among Trumpists and their ilk elsewhere, think again: liberals and the Left are hardly immune to groupthink, or to a politics based as much on allegiance and loyalty as rational interests and ideology. In the twentieth century, left-wing sectarian parties often practiced excommunication as a means of purging their ranks of dissenting elements. Today's leftist cosmopolites would hardly countenance a recourse to banishment or ostracism as the price of dissidence, and yet . . . one does not have to be a Fox News devotee to acknowledge that a trip-wire sensitivity to ideological deviance can also give rise to cancel-provoking moral outrage on the left, just as it can on the right. Indeed, the very nature of a group which sees itself as occupying the high ground of moral rectitude is virtually constitutionally disposed to regard any deviance under the sign of betrayal as opposed to mere dissent. Try this experiment, which might bear this out: if you're on the right, voice some qualms about your tribe's view of the Second Amendment; if on the left, gently query a woman's absolute right to an abortion.

The pertinent question is whether tribal politics is a breeding ground for resentment. To be sure, a range of emotions is produced as opposing tribes regard each other—anger, incomprehension, impatience, even hatred. Resentment emerges precisely because of the self-constituting moral character of each group—its nature as not just a collection of interests or even a bundle of aspirations but, rather, a moral stance in the world—as well as the moral outrage each provokes in the eyes of the other. The very existence of each tribe is an obstacle to the realization of all that could be good and right with the world. Here it's not so much a matter of feeling left behind as having your moral position in the world—the moral integrity of you and your kindred spirits—threatened by those who would thwart it.

In a polarized environment characterized by tribal politics, resentment is more evenly distributed than one might suspect or admit. Still, it can't be resentment "all the way down," which suggests a question: What, even with this expansive notion of this emotion's reach, lies beyond it? Would it be helpful to think of what sort of strong emotions or psychological dispositions, those resembling resentment in their affects, nevertheless lack something essential to it? This returns us to a consideration of the difference between anger and resentment, which I touch upon in the introduction. It might finally help us be more precise about the elusive distinctiveness of resentment.

*   *   *

> . . . I tell you—and I tell this gentleman, and these young ladies, if they are friends of yours—that if I took my wrongs in any other way, I should be driven mad! It is only by resenting them, and by revenging them in my mind, and by angrily demanding the justice I never get, that I am able to keep my wits together. It is only that!
>
> MR. GRIDLEY, a character in Charles Dickens's *Bleak House*[31]

We might surmise that people trapped in conditions of extreme poverty with very little hope in the way of improved circumstances, or who are otherwise profoundly limited in terms of their life prospects, experience a range of emotions and outlooks—despair, anger, a nihilistic attitude toward life . . . perhaps, too, resentment, insofar as they look around them at a society of enormous wealth and endless possibilities and cannot help but feel resentful of those who have it so much better. But I'm not sure that we can conflate despair, reckless anger, or a nihilistic outlook on life with resentment. I would, in fact, argue that resentment is a "value added" which has the potential to lift people from mere anger, despair, or nihilism to a more meaningful disposition. Does it have then a purpose? Perhaps we should recall Kant's dictum regarding the quality of the aesthetic: it reveals "purposiveness without purpose" (*Zweckmassigkeit ohne Zweck*), which is to say a phenomenon that fulfills something for those who experience it but does not accomplish something ("purpose") in the conventional sense. Nothing is achieved, but something is created nevertheless. In terms of resentment, we might also recall something mentioned in chapter 6 regarding the function of resentment in creating a "holding environment" for aggrieved victims who find it difficult to accept the overtures for forgiveness from their former oppressors. D. W. Winnicott, the pediatrician and psychoanalyst most identified with this concept, posited it as a therapeutic space of safety, most evident as exemplified by the "good enough" mother. With some adjustments, I think we can see resentment as "purposive" in this sense, especially in fostering a group identity, where the group—or, in our context, the political "tribe"—stands for something. Resentment, in other words, endows the tribe with a collective attitude that can raise individuals from the depths of despair, mere rage, or nihilism. It provides a kind of moral ballast, a meaningfulness which emerges, not entirely from the group itself but more from the antagonistic relationship with the opposing tribe. As with Dickens's Mr. Gridley, it contributes to people's capacity to "keep their wits together" in the face of moral outrage—which is to say their opponents' equally intractable moral stance.

Thus, in many, though certainly not all, instances, I would suggest that there is a misfit between a foreshortened sense of possibilities and resentment, that resentment, for all the inwardness, paralysis, and twisted thinking that often characterizes it, still maintains a hold on the potential realization of something different. Resentment is deeply invested in time, in the sense of "before," "now," and "beyond." "Before" is the time of the "once was," when things were good and right. "Now" denotes a fall from that time, the now of being "left behind," itself a notion deeply rooted in a sense of time. And the "beyond" is the time after, when all—the correct order of things—will be restored. Even the "superannuated" old, who might feel resentful of the young passing them by, are not thereby necessarily bereft or in the grip of despair: their resentment stems precisely from a status once secure but now challenged. It is by no means clear that they have given up. Time inflects modes and degrees of resentment differently, with some promoting a greater sense of futurity than others. But I would argue that absent a prospective orientation offering the possibility of improvement, restoration, rectification, or some other positive modification of one's circumstances, whatever strong emotion we are dealing with is not resentment.

If I am correct, this suggests that without a sense of different or imagined possibilities, there can be anger or rage and all that it might produce in terms of violence, transgression, or a desperate outlook on life, but not resentment. Conversely, this, then, endows resentment with a quality that is likely to be overlooked by those who only think of this emotion negatively. For one thing, it brings us back to Nietzsche, who for all his disparagement of *ressentiment*, still acknowledged its creative role in transforming values with world-changing implications (to his chagrin, of course). We don't need Nietzsche to appreciate that resentment can be a goad to purposeful action, if often that purpose is woefully off the mark. But this appreciation also should prompt us to esteem resentment differently, that is, as a disposition which rises above inchoate expressions of rage or anger. It is not "nihilistic."

All of this might also prompt us to think somewhat differently, for example, about the January 6 insurrection at the US Capitol, an event which at this writing still haunts many of us like a bad dream. Just afterward, a good friend commented on this mob of "meth-heads." My thought was: would it were so. It was, of course, a mixed bag of Trump supporters, including many clearly very mixed up, just there to do whatever happened, especially if it meant breaking things and maybe even breaking in. And at this writing we are only beginning to learn more about the social profile of the participants and their varied aspirations. But by and large the insurrectionaries not only came with a very particular purpose—to "Stop the Steal"—but they were also imbued with an overall sense of purposefulness hardly characteristic of a mindless hoard of ne'er do-wells. In the early years of the Nazis' rise to power, many supposedly well-informed Germans dismissed them as just a band of thugs. Again, would it had been so. In short, we cannot afford to write off or underestimate a movement on the grounds that it is infused with the sentiment of resentment. On the contrary, this disposition is all the more reason why it must not only be taken seriously but also approached with a measure of understanding and, dare I say, empathy, as distasteful as this might seem to many. And lest empathy seem not only distasteful but impossible, given the subject (and subjects) at hand, I would only raise (again) the point I have been rather insistent upon making—that resentment's reach can touch all of us.

Is one to conclude, then, that resentment is everywhere, at least today, and leave it at that? Clearly, as I hope I have demonstrated, there are different modes and degrees of resentment, from a resentment infused with rectitude, as expressed by Joseph Butler and embodied in the stance of victimized plaintiffs in several Truth and Reconciliation Commissions, to the bitter ranks of the "left behind" and contemporary racists whose sense of white supremacy is more than tinged with the animus of racial resentment—and everything in between. Stretching the reach of resentment across this range might well dilute its specificity to the point where it is rendered meaningless as a useful concept. Indeed, as I note at the start of this book, one of my concerns in exploring this subject was a niggling sense that we have been doing just that: applying resentment with a very wide brush across just too many political phenomena, thus obscuring much that needs to be looked at more carefully.

On the other hand, I would still suggest that we take seriously resentment's reach across the psychological landscape of our currently benighted political culture. This vexed disposition has seeped into the cracks and crevices of our collective mindset; no amount of fine-tuning or analytical care can obviate the sense that it resides among us, like a low-lying fog. Like a popular tune that has managed to become an earworm even to those who try to resist it, it will not be simply dispelled or pushed away as irrelevant to "our" way of thinking. Perhaps too, as I suggest at the end of chapter 8, it has evolved into such a reigning concept that we are now disposed to find it everywhere, simply because, like Beyoncé in her 2006 song "Resentment," we are "much too full of resentment." Or maybe this merely describes the author of this book: Have I become like the proverbial man with a hammer, for whom everything is a nail?

Resentment is a loaded concept: it must be handled with care. Resentment is a complex, many-leveled emotion: it should not serve as a pretext for facilely dismissing the grievances of people in its grip. The potential reach of resentment is wide, prompting us to be wary of ascribing it merely to those "others"—whoever they might be.

Notes

INTRODUCTION

1. Thomas B. Edsall, "The Resentment That Never Sleeps," *New York Times*, December 9, 2020.

2. David Brooks, "Scorn and the American Story," *New York Times*, October 14, 2021.

3. Maggie Haberman, "Trump Adds to Playbook Stoking White Fear and Resentment," *New York Times*, July 6, 2020.

4. Josephine Harvey, "Obama Says Trump Has Accelerated 'Truth Decay' in America," *Huffington Post*, November 16, 2020.

5. Edward-Isaac Dovere, "Joe Biden Names His Enemies," *Atlantic*, June 2, 2020.

6. Tom Switzer, "Trump Fans Flames of Resentment and Anger," *Sydney Morning Herald*, June 1, 2020.

7. David Remnick, "An American Tragedy," *New Yorker*, November 9, 2016.

8. Quoted in Thomas Frank, *The People, NO: A Brief History of Populism* (New York: Metropolitan Books, 2020), 236.

9. Leon Wieseltier, "Stay Angry: That's the Only Way to Uphold Principles in Trump's America," *Washington Post*, November 11, 2016, emphasis added.

10. German Lopez, "The Past Year of Research Has Made It Very Clear: Trump Won Because of Racial Resentment," Vox, December 15, 2017. Other examples of resentment invoked in various journalistic commentaries: ". . . certain forms of Republican insouciance about Covid are forged in the fires of cultural resentment." Ross Douthat, "How Will Blue America Live with Covid?" *New York Times*, October 20, 2021. A more recent quote reads: "On the right, meanwhile, nativism was growing. For those who were already stewing in economic or racial resentment, it had to do less with ideology than with a rootlessness of the mind—a loss of purpose, inspiration, and community." Evan Osnos, *Wildland: The Making of America's Fury* (New York: Farrar, Straus and Giroux, 2021), 316. Jamelle Bouie wrote in *Slate*, "Trump has never been . . . more clearly the head of the party of resentment" ("How Trump Happened," September 1, 2017). In 2018, Obama offered an unusual public commentary on his successor: the president was "capitalizing on resentment that politicians have been fanning for years," he said before an audience at the University of Illinois Urbana–Champaign. (Dan Merica, "Obama Slams Republicans: Trump is 'Capitalizing on Resentment,'" CNN News, Septem-

ber 8, 2018). "Trump Keeps Playing the Resentment Card," announced the title of an opinion piece by Albert R. Hunt in Bloomberg News in February 2019. "Trump is riding a powerful wave of white resentment," echoed the *Times of London* several months later in an article with that headline written by Gerald Baker (July 19, 2019). An opinion piece in the *Daily News* in January 2020 widened the scope of the indictment, targeting not only Trump but also politicians and others who attack him, from Bernie Sanders to the actor Robert De Niro. S. E. Cupp, "The Age of Haters: Our Politics and Culture Need to Break Free of Resentment," *New York Daily News*, January 29, 2020. The *Financial Times* linked the American president with Britain's notorious press baron using the same term: "Rupert Murdoch, Donald Trump and the Politics of Resentment" (Edward Luce, May 2, 2018). Michael Gerson, George W. Bush's former speechwriter, wrote in the *Washington Post*: "One of the United States' venerable, powerful political parties has been overtaken by people who make resentment against outsiders the central element of their appeal." Quoted in Thomas L. Friedman, "Lady Liberty Should Still Be Afraid," *New York Times*, March 31, 2021.

11. Quoted in Ronald Brownstein, "Trump's War on Expertise is Only Intensifying," *Atlantic*, November 21, 2019

12. Osita Nwanevu, "Cultural Resentment is Conservatives' New Religion," *New Republic*, October 22, 2020.

13. Andrew Higgins, "Wigan's Road to 'Brexit': Anger, Loss and Class Resentments," *New York Times*, July 5, 2016.

14. John Lichfield, "Just Who Are the Gilets Jaunes?" *Observer*, February 9, 2019.

15. Dayna Tortorici, "Reckoning with a Culture of Male Resentment," *Guardian*, December 19, 2017.

16. Roberto Stefan Foa and Jonathan Wilmot, "The West Has a Resentment Epidemic," *Foreign Policy*, September 18, 2019.

17. Ben Smith, "Obama on Small-Town Pa.: Clinging to Religion, Guns, Xenophobia," *Politico*, April 11, 2008.

18. Mayhill Fowler, *Huffington Post*, November 7, 2008.

19. Leo P. Ribuffo, "What Underlies Obama's Analysis of the 'People,'" *History News Network*, April 30, 2008. See also Robert Wuthnow's comment on Obama's "ill-advised 2008 remark," in *The Left Behind: Decline and Rage in Small-Town America* (Princeton, NJ: Princeton University Press, 2018), 3. In his memoir, *A Promised Land*, Obama himself admits that his comments were poorly conceived. There he writes, "I want to take that sentence back and make a few simple edits. I would say in my revised version, 'and they look to the traditions and way of life that have been constants in their lives, whether it's their faith, or hunting, or blue-collar work, or more traditional notions of family and community. And when Republicans tell them we Democrats despise these things—or when we give these folks reason to believe that we do—then the best policies in the world don't matter to them.'" *A Promised Land* (New York: Crown, 2020), 144–45.

20. William Shakespeare, *Othello, The Moor of Venice*, in *Shakespeare, Complete Works*, ed. W. J. Craig (London: Oxford University Press, 1965), act 3, scene 3, 959.

21. The bibliography on the historical study of emotions is by now vast and

growing by the day. Here is a sampling of some of the leading works: Carol Zisowitz Stearns and Peter N. Stearns, *Anger: The Struggle for Emotional Control in American History* (Chicago: University of Chicago Press, 1986); William M. Reddy, *The Navigation of Feeling: A Framework for the History of Emotions* (New York: Cambridge University Press, 2001); Thomas Dixon, *From Passions to Emotions: The Creation of a Secular Psychological Category* (Cambridge: Cambridge University Press, 2003); Barbara H. Rosenwein, *Emotional Communities in the Early Middle Ages* (Ithaca: Cornell University Press, 2006); Jan Plamper, *The History of Emotions: An Introduction*, trans. Keith Tribe (Oxford: Oxford University Press, 2015); Ute Frevert, *The Politics of Humiliation: A Modern History*, trans. A. Bresnahan (Oxford: Oxford University Press, 2020). See also Robert A. Schneider, ed., with Nicole Eustace, Eugenia Lean, Julie Livingston, Jan Plamper, William Reddy, and Barbara H. Rosenwein, "AHR Conversation: The Historical Study of Emotions," *American Historical Review* 117, no. 5 (December 2012), 1487–1531.

22. Plamper, *The History of Emotions*, 23.

23. "Fascism bears a different relation to ideas than the nineteenth-century "isms," . . . intellectual positions (not basic mobilizing passions like racial hatreds, of course) were likely to be dropped or added according to the tactical needs of the moment. All "isms" did this, but only fascism had such contempt for reason and intellect that it never even bothered to justify its shifts." Robert O. Paxton, *The Anatomy of Fascism* (New York: Alfred A. Knopf, 2004), 214.

24. Plamper, *History of Emotions*, 11.

25. Owen Flanagan, "Introduction," in *The Moral Psychology of Anger*, ed. Myisha Cherry and Owen Flanagan (London: Rowman and Littlefield, 2019), x.

26. P. F. Strawson, "Freedom and Resentment," republished in P. F. Strawson, *Freedom and Resentment and other Essays* (New York: Routledge, 2008 ed.), 1–28.

27. David Shoemaker, "You Oughta Know: Defending Angry Blame," in *The Moral Psychology of Anger*, ed. Myisha Cherry and Owen Flanagan (London: Rowman and Littlefield International, 2019) 69–70.

28. Pankaj Mishra, *The Age of Anger: A History of the Present* (New York: Farrar, Straus and Giroux, 2017).

29. Keith Oatley, "Why Fiction May Be Twice as True as Fact: Fiction as Cognitive and Emotional Simulation," *Review of General Psychology* 3, no. 2 (1999): 101–117.

30. All Bible verses from *The English Bible, King James Version: The Old Testament*, ed. Herbert Marks (New York: W.W. Norton, 2012).

31. *The English Bible: The Old Testament*, ed. Herbert Marks (New York: W.W. Norton, 2012), 83, note to Gen. 37:1–50:26.

32. Thomas Mann, *Joseph and His Brothers*, trans. John E. Woods (New York: Alfred A. Knopf, 2005), 423.

33. *The English Bible*, 84, note.

34. On this, see especially Bryan S. Turner, "Norbert Elias and the Sociology of Resentment," In *Emotions and Social Change*, eds. David Lemmings and Ann Brooks (New York: Routledge, 2014) chap. 10.

CHAPTER ONE

1. Robert C. Solomon, *The Passions: Emotions and the Meaning of Life* (Indianapolis: Hackett, 1993), 290ff.

2. All from Lina Minou, "To Take Ill: Resentment in Eighteenth-Century Context," in *On Resentment: Past and Present*, ed. Bernardino Fantini, Dolores Martín Moruno, and Javier Moscoso (Newcastle upon Tyne, UK: Cambridge Scholars Publishing, 2013), 73–74.

3. Thomas Dixon, *From Passions to Emotions: The Creation of a Secular Psychological Category* (Cambridge: Cambridge University Press, 2003), 3.

4. Minou, "To Take Ill," 74.

5. Robert G. Ingram, *Religion, Reform and Modernity in the Eighteenth Century: Thomas Secker and the Church of England* (Woodbridge, UK: Boydell Press, 2007), 52, note 41.

6. On Butler, see Christopher Cunliffe, ed., *Joseph Butler's Moral and Religious Thought: Tercentenary Essays* (Oxford: Clarendon Press, 1992); Bob Tennant, *Conscience, Consciousness and Ethics in Joseph Butler's Philosophy and Ministry* (Woodbridge, UK: Boydell Press, 2011); Terence Penelhum, *Butler* (London: Routledge, 1985). For the sermons, I have used *Joseph Butler: Fifteen Sermons and Other Writings on Ethics*, ed. David McNaughton (Oxford: Oxford University Press, 2017). The page numbers in the text refer to this edition.

7. Paul Avis, *In Search of Authority: Anglican Theological Method from the Reformation to the Enlightenment* (London: Bloomsbury, 2014), 308.

8. G. J. Barker-Benfield, *The Culture of Sensibility: Sex and Society in Eighteenth-Century Britain* (Chicago: University of Chicago Press, 1992), 103. On Butler as reacting to the controversial but ultimately quite influential views expressed in Bernard Mandeville, "*The Fable of the Bees: Or, Private Vices, Publick Benefits* (1723), see E. G. Hundert, *The Enlightenment's Fable: Bernard Mandeville and the Discovery of Society* (New York: Cambridge University Press, 1994), 126–39.

9. Paul Langford, *A Polite and Commercial People* (Oxford: Oxford University Press, 1989) 5.

10. Adam Smith, *The Theory of Moral Sentiments*, ed. D. D. Raphael and A. L. Macfie (Indianapolis: Liberty Classics, 1982), 110. Henceforth, *TMS*.

11. Quoted in Ashraf H. A. Rushdy, *After Injury: A Historical Anatomy of Forgiveness, Resentment, and Apology* (New York: Oxford University Press, 2018), 134. Rushdy's study is an important contribution not only to eighteenth-century understandings of resentment but also to more modern scholarship.

12. *TMS*, 37. For resentment and other "unsocial passions," see book 1, section 2, chap. 7, 34–38.

13. *TMS*, 34–35.

14. *TMS*, 34–35.

15. *TMS*, 95–96.

16. *TMS*, 84–85.

17. *TMS*, 76.

18. *TMS*, 76.

19. *TMS*, 340.

20. J. Y. T. Greig, ed. *The Letters of David Hume*, vol. 2 (Oxford: Oxford University

Press, 1932), Letter 406, 163; cited by Glen Pettigrove, "Hume on Forgiveness and the Unforgiveable," *Utilitas* 19, no. 4 (December 2007): 453, note 26.

21. David Hume, *A Treatise of Human Nature*, ed. David Fate Norton and Mary J. Norton (Oxford: Oxford University Press, 2000), 268.

22. Hume, *Treatise*, 268.

23. John Mullan, *Sentiment and Sociability: The Language of Feeling in the Eighteenth Century* (Oxford: Oxford University Press, 1990), 22.

24. Hume, *Treatise*, 268.

25. Hume, *Treatise*, 266.

26. Hume, *Treatise*, 268.

27. Hume, *Treatise*, 226.

28. Hume, *Treatise*, 206, emphasis added.

29. Hume, *Treatise*, 243.

30. Robert C. Solomon, "One Hundred Years of *Ressentiment*: Nietzsche's *Genealogy of Morals*," in *Nietzsche, Genealogy, Morality: Essays on Nietzsche's* On the Genealogy of Morals, ed. Richard Schacht (Berkeley, CA: University of California Press, 1994), 116.

31. John Rawls, *A Theory of Justice* (Cambridge, MA: Belknap Press, 1971), 533.

32. David Hume, "Essay X: Of Superstition and Enthusiasm," *Essays Moral, Political and Literary*, ed. Eugene F. Miller (Indianapolis: Liberty Fund, 1987), 73-79. First published 1777.

CHAPTER TWO

1. Paul Boyer and Stephen Nissenbaum, *Salem Possessed: The Social Origins of Witchcraft* (Cambridge, MA: Harvard University Press, 1974), 180.

2. Page numbers in the text refer to the online publication of *Publications of the Colonial Society of Massachusetts*, vol. 66, *The Sermon Notebooks of Samuel Parris, 1689–1694*, ed. James F. Cooper and Kenneth P. Minkema, distributed by the University of Virginia Press, 1993. https://www.colonialsociety.org/node/1188.

3. Boyer and Nissenbaum, *Salem Possessed*, 166.

4. Karlsen, *The Devil in the Shape of a Woman: Witchcraft in Colonial New England* (New York: W.W. Norton, 1987), 216, 217.

5. Karlsen, *Devil*, 217.

6. Paul Boyer and Stephen Nissenbaum, "*Salem Possessed* in Retrospect," *William and Mary Quarterly* 65, no. 3 (June 2008).

7. Erasmus, *In Praise of Folly* (London: Reeves & Turner, 1976), 132.

8. Erasmus, *The Complaint of Peace* (Oxford, 1802 ed.), 21.

9. Pauline M. Smith, *The Anti-Courtier Trend in Sixteenth-Century French Literature* (Geneva: Librairie Droz, 1966), 105.

10. Perez Zagorin, *The Court and the Country: The Beginning of the English Revolution of the Mid-Seventeenth Century* (New York: Atheneum, 1970), 44.

11. Zagorin, *Court and the Country*, 44.

12. See chapter 8.

13. Norbert Elias, *The Germans*, trans. Eric Dunning and Stephen Mennell (New York: Columbia University Press, 1998), 184.

14. P. W. Thomas, "Two Cultures? Court and Country under Charles I," in *The

Origins of the English Civil War, ed. Conrad Russell (London: Macmillan Press, 1973), 176.

15. Zagorin, *Court and the Country*, 92

16. H. R. Trevor-Roper, *The Gentry 1540–1640*, supplement 1 to the *Economic History Review* (London: Cambridge University Press, 1953), 26. To account partly for the continuity between late-Elizabethan and early-Jacobean cynicism in the Essex circle, Malcolm Smuts notes that, after the king's ascension, "Robert Cecil and his allies consolidated the dominance of the Privy Council they had achieved after Essex's fall—and Cecil's many enemies thus had reason to nurse their resentments" as the new reign unfolded. Malcolm Smuts, "Court-Centered Politics and the Uses of Roman Historians ," in *Culture and Politics in Early Stuart England*, ed. Kevin Sharpe and Peter Lake (Redwood City, CA: Stanford University Press, 1994), 35.

17. Passages from *Hamlet* taken from W. J. Craig, ed., *The Oxford Shakespeare Complete Works,* (London: Oxford University Press, 1974), 873.

18. Richard Van Oort, *Shakespeare's Big Men: Tragedy and the Problem of Resentment* (Toronto: University of Toronto Press, 2016), 68.

19. Van Oort, *Shakespeare's Big Men*, 86.

20. Van Oort, *Shakespeare's Big Men*, 67.

21. In Johann Wolfgang von Goethe, *Wilhelm Meister's Apprenticeship*, vol. 14, Harvard Classics Shelf of Fiction (New York: P.F. Collier & Son, 1917), https://www.bartleby.com/314/, 2000, 143.

22. Friedrich Nietzsche, *On the Genealogy of Morality*, ed. Keith Ansell-Pearson, trans. Carol Diethe (Cambridge: Cambridge University Press, 1997), 21.

23. E. P. Thompson, *The Making of the English Working Class*, (New York: Vintage Books, 1963), 12.

24. E. J. Hobsbawm, "The Machine Breakers," *Past and Present*, no. 1 (February 1952): 66.

25. Quotation in Adrian J. Randall, "The Philosophy of Luddism: The Case of the West of England Woolen Workers, ca. 1790–1809," *Technology and Culture* 27, no. 1 (January 1986): 12.

26. Jeffrey Wasserstrom, "'Civilization' and its Discontents: The Boxers and Luddites as Heroes and Villains," *Theory and Society* 16, no. 5 (September 1987): 680.

27. Karl Marx, *Capital*, ed. Frederick Engels, vol. 1, *A Critical Analysis of Capitalist Production* (New York: International Publishers, 1967), 429.

28. George Rudé, *The Crowd in History: A Study of Popular Disturbances in France and England, 1730–1848* (London: John Wiley and Sons, 1964), 227–228; see also Sophia Rosenfeld, *Democracy and Truth: A Short History* (Philadelphia: University of Pennsylvania Press, 2018), especially chap. 3.

29. David F. Noble, *Progress without People: New Technology, Unemployment, and the Message of Resistance* (Toronto: Between the Lines, 1995), 221.

30. Charlotte Brontë, *Shirley* (London: Penguin, 1994 ed.), 23.

31. Brontë, *Shirley*, 287.

32. See more descriptions of workers in *Shirley*, pp. 101–103: Moore calls Moses a "drunkard and swindler. . . . You no more sympathise with the poor who are in

distress than you sympathise with me. You incite them to outrage for bad purposes of your own. . . . [Referring to Moses's partner] You two are restless, meddling, impudent scoundrels, whose chief motive-principle is a selfish ambition, as dangerous as it is puerile. The persons behind you [referring to the group of men with him] are some of them honest although misguided men, but you two I count altogether bad."

33. Fredric Jameson, *The Political Unconscious: Narrative as a Socially Symbolic Act* (Ithaca, NY: Cornell University Press, 1981), 202.

34. Francis Bacon, "Of Envy," essay 9, in *Essays, Civil and Moral* (New York: P. F. Collier & Son, 1909–1914).

35. Robert Darnton, "The High Enlightenment and the Low-Life of Literature in Pre-Revolutionary France," *Past and Present*, no. 51 (May 1972): 81–115. For critical assessments of Darnton's view, see Haydon T. Mason, ed. *The Darnton Debate: Books and Revolution in the Eighteenth Century* (Oxford: The Voltaire Foundation, 1998).

36. Darnton, "High Enlightenment," 97.

37. Darnton, "High Enlightenment," 98.

38. Darnton, "High Enlightenment," 115.

39. "Distrust and anger against a government putting all fortunes at risk, rancor and hostility against a nobility barring all roads to popular advancement are, then, the sentiments developing themselves among the middle class solely due to their advance in wealth and culture." Hippolyte Taine, *Les origines de la France contemporaine* (Paris: Robert Laffont, 2011 ed.), 234.

40. Taine, *Les origins*, 237.

41. Pierre Augustin Caron de Beaumarchais, *The Follies of the Day; or, The Marriage of Figaro*, trans. Thomas Holcroft (London: G. G. J. and Robinson, 1785), act 5, scene 1, https://www.gutenberg.org/files/64953/64953-h/64953-h.htm#ACT_V.

42. David Bien's penetrating study of the Ségur reform highlights the cleavage within the ranks of the nobility, not between noblemen and the bourgeoisie. David D. Bien, "La reaction aristocratique avant 1789: l'exemple de l'armée," *Annales: économies, sociétés, civilisations* 29, no. 1/2 (1974) : 23–48, 505–34.

43. William H. Sewell Jr., *A Rhetoric of Bourgeois Revolution: The Abbé Sieyes and "What Is the Third Estate?"* (Durham, NC: Duke University Press, 1994), 64.

44. Sewell, *Rhetoric*, 7.

45. Emmanuel Joseph Sieyès, *What Is the Third Estate?* trans. M. Blondel (New York: Pall Mall, 1965), 61.

46. Sewell, *Rhetoric*, 61. See Sarah Maza, *The Myth of the French Bourgeoisie* (Cambridge, MA: Harvard University Press, 2005), 77, on Sieyès calling the nobility "counterfeit."

47. Sieyès, *Third Estate*, 174.

48. Marc Ferro, *Resentment in History*, trans. Steven Rendall (Cambridge, UK: Polity, 2010), 21.

49. William M. Reddy, *The Navigation of Feeling: A Framework for the History of Emotions* (Cambridge: Cambridge University Press, 2001), 198.

50. Quoted in Arno J. Mayer, *The Furies: Violence and Terror in the French and Russian Revolutions* (Princeton, NJ: Princeton University Press, 2000), 134.

51. Sheila Fitzpatrick, "Violence and Ressentiment in the Russian Revolution," *French Historical Studies* 24, no. 4 (Fall 2001): 588.

52. Albert Camus, *The Rebel*, trans. Anthony Bower (New York: Alfred A. Knopf, 1956), 17–18

CHAPTER THREE

1. Quoted in Frances Wilson, "You Can't Silence D. H. Lawrence," *UnHerd*, April 19, 2021, https://unherd.com/2021/04/you-cant-silence-d-h-lawrence/.

2. Brian Bailey, *The Luddite Rebellion* (New York: New York University Press, 1998), 42–43, 163. See also, Benita Eisler, *Byron: Child of Passion, Fool of Fame* (New York: Alfred A. Knopf, 1999), 324–30. In the aftermath of this episode, Byron penned "An Ode to the Framers of the Frame Bill," which ends with the following verse:

Some folks for certain have thought it was shocking,
When Famine appeals, and when Poverty groans,
That life should be valued at less than a stocking,
And breaking of frames lead to breaking of bones.
If it should prove so, I trust by this token,
(And who will refuse to partake in the hope?)
That the frames of the fools may be first to be *broken*,
Who, when asked for a *remedy*, sent down a *rope*.
(Eisler, *Byron*, 329–40.)

3. Charles Baudelaire, "The Painter of Modern Life," in *The Painter of Modern Life and Other Essays*, trans. and ed. Jonathan Mayne (London: Phaidon, 1995), 9. This essay was originally published in *Le Figaro* in 1863. Baudelaire is actually describing a "Monsieur G."

4. Charles Baudelaire, "Eyes of the Poor," in *Paris Spleen*, trans. Louise Varèse (New York: New Directions, 1970), 52–53. For a brilliant gloss on this text, see Marshall Berman, *All That Is Solid Melts into Air* (New York: Simon and Schuster, 1982).

5. Friedrich Nietzsche, *Thus Spoke Zarathustra: A Book for Everyone and No One*, trans. R. J. Hollingdale (New York: Penguin, 1969; 1980 printing), 86.

6. Friedrich Nietzsche, *Beyond Good and Evil*, trans. Walter Kaufmann (New York: Penguin, 1989), 115–17.

7. With apologies to that eminent contemporary political thinker, James Carville (1944–).

8. C. McEvedy and R. Jones, *Atlas of World Population History* (Harmondsworth, UK: Penguin, 1978), 18 and passim.

9. Quoted in John Carey, *The Intellectuals and the Masses: Pride and Prejudice among the Literary Intelligentsia, 1880–1939* (New York: St. Martin's Press, 1993), 3.

10. George Rudé, *The Crowd in History: A Study of Popular Disturbances in France and England, 1730–1848* (London: John Wiley and Sons, 1964), 5.

11. Charles Tilly, Louise Tilly, and Richard Tilly, *The Rebellious Century, 1830–1930* (Cambridge, MA: Harvard University Press, 1975).

12. Matthew Arnold, *Culture and Anarchy* (London, 1889; Cambridge: Cambridge University Press, 1971), 203.

13. Quoted in Carey, *Intellectuals and the Masses*, 7.

14. Quoted in Carey, *Intellectuals and the Masses*, 55.

15. For the deployment of this metaphor in the seventeenth century, see Robert A. Schneider, *Dignified Retreat: Writers and Intellectuals in the Age of Richelieu* (New York: Oxford University Press, 2019), chap. 3.

16. Peter Gay, *The Bourgeois Experience, Victoria to Freud*, vol. 3, *The Cultivation of Hatred* (New York: W.W. Norton, 1993), 221.

17. Jules Michelet, *The People*, trans. John P. McCay (Champaign: University of Illinois Press, 1973), 18.

18. Michelet, *The People*, 21–22.

19. Michelet, *The People*, 121.

20. Michelet, *The People*, 49.

21. Heinrich Heine, Michelet's contemporary, shared his sentimental view of the people. Viewing Delacroix's famous painting *Liberty at the Barricades*, he rhapsodized, "And here we have it! A great thought has ennobled and sainted these common people, this *crapule*, and again awakened the slumbering dignity of their souls." Quoted in Ronald Paulson, *Representations of Revolution* (New Haven, CT: Yale University Press, 1983), 21–22. See also Raymond Grew, "Picturing the People: Images of the Lower Orders in Nineteenth-Century French Art," *Journal of Interdisciplinary History* 17, no. 1 (Summer 1986): 203–31.

22. Nietzsche, *Beyond Good and Evil*, 193.

23. Quoted in Susanna Barrows, *Distorting Mirrors: Visions of the Crowd in Late Nineteenth-Century France* (New Haven, CT: Yale University Press, 1981) 87.

24. Hippolyte Taine, *La Révolution*, 2 vols. (Paris, 1878), vol 1, 81–89. Gabriel Tarde, writing mostly in the 1890s and the early years of the twentieth century, was probably the most sophisticated of the practitioners of the new discipline of sociology. He acknowledged Taine's influence, especially the historian's "never-to-be forgotten" description of the taking of the Bastille. And like Taine, despite the considerable subtlety of his analysis, he echoed the common trope of the crowd as a sort of beast. The mob, he writes, "is a strange phenomenon. It is a gathering of heterogeneous elements, unknown to one another, but as soon as a spark of passion, having flashed out from one of these elements, electrifies this confused mass, there takes place a sort of sudden organization, a spontaneous generation. This incoherence becomes cohesion, this noise becomes a voice, and these thousands of men crowded together soon form but a single animal, a wild beast without a name, which marches to its goal with an irresistible finality." Barrows, *Distorting Mirrors*, 141.

25. Charles Féré, *La famille névropathique* (Paris, 1884) 449; cited in Ruth Harris, *Murders and Madness: Medicine, Law, and Society in the* Fin de Siècle (Oxford: Clarendon Press, 1989), 69.

26. Harris, *Murders and Madness*, 78.

27. Quoted in Barrows, *Distorting Mirrors*, 164.

28. Gustave Le Bon, *The Crowd: A Study of the Popular Mind* (London, 1896), 16.

29. Interestingly, Le Bon contemplates a counter-factual version of the past,

one in which democracy prevailed long ago. Then, he surmises, such technological innovations as the mechanized factory and the railroad would not have been
possible, "or would have been achieved at the cost of revolutions and repeated
massacres. . . . It is fortunate for the progress of civilization that the power of
crowds only began to exist when the great discoveries of science and industry
had already been effected." (Le Bon, *The Crowd*, 56). Like Marx and Engels, he is
a willing witness to a new age characterized by class polarization, only for Le Bon
this advent is the result of the rise of the crowd, not the development of capitalism: "At the bottom of the social ladder the system creates an army of proletari-
ans discontented with their lot and always ready to revolt, while at the summit it
brings into being a frivolous bourgeoisie, at once skeptical and credulous, having
a superstitious confidence in the State . . ." (Le Bon, *The Crowd*, 93). Both an anti-
liberal and a cynic, Le Bon had little faith in historical progress and was downright contemptuous of notions of equality and liberty. He was, for the most part,
a reactionary, but he was nevertheless fascinated by the dynamics of a mass society and the likelihood that the crowd's fickleness and essential passivity would
naturally lead to "despotism"—an outcome he did not necessarily bemoan. It is
easy to see in Le Bon's steely observations of his contemporaries a harbinger of
fascist theories in the early part of the twentieth century.

30. Alexis de Tocqueville, *Democracy in America*, ed. Thomas Bender (New
York: Modern Library, 1981), 7.

31. Alexis de Tocqueville, *The Old Regime and the French Revolution*, trans. Stuart Gilbert (New York: Doubleday, 1955), 81.

32. Tocqueville, *Democracy*, 108–9.

33. Tocqueville, *Old Regime*, 77.

34. Tocqueville, *Old Regime*, 204.

35. See chapter 1.

36. Emile Durkheim, *Suicide: A Study in Sociology*, trans. John A. Spaulding and
George Simpson (New York: Routledge, 1951), 253.

37. Søren Kierkegaard, *The Present Age: On the Death of Rebellion*, trans. Alexander Dru (New York: Harper and Row, 1962), 33.

38. Kierkegaard, *Present Age*, 38.

39. Kierkegaard, *Present Age*, 20–21. Kierkegaard did not use the word *ressentiment*, and other translators have rendered the Danish *misundelse* as "envy." The
philosopher Sjoerd van Tuinen writes, however, "The way Kierkegaard uses it—a
reflection that imprisons the will and prevents it from coming to a decision—is
in fact already closer to *ressentiment*." Sjoerd van Tuinen, "Introduction," *The Polemics of Ressentiment: Variations on Nietzsche*, ed. Sjoerd van Tuinen (London:
Bloomsbury Academic, 2018), 13, note 22.

40. Kierkegaard, *Present Age*, 21.

41. Kierkegaard, *Present Age*, 23.

42. Kierkegaard, *Present Age*, 23. Emphasis in the original.

43. Nietzsche, *Beyond Good and Evil*, 340–41.

44. Michael André Bernstein, *Bitter Carnival: Ressentiment and the Abject Hero*
(Princeton, NJ: Princeton University Press, 1992), 7.

45. Dostoyevsky, *Notes from Underground, White Nights, The Dream of a Ridicu-*

lous Man and Selections from The House of the Dead, trans. Andrew R. MacAndrew (New York: Signet Classics, 1961), 92.

46. Dostoyevsky, *Notes from Underground*, 135.

47. Dostoyevsky, *Notes from Underground*, 136.

48. I discuss some aspects of these figures in relationship to resentment in the last chapter of the book.

49. Sander L. Gilman and James M. Thomas, *Are Racists Crazy? How Prejudice, Racism, and Antisemitism Became Markers of Insanity* (New York: New York University Press, 2016), 75.

50. Fredrich Nietzsche, *The Will to Power*, trans. Walter Kaufmann and R. J. Hollingdale (New York: Vintage, 1968), 287.

51. The literature on nineteenth-century populism is vast, especially for the US. See the synthetic work by Michael Kazin, *The Populist Persuasion: An American History* (New York: Basic Books, 1995). Richard Hofstadter, *The Age of Reform: From Bryan to F.D.R.* (New York: Vintage, 1955) is controversial precisely because he sees nativistic and anti-Semitic sentiments as prominent in the movement. I deal with Hofstadter and his contemporaries who looked upon populism as, indeed, inflected with resentment in a subsequent chapter. For France, see Philip G. Nord, *Paris Shopkeepers and the Politics of Resentment* (Princeton, NJ: Princeton University Press, 1985). For Germany, Shulamit Volkov, *The Rise of Popular Antimodernism in Germany: The Urban Master Artisans, 1873–1896* (Princeton, NJ: Princeton University Press, 1978).

52. This is not to ignore the presence of anti-Semitism on the Left, in France and elsewhere, especially as many socialists were prepared to associate Jews primarily with the bourgeoisie.

CHAPTER FOUR

1. The historian's sense of a "moment" defies most people's understanding of time and duration. A notable case in point is J. G. A. Pocock's classic study *The Machiavellian Moment* (1975), which stretched its temporal sweep over a period of more than three centuries. Some moment! It might be said that this peculiar concept, despite its patent reference to time, rejects temporal constraints; it suggests a configuration not so much as a *durée* than as a cluster of meaningful associations which cohere over a period of an indeterminate temporal length, whether momentary or across the centuries. Perhaps this is best captured in recalling that the Latin root of "moment" is "momentum," connoting movement and motion. A historical "moment" was certainly set in motion in the last decades of the nineteenth century, when the concept of *ressentiment* caught the attention of a range of philosophers and assorted moralists. It is a moment that has waxed and waned but, in a sense, still has not come to an end.

2. Gottfried Benn, "Nietzsche after 50 Years," *New Nietzsche Studies* 4, no. 3/4 (2000–2001): 127.

3. There is no comparable term in German: *Groll* (rancor) does not convey the same sentiment as either the English or the French. Nietzsche preferred the French (*ressentiment*), although translators of his works into English have used

both the French and the English. Some argue for a distinction between "resentment" and "*ressentiment*," asserting that that the latter conveys a stronger sense of lingering hatred. For the most part in this book, "resentment" will be the default term, although the French may appear, especially when discussing Nietzsche, and certainly when quoting him directly.

4. Arthur Danto "Some Remarks on *The Genealogy of Morals*," in *Reading Nietzsche*, ed. Robert C. Solomon and Kathleen M. Higgins, (New York: Oxford University Press, 1988), 18.

5. For a discussion concerning translating Nietzsche's *Umwerthung* as either "transvaluation" or "revaluation," see Duncan Large, "A Note on the Term 'Umwerthung,'" *Journal of Nietzsche Studies* 39, no. 1 (2010): 5–11: "Whereas 'transvaluation' was initially used, the modern consensus favors 'revaluation,' which is preferred in almost all postwar English translations," 5.

6. Citations in the text are from Friedrich Nietzsche, *On the Genealogy of Morality*, ed. Keith Ansell-Pearson, trans., Carol Diethe (Cambridge: Cambridge University Press, 2017).

7. On the role of the priests, see R. Lanier Anderson, "On the Nobility of Nietzsche's Priests," in *Nietzsche's* On the Genealogy of Morality: *A Critical Guide*, ed. Simon May (Cambridge: Cambridge University Press, 2011), 24–55.

8. This is why, as some commentators have pointed out, a certain vulgarization of the Nietzschean master can be found in images of the warrior "superhero" in popular culture.

9. *Stanford Encyclopedia of Philosophy*, s.v. "Max Scheler," revised October 18, 2018, https://plato.stanford.edu/entries/scheler/.

10. All citations in the text are from Max Scheler, *Ressentiment*, trans. Lewis Coser (Milwaukee, WI: Marquette University Press, 1994).

11. Later he would turn away from Christianity.

12. This is to repeat the theme sounded by both Hume and Tocqueville.

13. Quoted in Richard Wolin, *The Seduction of Unreason: The Intellectual Romance with Fascism from Nietzsche to Postmodernism* (Princeton, NJ: Princeton University Press, 2004), 53.

CHAPTER FIVE

1. Founded by businessman Robert Welch in 1958 in Indianapolis, the John Birch Society was a national organization devoted to combatting what it saw as the steady encroachment of communism, socialism, collectivism, and other "subversive" elements in the United States. It opposed civil rights, the income tax, and anything having to do with the New Deal, and it saw American liberalism as nothing more than a domestic face of worldwide communism. Many of its supporters and adherents found a way into mainstream—or at least party—politics with the presidential campaign of Barry Goldwater. (On this see Lisa McGirr, *Suburban Warriors: The Origins of the New American Right* (Princeton, NJ: Princeton University Press, 2001.) After lying dormant for several decades, it has now experienced something of a resurgence in popularity. There are several more recent works on the Birchers, but Westin's essay, "The John Birch Society: 'Radi-

cal Right' and 'Extreme Left' in the Political Context of Post World War II (1962)," in Daniel Bell, ed., *The Radical Right* (Garden City, NY: Doubleday, 1963), 239–268, is as good a start as any, at least from the contemporary perspective.

2. On the funding of the essays in *The Radical Right*, see Bell's preface, xi. The Fund for the Republic distributed one thousand copies of Hofstadter's essay, "Pseudo-Conservative Revolt" (republished in *The Radical Right*) to civic leaders, businessmen, and school superintendents. On this, see David S. Brown, *Richard Hofstadter: An Intellectual Biography* (Chicago: University of Chicago Press, 2006), 150. According to Brown, Hofstadter and the other contributors to this book were not aware of the connection between the Fund and the CIA. On the seminar, see Ira Katznelson, *Desolation and Enlightenment: Political Knowledge after Total War, Totalitarianism, and the Holocaust* (New York: Columbia University Press, 2003), chap 3; and William E. Leuchtenburg, "The Uses and Abuses of History," *History and Politics Newsletter* 2 (Fall 1991): 6–7. Hofstadter's biographer writes, "The seminar proved a perfect opportunity for Hofstadter to selectively organize the insights of Merton, Mannheim, Weber and Adorno into an exploration of the social-psychological conditions that gave rise to McCarthyism." Brown, *Richard Hofstadter*, 93. At the time of the publication of *The Radical Right*, Bell, Hofstadter, Westin, and Hyman were on the faculty at Columbia. Riesman and Parsons were at Harvard. (Parsons helped found the Department of Sociology at Harvard.) Viereck taught at Mount Holyoke. The oddest of the bunch, he was a poet and identified himself as a conservative (although not of the Goldwater persuasion); his father had been a Nazi fellow traveler. Lipset was on the faculty at Berkeley. Glazer had been associated with Harvard, Berkeley, Smith, and Columbia, but in 1962 he was serving in the Kennedy Administration in the Housing and Home Finance Agency (the predecessor to the Department of Housing and Urban Development). Bell also had been the managing editor of *The New Leader* and the director of the international seminar program at the Congress for Cultural Freedom in Paris. (In 1965 he would join with Irving Kristol as coeditor of *The Public Interest*.) Westin was a member of the National Board of Directors of the American Civil Liberties Union (ACLU). Hyman was the associate director of the Bureau of Applied Social Research at Columbia and was past president of the American Association for Public Opinion Research. Lipset was the Director of the Institute of International Studies at the University of California at Berkeley.

3. These academics were largely of the same generational cohort. Six of the nine were born between 1916 and 1923. Except for Parsons and Viereck, all were Jewish or, in the case of Hofstadter, half-Jewish. Most were sons of working-class immigrants.

4. Thomas S. Kuhn, *The Structure of Scientific Revolutions* (Chicago: University of Chicago Press, 1962).

5. David B. Truman, "Disillusion and Regeneration: The Quest for a Discipline," *American Political Science Review* 59, no. 4 (December 1965): 865–73.

6. Richard Hofstadter, *The Progressive Historians: Turner, Beard, Parrington* (New York: Knopf, 1968), xv.

7. Talcott Parsons, *The Structure of Social Action: Marshall, Pareto, Durkheim* (New York: McGraw-Hill, 1937). The second part of *The Structure of Social Action* is

devoted to Weber. For a highly critical view of Parsons's understanding of Weber, see Jere Cohen, Lawrence E. Hazelrigg, and Whitney Pope, "De-Parsonizing Weber: A Critique of Parsons's Interpretation of Weber," *American Sociological Review* 40, no. 2 (April 1975): 229–41.

8. Here the essential work is Uta Gerhardt, ed., *Talcott Parsons on National Socialism* (New York: Aldine de Gruyter, 1993), which contains fourteen essays Parsons wrote on the subject in the 1930s and '40s; Gerhardt also supplies an excellent introduction. See also Gerhardt, *Talcott Parsons: An Intellectual Biography* (Cambridge: Cambridge University Press, 2002). While I am emphasizing Parsons's public writings in the immediate prewar and wartime periods as demonstrating the impact of contemporary events on his thinking, a case can be made that Parsons was an intellectual committed to social reform and, indeed, embodied many of the reformist principals of the Progressives. On this, see especially Howard Brick, "The Reformist Dimension of Talcott Parsons's Early Social Theory," in *The Culture of the Market: Historical Essays*, ed. Thomas L. Haskell and Richard F. Teichgraeber III (Cambridge: Cambridge University Press, 1993), 357–96. It is evident that this engagement yielded a turn in Parsons's thinking which, while grounded in his previous scholarship, does not flow seamlessly from the pages of *The Structure of Social Action*. It was a direct response to the challenge of National Socialism. Here he was active on many fronts and in many organizations and ad-hoc committees, some in Cambridge, others in Washington, all directly related to the war effort and the combat against fascism and anti-Semitism. Just a sampling: In 1937 he was part of a discussion group at Harvard among faculty and students on National Socialist propaganda. In April 1940 he spoke at an anti-pacifist rally at Harvard sponsored by the Committee for Militant Aid to Britain. Later that year he joined, along with many other social scientists, the Council of Democracy, whose goal was to inform the American public about the fascist threat. As part of his work with this group, he wrote a "memorandum," "The Development of Groups and Organizations Amenable to Use against American Institutions and Foreign Policy and Possible Measures of Prevention" (later published as "Propaganda and Social Control," *Psychiatry* 5 (1942): 551–72; also in *Talcott Parsons on National Socialism* chapter 11). At the same time, he helped found the American Defense Harvard Group, which aimed to place the intellectual resources of Harvard's professors and students in service of democracy against the totalitarian threat. During several months in 1940 and 1941, he commented on contemporary events over the air at a local radio station, WRUL. In early 1941, he served as chairman of the American Defense Committee on National Morale, which sponsored discussions on the social structure of Nazi Germany, with an eye toward formulating American postwar policy and planning. Gerhardt, "Introduction" to *Parsons on National Socialism*, 22. In 1944, he could be found among the members of the Joint Committee of Post War Planning, whose proceedings were published in the *Journal of Orthopsychiatry*, an indication of the disciplinary orientation of most of the participants. That same year he participated in a Conference on Anti-Semitism organized by the American Jewish Committee. Gerhardt, Introduction to *Parsons on National Socialism*, 12–40.

9. Talcott Parsons, "The Sociology of Modern Anti-Semitism," in Gerhard, *Parsons on National Socialism*, 143–44, 146.

10. Erich Fromm, *Escape from Freedom* (New York: Farrar and Rinehart, 1941), 37.

11. Fromm, *Escape from Freedom*, 235. Fromm cites Lasswell's article, "The Psychology of Hitlerism," *Political Quarterly* 4 (1933): 374.

12. Fromm, *Escape from Freedom*, 241.

13. On this, see Stuart Jeffries, *Grand Hotel Abyss: The Lives of the Frankfurt School* (London: Verso, 2016), chap. 13. Martin Jay, *The Dialectical Imagination: The History of the Frankfurt School and the Institute of Social Research, 1923–1950* (Boston: Little, Brown, 1973) is still indispensable.

14. Max Horkheimer, preface to *The Authoritarian Personality*, by T. W. Adorno, Else Frenkel-Brunswik, Daniel J. Levinson, and R. Nevitt Sanford (New York: Harper and Brothers, 1950), lxxi.

15. Peter E. Gordon, introduction to *The Authoritarian Personality*, by Theodor Adorno, Else Frenkel-Brunswik, Daniel J. Levinson, and R. Nevitt Sanford (New York: Verso, 2019), xxx.

16. Gordon, introduction, xxxv–xxxvi.

17. Richard Hofstadter, "The Pseudo-Conservative Revolt (1955)," in Bell, *Radical Right*, 81.

18. Recalling the importance of Max Weber's influence and his concept of status in particular, Daniel Bell said, "It was basically Weber's influence on status politics which Marty Lipset picked up, I picked up and Dick [Richard Hofstadter] very quickly took the lead." Quoted in Brown, *Hofstadter*, 91. C. Wright Mills and Robert Merton, both at Columbia, were important in developing Weber's concept of status and conveying it to their colleagues. See Mills, *White Collar: The American Middle Class* (New York: Oxford University Press, 1951); and Merton, *Social Theory and Social Structure* (New York: Free Press, 1949).

19. In a passage where he discusses the contrasting world views and aspirations of "positively privileged" and "negatively privileged" strata, Weber alludes to Nietzsche's concept of *ressentiment*. The former "live for the present and by exploiting their great past. . . . The sense of dignity of the negatively privileged strata naturally refers to a future lying beyond the present, whether it is of this life or of another. In other words, it must be nurtured by a belief in a providential 'mission' and by a belief in a specific honor before God. The 'chosen people's' dignity is nurtured by a belief either that in the beyond 'the last will be first,' or that in this life a Messiah will appear to bring forth into the light of the world which has cast them out the hidden honor of a pariah people." Weber adds, however, that he does not see in this reaction the "'resentment' which is so strongly emphasized in Nietzsche's much admired construction in the *Genealogy of Morals*." Weber, "Class, Status, Party," in *From Max Weber: Essays in Sociology*, ed. and trans. H. H. Gerth and C. Wright Mills (New York: Oxford University Press, 1946), 190.

20. Lipset, "The Sources of the 'Radical Right' (1955)," in Bell, *Radical Right*, 308–9. See also Lipset and Reinhard Bendix, "Social Status and Social Structure," *British Journal of Sociology* 2, no. 3 (September 1951): esp. 230–33.

21. Bell, "Interpretations of American Politics (1955)," in Bell, *Radical Right*, 59.

22. After 1945, psychoanalysis went through a "golden age of popularization." Nathan G. Hale Jr., *The Rise and Crisis of Psychoanalysis in the United States: Freud and the Americans, 1917–1985* (New York: Oxford University Press, 1995), chap. 16.

See also Louis Menand, "Freud, Anxiety, and the Cold War," in *After Freud Left: A Century of Psychoanalysis in America*, ed. John Burnham (Chicago: University of Chicago Press, 2012), 189–207. W. H. Auden on Freud: "To us he is no more a person/Now but a whole climate of opinion. . . . Whatever we may think of that famous trio Ego, Super-Ego and Id, we see that they are like Prince Tamino, Zorastro and the Queen of the Night and not like mathematical equations." Quoted in Hale, *Rise and Crisis*, 284.

23. Dorothy Ross, "Freud and the Vicissitudes of Modernism in the United States, 1940–1980," in Burnham, *After Freud Left*, 163–88; and Ross, "American Modernities, Past and Present," *American Historical Review* 116, no. 3 (June 2011): 702–14.

24. Quoted in Brown, *Hofstadter*, 88.

25. Lasch's comments are, to be sure, critical. He continues, "This procedure excused them from the difficult work of judgment and argumentation. Instead of arguing with opponents, they simply dismissed them on psychiatric grounds." Quoted in an interview in Casey Blake and Christopher Phelps, "History as Social Criticism: Conversations with Christopher Lasch," *Journal of American History* 80, no. 4 (March 1994): 1317–18.

26. Hofstadter, "Pseudo-Conservative Revolt," 76.

27. Hofstadter, "Pseudo-Conservative Revolt," 78.

28. Lipset, "Three Decades of the Radical Right: Coughlinites, McCarthyites and Birchers (1962)," in Bell, *Radical Right*, 411.

29. Bell, "Dispossessed," 13–14.

30. Parsons, "Social Strains in America (1955)," in Bell, *Radical Right*, 218.

31. The intellectual influence of Merton, independent of *The Authoritarian Personality*, should not be underestimated. For an excellent treatment of the wide range of social science theories that Hofstadter in particular acknowledged as influential, see Daniel Joseph Singal, "Beyond Consensus: Richard Hofstadter and American Historiography," *American Historical Review* 89, no. 4 (October 1984): 976–81.

32. Parsons, "Social Strains in America (1955)," 217.

33. It is somewhat doubtful that these authors embraced the concept of a "mass society," at least for the American context in the twentieth century. Arendt herself, perhaps reflecting a marginal sense of optimism regarding her new country, excluded America from this diagnosis: "America, the classical land of equality of condition and of general education with all its shortcomings knows less of the modern psychology of the masses than perhaps any other country in the world." Arendt, *The Origins of Totalitarianism* (New York: Harcourt, Brace, 1951), 316. Both Bell and Lipset, who, like many of their contemporaries, saw America through the powerful gaze of Tocqueville, who emphasized the strong associational tendencies of Americans, were less entranced by the concept of mass society. See Bell, "America as a Mass Society," in *The End of Ideology* (Glencoe, IL: The Free Press, 1960), 21; Lipset, *Political Man: The Social Basis of Politics* (Garden City, NY: Doubleday, 1960), 53. On this as well, see Alan Wolfe, *The Politics of Petulance: America in an Age of Immaturity* (Chicago: University of Chicago Press, 2018), 68–69.

34. Bell, "Dispossessed," 42.

35. Parsons, "Social Strains in America: A Postscript (1962)," in Bell, *Radical Right*, 233.

36. Bell, *The Coming of Post-Industrial Society: A Venture in Social Forecasting* (New York: Basic Books, 1973), 453.

37. Brinkley, "Richard Hofstadter's *The Age of Reform*: A Reconsideration," *Reviews in American History* 13, no. 3 (September 1985): 462. See also Michael Kazin, "Hofstadter Lives: Political Culture and Temperament in the Work of an American Historian," *Reviews in American History* 27, no. 2 (June 1999): 334–48; Alan Brinkley, "Liberalism and Belief," in *Liberalism for a New Century*, ed. Neil Jumonville and Kevin Mattson (Berkeley: University of California Press, 2007), 82ff.

38. See, for example, Vernon L. Parrington, *Main Currents in American Thought: The Beginnings of Critical Realism in America, 1860–1929*, vol. 3 (New York: Harcourt, Brace, 1930); John D. Hicks, *The Populist Revolt: A History of the Farmers' Alliance and the People's Party* (Minneapolis: University of Minnesota Press, 1931); C. Vann Woodward, *Tom Watson, Agrarian Rebel* (New York: Macmillan, 1938).

39. Richard Hofstadter, *The Age of Reform: From Bryan to F.D.R.* (New York: Vintage, 1955), 19.

40. Hofstadter, *Age of Reform*, 61.

41. Hofstadter, *Age of Reform*, 80.

42. Parsons, "Social Strains in America (1955)," 225.

43. Riesman, "Intellectuals and Discontented Classes," (1962), in Bell, *Radical Right*, 141.

44. Bell, "Dispossessed," 3.

45. The title of Hofstadter's best-selling book published in 1948, in which FDR figures as the culminating figure in a line of "the men who made it" (the subtitle), starting with the Founding Fathers.

46. Arthur Schlesinger Jr., *The Vital Center: The Politics of Freedom* (Boston: Houghton Mifflin, 1949). See Brinkley's essay, "Liberalism and Belief," 75–89; 83 on Schlesinger.

47. Bell, *The End of Ideology*, 400–2.

48. Hofstadter, *The American Political Tradition* (New York: Vintage, 1948), 261. This in reference to William Jennings Bryan.

49. On the so-called consensus school, see especially Peter Novick, *That Noble Dream* (Cambridge: Cambridge University Press, 1988), 332ff. For a genealogy of the relationship between elitism and liberalism, see Robert Hollinger, *The Dark Side of Liberalism: Elitism vs. Democracy* (Westport, CT: Praeger, 1996).

50. Russell Jacoby, *Social Amnesia: A Critique of Contemporary Psychology* (Boston: Beacon, 1975), 2.

51. Of course, there were notable and influential feminist psychoanalysts, both theorists and practitioners, who remained largely faithful to Freud's teachings, although reworking them in the light of a feminist perspective. For an early example of this, see Nancy J. Chodorow, *The Reproduction of Mothering: Psychoanalysis and the Sociology of Gender* (Berkeley, CA: University of California Press, 1978). See also the brilliant work of the historian Lyndal Roper, *Oedipus and the Devil: Witchcraft, Sexuality, and Religion in Early Modern Europe* (London: Routledge, 1994).

52. This paragraph relies mostly, though not entirely, on Hale's comprehen-

sive study, *The Rise and Crisis of Psychoanalysis*, especially chap. 17. See also the essays in Burnham, *After Freud Left*. To be sure, the 1980s were the high-water mark of psychohistory, a method of exploring the past that often relied upon Freudian categories. This should give us pause before concluding a decisive turn away from psychoanalysis in particular or the path of psychologizing more generally. But psychohistory's star turned out to be more meteor-like than astral: it fell as rapidly as it rose. By the end of the twentieth century, it was a very marginal scholarly pursuit. For an early treatment of the "forgetting" of the critical aspects of psychoanalysis, especially for social theory, see Jacoby, *Social Amnesia*.

53. Woodward, "The Populist Heritage and the Intellectual," *American Scholar* 29, no. 1 (Winter 1959–60): 63; reprinted in Woodward, *The Burden of Southern History* (Baton Rouge: Louisiana State University Press, 1968 ed.).

54. Woodward, "Populist Heritage," 58. In a letter to Merle Curti, Hofstadter admitted that he exaggerated the element of anti-Semitism among the Populists because it had been so blatantly ignored by others. Novick points out that those critical of the Populists were Jewish and from the Northeast, while the historians who took umbrage with his critique were from the South and Midwest. (Parsons, among the former, and Norman Pollack, among the latter group are the exceptions.) He adds, "This feature of the controversy was well known to the participants and many contemporary observers, but was usually mentioned only obliquely, if at all. It tacitly raised issues of perspectivism and universalism which, for the moment, the profession preferred not to discuss openly." *That Noble Dream*, 338, 339.

55. This case against the earlier view of Populism is summarized in Robert C. McMath Jr., *American Populism: A Social History, 1877–1898* (New York: Hill and Wang, 1993), 13.

56. Undoubtedly one of the most significant historical works on Populism, Lawrence Goodwyn's *Democratic Promise: The Populist Movement in America* (New York: Oxford University Press, 1976). Like Hofstadter and his fellow travelers, who looked at the past through a presentist lens tinted with McCarthyism, Goodwyn and other historians of the 1960s were inspired by the Civil Rights Movement to recover an indigenous tradition of social protest and political radicalism. What emerges in Goodwyn's study of (mostly) Texas Populism, focusing on the Southern Farmers' Alliance, is a grassroots network of organizations—farmers' cooperatives—that formed the infrastructure of the Populist movement. Following the approach of contemporary historical sociologists, Goodwyn essentially posits an organizational pyramid constructed over time, from farmers' cooperatives which formed the cell structure of the Farmers' Alliance to the People's Party and an ideology of reform, which was their political expression. No anomie, no mass society, few irrational or extreme claims, and little evidence of deep-seated resentment characterized this sustained popular mobilization. Along the way, he takes several swipes at Hofstadter, barely disguising his contempt for the Columbia professor's view of Populism and what he calls the failure of the "American academic mainstream" "to uncover mass striving and mass defeat." He makes it absolutely clear that the reason is political. In a long footnote, he writes, "It is simpler to dismiss moments of unseemly discord as [quoting the novelist Dean Howells] 'blind groping for fairer conditions,' or, in Hofstadter's [phrase] as the

irrationalities of people who saw themselves as 'innocent pastoral victims of conspiracies hatched in the distance.'" The work of Charles Tilly is crucial here. See, for example, *From Mobilization to Revolution* (Reading, MA: Addison-Wesley, 1978). For a more explicit use of historical sociology, especially the work of Tilly, see Donna A. Barnes, *Farmers in Rebellion: The Rise and Fall of the Southern Farmers Alliance and People's Party in Texas* (Austin: University of Texas Press, 1984), chap. 2.

57. Kazin, *The Populist Persuasion: An American History* (New York: Basic Books, 1995), 196.

58. Wolfgang Sachs, "The Archeology of the Development Idea," *INTERculture* 23, no. 4 (Fall 1990): 1. Extremely enlightening on this whole topic is Nick Cullather, "Development? It's History," *Diplomatic History* 24, no. 4 (Fall 2000): 641–53. For a thorough review of the literature on this topic, see Joseph Morton Hodge, "Writing the History of Development (Part I: The First Wave)," *Humanity* 6, no. 3 (Winter 2015): 429–63.

59. James C. Scott, *Seeing Like a State: How Certain Schemes to Improve the Human Condition Have Failed* (New Haven, CT: Yale University Press, 1998).

CHAPTER SIX

1. James C. Scott, *Weapons of the Weak: Everyday Forms of Peasant Resistance* (New Haven, CT: Yale University Press, 1985).

2. All references in the text from Jean Améry, "Resentments," in *At the Mind's Limits: Contemplations by a Survivor on Auschwitz and Its Realities*, ed. and trans. Sidney Rosenfeld and Stella P. Rosenfeld (Bloomington: Indiana University Press, 1980).

3. See Jean Améry, "Sartre: Greatness and Failure," in Jean Améry, *Selected Essays*, ed. and trans. Sidney Rosenfeld and Stella P. Rosenfeld (Bloomington: Indiana University Press, 1984), 118–34.

4. An obvious reference to Nietzsche's *Beyond Good and Evil*.

5. Trans. Sidney Rosenfeld and Stella P. Rosenfeld (Bloomington: Indiana University Press, 1980). Page numbers in the text from this edition.

6. Martin Walser, "Our Auschwitz," in *The Burden of the Past: Martin Walser on Modern Germany; Texts, Contexts, Commentary*, ed. and trans., Thomas A. Kovach (Rochester, NY: Camden House, 2008), 10. This publication contains Walser's public comments on this subject from 1965 to 1998.

7. Walser, "Our Auschwitz," 7. See also Walser, "Handshake with Ghosts," (1979), quoted in Kovach, *Burden of the Past*, 104.

8. Quoted in Yascha Mounk, *Stranger in My Own Country: A Jewish Family in Modern Germany* (New York: Farrar, Straus and Giroux, 2014), 130.

9. Charles S. Maier, *The Unmasterable Past: History, Holocaust, and German National Identity* (Cambridge, MA: Harvard University Press, 1988), 12.

10. Richard J. Evans, *In Hitler's Shadow: West German Historians and the Attempt to Escape from the Nazi Past* (New York: Pantheon, 1989), 19.

11. "The Germans and their past: no really new theme there. But it is apparently not wearing thin; rather the opposite . . . the question that is now thrown open is: should the Third Reich be treated historiographically so that it no longer

blocks the way to our past like some somber and monstrous monument, but rather itself becomes "history," past time, one epoch among other epochs? Or should it simultaneously remain as some admonitory memorial . . . because, in the speech of biblical simile, this stone actually became the cornerstone of the new beginning after the Second World War? And should history provide orientation, awaken pride and self-consciousness, and thus become a starting point for "identity" and "national consciousness"—or is its task much more one of unsettling what is customary, throwing into question what persists, and sharpening our vision for the future?" Hermann Rudolph, quoted in Maier, *Unmasterable Past*, 9.

12. Quoted in Evans, *Hitler's Shadow*, 26. Nolte pursued his case on several fronts. He argued that Auschwitz was not unique, evoking previous atrocities such as the Armenian genocide at the hands of the Ottoman Turks and, especially, the Soviet "Gulag Archipelago" (recently documented by Solzhenitsyn) and other crimes committed against the German people themselves by the Communist regime in the interwar period. Hitler's "Final Solution," he said, was really devised in imitation of the "social extermination" practiced by the Bolsheviks—"the exact counterpart of the attempt at the complete destruction of a universal class, and thus the biologically transposed copy of the social original" (quoted in Evans, 29). His central thesis proposed that because Germany was threatened by this "Asiatic" menace, Hitler was justified in adopting similar measures as a defensive response. His case, then, hinges on making the Communists into the prime movers in the historical emergence of Fascism. The Nazi regime, indeed the whole war, was merely a reaction to the threat from the barbarian East. But he goes even further, asserting that there were grounds for Hitler's animus of the Jews—that they were out to destroy him, citing Chaim Weizmann's avowal at the World Zionist Congress of 1939 that Jews from throughout the world would join Britain in its fight against Germany. In his book *The European Civil War*, he claims that historical writings on the Holocaust have been produced primarily by "Jewish authors," who have, consequently, perpetuated a simple "perpetrator-victim" pattern (Evans, 33). The Germans, too, were victims—those subjected to allied bombing raids, those soldiers exposed to the atrocities on the Eastern front, and those ethnic Germans expelled from Eastern lands after the war. The fact that this suffering had not been acknowledged was clearly a source of bitterness and resentment for Nolte and those who shared his views.

13. Jacob Heilbrunn, "Germany's New Right," *Foreign Affairs*, November/December 1996, 86.

14. Heilbrunn, "Germany's New Right," 89.

15. Heilbrunn, "Germany's New Right," 87.

16. Heilbrunn, "Germany's New Right," 94. See "Forum: The *Historikerstreit* Twenty Years On," *German History* 24, no. 4 (October 2006): 587–607, and the comments by Nicholas Stargardt: "Thanks to the recent work of cultural historians of the 1950s, we've all become aware of the huge undertow of *ressentiment* in West German discussions of the 1950s, much of it with official encouragement" (596); and Michael Geyer: ". . . The desire of so many Germans to be victims . . . it is remarkable for the recrudescence of national resentment" (602).

17. Martin Walser, "Experiences while Composing a Sunday Speech (1998)," in Kovach, *Burden of the Past*, 85.

18. Walser, "Sunday Speech," 85–86.

19. Walser, "Sunday Speech," 88.

20. Walser, "Sunday Speech," 89.

21. Walser, "Sunday Speech," 91.

22. Walser, "Sunday Speech," 91.

23. Walser, "Sunday Speech," 92.

24. Walser, "Sunday Speech," 93.

25. Lutz Niethammer, quoted in Aleida Assmann, "Two Forms of Resentment," *New German Critique*, special issue, *Taboo, Trauma, Holocaust*, no. 90 (Autumn 2003): 129.

26. Assmann, "Two Forms," 131.

27. On this, see the very pertinent and insightful remarks of Stefan-Ludwig Hoffmann, "Human Rights and History," *Past and Present*, no. 232 (August 2016): 279–310.

28. John Torpey, *Making Whole What Has Been Smashed: A Reparations Politics* (Cambridge, MA: Harvard University Press, 2006).

29. Leon Wessels, "Good Faith is not enough: we have to dialogue," *In the Balance: South Africans Debate Reconciliation*, ed. Fanie du Toit and Erik Doxtader (Auckland Park, South Africa: Jacana Media, 2010), 11.

30. Hannah Arendt, preface to the first edition of *The Origins of Totalitarianism* (New York: Harcourt, Brace, 1951), ix. See also Alain Cairns, "Coming to Terms with the Past," in *Politics and the Past: On Repairing Historical Injustices*, ed. John Torpey (Lanham, MD: Rowman and Littlefield, 2003), 69: "Nazism, fascism, communism, Japanese militarism, rule by junta, domestic and overseas imperialism have all reinforced the idea that millions, in fact hundreds of millions, were properly ruled by others, and in extreme cases were expendable on the road to utopia."

31. For these and others, see Priscilla B. Hayner, *Unspeakable Truths: Confronting State Terror and Atrocity* (New York: Routledge, 2001), 14–15.

32. Desmond Tutu, *No Future without Forgiveness* (New York: Doubleday, 1999).

33. Amélie Oksenberg Rorty, "The Dramas of Resentment," *Yale Review* 88, no. 3 (July 2000): 95–96.

34. Martha Minow, *Between Vengeance and Forgiveness: Facing History after Genocide and Mass Violence* (Boston: Beacon Press, 1998), 18.

35. Jeffrie Murphy, "Forgiveness and Resentment," in *Forgiveness and Mercy*, by Jeffrie G. Murphy and Jean Hampton (Cambridge: Cambridge University Press, 1988), 17.

36. Friedrich Nietzsche, *On the Genealogy of Morality*, ed. Keith Ansell-Pearson, trans. Carol Diethe (Cambridge: Cambridge University Press, 1997), 22.

37. Jeffrie Murphy, "Forgiveness and Resentment," in *Social and Political Philosophy*, ed. Peter A. French, Theodore E. Uehling Jr., and Howard K. Wettstein, Midwest Studies in Philosophy 7 (Minneapolis: University of Minnesota Press, 1982), 505.

38. Desmond Tutu, *No Future Without Forgiveness* (New York: Doubleday, 1999), 31.

39. Pregs Govender, "Truth, Reconciliation and Women in South Africa," in du Toit and Doxtader, *In the Balance*, 75.

40. Pumla Gobodo-Madikizela, "Reconciliation: A Call to Reparative Humanism, in du Toit and Doxtader, *In the Balance*, 137.

41. Glen Sean Coulthard, *Red Skin, White Masks: Rejecting the Colonial Politics of Reconciliation* (Minneapolis: University of Minnesota Press, 2014), 109.

42. Coulthard, *Red Skin, White Masks*.

43. David W. McIvor, "The Mendacity of Reconciliation in an Age of Resentment," *American Journal of Economics and Sociology* 76, no. 5 (November 2017): 1144.

44. Fanon, *Black Skin, White Masks*, trans. Richard Philcox (New York: Grove Press, 2008 ed.), 101.

45. Fanon, *Black Skin, White Masks*, 90.

46. Fanon, 92.

47. Fanon, 95.

48. Fanon, 91.

49. Fanon, 91.

50. Fanon, 93.

51. Fanon, 95.

52. Fanon, 96.

53. Fanon, 101.

54. Fanon, 118.

55. Fanon, 119.

56. Fanon, 195, note 10.

57. Fanon, 193.

58. Fanon, 197.

59. Fanon, 197.

60. Frantz Fanon, *Wretched of the Earth*, trans. Constance Farrington (New York: Grove Press, 1963), 136, 139.

61. Jean-Paul Sartre, preface to Fanon, *Wretched of the Earth*, 7–8.

62. Sartre, preface, 21.

63. Fanon, *Wretched of the Earth*, 94.

CHAPTER SEVEN

1. Howard Zinn, "Marxism and the New Left," in *Dissent: Explorations in the History of American Radicalism*, ed. Alfred L. Young (DeKalb: Northern Illinois University Press, 1968), 371. Quoted in Staughton Lynd, "The New Left," *Annals of the American Academy of Political and Social Science* 382 (March 1969): 68. Rick Perlstein, Nixonland: The Rise of a President and the Fracturing of America (New York: Scribner, 2008), 21.

2. Arthur Marwick describes this "sixties" in terms of a grab bag of tendencies, values, and movements: "Black civil rights, youth culture and trend setting by young people; idealism, protest, and rebellion; the triumph of popular music based on Afro-American models and the emergence of this music as universal language, with the Beatles as the heroes of the age; the search for inspiration in the religions of the Orient; massive changes in personal relationship and sexual

behavior, a general audacity and frankness in books and in the media, and in ordinary behavior, relaxation of censorship, the new feminism, gay liberation; the emergence of 'the underground' and the 'counter culture;' optimism and genuine faith in the dawning of a better world." Marwick, *The Sixties: Cultural Revolutions in Britain, France, Italy, and the United States* (New York: Oxford University Press, 1998), 3–4.

3. *Funny Face* (1957). I owe this reference to Robert Zaretsky.

4. Quoted in George Cotkin, *Existential America* (Baltimore: Johns Hopkins University Press, 2003), 126–27.

5. Lionel Trilling, *Sincerity and Authenticity* (Cambridge, MA: Harvard University Press, 1973).

6. Marshall Berman, *The Politics of Authenticity: Radical Individualism and the Emergence of Modern Society* (New York: Atheneum, 1970), x.

7. Quoted in Tom Hayden, "Participatory Democracy: From the Port Huron Statement to Occupy Wall Street," *The Nation*, March 27, 2012, https://www .thenation.com/article/archive/participatory-democracy-port-huron-statement -occupy-wall-street/.

8. It is true that Camus himself disavowed an identification with the so-called existentialists. Nevertheless, despite this, he is usually placed within their ranks.

9. Tom Hayden, *Reunion: A Memoir* (New York: Random House, 1988).

10. Albert Camus, *The Plague*, quoted in Hayden, *Reunion*, 76.

11. Hayden, *Reunion*, 82.

12. Hayden, *Reunion*, 94.

13. *The Port Huron Statement*, https://www.ssc.wisc.edu/~wright/929-utopias -2013/Real%20Utopia%20Readings/Port%20Huron%20Statement.pdf.

14. *Port Huron Statement*, 7. The statement is more than a critique of the establishment and the American status quo; it offers a reformist vision for the radical restructuring of the political and economic order encompassed by a total recasting of the American system of values. In politics, the students urge "participatory democracy," which will not only transform the mechanics of politics but also bring "people out of isolation and into community," providing them with "outlets for the expression of personal and grievance and aspirations" (19). In economics, they look forward to work that is "educative, not stultifying, creative, not mechanical, self-directive, not manipulative," which endows workers with a "sense of dignity." The economy itself should be subject to democratic regulation (20). Overall, they call for social institutions to be organized with the "well-being and dignity of man as the essential measure of success" (21).

15. *Port Huron Statement*, 6.

16. *Port Huron Statement*, 5–6.

17. Todd Gitlin, *The Sixties: Years of Hope, Days of Rage* (New York: Bantam, 1987), 108.

18. In his later years, Hayden reflected on the turn taken by the students and other sixties radicals toward ideological absolutes, sectarianism, violence, and the adulation of such dubious revolutionary "heroes" as Che Guevara, Castro, Mao, and Ho Chi Minh. "The early spirit of pragmatism and experimentation was steadily replaced by the adoption of more radical, abstract and ultimately paralyzing ideology." Camus was forgotten in favor of others more single mindedly

committed to the prospect of revolution, such as Sartre and Herbert Marcuse. He concludes wistfully, "Camus had warned against the politics of resentment I was beginning to embody, calling it an 'evil secretion, in a sealed vessel, of prolonged impotence.'" *Reunion*, 297.

19. Gitlin, *The Sixties*, 374.

20. Robin Morgan, ed., *Sisterhood is Powerful* (New York: Random House, 1970), xxiii.

21. Betty Friedan, *The Feminine Mystique* (New York: W.W. Norton, 1963). All page numbers in the text refer to this edition.

22. Ellen Goodman, "How Friedan Pulled the Trigger on History," *Baltimore Sun*, February 13, 2006. https://www.baltimoresun.com/news/bs-xpm -2006-02-13-0602130026-story.html.

23. "Ten Most Harmful Books of the 19th and 20th Centuries," *Human Events*, May 31, 2005, https://humanevents.com/2005/05/31/ten-most-harmful-books-of -the-19th-and-20th-centuries/.

24. According to Tom Hayden, Robert Moses was "perhaps the single greatest influence on the early SDS and SNCC, a Socratic Existentialist." Hayden, "Participatory Democracy."

25. Cotkin, *Existential America*, 231.

26. For a very intelligent reading of Camus's *The Rebel*, see Jeffrey C. Isaac, *Arendt, Camus, and Modern Rebellion* (New Haven, CT: Yale University Press, 1992).

27. Sally Belfrage, *Freedom Summer* (Charlottesville: University Press of Virginia, 1965), 11.

28. There are three PDFs of transcripts from an unspecified archive. The tapes of the interview have been made available by the Robert Penn Warren Oral History Archive, Louis B. Nunn Center for Oral History, University of Kentucky Libraries, https://nunncenter.net/robertpennwarren/exhibits/show/interviews -with-civil-rights-l/item/118.

29. Albert Camus, *The Rebel*, trans. Anthony Bower (New York: Alfred A. Knopf, 1956), 166–73. As Jeffrey Isaac points out (*Arendt, Camus, and Modern Rebellion*, 291), Camus's source on this is Boris Savinkov, *Memoirs of a Terrorist* (New York: A. C. Boni, 1931), 71–117.

30. Stokely Carmichael with Ekwueme Michael Thelwell, "A Band of Brothers, a Circle of Trust," chap. 14 in *Ready for Revolution: The Life and Struggles of Stokely Carmichael (Kwame Ture)* (New York: Scribner, 2003), 311–12.

31. Quoted in Cotkin, *Existential America*, 235.

32. Frantz Fanon, *Black Skin, White Masks*, trans. Richard Philcox (New York: Grove Press, 2008 ed.), 95.

33. Huey P. Newton, *Revolutionary Suicide* (New York: Random House, 1973). On the influence of Nietzsche on Newton's thinking more generally, see Jennifer Ratner-Rosenhagen's pathbreaking study, *American Nietzsche: A History of an Icon and his Ideas* (Chicago: University of Chicago Press, 2012), 258–60.

34. Newton, *Revolutionary Suicide*, 164.

35. Newton, 165.

36. Newton, 168.

37. Newton, 168.

38. Martin Luther King Jr., "Letter from a Birmingham Jail," August 1963, https://www.csuchico.edu/iege/_assets/documents/susi-letter-from-birmingham-jail.pdf, 4.

39. Martha C. Nussbaum, *Anger and Forgiveness: Resentment, Generosity, Justice* (New York: Oxford University Press, 2016), 221–22.

40. Peniel E. Joseph, *The Sword and the Shield: The Revolutionary Lives of Malcolm X and Martin Luther King Jr.* (New York: Basic Books, 2020), 9.

41. Joseph, *Sword and the Shield*, 16–17, emphasis in the original.

42. Democracy Now! "Atonement and James Baldwin," October 17, 1997, https://www.democracynow.org/1997/10/17/atonement_and_james_baldwin.

43. Joseph, *Sword and the Shield*, 163.

44. On the place of resentment in this context, see especially Jeremy Engels, *The Politics of Resentment: A Genealogy* (University Park: University of Pennsylvania Press, 2015).

45. Rick Perlstein, *Nixonland: The Rise of a President and the Fracturing of America* (New York: Scribner, 2008), 434–35. See Bill Schwarz, "The Silent Majority: How the Private Becomes Political," in *Inventing the Silent Majority in Western Europe and the United States*, ed. Anna von der Golz and Britta Waldschmidt-Nelson, (Cambridge: Cambridge University Press, 2017), 154, note 14. George Meany had previously used the phrase, referring to pro-war labor, "the vast, silent majority of the nation." On viewing audience, p. 155; and Jeremy Varon, *Bringing the War Home* (Los Angeles: University of California Press, 2004), 134; and Richard Reeves, *President Nixon: Alone in the White House* (New York: Simon and Schuster, 2001), 320–21. See Haldeman's account of Nixon's ruminations: Haldeman, *The Haldeman Diaries* (New York: G.P. Putnam's Sons, 1994), 631–32; cited in Schwarz, p. 156, note 24. See Martin H. Geyer, "Elisabeth Noelle-Neumann's 'Spiral of Silence,' the Silent Majority, and the Conservative Moment of the 1970s," in von der Golz and Waldschmidt-Nelson, *Inventing the Silent Majority*, p. 264, note 45 on the "game plan" for the Silent Majority speech media campaign: "This included the letters and telegrams that flooded the White House (not least thanks to pre-arranged special rates with AT&T), the page-long newspaper articles by supporters who spoke out for the silent majority, and the film by the U.S. Information Agency." On the German "silent majority," see Elisabeth Noelle-Neumann, *Spiral of Silence* (Chicago: University of Chicago Press, 1993), the main focus of Geyer's essay.

46. Perlstein, *Nixonland*, 431.

47. Perlstein, *Nixonland*, 432. In other comments, Agnew also fed the flames of racial animus. As the sociologist Jonathan Rieder noted, he was especially popular among "resentful Middle Americans" because of "the opportunity he gave them to participate in verbal retaliation against black adversaries." Rieder, *Canarsie: The Jews and Italians of Brooklyn against Liberalism* (Cambridge, MA: Harvard University Press, 1987), 174.

48. "Man and Woman of the Year: The Middle Americans," *Time*, January 5, 1970, http://content.time.com/time/subscriber/article/0,33009,943113,00.html.

49. Quoted in "Man and Woman of the Year."

50. In "George F. Will: By the Book, *New York Times*, May 31, 2019. The con-

servative columnist Will cited *The True Believer* as one of the "books that best capture your own political principles."

51. Eric Hoffer, *The Temper of Our Time* (New York: Harper and Row, 1966), 69.

52. Hoffer, *Temper of Our Time*, 71–72.

53. Eric Hoffer, *First Things, Last Things* (New York: Harper and Row, 1971), 72.

54. Hoffer, *First Things, Last Things*, 77.

55. Hoffer, *First Things, Last Things*, 78.

56. Hoffer, *Temper of our Times*, 47.

57. Hoffer, *Temper of our Times*, 47.

58. Hoffer, *First Things, Last Things*, 110.

59. Hoffer, *First Things, Last Things*, 111.

60. John Updike, *Rabbit Redux* (New York: Alfred A. Knopf, 1971), 13.

61. "This is Updike's most topically attuned novel, trying too deliberately to take on the whole sixties scene . . ." Morris Dickstein, "Fiction and Society, 1940–1990," in *The Cambridge History of American Literature*, ed. Sacvan Bercovitch, vol. 7, *Prose Writing, 1940–1990* (Cambridge: Cambridge University Press, 1994), 193.

62. *Rabbit Redux*, 47.

63. *Rabbit Redux*, 248–49.

64. *Rabbit Redux*, 341.

65. Dickstein, "Fiction and Society," 188.

66. *Rabbit Redux*, 83.

67. In response to a query from a British paper in 1966, he wrote, "Like most Americans I am uncomfortable about our military adventure in South Vietnam. . . . I am for our intervention if it does some good. . . . I don't see that we can abdicate our burdensome position in South Vietnam." Quoted in Adam Begley, *Updike* (New York: Harper, 2014), 275–76.

68. On this, see Ian Haney Lopez, *Dog Whistle Politics* (New York: Oxford University Press, 2013), 24–26ff.

69. Kevin Phillips, *The Emerging Republican Majority* (New Rochelle, NY: Arlington House, 1969), 39–40, 470.

70. Phillips, *Emerging Republican Majority*, 184, 195.

71. See especially Susan Faludi, *Backlash: The Undeclared War Against American Women* (New York: Crown, 1991).

72. Matthew D. Lassiter, *The Silent Majority: Suburban Politics in the Sunbelt South* (Princeton, NJ: Princeton University Press, 2007), 10.

73. Lassiter, *Silent Majority*, 227.

74. Katharine Q. Seelye, "Molly Ivins, Columnist, Dies at 62," *New York Times*, February 1, 2007, https://www.nytimes.com/2007/02/01/washington/01ivins.html.

75. Mark Lilla, *The Once and Future Liberal* (New York: HarperCollins, 2017), 39.

76. Seymour Martin Lipset, "Beyond the Backlash," *Encounter* 83 (1964): 24. "The groups now reacting with such desperation are desperate precisely because they are growing less influential and less numerous" (23). Lipset does acknowledge that the "Negro Revolution and the success of the Civil Rights movement have increased the fears of large sections of the white population" (21). Lipset writes that many whites are worried about "Negroes" moving next door, integrating their schools, or demanding their jobs. But in the next breath he insists

that "there is simply no evidence that dogmatic conservatism, racial bigotry, or xenophobic nationalism have become more popular in the country" (23).

77. Faludi, *Backlash*, 11.

78. Faludi, *Backlash*, 243.

79. Faludi, *Stiffed: The Betrayal of the American Man* (New York: William Morrow, 1999).

CHAPTER EIGHT

1. Emily Wang with Matthew Shen Goodman, "A Note on Resentment," *Triple Canopy*, https://www.canopycanopycanopy.com/contents/a-note-on-resentment.

2. Here are some of the scholarly books published since 2015 in which "resentment" figures as a term of analysis: Jeremy Engels, *The Politics of Resentment: A Genealogy* (University Park: University of Pennsylvania Press, 2015); Katherine J. Cramer, *The Politics of Resentment: Rural Consciousness in Wisconsin and the Rise of Scott Walker* (Chicago: University of Chicago Press, 2016); Martha Nussbaum, *Anger and Forgiveness: Resentment, Generosity, and Justice* (New York: Oxford University Press, 2016); Francis Fukuyama, *Identity: The Demand for Dignity and the Politics of Resentment* (New York: Farrar, Strauss & Giroux, 2018); Sjoerd van Tuinen, ed., *The Polemics of* Ressentiment: *Variations on Nietzsche* (London: Bloomsbury Academic, 2018); Jonathan M. Metzl, *Dying of Whiteness: How the Politics of Racial Resentment is Killing America's Heartland* (New York: Basic Books, 2019); Rory McVeigh and Kevin Estep, *The Politics of Losing: Trump, the Klan, and the Mainstreaming of Resentment* (New York: Columbia University Press, 2019); Lawrence Rosenthal, *Empire of Resentment: Populism's Toxic Embrace of Nationalism* (New York: The New Press, 2020); Michelle Schwarze, *Recognizing Resentment: Sympathy, Injustice, and Liberal Political Thought* (Cambridge: Cambridge University Press, 2020).

3. Pakasj Mishra, "Politics in the Age of Resentment: The Dark Legacy of the Enlightenment," in *The Great Regression*, ed. Heinrich Geiselberger (Cambridge: Polity, 2017), 110.

4. Arlie Russell Hochschild, *Strangers in Their Own Land: Anger and Mourning on the American Right* (New York, New Press, 2018), 139.

5. Pooneh Rohi with Kira Josefesson and Kaneza Schaal, "The Victor." The video is described in the text: https://www.canopycanopycanopy.com/contents/the-victor/#title-page.

6. On this, see most recently, Gary Gerstle's magisterial study, *The Rise and Fall of the Neoliberal Order: America and the World in the Free Market Era* (New York: Oxford University Press, 2022).

7. See Jon Swaine, "White, Working Class and Angry: Ohio's Left-Behind Helped Trump to Stunning Victory," *Guardian*, November 9, 2016; "The 'angry working class' had helped Trump to an angry victory." Jon Daniel Davidson, "Trump Is No Fascist. He's a Champion for the Forgotten Millions," *Guardian*, February 4, 2017.

8. "Trump retained the overwhelming majority of Republican voters but also made a wider incursion into the Democratic electorate, winning 13 per cent of

Obama's 2012 voters. This suggests that while 2.5 million Romney supporters switched to Clinton, more than 8 million of Obama's voters went to Trump, allowing him to win four states that Obama had carried in both 2008 and 2012.The key switchers were white without degrees." Roger Eatwell and Matthew Goodwin, *National Populism: The Revolt against Liberal Democracy* (London: Pelican, 2018), 248–49.

9. Rory McVeigh and Kevin Estep, *Trump, the Klan and the Mainstreaming of Resentment* (New York: Columbia University Press, 2019), 107.

10. "Full Text: 2017 Donald Trump Inauguration Speech Transcript," *Politico*, January 20, 2017, https://www.politico.com/story/2017/01/full-text-donald-trump -inauguration-speech-transcript-233907.

11. Joan C. Williams, *White Working Class: Overcoming Class Cluelessness in America* (Boston: Harvard Business Review Press, 2017). She cites Nate Silver's May 2016 piece on his website, *FiveThirtyEight*, "The Mythology of Trump's Working Class Support": "It's been extremely common for news accounts to portray Donald Trump's candidacy as a 'working-class' rebellion against Republican elites. His voters are better off economically than most Americans."

12. Stephen Hawkins, Daniel Yudkin, Miriam Juan-Torres, and Tim Dixon, *Hidden Tribes: A Study of America's Polarized Landscape*, More in Common, 2018), 54.

13. Daniel Cox, Rachel Lienesch, and Robert P. Jones, "Beyond Economics: Fears of Cultural Displacement Pushed the White Working Class to Trump," *PRRI/ The Atlantic Report*, May 9, 2017, https://www.prri.org/research/white-working -class-attitudes-economy-trade-immigration-election-donald-trump/. See also the important research of Diana C. Mutz, "Status Threat, not Economic Hardship, Explains the 2016 Vote," *Proceedings of the National Academy of Sciences of the United States of America (PNAS)* 115, no. 19 (May 8, 2018). https://www.pnas.org /content/115/19/E4330.

14. John R. Hibbing, *The Securitarian Personality: What Really Motivates Trump's Base and Why It Matters for the Post-Trump Era* (New York: Oxford University Press, 2020), 166.

15. Many years ago, the American social scientist James C. Davies proposed the model of the "J-curve" as an explanation for revolutionary movements. "Revolutions are most likely to occur when a prolonged period of objective economic development is followed by a short period of sharp reversal," he wrote in his 1962 article "Toward a Theory of Revolution," *American Sociological Review* 27, no. 1 (1962): 5–19. "People then subjectively fear that ground gained with great effort will be quite lost . . ." (The "J" was configured as upside down, thus suggesting the rise and then fall of expectations.) The theory was not entirely original, as it was central to Tocqueville's interpretation of the cause of the French Revolution.

16. Eatwell and Goodwin, *National Populism*, 219.

17. There are some qualifications. In their study *The Tea Party and the Remaking of Republican Conservatism* (New York: Oxford University Press, 2012), Theda Skocpol and Vanessa Williamson show that while members think poorly of Blacks, especially when it comes to work and discipline, they also disparage the behavior of many lower-class whites. And though many are imbued with an "us" versus "them" attitude along racial lines, they are most energetic in denounc-

ing the threat from Muslims and immigrants (69). In another study of the Tea Party, *Change They Can't Believe In: The Tea Party and Reactionary Politics In America* (Princeton, NJ: Princeton University Press, 2013), Christopher S. Parker and Matt A. Barreto prefer to characterize its members as "reactionary conservatives," that is, as part of a long-standing current in American political culture, rather than emphasize racism or disapproval of Obama for his race (150–51).

18. Parker and Barreto, *Change*, 209. A CNN/ORC poll at the end of Obama's second term revealed that 54 percent of Trump's supporters, and 43 percent of all Republicans, believed that Obama was a Muslim. Robert P. Jones, *White Too Long: The Legacy of White Supremacy in American Christianity* (New York: Simon and Schuster, 2020), 14.

19. Parker and Barreto, *Change*, 238.

20. Parker and Barreto, *Change*, 8.

21. Michèle Lamont, *The Dignity of Working Men: Morality and the Boundaries of Race, Class, and Immigration* (Cambridge, MA: Harvard University Press, 2000), 61.

22. John R. Hibbing, *The Securitarian Personality: What Really Motivates Trump's Base and Why It Matters for the Post-Trump Era* (New York: Oxford University Press, 2020), 117.

23. Cornell Belcher, *A Black Man in the White House: Barack Obama and the Triggering of America's Racial-Aversion Crisis* (Healdsburg, CA: Water Street, 2016), 126–27.

24. In Yuri Slezkine's terms, in his remarkable book, *The Jewish Century* (Princeton, NJ: Princeton University Press, 2004), they are a "Mercurian" people, as opposed to the "Apollinian" gentiles.

25. Götz Aly, *Europe against the Jews, 1880–1945*, trans. Jefferson Chase (New York: Metropolitan Books, 2020), 335.

26. David C. Wilson and Darren W. Davis, "Reexamining Racial Resentment: Conceptualization and Content," *Annals of the American Academy of Political and Social Science*, 634, no. 1 (2011): 119, 128. See also their book *Racial Resentment in the Political Mind* (Chicago: University of Chicago Press, 2022).

27. Martin Luther King Jr., "The Other America," April 14, 1967, Stanford University, https://www.crmvet.org/docs/otheram.htm.

28. Larry Glickman, "How White Backlash Controls American Progress," *Atlantic*, May 21, 2020, https://www.theatlantic.com/ideas/archive/2020/05/white-backlash-nothing-new/611914/.

29. Jones, *White Too Long*, 15.

30. Recent decades have seen the emergence of what has been called the "new racism," which focuses on "cultural threats" to national identity—the idea that immigration and ethnic change present an imminent risk to the cultural distinctiveness of the national group, to national values, identity, and ways of life. Eatwell and Goodwin, *National Populism*, 73; see also chap. 2, note 28; Bradley Jones and Jocelyn Kiley, "More 'Warmth' for Trump among GOP Voters Concerned by Immigrants, Diversity," Pew Research Center, June 2, 2016, https://www.pewresearch.org/fact-tank/2016/06/02/more-warmth-for-trump-among-gop-voters-concerned-by-immigrants-diversity/.

31. Sarah Wildman, "'You Will Not Replace Us': A French Philosopher Explains the Charlottesville Chant," Vox, August 15, 2017, https://www.vox.com/world

/2017/8/15/16141456/renaud-camus-the-great-replacement-you-will-not-replace-us
-charlottesville-white.

32. Hibbing, *The Securitarian Personality*, 109. On the other side, opposed to
the "securitarians," are the "unitarians" (with apologies to the religious group
so-named) who are governed by a desire to protect outsiders from insider
threats—to be guardians, so to speak, of those susceptible to discrimination or
persecution by the either the majority or the powers that be (89).

33. Hibbing, *The Securitarian Personality*, 104.

34. Lamont, *Dignity of Working Men*, 147.

35. J. D. Vance, *Hillbilly Elegy: A Memoir of a Family and Culture in Crisis* (New
York: HarperCollins, 2016), 139.

36. Williams, *White Working Class*, 13.

37. Williams, *White Working Class*, 16.

38. Vance, *Hillbilly Elegy*, 139.

39. Williams, *White Working Clas*, 22.

40. Lamont, *Dignity of Working Men*, 25.

41. Quoted in Williams, *White Working Class*, 26.

42. Hochschild, *Strangers in Their Own Land*, 227.

43. Jacob Jarvis, "Mitch McConnell, Amy McGrath Make Final Case to Kentucky Voters as Polls Show Big GOP Lead," *Newsweek*, November 3, 2020, https://
www.newsweek.com/mitch-mcconnell-amy-mcgrath-final-case-kentucky-voters
-gop-lead-1544362.

44. For this, I refer again to Kevin Phillips: "Beyond race, Phillips joined with
the Democratic strategists Seammon and Watenberg in seeing a host of 'social
issues' as driving a permanent wedge through the Democratic Party. Phillips
looked forward to a 'great electoral bastion of a Republicanism that is against
aid to blacks, against aid to big cities and against the liberal life-style it seems
typified by purple glasses, beards, long hair, bralessness, pornography, coddling
of criminals and moral permissiveness run riot.' Here we see a distinct meaning
of 'liberal' emerge: now not as a stance regarding good government and the dan-
gers of concentrated wealth, but liberalism as 'moral permissiveness,' especially
around issues of crime, gender, sexual orientation and religion." James Boyd,
"Nixon's Southern Strategy: It's All about the Charts," *New York Times*, May 17,
1970. See Phillips, *Emerging Republican Majority*, 22, 39–40, 470.

45. Hochschild, *Strangers in Their Own Land*, 165, 162.

46. Hochschild, *Strangers in Their Own Land*, 227.

47. Jessica Murphy, "Toronto Professor Jordan Peterson Takes On Gender-
Neutral Pronouns," BBC News, November 4, 2016, https://www.bbc.com/news
/world-us-canada-37875695.

48. Pippa Norris and Ronald Inglehart, *Cultural Backlash: Trump, Brexit, and
Authoritarian Populism* (Cambridge: Cambridge University Press, 2019).

49. Anthony Gerace, "These Eight Conservative Men are Making No Apologies," *New York Times*, April 18, 2022.

50. Katherine J. Cramer, *The Politics of Resentment: Rural Consciousness in Wisconsin and the Rise of Scott Walker* (Chicago: University of Chicago Press, 2016), 7.
"Resentment toward fellow citizens is front and center. People understand their

circumstances as the fault of guilty and less deserving people, not as the product of broad social, economic, and political forces" (61).

51. Quoted in Robert Wuthnow, *The Left Behind: Decline and Rage in Rural America* (Princeton, NJ: Princeton University Press, 2018), 2.

52. Wuthnow, *Left Behind*, 6.

53. See Wuthnow, *Left Behind*, 38, on the fear of outsiders.

54. David Goodhart, *The Road to Somewhere: The Populist Revolt and the Future of Politics* (London: Hurst, 2017), 3.

55. Quoted in Michael J. Sandel, *The Tyranny of Merit: What's Become of the Common Good?* (New York: Farrar, Straus and Giroux, 2020), 101.

56. Quoted in William A. Galston, *Anti-Pluralism: The Populist Threat to Liberal Democracy* (New Haven, CT: Yale University Press, 2018), 37.

57. Quoted in Alexandra Homolar and Georg Löfflmann, "Populism and the Affective Politics of Humiliation Narratives," *Global Studies Quarterly* 1, no. 1 (March 2021): 8.

58. Joseph McCarthy, speech before the Women's Republican Club, Wheeling, West Virginia, February 9, 1950, in Richard A. Schwartz, *Eyewitness History: The 1950s* (New York: Facts on File, 2003), 428.

59. Ronald Brownstein, "Trump's War on Expertise is Only Intensifying," *Atlantic*, November 21, 2019, https://www.theatlantic.com/politics/archive/2019/11/trump-attack-vindman-yovanovitch-hill/602383/.

60. Jan-Werner Müller, *What is Populism?* (Philadelphia: University of Pennsylvania Press, 2016), 3.

61. Müller, *What is Populism?* 3.

62. Yascha Mounk, *The People vs. Democracy: Why Our Freedom Is in Danger and How to Save It* (Cambridge, MA: Harvard University Press, 2018).

63. Thomas Frank, *The People, NO: A Brief History of Anti-populism* (New York: Metropolitan Books, 2020), 255.

64. Müller, *What is Populism?* 16.

65. Galston, *Anti-Pluralism*, 126.

66. Mounk, *People vs. Democracy*, 97.

67. Sandel, *Tyranny of Merit*, 135.

68. Sandel, *Tyranny of Merit*, 152.

69. Sandel, *Tyranny of Merit*, 118.

70. This is the title of chapter 4 in Sandel, *Tyranny of Merit*.

71. Michael Salter, "The Problem with a Fight against Toxic Masculinity," *Atlantic*, February 27, 2019, https://www.theatlantic.com/health/archive/2019/02/toxic-masculinity-history/583411/.

72. Indeed, its origins in reaction is one among several reasons why Nietzsche denigrated it as a sign of slavish dependence and an obstacle to self-realization.

73. William E. Connolly, *Aspirational Fascism: The Struggle for Multifaceted Democracy under Trumpism* (Minneapolis: University of Minnesota Press, 2017), 64. See Thomas B. Edsall's column, "'It's Become Increasingly Hard for Them to Feel Good About Themselves,'" *New York Times*, September 22, 2021. Edsall cites Adam Enders, a professor of political science at the University of Louisville, who attributes young white men's troubles to partisan resentment. "My take is that

lower-class white males likely have lower trust in institutions of higher education over time. This bears out in the aggregate," he writes, referencing a Pew Research Survey: "Part of the reason for this—at least among some conservative males—is the perception that colleges are tools for leftist indoctrination—a perception increasingly fueled by the Right, including top Republican and conservative leaders. Indeed, there is a hefty split between Democrats and Republicans in their orientations toward the education system. Republicans became more negative than positive about education since around 2016."

74. Masood Farivar, "Researchers: More Than a Dozen Extremist Groups Took Part in Capitol Riots," VOA, January 16, 2021, https://www.voanews.com/2020-usa -votes/researchers-more-dozen-extremist-groups-took-part-capitol-riots.

75. My three major sources on the Incels are Jia Tolentino, "The Rage of the Incels," *New Yorker*, May 15, 2018, https://www.newyorker.com/culture/cultural -comment/the-rage-of-the-incels; Amia Srinivasan, "Does Anyone Have the Right to Sex? *London Review of Books* 40, no. 6 (March 22, 2017), https://www.lrb.co.uk /the-paper/v40/no6/amia-srinivasan/does-anyone-have-the-right-to-sex; and Jennifer Wright, "Why Incels Hate Women," *Harper's Bazaar*, April 27, 2018, https:// www.harpersbazaar.com/culture/politics/a20078774/what-are-incels/. All the quotes in these paragraphs are from these sources. See also Wendy Brown, *In the Ruins of Neoliberalism: The Rise of Antidemocratic Politics in the West* (New York: Columbia University Press, 2019), 172.

76. Tolentino, "Rage of the Incels."

77. Tolentino, "Rage of the Incels."

78. Vladimir Putin, *First Person: The Astonishingly Frank Self-Portrait by Russia's President Vladimir Putin*, trans. Catherine A. Fitzpatrick (New York: Public Affairs, 2000), 18.

79. David Caplan, "Shirtless Vladimir Putin Takes Dip in Icy Russian Lake for the Epiphany," ABC News, January 18, 2018, https://abcnews.go.com/Politics /shirtless-vladimir-putin-takes-dip-icy-russian-lake/story?id=52450562.

80. Masha Gessen, The Man Without a Face: The Unlikely Rise of Vladimir Putin (New York: Riverhead Books, 2013), chap. 3.

81. David Brooks, "This Is Why Putin Can't Back Down," *New York Times*, March 10, 2022, https://www.nytimes.com/2022/03/10/opinion/putin-ukraine -russia-identity.html.

82. Paul Berman, "The Intellectual Catastrophe of Vladimir Putin," *Foreign Policy*, March 13, 2022, https://foreignpolicy.com/2022/03/13/putin-russia-war -ukraine-rhetoric-history/.

83. Jane Burbank, "The Grand Theory Driving Putin to War," *New York Times*, March 22, 2022, https://www.nytimes.com/2022/03/22/opinion/russia-ukraine -putin-eurasianism.html.

84. Liah Greenfeld, *Nationalism: Five Roads to Modernity* (Cambridge, MA: Harvard University Press, 1002).

85. Greenfeld, *Nationalism*, 261.

86. Max Fisher, "Putin's Case for War, Annotated," *New York Times*, February 24, 2022.

87. On Dugin's influence and particularly on Putin, see Charles Clover, "Pu-

tin's Grand Vision and Echoes of '1984,'" *Financial Times*, October 4, 2011; and Amit Varshizky, "To Understand Putin, You First Need to Get Inside Aleksandr Dugin's Head," *Ha'aretz*, March 22, 2022.

88. Varshizky, "To Understand Putin."

89. Quoted in Masha Gessen, *The Future is History: How Totalitarianism Reclaimed Russia* (New York: Riverhead, 2017), 388–89.

90. Greenfeld, *Nationalism*, 261.

91. Bernard Lewis, "The Roots of Muslim Rage: Why So Many Muslims Deeply Resent the West, and Why Their Bitterness Will Not Be Easily Mollified," *Atlantic*, September 1990, https://www.theatlantic.com/magazine/archive/1990/09/the-roots-of-muslim-rage/304643/.

92. Lewis, "Roots of Muslim Rage," 48.

93. Lewis, "Roots of Muslim Rage," 52.

94. Lewis, "Roots of Muslim Rage," 59.

95. Lewis, "Roots of Muslim Rage," 60.

96. Lewis, "Roots of Muslim Rage," 59. Jurgen Habermas, whose ideological orientation is quite different from Lewis's, nevertheless shared something of this analysis. In a 2001 speech, he described the 9/11 attacks as a reaction to "an accelerated and radically uprooting modernization." Edward Skidelsky, "Habermas vs The Pope," *Prospect*, November 20, 2005, https://www.prospectmagazine.co.uk/magazine/jurgen-habermas-pope-benedict-xvi-ratzinger.

97. George W. Bush, "An Address to a Joint Session of Congress," September 21, 2001, https://www.govinfo.gov/content/pkg/CDOC-107hdoc122/html/CDOC-107hdoc122.htm.

98. Slavoj Žižek, *Violence: Six Sideways Reflections* (New York: Picador, 2008), 83.

99. Žižek, *Violence*, 85.

100. Slavoj Žižek, *Trouble in Paradise: From the End of History to the End of Capitalism* (Brooklyn, NY: Melville House, 2015), 100.

101. See Axel Honneth, *The Struggle for Recognition: The Moral Grammar of Social Conflicts*, trans. Joel Anderson (Cambridge, MA: Harvard University Press, 1996) on *thymos*.

102. On the similarity between some commentators in the Islamic fundamentalist tradition and critics of modernity, etc., in the West, see the important work by Roxanne L. Euben, *Enemy in the Mirror: Islamic Fundamentalism and the Limits of Modern Rationalism* (Princeton, NJ: Princeton University Press, 1999).

103. Jonah Goldberg, "The Real Danger of Categorical Politics," *National Review*, July 12, 2019, https://www.nationalreview.com/2019/07/identity-politics-danger-group-loyalty/.

104. Todd Gitlin, "The Rise of 'Identity Politics': An Examination and a Critique," ed. Michael Bérubé and Cary Nelson, *Higher Education Under Fire: Politics, Economics and the Crisis of the Humanities* (New York: Routledge, 1995), 308.

105. Todd Gitlin, "The Rise of Identity Politics," *Dissent*, Spring 1993, https://www.dissentmagazine.org/article/the-rise-of-identity-politics.

106. Mark Lilla, "The End of Identity Liberalism," *New York Times*, November 18, 2016, https://www.nytimes.com/2016/11/20/opinion/sunday/the-end-of-identity-liberalism.html.

107. William Cummings, "Bannon: If Left Focuses on Race, 'We Can Crush the Democrats,'" *USA Today*, August 16, 2017, https://www.usatoday.com/story/news /politics/onpolitics/2017/08/16/bannon-interview/574845001/.

108. Francis Fukuyama, *Identity: The Demand for Dignity and the Politics of Resentment* (New York: Macmillan, 2018). See also his *The End of History and the Last Man* (New York: Free Press, 1992) for an even fuller treatment of *thymos*.

109. Ken Gewertz, "Harvey Mansfield on Politics, the Humanities, and Science," *Harvard Gazette*, October 11, 2007, https://news.harvard.edu/gazette/story /2007/10/harvey-mansfield-on-politics-the-humanities-and-science/.

110. Fukuyama, *Identity*, 7.

111. Fukuyama, *Identity*, 115.

112. Fukuyama, *Identity*, 170.

113. Wendy Brown, *States of Injury: Power and Freedom in Late Modernity* (Princeton, NJ: Princeton University Press, 1995).

114. Brown, *States of Injury*, 62.

115. Brown, *States of Injury*, 26.

116. Brown, *States of Injury*, 25.

117. Honneth, *Struggle for Recognition*. Among others, the philosopher Katie Stockdale, in "Collective Resentment," *Social Theory and Practice* 39, no. 3 (July 2013): 501–21, has made a strenuous case for collective resentment as describing the disposition of Indigenous Canadians not only in defense of their rights and traditions, and not merely to demand redress for their injuries, but as an assertion of their very existence as a people. She makes a distinction between particular grievances, like the residential schools that inflicted so much physical and psychological damage on young native children who were taken from their families, denied their language and traditions, and forced to "assimilate" into mainstream Canadian culture; and a collective resentment against "the assimilationist project of manipulating not only the identities of indigenous children, but of annihilating whole cultures, traditions, languages and spiritualities" (513). Reading a text by the indigenous scholar Taiaiake Alfred, "Colonial Stains on our Existence," she finds a wholesale litany of objects of resentment: "monotheistic religiosity, liberal political theory, neo-liberal capitalist economics, presumptions of racial superiority, and false assumptions about Euro-American cultural superiority" (511). This, then, is not a piecemeal indictment but a fully conceived assertion of a separate identity grounded in an alternative worldview. It transcends both the personal and the particular grievance. Resentment of this sort does not depend upon having personally suffered an injury; it only presupposes belonging to the collectivity which has suffered, for it is the threat to the *identity* of the group itself which is the real concern. She even asserts that particular members of the threatened group might be criticized for failing to feel resentful, presumably because this failure demonstrates a lack of emotional investment in the collectivity's existence. Here we are getting perilously close to the kind of psychological coercion often exhibited by political groups where the demand for absolute consensus often works to stifle personal preferences. In any case, Stockdale's reading of Indigenous Canadians' programmatic statements moves her to conclude that resentment is not only appropriate as a description of the disposi-

tion of a beleaguered group but also constitutive of its collective identity. Indeed, contrary to Brown's claim that resentful identity politics is restrictive in its range of political concerns, Stockdale's representation of an indigenous identity movement suggests resentment as doing precisely the opposite—moving beyond the particular injury to an existential claim regarding the group's very being.

118. René Girard, *I See Satan Fall Like Lightning*, trans. James G. Williams (Maryknoll, NY: Orbis, 2001), 9.

119. Quoted in Elisabetta Brighi, "Sentiments of Resentment: Desiring Others, Desiring Justice," *Contagion: Journal of Violence, Mimesis and Culture* 26 (2019): 182. See also Brighi, "The Globalisation of Resentment: Failure, Denial, and Violence in World Politics," *Millennium: Journal of International Studies* 44, no. 3 (2016): 411–32.

120. Brighi, "Sentiments of Resentment," 184.

121. "Foreword by René Girard" in Stefano Tomelleri, *Ressentiment: Reflections on Mimetic Desire and Society* (East Lansing: Michigan State University Press, 2015).

122. Tomelleri, *Ressentiment*, 72, 92, quoted in Brighi, "Sentiments of Resentment," 184.

123. Alexis de Tocqueville, *Democracy in America*, ed. Thomas Bender (New York: Modern Library, 1981), 108–109.

CONCLUSION

1. William Ian Miller, *Humiliation* (Ithaca, NY: Cornell University Press, 1993), 94.

2. Keith Payne, *The Broken Ladder: How Inequality Affects the Way We Think, Live, and Die* (New York: Penguin, 2017).

3. Rawls, *Theory of Justice*, 533.

4. Jameson, *Political Unconscious*, 202.

5. Leon Wieseltier, "Stay Angry: That's the Only Way to Uphold Principles in Trump's America," *Washington Post*, November 11, 2016, emphasis added.

6. Sjoerd van Tuinen, "The Resentment-Ressentiment Complex: A Critique of Liberal Discourse," *Global Discourse*, no. 2–3 (May 2020): 237–53.

7. William E. Connolly, *Aspirational Fascism: The Struggle for Multifaceted Democracy under Trumpism* (Minneapolis: University of Minnesota Press, 2017), 64–68.

8. Katie Reilly, "Read Hillary Clinton's 'Basket of Deplorables' Remarks about Donald Trump's Supporters," *Time*, September 10, 2016, https://time.com/4486502/hillary-clinton-basket-of-deplorables-transcript/.

9. Tim Haines, "Charles Murray: Hillary Clinton's 'Deplorables' Comment May Have Changed the Course of World History," RealClear, April 25, 2017, https://www.realclearpolitics.com/video/2017/04/25/charles_murray_hillary_clintons_deplorables_comment_may_have_changed_the_course_of_world_history.html.

10. David Jackson, "Trump Seeks to Profit from Clinton's 'Deplorables' Remark," *USA Today*, September 15, 2016, https://www.usatoday.com/story/news/politics/elections/2016/09/15/donald-trump-hillary-clinton-basket-of-deplorables/90352670.

11. Tim Haines, "Pence: Clinton Expressing 'Disdain' and 'Contempt' for Ev-

eryday Americans 'Disqualifies Her,'" RealClear, September 13, 2016, https://www.realclearpolitics.com/video/2016/09/13/pence_for_clinton_to_express_disdain_for_everyday_americans_disqualifies_her.html.

12. Ben Smith, "Obama on Small-Town Pa.: Clinging to Religion, Guns, Xenophobia," *Politico*, April 11, 2008.

13. "Speech Highlights: Convention Day 3," *Tampa Bay Times*, September 4, 2008, https://www.tampabay.com/archive/2008/09/04/speech-highlights-convention-day-3/#.

14. Barack Obama, *A Promised Land* (New York: Crown, 2020), 169–70.

15. See Nancy Isenberg's list in *White Trash*: "Offscourings, Bogtrotters, Rascals, Rubbish, Squatters, Crackers, Clay-eaters, Hillbillies, Rednecks. And white trash." Isenberg, *White Trash: The 400-Year-Old Untold History of Class in America* (New York: Viking, 2016).

16. Alexis de Tocqueville, *The Old Regime and the French Revolution*, trans. Stuart Gilbert (Garden City, NJ: Doubleday, 1955), 180.

17. "Text of Trump['s] Address to the National Guard Association of the United States," *Capital Gazette* (Baltimore), September 12, 2016, https://www.capitalgazette.com/politics/bs-md-trump-text-of-address-20160912-story.html.

18. "Speech: Donald Trump in Naples, FL, October 23, 2016," FactBase, https://factba.se/transcript/donald-trump-speech-naples-fl-october-23-2016.

19. "Full Text: Donald Trump 2016 RNC Draft Speech Transcript," Politco, July 21, 2016, https://www.politico.com/story/2016/07/full-transcript-donald-trump-nomination-acceptance-speech-at-rnc-225974.

20. Donald Trump, "Remarks at the Southeastern Livestock Pavilion in Ocala, Florida," October 12, 2016, The American Presidency Project, https://www.presidency.ucsb.edu/documents/remarks-the-southeastern-livestock-pavilion-ocala-florida.

21. Brian Naylor, "Read Trump's Jan. 6 Speech, a Key Part of Impeachment Trial," NPR, February 10, 2021, https://www.npr.org/2021/02/10/966396848/read-trumps-jan-6-speech-a-key-part-of-impeachment-trial.

22. "Transcript: 'Go Home': Trump Tells Supporters Who Mobbed Capital to Leave, Again Falsely Claiming Election Victory," WBUR (Boston), January 6, 2016, https://www.wbur.org/news/2021/01/06/go-home-trump-supporters-us-capitol-transcript.

23. "EU Referendum: Boris Johnson Stands by Hitler EU Comparison," BBC News, May 16, 2016, https://www.bbc.com/news/uk-politics-eu-referendum-36295208.

24. On this, see especially Wolfgang Schivelbusch, *The Culture of Defeat: On National Trauma, Mourning, and Recovery*, trans. Jefferson Chase (New York: Metropolitan Books, 2003), chap. 1.

25. Omer Bartov, *Anatomy of a Genocide: The Life and Death of a Town Called Buczacz* (New York: Simon and Schuster, 2018), 153. On this and the general relationship between humiliation and resentment, I have been much informed by Alexandra Homolar and Georg Löfflmann, "Populism and Affective Politics of Humiliation Narratives," *Global Studies Quarterly* (2021): 1–11.

26. Vivian Gornick, "Put on the Diamonds: Notes on Humiliation," *Harper's Magazine*, October 2021.

27. Elias Canetti, *Crowds and Power* (New York: Seabury Press, 1978), 262.

28. Matthew Newsom Kerr, "Frustration, Anger and Deaths Won't Convince the Unvaccinated," *Washington Post*, October 5, 2021.

29. David Frum, "Vaccinated America Has Had Enough," *Atlantic*, July 23, 2021.

30. Frum, "Vaccinated America."

31. Charles Dickens, *Bleak House* (New York: Oxford University Press, 1998 ed.), 230. Mr. Gridley, alas, ultimately commits suicide.

Index

on, 4; Nietzsche on, 4–5, 8, 13, 61,
80–88, 112, 116–17, 133–35, 150–51, 191,
211–12, 220, 233–34, 247–48n3, 251n19;
term, usage, 5, 246n39, 247–48n3
Ressentiment (Scheler), 13, 248n10
ressentir (reaction/repetition), 9, 196
retaliation, 19, 158
retribution, 127, 152, 199
Reunion (Hayden), 142, 259–60n18,
259n9
revenge: and hatred, 23, 81, 87; and
malice, 22–23; and resentment, 12,
19, 22–24, 27–28, 30–31, 55, 79–81, 85,
127–28, 133; and retribution, 152. *See
also* vengeance
revolution: and anger, 50–51; and
contentious resentment, 12–13,
50–58; and degeneration, 66; and
democracy, 76–77; and emotions/
sentiment, 55; ethos of, 227; in
Europe, 62–63; and mobilization,
57–58, 254–55n56; populism, 76;
and rebellion, 56; and resentment,
55–56; and vengeance, 55–56; and
violence, 133–34
Revolutionary Suicide (Newton), 150,
260n33
Rhetoric of Bourgeois Revolution, A
(Sewell), 54, 243n43
Ribuffo, Leo, 2, 238n19
Rieder, Jonathan, 164, 261n47
Riesman, David, 92, 102, 104, 249n2,
253n43
right-wing movements, xii, 77, 88, 90,
92, 98, 104, 166, 170, 191
"Rise of 'Identity Politics,' The"
(Gitlin), 209, 269n104
Robertson, Pat, 165
Robespierre, Maximilien, 64
Rodger, Elliot, 198–99
Rogin, Michael, 107
Röhl, Klaus Rainer, 119–20
*Role of Ressentiment in the Structure of
Morals, The* (Scheler), 84
Romney, Mitt, 175, 263–64n8
Roosevelt, Theodore, 66–67

"Roots of Muslim Rage, The" (Lewis),
205, 269n91–96
Rorty, Amélie Oksenberg, 125, 257n33
Ross, Dorothy, 100, 252n23
Rousseau, Jean-Jacques, 24–25, 49,
140, 211
royal court, English, and contentious
resentment, 38–44. *See also* nobility
Rudé, George, 62, 242n28, 244n10
Rudolph, Hermann, 255–56n11
rural consciousness, and resentment,
188
Rushdy, Ashraf H. A., 240n11
Russia: Asiatic Communist, 119; and
Eurasian vision of continental
hegemony, 202; national identity/
nationalism in, 201–2; and resentment, historical drama of, 200–203;
terrorists of 1905, 148

Sachs, Wolfgang, 108–9, 255n58
sadness, and resentment, 3, 29
*Salem Possessed: The Social Origins of
Witchcraft* (Boyer and Nissenbaum),
35–36, 241n1, 241n3, 241n6
Salem witch trials (1692), 34–38, 207
Salinger, J. D., 141
Salter, Michael, 196, 267n71
Sandel, Michael, 194–95
Sanford, R. Nevitt, 98, 251n14–15
Sartre, Jean-Paul, 113, 130–31, 133, 140,
149, 259–60n18
schadenfreude, 230
Scheler, Max, 4, 13, 84–89, 90, 111–15,
214, 248n9–10
Schlesinger, Arthur, Jr., 104–5, 253n46
Schroeder, Gerhard, 121
Scott, James C., 109, 112, 255n1, 255n59
SDS. *See* Students for a Democratic
Society (SDS)
Second Sex, The (Beauvoir), 144, 146–47
sectarianism, 212–13, 259n18
secularism, 87, 203, 205
secularization, and modernity, 101–2
Securitarian Personality, The (Hibbing),
182, 264n14, 265n22, 266n32–33

Voltaire (Arouet, François-Marie),
47, 49
Vox (news site), 2

Walker, Scott, 187
Wall Street Journal, 206
Walser, Martin, 117–18, 120–24, 135,
255n6–7, 257n17–24
Wang, Emily, 169, 263n1
Warren, Robert Penn, 148, 151, 260n28
Washington Post (newspaper), 1–2,
237n9, 238n10, 271n5, 273n28
Watts, Isaac, 21
Weber, Max, 87, 94–95, 99, 101–2, 170,
211, 249–50n7, 249n2, 251n18–19
Weizmann, Chaim, 256n12
Welch, Robert, 248–49n1
well-being, 96, 103, 109, 173, 176–77,
218, 224, 229, 259n14
Wells, H. G., 62
"West Has a Resentment Epidemic,
The" (Foa and Wilmot), 2, 238n16
Westin, Alan, 92, 248–49n1, 249n2
Weyrich, Paul, 165
What Is the Third Estate? (Sieyès), 53–
54, 243n43, 243n45
What's the Matter with Kansas?
(Frank), 187–88, 191
White Collar (Mills), 102, 251n18
white privilege, 224
white supremacy, 180–81, 197, 234
White Working Class (Williams), 184,
264n11
Wieseltier, Leon, 1–2, 220–21, 237n9,
271n5
"Wigan's Road to Brexit: Anger, Loss
and Class Resentments" (Higgins),
2, 238n13
Will, George F., 261–62n50
Williams, Joan C., 184, 264n11
Williams, William A., 107
Williamson, Vanessa, 264n17

Will to Power, The (Nietzsche), 89, 133,
150–51
Wilmot, Jonathan, 238n16
Wilson, David C., 179, 265n26
Winnicott, D. W. (Donald), 129, 232–33
witches/witchcraft: and contentious
resentment, 12–13, 32, 34–38, 207
witch hunts: in England, 35, 38; in
Europe (16th and 17th centuries),
34–35; in New England (16th and
17th centuries), 34–38, 207
wokeness, 229
Wolin, Richard, 89, 248n13
Women's Liberation Movement, 106,
144–45
Woodward, C. Vann, 107–8, 253n38,
254n53–54
Woolf, Virginia, xii
working class: and bourgeoisie, 63;
complacency of, 183; in Europe,
67–68; and populism, 46–47, 107–8;
and protest, 46; and racism, 158;
and resentment, 2, 163–64, 174–75,
183–85, 221; Southern, 163; white,
158, 174–75, 177, 183–84, 221, 223. *See
also* lower class; middle class
Wretched of the Earth, The (Fanon),
130, 133–34, 227, 258n60
Wuthnow, Robert, 188–89, 238n19,
267n51–53

xenophobia, 2, 76, 181, 183, 221–22,
262–63n76

Yellow Vest movement, in France, 2
Young, Michael, 194

Zarathustra, 60, 244n5
Zinn, Howard, 137, 258n1
Zitelmann, Rainer, 120
Žižek, Slavoj, 206–8, 269n98–100
Zola, Emile, 76